MW00532871

American Sports History Series

edited by
David B. Biesel

1. *Effa Manley and the Newark Eagles* by James Overmyer, 1993.
2. *The United States and World Cup Competition: An Encyclopedic History of the United States in International Competition* by Colin Jose, 1994.
3. *Slide, Kelly, Slide: The Wild Life and Times of Mike "King" Kelly, Baseball's First Superstar* by Marty Appel, 1996.
4. *Baseball by the Numbers* by Mark Stang and Linda Harkness, 1997.
5. *Roller Skating for Gold* by David H. Lewis, 1997.
6. *Baseball's Biggest Blunder: The Bonus Rule of 1953–1957* by Brent Kelley, 1997.
7. *Lights On! The Wild Century-Long Saga of Night Baseball* by David Pietrusza, 1997.
8. *Windy City Wars: Labor, Leisure, and Sport in the Making of Chicago* by Gerald R. Gems, 1997.
9. *The American Soccer League 1921–1931: The Golden Years of American Soccer* by Colin Jose, 1998.
10. *The League That Failed,* by David Quentin Voigt, 1998.
11. *Jimmie Foxx: The Pride of Sudlersville* by Mark R. Millikin, 1998.
12. *Baseball's Radical for All Seasons: A Biography of John Montgomery Ward* by David Stevens, 1998.
13. *College Basketball's National Championships: The Complete Record of Every Tournament Ever Played* by Morgan G. Brenner, 1998.
14. *Chris Von der Ahe and the St. Louis Browns* by J. Thomas Hetrick, 1999.
15. *Before the Glory: The Best Players in the Pre-NBA Days of Pro Basketball* by William F. Himmelman and Karel de Veer, 1999.
16. *For Pride, Profit, and Patriarchy: Football and the Incorporation of American Cultural Values* by Gerry Gems, 2000.

Chris Von der Ahe's life-size monument at St. Louis' Bellefontaine Cemetery. (*Reprinted by permission of Jim Rygelski.*)

Chris Von der Ahe and the St. Louis Browns

J. Thomas Hetrick

American Sports History Series, No. 14

The Scarecrow Press, Inc.
Lanham, Maryland, and London
1999

SCARECROW PRESS, INC.

Published in the United States of America
by Scarecrow Press, Inc.
4720 Boston Way, Lanham, Maryland 20706
http://www.scarecrowpress.com

4 Pleydell Gardens, Folkestone
Kent CT20 2DN, England

British Library Cataloguing in Publication Information Available

Library of Congress Cataloging-in-Publication Data

Hetrick, J. Thomas 1957–
Chris Von der Ahe and the St. Louis Browns / by J. Thomas Hetrick.
p. cm. — (American sports history series ; no. 14)
Includes bibliographical references (p.) and index.
ISBN 0-8108-3473-1 (alk. paper)
1. St. Louis Browns (Baseball team)—History. 2. Von der Ahe, Chris. I. Title. II. Series.
GV875.S72H48 1999
796.357′64′0977866—dc21 99-25095
CIP

™ The paper used in this publication meets the minimum requirements of American National Standard for Information Sciences—Permanence of Paper for Printed Library Materials, ANSI/NISO Z39.48–1992.
Manufactured in the United States of America.

For my father and mother

Joseph Streamer Hetrick (1932–1998)
Rachel Ann Perri (1930–1987)

"The man who dies . . . rich dies disgraced."

—Andrew Carnegie

On Ballplayers:

". . . a shiftless member of the laboring class, prone to drink, having a loose moral code and preferring to avoid an honest days work by playing ball."

—*The New York Times*, 1870s

Contents

The Later Years

Appendices

Foreword

Growing up as a fan of the St. Louis Cardinals in the late 1950s was a challenge, particularly for someone like me, who lived a long walk from the Redbirds' home at Busch Stadium, a rechristened ball yard my father and other old-timers still called Sportsman's Park.

Oh, the Cardinals then were always good, but never good enough when it came to the final standings. I often countered my disappointment by reading of the Cardinals' championship squads of the '20s, '30s, and '40s. While I'd been born only three years after their 1946 championship season, I began to wonder, even at an early age, if I'd ever see St. Louis win the pennant. More importantly, I wondered if St. Louis had been a Johnny-come-lately in baseball history, a lucky blip on the chart.

One morning, after a defeat that showed clearly why the Cardinals wouldn't win that year, I trudged to the bookmobile near school. Going straight to the sports section, I discovered Fred Lieb's book, *The St. Louis Cardinals*.

I learned not only that baseball had been played in the 1800s—a time formerly reserved in my mind for cowboys and Indians—but also that a team representing my hometown, the St. Louis Browns, had been one of the best of that formative era.

Why, the Cardinals were the direct descendants of those Browns, who'd won four pennants in a row, 1885 through 1888, in a league called the American Association, part of which was absorbed by the National League. The Browns had played in Sportsman's Park and had Charley Comiskey, after whom Comiskey Park in Chicago was named, as their manager and first baseman.

But most notable, and memorable as it turned out, was the Browns' owner, a funny-looking round man named Chris Von der Ahe, a German immigrant who said many outrageous things while raking in money from his four-time champions and then wasting it all on wine, beer, women, and shoot-the-chutes.

Gussie Busch, the flamboyant brewer who owned the Cardinals of my youth, had nothing—particularly success—on Chris Von der Ahe.

The Cardinals of the 1960s recaptured their lost glory, taking three pennants and two World Series titles. It became easy to forget the past in the heroics of the present, but every once in a while, I'd come across a reference to Chris Von der Ahe and his Browns in the popular baseball histories of the day. They all treated the nineteenth-century as if it had been a joke, led by the great comedian Chris Von der Ahe.

A quarter century after my first encounter with Von der Ahe and his Von der Boys, I was strolling near an old South St. Louis park when the year 1885, chiseled into one of its stone entrances, caught my eye. Wasn't that the first of the Browns four championship years? The fact that it was 1985, a season the Cardinals would win the pennant, spurred my interest into some serious research.

In my reading of contemporary news accounts, I found the baseball world of the century before to be livelier—and taken more seriously by both player and fan—than the popular histories had portrayed it. The Browns were indeed a big part of the long-forgotten American Association, even in years they hadn't won the pennant. And they were a most important part of St. Louis.

Chris Von der Ahe was at the center of it all, win or lose. Yes, he was funny, as when he railed against the Association's wanting to pay players a $1,000 minimum salary because he'd mistook it as a maximum and said it would be an insult, or when he fined third baseman Arlie Latham for "singing and otherwise acting up" during a game.

But another side of Chris Von der Ahe emerged from my delving into the past. He believed in honor—even if he made excuses for his own detours from it, as with his mistresses—and demanded that his players show that honor on and off the field. He was generous, as evidenced by the times he bought each of his players a new suit of dress clothes.

He was also a much smarter baseball team owner than later writers had portrayed him. He had to have been, or he never could have built the dynasty St. Louis baseball fans enjoyed watching in the 1880s.

But that business sense got him into trouble. He fined players for the slightest infractions, causing his champions of the '80s to bolt when they had the chance after the Association collapsed. When he paid their replacements poorly, causing the team to tumble in the standings, his answer to sagging attendance was to build a new ballpark and add bicycle races and night horse racing.

Famed SABRmetrician Bill James wrote, in his *Historical Baseball Abstract,* that a very good movie could be made about baseball in St. Louis in the 1880s. J. Thomas Hetrick, luckily, has written a very good book about baseball in St. Louis in not only the 1880s but also the 1890s, the two decades in which Chris Von der Ahe drove his team and its fans to both the heights and depths.

Many other Americans have achieved either fame or infamy through baseball, but few have had both in the way that Chris Von der Ahe did, and no writer before J. Thomas Hetrick has probed the factors that led to Von der Ahe to do what he did.

We see a much fuller side to Von der Ahe and his players—Commy, Tip, Icebox, the Dude, and Parisian Bob—among those with the more colorful nicknames. He loved them as sons, even as he battled them like an overbearing father would his offspring. Though they whined, wailed, and even rebelled against him, leaving him behind for greener pastures most never found elsewhere, they never forgot him.

The St. Louis Browns of the last two decades of the nineteenth-century weren't just some fabled group of ball tossers. They were closer to the players of today than we'd suspect, being led by the same desires that fuel today's stars—money, admiration, and distrust of the magnates that hold the purse strings. Von der Ahe was no classic clown but a man that modern club owners such as Charley Finley and George Steinbrenner have emulated, even if they didn't realize it.

Chris Von der Ahe and the St. Louis Browns brings back a story baseball fans need to read and never forget.

—Jim Rygelski

Preface

When the *Macmillan Baseball Encyclopedia* was first published in 1969, it was the most comprehensive document of baseball statistics available. The gargantuan computer database contained records of more than 10,000 players in the major leagues—their dates and places of birth, injuries, extraordinary accomplishments, and yearly averages. Behind this wealth of information are flesh-and-blood human beings who played these simple games that, for them, meant the world.

Christian Frederick Wilhelm Von der Ahe is one such story. Although he probably never caught or threw a baseball, his impact on the game remains unique.

An obscure German immigrant, Von der Ahe began as a grocer and saloon keeper in late nineteenth-century St. Louis. He invested his money in local real estate and later became involved in baseball as a way to increase his beer profits. As owner of the famous St. Louis Browns, he earned hundreds of thousands of dollars with his baseball industry; then, because of his megalomaniacal personality and a series of staggering professional and personal calamities, he lost nearly every penny.

Von der Ahe lived a full life. He embodied the German work ethic to build his fortune. He played even harder, indulging in extraordinary extravagances for himself and his baseball team. Unfortunately, his excesses overwhelmed him, his family, his baseball team, and even the city itself. By the time he died, he was all but forgotten in the St. Louis that he loved.

What follows is Von der Ahe's strange baseball odyssey, warts and all.

—J. Thomas Hetrick
Clifton, VA

Acknowledgments

This study of the baseball life of Chris Von der Ahe would have not have been possible without the assistance of several outstanding individuals. I would be remiss without acknowledging their contributions.

My sincere thanks extend to the following major contributors: illustrator Michael D. Arnold, Brian Hohlt of St. Louis University, Fred Ivor-Campbell of the Society for American Baseball Research, the Library of Congress, the Missouri Historical Society, the National Baseball Hall of Fame Library, baseball historians John Phillips and David Pietrusza, Matthew J. Riley, illustrator John Schleith, curator Michael Tiemann of Bellefontaine Cemetery in St. Louis, and nineteenth-century baseball expert Robert Tiemann.

In addition, I'm also grateful for the inspiration from Bowling Green University Press, which published Daniel Pearson's *Baseball in 1889*. Encouraging words, material, and assistance were provided by Bob Broeg, Jack Carlson, Francis Certo, Allison Cobb, Richard Crespo, Robert Davids, James Floto, Sue Fuerst, George Mason University, Steve Gietschier, Roger Godin, Michael Hardcastle, Robert Harley, Ralph Horton, Jack Kavanaugh, Jack Little, Norman Macht, Andy McCue, William Mead, Heather Miller, Gaston Naranjo, David Nemec, Michelle Reiche, Steven Riddle, John Roca, Jeffrey Samoray, Mike Sparrow, Dean Sullivan, Ron Willnow and Susan Luberda of the *St. Louis Post-Dispatch,* the St. Louis Public Library, Chris Thaiss, Richard Topp, David Vincent, and Russell Von der Ahe.

Technical assistance was provided by Guido Cafasso, Emery Conrad, John Gratz, Namita Magoon, Shane Morris, and Ray Rybicki.

Long ago, a little boy named Billy Trusty helped fan my interest in baseball.

I must also thank my wife, Mi Ae, and my daughter, Alicia, for enduring so much time away from their husband/father.

Without question, the work could not have been completed without the sterling efforts of my editor, Dave Biesel.

Finally, a special debt of gratitude should be paid Jim Rygelski, a suburban St. Louis newspaper editor and fellow Von der Ahe aficionado. In 1994, Rygelski wrote a play about Chris Von der Ahe. It was Jim who pushed and prodded the project along, especially when the author seemed as troubled as his subject. On several occasions, Mr. Rygelski suggested to me that he'd like to share some suds and conversation with the old bartender himself. We'd talk over old times and the glories of the Browns. Of course, that cannot happen. However, here's to hoping that this biography serves as a final toast.

Ein Prosit, Herr Von der Ahe!

—J. Thomas Hetrick

The Early Years

1

A Not-So Modest Grocer

The beer flowed, and congratulatory toasts echoed into the night. Curt Welch's dusty dash to home plate that afternoon had made world champions of the St. Louis Browns and helped Christian Frederick Wilhelm Von der Ahe—a German immigrant, saloon keeper, and self-proclaimed "boss president" of that baseball team, achieve his American dream. The portly Von der Ahe lit another cigar, brushed the frothy amber from his walrus moustache, placed his feet up on the table, and grinned. In late October 1886, the city of St. Louis was his, and Von der Ahe was enjoying it more than any other conquest he'd made in his thirty-five years.

Coming to the United States alone from the historically plundered area of Westphalia, the teenage Chris settled in New York City for a few weeks before migrating to St. Louis. His father was a grain dealer and merchant. Farmers, grocers, and a religious teacher comprised Von der Ahe's ancestry. Chris was like millions of other Europeans who emigrated to the United States because of crop failures, social discontent, and political repression. Sometimes whole villages of peasants headed by their pastors left for the New World.

Many Germans had been lured to America by romantic propaganda. Often, ads were run in German newspapers by Germans who wanted to develop communities in the United States. One such author was Gottfried Duden, a lawyer/doctor, originally from the Rhineland, who had settled in Missouri in 1824. Concerned with the worsening German economy due to constant rebellions and war, Duden envisioned a widespread migration to the United States. He wrote glowing testimonials on the rich soil, agreeable climate, and political freedoms. Skilled German workers, deprived of positive conditions in their home country, flocked to America with its promise of a better business environment.

Chris Von der Ahe seemed determined to make good. It wouldn't be easy in a new country with many unknowns and so many people arriving for the same slice of pie. Immigrants were often met with hostility and resentment. Many Americans disliked German speech, habits, and supposed political radicalism. However, young Von der Ahe possessed a heady lust for life and an entrepreneurial spirit.

After finding his bearings in St. Louis about 1867, Von der Ahe found a job as a grocery clerk in the West End part of town. Within a few years, he became co-owner and then proprietor of his own delicatessen and saloon at Sullivan and Spring Avenues. At first, Von der Ahe's business was modest. However, with a burgeoning German population, pretzels, pumpernickel, and sauerkraut soon began to find their way into the arms of eager buyers. And why not? Von der Ahe was equal parts ambition, pluck, and conversation. He loved to talk, and his customers came to listen. Like many immigrants, his accent was as thick as his cheese. Von der Ahe and his fellow Germans were helping to establish the community. Nearly all German settlers retained their native language, setting up churches, schools, and theaters. Singing societies, sharpshooter's clubs, and beer drinking clubs made life tolerable. Von der Ahe's delicatessen also catered to large gangs of quarrymen who were stabling in town.

On March 3, 1870, the 18-year-old Von der Ahe married Emma Hoffman, a Missouri-born woman of German ancestry. That same year, the young couple had a son whom they named Edward.

Young Von der Ahe eventually bought out his partner, Samuel J. P. Anderson, in 1872 for $1125. Von der Ahe's business was booming. To increase his capital, Von der Ahe began to loan money. One such transaction resulted in a rather fortuitous deal. In 1873, Mr. James Nash, one of Von der Ahe's debtors, died. With the heirs unable to pay off the remaining debt, the Nash property became available at auction. Von der Ahe acquired the property and quickly had another lot next to his own.

By the early 1870s, Chris Von der Ahe was ready to expand. Converting his profits into real estate purchases and later boardinghouses, he moved his delicatessen a block south, to the northwest corner of Grand Boulevard and St. Louis Avenue. Von der Ahe's new establishment was a two-and-one-half story structure. The locale was to serve a new purpose. In addition to being a popular food market, a saloon and beer garden were added to quench the thirst. The location was odd, considering the area was a practical wilderness, but soon it became a bustling business district and property values began to climb.

Von der Ahe's reputation as a businessman, host, and talker supreme grew. So did his patronage. By day, the shop in north St. Louis served those in the market for sustenance. By night, it was Von der Ahe's headquarters for political and social exchange—all with the help of foamy steins of beer. Von der Ahe not only poured and served the drinks, but he took libation as well.

Life was good for Chris Von der Ahe. He owned a considerable interest in the area. To promote his business and keep the West End prosperous, Chris entered local politics. For several years he served as chairman of the Eighth Congressional District Committee. In this arena, Von der Ahe made a crucial political connection, befriending Congressman John J. O'Neill.

By the spring of 1880, Von der Ahe began to notice the daily shouts of boys playing ball across the street in a vacant lot. The grounds were the site of Grand Avenue Park, an old-time German shooting park laid out by sportsman August "Gus" Solari in 1866. Amateur, semipro, and professional baseball had been played in St. Louis for years after Jeremiah Fruin laid out the first diamond.

Shortly after the Civil War, St. Louis baseball was characterized by a series of starts and stops. In the 1860s, amateur clubs such as the Empires, Unions, and Turners competed for sporting glory. In 1873, grocer Thomas McNeary and his brother Frank organized and financed a club called the St. Louis Red Stockings. The Red Stockings played their games at Grand Avenue Park and the smaller Compton Park. Two years later, McNeary's club toured Chicago. On the train ride back to St. Louis, Andy Blong got suckered into a card game and managed to lose the club's earnings. When Blong's teammates discovered that their money was gambled away, they recovered their earnings by brandishing baseball bats against the perpetrators.

In 1875, the club joined the National Association, a loose-knit professional organization. However, their experience was short-lived. Insisting on fielding a team composed of local talent, McNeary's boys eventually succumbed to a rival bunch called the St. Louis Browns, who saw no problems with importing players from other locales. In one seven-week period, the Browns pasted a strong Chicago squad 10–0 before a huge St. Louis throng and beat clubs from Boston, Hartford, New York, and Philadelphia. Local St. Louis papers reveled in the Chicago win, exhorting civic-minded citizens to stand up and support the Browns. The Red Stockings weren't so fortunate and dropped out of the National Association after July 4, 1875, for financial reasons. The team suffered further when the Browns refused to play them. Undaunted, Tom McNeary raised $10,000 capital for the 1876 edition of his Red Stockings. However, this club was later forced to play its games exclusively in St. Louis, to sparse crowds. That same year of 1876, the St. Louis Brown Stockings began their two-year association with the fledgling National League. The Brown Stockings were owned by St. Louis merchant Charles Fowle and manned by players such as pitcher George Washington Bradley. On July 15, 1876, Bradley tossed the league's first no-hit game, a 2–0 masterpiece against Hartford. Second baseman-outfielder Lipman Pike, shortstop Dickey Pearce, infielder Davy Force, and the not-so-aptly named pitcher Tricky Nichols also toiled for St. Louis. The 1876 edition was second to Al Spalding's mighty Chicago squad but slipped to fourth place the next season.

Unfortunately for St. Louis ball cranks, a scandal forced the team out of the league. Four Louisville players—Bill "Butcher" Craver, Jim "Terror" Devlin, "Gentleman George" Hall, and Al "Slippery Elm" Nichols—who had recently found themselves in St. Louis, were banished for life for conspiring to fix league games in favor of Boston. In disgust, the St. Louis owners took their money and quit.

2

Baseball Discovers Von der Ahe

After numerous saloon meetings with ballplayer Ned Cuthbert and St. Louis sports writers Al Spink and George Munson, Von der Ahe was persuaded to finance the Browns. It's likely that the men appealed to Von der Ahe's vanity by using flattery. They convinced him that by sponsoring a team, Von der Ahe would be famous. As the leaves changed in the fall of 1880, a back room in Von der Ahe's tavern was the scene of a meeting between Chris Von der Ahe, the *Missouri Republican*'s Al Spink, saloon owner John Peckington, brewer William F. Nolker, and Congressman John J. O'Neill. It was here that the Sportsman's Park Club and Association was formed. Von der Ahe was to be president. Al Spink was voted secretary. After taking over the $6,500 lease of the ballpark from August Solari, the club was to oversee the renovation of the newly named Sportsman's Park.

The former Grand Avenue Park had long since fallen into disuse. Remote from St. Louis proper, the unpaved roads to the park were too bumpy for travel by carriage. With monies from the Sportsman's Park Club and Association, the rotten benches were replaced with a double-decker grandstand and bleachers. Capacity was 8,000, including comfortable chairs for ladies and a special section dedicated exclusively to the "howling" element of fandom. The park was also available for pleasure parties and outdoor events. At about this time, Von der Ahe acquired the concession rights at the park. Al Spink and brother William would also promote other baseball teams in the city under the auspices of the St. Louis Baseball Association.

The Spink brothers were no strangers to baseball promotion. Originally hailing from Quebec, Canada, the family boasted no less than four cricket-playing siblings—Al, William, Fred, and Charles. During the Civil War, the Spinks moved south to Chicago. In their new country, the brothers' love for cricket was replaced by a passion for baseball. After some time, William departed Chicago to become a telegraph operator in St. Louis. Al Spink followed shortly thereafter. A failed telegraphers' union strike forced William to quit his Western Union post and become a newsman. William's interests eventually earned him the sports editorship of the *St. Louis Globe-Democrat*. Al, meanwhile, used his good temperament to land a job at Joseph Pulitzer's *Post-Dispatch* and the *Missouri Republican*. When Al inked a deal with a third newspaper, the *St. Louis Chronicle*, he became sports editor as well. William and Al's newspaper experience and subsequent "barroom" fraternity in the St. Louis sporting subculture proved invaluable. Their contacts included local politicians, police, saloon keepers, and landlords. Along the way, the Spinks counted gambling, horse racing, boxing, and the theater among their interests.

Three years after organizing the first pro club in the city, the 1875 St. Louis Browns, the Spinks tried again. Unfortunately, the city baseball climate had changed, for the worse. The Louisville gambling scandal had left a bad taste in the mouths of would-be baseball supporters. Al believed that the Louisville debacle implied guilt on the part of the St. Louis sporting public. Against this backdrop, Al and William formed the new St. Louis Browns, a co-operative club composed of ex-professionals. The club played their games on Sunday afternoons at Grand Avenue Park and Compton Park. Despite coaxing the International Association champion Indianapolis Browns to St. Louis in 1878, the club flopped. Few ball cranks seemed interested, and the Spink venture foundered.

By early spring 1881, Al and William Spink and Ned Cuthbert were busy organizing the new St. Louis Browns team. Promoting the club in their respective newspapers, the brothers recruited veterans George Seward, George McGinnis, Jack and Bill Gleason, and Harry McCaffrey. The semipro Browns' main mission was to "boom the game" in the city by emphasizing promptness and fair play. At first, the Browns scheduled exhibition contests among themselves. Only modest financial results followed, but that would soon change. O. P. Caylor, a Cincinnati baseball writer, was asked by Al Spink to organize a squad of the best Ohio players. Al Spink then invited the new Cincinnati Reds to St. Louis to play the Browns. On May 22, 1881, at Sportsman's Park, the Browns defeated the Reds, 15–8. Though the affair was less than artistic, the enthusiastic crowd made the day a success. The availability of beer for the event certainly didn't hurt. The Spink brothers scheduled the games on Sunday to take advantage of the spectators' leisure time.Under a percentage plan, over 50 percent of the gate receipt monies went to the players; 40 percent was for a neophyte industry called advertising. The remainder was for expenses and profits. Von der Ahe, provided the refreshments from his saloon across the street.

It is unlikely that baseball pleased Von der Ahe the way it did many Germans. The sport was known for its "geometric order, its requirement of technical skills as well as brute strength and quick reflexes, its disciplined pattern." Baseball "appealed to something in the German psyche." From the beginning, Von der Ahe's investment seemed based on selling his foamy mugs. At the conclusion of the Browns-Reds exhibition, Von der Ahe said to Al Spink, "Vot a fine pig crowd. But the game, Al. How vas the game? Vas it a goot game? You know, I know nawthing." Von der Ahe's honest remarks revealed several facets about the man. His thick German accent and baseball naïveté would become a source of amusement for writers and readers alike. A fun-loving personality also emerged. These character traits would be praised by Von der Ahe's supporters and damned by his enemies for years to come.

By the end of the summer, the Browns challenged all comers. Teams from Chicago and Akron, Ohio, visited St. Louis. One Chicago club was so eager to play that they arrived with only seven men. Two St. Louis lads named Henry Oberbeck and Kid Baldwin served as the battery for the Chicago team. The receipts were so profitable that clubs from Brooklyn and Philadelphia traveled a thousand miles by rail to square off with the Browns. It was the arrival of the Dubuque (Iowa) Rabbits, though, that changed baseball in St. Louis for a decade. The Rabbits, not much more than a sandlot bunch, were organized by railroad concessionaire and nonstop baseball promoter Ted Sullivan.

Dubuque's first baseman was Sullivan's college buddy from St. Mary's, Kansas. His name was Charlie Comiskey, a kid pitcher who learned his baseball on Milwaukee diamonds. Comiskey played ball when he wasn't hustling reading material and confections for patrons of the Illinois Central Railroad. His talents went beyond his physical abilities. Having been a regular on the Rabbits since 1878, Comiskey studied the fine points of the game. He was fortunate enough to have had good teachers; his Dubuque teammates included pitcher Charles Radbourne, infielder Bill Gleason, and outfielder Tom Loftus. As a pitcher, Comiskey possessed underhand speed and a fadeaway curve ball. His catchers often complained of having to stop his swift tosses. Unfortunately, Comiskey developed a sore arm and in 1880 he switched to first base, a position at which he seemed a natural. Believing baseball to be a game of anticipation and quick thinking, Comiskey became an early innovator at the position. One such innovation was to have the pitcher cover first base on balls hit to the right side of the diamond. Player-manager Ted Sullivan had taught Comiskey to play off the bag at first base.

Although the hometowners easily defeated the Rabbits 9–1 on a sweltering July afternoon, Al Spink was most impressed with the errorless play of Comiskey, a "tall, lanky sort of lad with a serious face." That winter, Al Spink offered Comiskey a position on the Browns. Comiskey's first monthly contract paid him $75. One month later, Von der Ahe doubled Comiskey's salary to $150.

After the Browns cleared nearly $25,000 profit for 1881, Von der Ahe realized that baseball was an excellent adjunct to his grocery and saloon business. When the moment arrived to settle the accounts of the Sportsman's Park Club and Association at the end of the season, Von der Ahe had a surprise for the group. He presented them with a check for their stock in the club. Questioned by a stockholder, Von der Ahe calmly said, "Neffer mind who pought it. Here is der check of Chris Von der Ahe for $1,800." Von der Ahe's bold buyout effectively ended the St. Louis Baseball Association, which was absorbed by the Sportsman's Park Club and Association. Chris was beginning to like this "paseball" business.

3

A Working Man's League

Von der Ahe's coup was only the beginning of a larger scheme—the founding of a new baseball league. An element of luck played no small part in this endeavor. Philadelphia ball man Horace Phillips and the former president of the Cincinnati National League team, Justus Thorner, had good intentions. They sent several clubs invitations for an October 10, 1881, meeting in Pittsburgh. However, only baseball editor O. P. Caylor and a reporter with the *Enquirer* showed. Distraught by the lack of response, the men were consigned to failure. However, their fortunes changed when they bumped into an ex-ballplayer and Pittsburgh bartender named Al Pratt. After telling Pratt about their plan for a new baseball league, Pratt told the organizers of a Pittsburgh iron smelter named Denny McKnight. Within hours, the group ingeniously wired other clubs implying that their presence would complete the group at Pittsburgh.

On November 2, 1881, in Cincinnati, a meeting was called to formalize the American Association of Base Ball Clubs. Among the organizers were Chris Von der Ahe and five city representatives eager to earn sporting dollars. McKnight had been at work reorganizing the Allegheny club of Pittsburgh. Caylor had tried (and failed) to form a new league following expulsion of his beloved Cincinnati Red Stockings from the National League in 1880. Six cities were admitted to the Association: St. Louis, Louisville, Cincinnati, Pittsburgh, Philadelphia, and Baltimore. The timing and execution could not have been better. Whereas the National League existed to combat the alcohol and gambling influences of the defunct National Association (1871-1875), the new American Association planned to reverse the temperance trend with a series of deft marketing maneuvers.

First, beer and whiskey could be consumed at American Association ballparks. Originally, board members planned on banning "German tea." However, St. Louis and Cincinnati strongly objected, claiming that $4,000-$5,000 dollars per annum would be lost if the ban were upheld. Second, minimum ticket prices would be cut in half, from the National League's fifty cents to the American Association's twenty-five cents. Third, games would be contested every day, including Sundays, despite intense criticism from ministers and politicians. Fourth, players could be hired off National League blacklists. Fifth, Association teams could play outside clubs in exhibitions. Sixth, permanent umpire staffs would be employed and guaranteed a $140 monthly salary with $3.00 a day expenses. Umpires would be attired in uniforms of blue flannel jackets and caps. Umpires could be removed upon the objections of four Association clubs. Seventh, the American Association placed their teams in non-National League cities.

Visiting ball teams would be guaranteed $65 of the gate. On holidays, the receipts would be split 50-50. The Association also adopted a clause that permitted member teams to leave on their own volition. In effect, the American Association created a working man's baseball league by lowering prices and lifting restrictions on alcohol and Sunday baseball. Ironically, the Association constitution was almost an exact copy of the National League's, with stiff penalties to players for excessive drinking. Chris Von der Ahe and his fellow magnates reasoned that their old-fashioned, backslapping league was better suited for entertainment than the National League version.

The organizers of the Association had one common element: most of the teams were backed by beer money. It was no coincidence that large German, Irish, French, and Italian populations existed in the selected American Association cities. Von der Ahe's St. Louis group included Al Spink, who made money in gambling. Philadelphia, Louisville, Cincinnati, and Baltimore owners all had connections to either brewers, saloons, or gambling houses. At the conclusion of the meeting, McKnight was named president and James Williams was voted secretary. Chris Von der Ahe made the board of directors.

The prudish National League was quick to call its rivals a variety of epithets, including "The Beer and Whiskey Circuit" and "The American Beerball League." National League President William Hulbert telegrammed his rival McKnight: "You cannot afford to bid for the patronage of the degraded; if you are successful you must secure recognition by the respectable." The American Association responded that the National League was a "rich man's league." However warranted the names, it is likely that the National League had reason to fear their competition. American Association directors held their breath in anticipation of their first season.

To illustrate his point, Von der Ahe promoted alcohol sales at Sportsman's Park in a unique way. Combining American capitalism and leisure activities with German gemütlichkeit, Von der Ahe added an open-air beer garden in right field. The beer garden was a German institution for community gathering. As the gardens gained in popularity, some added concert bands, string orchestras, and stage headliners. They even became amusement parks with carnival attractions. Gus Solari's two-story house in the right-field corner was now the scene for people, picnic tables, and mugs of cold brew.

Those so inclined could try their hand at lawn bowling or handball. In the spring, 1882, electric light lawn parties were given at the park. Once a week, revelers could enjoy dancing to their hearts' content as fireworks burst overhead from a bamboo Japanese cannon. In a sense, all Sportsman's Park events would be just like Octoberfest.

Von der Ahe's baseball-beer garden vision didn't end there. Realizing that spectators at ball games enjoyed vicarious action, the beer garden was considered in play. Exactly how many baseballs plunked into beer schooners, scattered revelers, or rattled around picnic tables is conjecture. However arcane this seems today, the idea was perfectly within the rules. Balls retrieved from this area had to be relayed to the pitcher before the runner could be put out.

Von der Ahe and his Sportsman's Park Club cronies would have little difficulty getting their suds in St. Louis. As the large influx of Germans settled in town, their industrial and social habits came, also. Germans seemed to regulate their lives by the ebb and flow of the beer seasons. Beginning in the 1840s, brewers such as Lemp, Busch, and Anheuser populated St. Louis. The city's economy was boosted by this new business and production reached 1 million barrels in 1882. As the demand for beer increased, more factories opened. So popular was beer in St. Louis that one firm made a great business of erecting breweries.

The issue of ballpark alcohol sales cannot be underestimated. From baseball's earliest days, beer guzzling had been a postgame team ritual. Hot summer weather had made beer the refreshment of choice. Despite club rules to curb drinking, teams were lax in enforcement. To bring more cranks to the ballpark, beer was often sold on the premises. Baseball's first professional league, the National Association (1871-1875), discontinued play largely as a result of the excessive boozing of its players. The National League, formed in 1876, also sold the foamy froth in some parks; however, the league never could settle the paradox of selling liquor to patrons while forbidding players from imbibing. By the late 1870s, National League President William Hulbert was promoting a ban on ballpark liquor sales. Hulbert also banned Sunday ball, attempting to appeal to a higher class of fans and rid the game of negative elements. The beer ban extended to entire franchises. Cincinnati, a city with a large German population, was expelled from the league in 1880 after insisting on liquor sales at its park.

Baseball and saloons also shared a common bond. Oppressed workers endured ten to twelve-hour workdays, low wages, and autocratic bosses. Baseball acted as diversion and catharsis for the masses. At a ball game, the downtrodden worker could cheer for his favorite players and teams against not only the opposition but the umpire, who symbolized authority. A spectator could also enjoy heated on-field arguments with the umpires, fantasizing that the arbiter was, for just a moment, his hated boss. Inside the watering hole, one could enjoy popular music, share baseball scores and stories, and tell jokes. Conversations often turned to ill-perceived authority figures: dishonest police, corrupt politicians, pompous judges, and clergy. Germans, in particular, wielded a large influence on middle-class drinking habits.

On April 2, 1882, the Browns played their first exhibition game against a local outfit called the Standards. It was an inauspicious beginning. The Standards won the contest, 4-2. Their president? Alfred Henry Spink. A week later, the Browns exacted their revenge by destroying the Standards.

4

Growing Pains

After a dozen exhibitions, opening day (May 2, 1882) finally arrived in St. Louis to inaugurate the American Association season. The weather cooperated for the 2,000 cranks. The opener was accompanied by much fanfare. President Chris Von der Ahe hired a local band to serenade the spectators and welcome the new players. St. Louis players appeared in uniforms of pure white, with brown caps, stockings, and trim. Opposing St. Louis were the Louisville Eclipse. The opposition came dressed to the nines in their light gray duds with red trim, gray hats, and red stockings. Following tradition, the Louisville players received a horse-drawn taxi ride to Sportsman's Park, but as they entered the park, St. Louis rooters greeted Louisville by flinging rocks, vegetables, and unkind words.

Although manager and captain Ned Cuthbert had scouted five eastern players for the St. Louis nine, the key members were homegrown. Infield brothers Bill and Jack Gleason, pitcher George McGinnis, outfielder George Seward, and catcher Tom "Sleeper" Sullivan all hailed from St. Louis. Also in the lineup was first baseman Charles Comiskey.

A local player, Charlie Houtz, was picked by the Browns to officiate. Houtz called together the captains for a pregame coin flip, Louisville lost the toss, and the Browns chose to take the field. George McGinnis took the box for St. Louis. His opponent was talented Tony Mullane. After six innings, the Browns held a comfortable 8–2 lead, but had to hold off a late Louisville rally to win their opener 9–7. Most in attendance would attest that a good time was had by all. Von der Ahe sent out a virtual army of vendors in white aprons balancing trays and hawking mugs of beer. For those inclined to stiffer spirits, wine by the glass and whiskey by the shot were also sold.

Von der Ahe's first American Association club was a modest aggregation that finished fifth in a six-team league. They won just 37 of 80 games. The Browns were managed by a handsome Philadelphian named Ned Cuthbert. A baseball pioneer, Cuthbert began his career as an amateur outfielder for the 1865 Philadelphia Keystones. Early on, Ned developed a knack for being involved in neophyte baseball leagues. The engaging flychaser helped inaugurate the National Association in 1871 with the Philadelphia Athletics, the National League St. Louis club in 1876, and the American Association St. Louis Browns in 1882. He would later become a member of the 1884 Baltimores of the Union Association. Affable and persuasive, Cuthbert loved to joke about his adventures on and off the diamond. In fact, Cuthbert spent hours in Von der Ahe's bar, convincing Chris to invest his grocery dollars to bring baseball back to St. Louis.

Not particularly strong in the infield or in the outfield, the Browns did possess one star. Local spectators marveled at the exploits of gentlemanly righthand pitcher George "Jumbo" McGinnis. Hailing from the Browns semi-pro team, McGinnis was only fifteen years old when he first played in 1879. George certainly didn't look his age. Mustachioed George was known for his portly physique. A winner in the Browns first American Association game, McGinnis impressed fans and opposition alike with his speedy tosses. "Jumbo" wasn't an overeater; his girth was due to his off-season occupation as glassblower. On the first St. Louis Association team, McGinnis won twenty-five contests. Unfortunately, a lack of pitching depth hurt St. Louis. When McGinnis went down with an ankle injury in July, the team fell out of the race.

This 1882 Browns team was a motley collection of baseball obscurities. Besides Cuthbert, McGinnis, Charlie Comiskey, and the brothers Gleason, virtually no one distinguished themselves in the majors. Three hurlers—John Shappert, Bert Dorr, and Ed Doyle—pitched only in 1882. Morrie Critchley claimed to have won twenty ball games for Albany in 1879 against one defeat. For the Browns, Critchley tossed four games and lost them all. Diminutive Bobby Mitchell would later brag that pitchers were much better in his day. Mitchell swore that his brethren should be able to stop Babe Ruth and Lou Gehrig.

The catching corps was utterly forgettable.

In the infield, Comiskey was just beginning his long stint in the majors. Shortstop "Brother Bill" Gleason was a six-year veteran of the baseball wars. A loud-mouthed coacher and singles hitter, Bill liked to run onto the infield to encourage his mates around the base paths. As a fielder, he didn't think twice about impeding opposing base runners with a knee or hip. Leadoff batter Jack Gleason, four years Bill's senior, wasn't as accomplished. Jack Gleason's fielding difficulties, especially on St. Louis' ruddy infield, helped shorten his career. Infielder Frank Decker quit baseball due to the wear and tear on his hands. Decker's major league resume showed all of five games. In the outfield, Ned Cuthbert was the only player worth mentioning.

It was a season of trial and error for Von der Ahe and his Browns. St. Louis fans were growing accustomed to the owner's starched shirts and bowler hats, which he wore on the hottest of days. Those reading the sports pages noted the German's disposition to become involved in all aspects of his team. Though the Browns weren't too talented, fan enthusiasm was high. A total of 179,000 attended their home and away games. Von der Ahe enjoyed active turnstiles, preferring to count the gate by the amount of beer sold. When Chris discovered that Cincinnati's beer sales were higher, he simply increased the size of the Sportsman's Park bar.

St. Louis cranks also enjoyed Von der Ahe's curious ignorance about the game. Chris' misunderstanding was gleefully reported in the local papers. As fellow American Association owners gathered with Chris at the dedication of Sportsman's Park, Von der Ahe boasted, "Look around chentlemen [sic], because this the largest dimundt in the welt ist."

Wincing, first baseman Comiskey softly whispered to his boss that all diamonds were of identical size.

"Vot I meant to say vas this the larchest infield in the welt ist."

At a meeting with Association owners, Von der Ahe vociferously complained that his team had too many scheduled rain outs, hampering his gate receipts. "I don't vant to be greedy, but next year let it rain in Zinzinnati or on that 'dumkopf' in Baltimore."

After a long hit to right field won a ball game for the Browns, Von der Ahe ordered Captain Comiskey to have his men "Hit all balls to right field." After a loss, a variation on the story was told.

Von der Ahe loved to savor his investment. While sitting on the roof of the grandstand with fellow Sportsman's Park Club directors, Chris would jump up to fine his men for batting, pitching, or fielding transgressions. In a team meeting, Von der Ahe once railed at the failure of shortstop Bill Gleason to stop a ball.

"Gleason, that will cost you a hundred."

The sphere had scooted twenty feet to the left of the fielder.

"But, Chris, he wasn't even near the ball," defended Comiskey.

"But, why wasn't he in front of it?" quizzed Von der Ahe.

Some people joked that Von der Ahe wasn't quite sure if the Browns won or lost the game. All too frequently, Chris had to ask.

In effect, thanks to Al Spink's promotional genius and Von der Ahe's own ignorance of the game, Von der Ahe's baseball persona was created. Early on, editors learned to depend on Von der Ahe for comments. Chris' words made news, created laughs, and sold newspapers. Many of Von der Ahe's quotes must be considered apocryphal, but, his words served to illuminate his personality. To exploit his character, Spink and others often printed Von der Ahe's quotations in a German-English dialect. To make the boss seem erudite, the press and Von der Ahe's own public relations men created a character quite capable of conversing in the King's English. Proof exists that many of these quotes were not quite authentic, due in part to their repetitive nature. Certain quotations were run year after year in St. Louis' local newspapers; often with theme intact but the wording slightly altered.

If Von der Ahe lacked baseball knowledge, he made up for it in ostentation. Chris knew how to throw a party. Before Sportsman's Park had a clubhouse, players were compelled to dress in their hotels or apartments. After donning their uniforms, the Browns would assemble at Von der Ahe's saloon. From there, the club marched up Sullivan Avenue to the ball yard, led by an overdressed Von der Ahe. At game's end, the parade route was reversed. With some ball cranks trailing along, the Von der Ahe entourage entered the saloon. Inside were foamy mugs of beer. Occasionally, Chris would buy drinks for the house, proclaiming in a loud voice, "Money, dot ist to schpend!"

Critical to the success of the Association was its relationship with the National League. All seemed smooth until two Association clubs signed two ex-National Leaguers, Samuel Washington Wise and John "Dasher" Troy. Both were infielders who had briefly played with Detroit in 1881. Soon afterward, the National League declared "war" on their rivals by re-inking Wise and Troy to National League deals. The Detroit Wolverines sent a letter to the American Association's Philadelphia Athletics to inform them that the league did not recognize the Association. In May 1882, the Association countered by adopting a "non-intercourse" policy with the league. Hence forward, the Association would play no more exhibition games with the league and ignore their "reserve" lists. Suspended or blacklisted leaguers were now free to apply to the Association board for reinstatement in that body. A round of lawsuits commenced. Though the Association did sign thirteen National Leaguers, almost all of them eventually returned to the league. The National League was far more successful in getting Association players to jump to the senior circuit.

Following the 1882 campaign, the American Association was pleasantly surprised to count its profits. All clubs finished with positive financial ledgers, including $15,000 for the champion Cincinnati Reds. This profit was largely because the Association had twice the population (2.37 million) in their cities than the eight-team National League. As a result, the Association expanded to eight clubs for 1883. The Columbus Buckeyes and New York Metropolitans were added.

Feeling bold, the Association's Cincinnati Reds played Cap Anson's mighty Chicago team in an unsanctioned championship series. The series lasted only two games before Association President Denny McKnight imposed a $100 fine on the Reds and ordered them to cease playing games with the Chicago nine. McKnight warned his champions that any more contests would result in the Reds' expulsion from the Association.

Realizing that a protracted war between leagues would result in inflated salaries among players, representatives of the National League, American Association, and the newly formed Northwestern minor league met in New York on February 17, 1883. This so-called Harmony Conference resulted in the formation of a new baseball document called the National Agreement or Tripartite agreement. The National Agreement stated that the three leagues were to honor each others' reserve lists, suspension and expulsion lists, and territorial rights. An arbitration committee was formed to settle any disputes that might arise among the signing parties. Representing each league were their respective presidents, Colonel Abraham Mills of the National League, Denny McKnight of the American Association, and Elias Matter of the Northwestern League.

In addition, each league was required to control its own internal affairs. All three leagues were to stand united on issues of player control, territoriality, and outside rivals. Blacklisted ballplayers were forbidden to sign with other clubs. A minimum salary of $1,000 per player was set, though this rule was never challenged. Von der Ahe thought the $1,000 minimum untenable and believed that talented men should be rewarded with larger salaries. The key issue of the meeting, though, was the reserve clause. The list of those covered by the clause was expanded from five to eleven men per team.

Suggested by National League mogul Arthur Soden at a secret gathering in the fall of 1879, the reserve rule bound a player to his team beyond the period of his contract and permitted the club exclusive rights to him for the next season. For the previous three years, the reserve rule had not been part of player contracts. However, with the National Agreement, the reserve clause entered into every contract signed in the three leagues. In theory, the reserve clause prevented raiding. Most importantly, agreed the delegates, the clause forced most players to accept management salaries. Under the plan, signing deals with the highest bidder would be almost impossible. The reserve rule was used as a leverage tool for baseball magnates. Those drunk, absent, insubordinate, or involved in salary disputes could simply be blacklisted or placed on reserve. To continue their careers, players would be compelled to sign on the terms of the owner.

5

A Near Miss

Disappointed with his 1882 Browns, Von der Ahe sought to improve the club in 1883. Acting on a tip from baseball men in Dubuque, Von der Ahe met with the versatile Ted Sullivan, confiding that money would be no object if Sullivan would reorganize and manage the St. Louis Browns. Nearly the same age as Von der Ahe, Sullivan was a determined Irish-born immigrant. Chris was looking for a leader and die-hard baseball man, and T. P., as he was called, certainly fit the description. Sullivan was just starting a long career as a baseball player, manager, owner, league organizer, promoter, and talent scout. The indefatigable Sullivan possessed one advantage over the Browns' owner: Ted knew his baseball.

With Sullivan in command, the reorganization of the Browns commenced. Ted's first hire was a diminutive Scottish-born outfielder named Hugh Nicol. Sullivan believed that Nicol was a fluid fly chaser and that, in time, his batting would improve. Excited about signing Nicol, Sullivan wired Von der Ahe, who was attending the American Association meeting in New York. As the news reached the other magnates about the promising Nicol, they attempted to convince Chris that Nicol was an amateur. Von der Ahe wired back to Sullivan, telling him to release Nicol at once. Sullivan stood his ground and remarked to his boss, "Don't let those wise boys kid you."

After signing Nicol, Sullivan revamped the rest of the squad. First came the pitchers. Tony Mullane, one of the Association's leading pitchers at Louisville, signed a $1,400 contract. Mullane's repertoire featured a fastball and a confounding drop ball often thrown out of the strike zone. Association batters seethed after swinging at Mullane's offerings. To further intimidate hitters, Mullane simply hit them with a pitch. Tony became famous for his dandified appearance (he sported a handlebar moustache and was a favorite of female cranks), his ambidexterity, which he used to his advantage on pickoff moves, his training methods, and his ego. Tony enjoyed practicing on the warmest of days while wearing two heavy sweaters. His ego contributed to many contract squabbles. In 1881, Mullane refused to try out for Detroit, his first major-league team, insisting on a regular contract. Unfortunately, Tony pitched poorly and ended with only a 1–4 record. "Jumbo" George McGinnis was retained, giving the Browns a formidable one-two punch. Ted Sullivan also secured St. Louis native Charlie Hodnett.

At catcher, the Browns weakest position the year before, veteran Pat Deasley was added from Boston. Sleeper Sullivan remained.

In the infield, Sullivan kept first baseman Charlie Comiskey and shortstop Bill Gleason. George Strief replaced the ineffective Bill Smiley at second base. Arlie Latham, acquired from Philadelphia, bumped third baseman Jack Gleason to the bench. An original character, Arlie began his big-league career in a most spectacular way. Playing center field for Buffalo on July 4, 1880, Latham broke up a scoreless tie in the tenth inning by doubling and then scoring the winning run on his teammate's double. His method of scoring was unique. Latham is said to have somersaulted into home plate, beginning ten feet from third base. Upon arriving at his destination, he excitedly faced the crowd and shouted, "The world is mine!"

The outfield corps was overhauled, but it remained chaotic throughout the season. Tom Dolan was penciled in to play right field. Tom Loftus was to captain the club and play center, but he fell ill and appeared in only six games. Tony Mullane patrolled the outer garden on days he didn't pitch. The aging Ned Cuthbert was assigned a backup role along with Harry McCaffrey. In mid-season, the Browns acquired the volatile Fred Lewis from Philadelphia and Tom Mansell from Detroit. Neither Lewis nor Mansell had hit well before, but both responded for Von der Ahe's Browns. Lewis hit .300 and Mansell slugged .400 in limited action. Unfortunately, Mansell's season was shortened due to a wild night on the town. He fell through an elevator shaft at a Cincinnati hotel.

Lewis lasted longer, despite his drinking proclivities and his habit of threatening his manager. During one escapade, Lewis stayed out late lushing with a teammate at a prizefighters' watering hole. After being KO'd by alcohol, the two men found themselves in jail overnight. The next morning, Von der Ahe showed up to see his ballplayers lying helpless on the floor. Chris reached in between the cell bars and poked his men in the ribs. "Say Fred, I tell you fellers to go to bed at 11 o'clock last nide. You got in der wrong room, didn't you."

At preseason training, Sullivan was all business. He drilled his charges in the morning and afternoon. Players were expected to report promptly and as a team, a far cry from 1882, when the club practiced at uneven times and with different colored socks! To change that attitude, Sullivan placed a gong on the grounds to signal the beginning of work. Sullivan's diligence and conditioning methods paid off. Von der Ahe was most appreciative. One afternoon at Sportsman's Park, Von der Ahe summoned Sullivan over to his private seat. The owner whispered to his manager that there was something waiting for him in Von der Ahe's office. After the ball game, Sullivan was given a plush box. Inside was a gold watch and chain with the inscription "C. Von der Ahe to T. P. Sullivan April 4th, 1883."

Throughout the summer, the Browns and Philadelphia battled for the Association pennant. Manager Lew Simmons' Philadelphians were led by the strong bat of first baseman Harry Stovey and the able pitching of Bobby Matthews. Philadelphia management drafted strict restrictions on player behavior. Among them were prohibitions against smoking after pregame dinners, consorting with girls while in uniform, and staying out past 11:00 P.M. on road trips.

The Browns' temperament was somewhat different. Though they earned praise for their play in St. Louis, they were scorned around the Association. *Sporting Life* found them intolerable, calling them ". . . the toughest and roughest gang that ever struck this city . . . Vile of speech, insolent in bearing . . . they set at defiance all rules, grossly insulting the umpire and exciting the wrath of the spectators." When the Browns weren't nasty, they beat opponents by being politely nasty.

Arlie Latham volunteered to coach a game in Cincinnati. Bespectacled Reds' right-hander Will White had puzzled St. Louis hitters all afternoon. Whereupon, Latham calmly offered this advice: "My dear Mr. White, we have been very courteous during the game, but as the Browns need a few runs, we will have to be rude to you for a while." The comment so unnerved White that the Browns began to knock his "raise ball" all over the yard.

Thanks to the success of the Browns, patrons of St. Louis baseball could not have been more rabid. To help sustain interest, Von der Ahe ordered a telephone connection from the club's downtown headquarters to the park. The connection relayed wire reports on ball games around the American Association, so fans could follow other Association games in progress. The numbers were then posted on giant bulletin boards, forerunners of scoreboards.

In fact, the word *fan* is said to have derived from Von der Ahe's mispronunciation of the word *fanatic*. A more plausible explanation is that the term originated with Ted Sullivan. The early word for the peculiar traits of baseball patrons was "crank." A dictionary defined the colloquial term as "a person who has odd, stubborn notions about something." "Fan" was also defined as a "wind-producing instrument," a term not far removed from the baseball appellation.

Thomas Lawson was one such crank. He would write a book entitled *The Krank: His Language and What it Means. Krank* was a novelty; the book was supposedly made of baseball skin, in the shape of a ball, and cost twenty-five cents. Lawson also invented a baseball game with cards, which he sold on trains. His book was equal parts parody and self-description. He described the crank as a bully who gobbled up every newspaper item he could about the game but then regurgitated the facts to everyone he met. The crank was obnoxious and argumentative, directing his barbs from the ticket taker to the turnstile custodian. Players, managers, and other cranks were hardly immune to his tirades. Lawson also wrote that the crank was a "heterogenous compound of flesh, bone and baseball, mostly baseball."

During the 1883 season, Ted Sullivan and Charles Comiskey were meeting at team headquarters when an unknown man strolled into the office. Without warning, he launched into a series of nonstop, unsolicited opinions about the Browns. Exhausting his comments of the locals, the stranger proceeded to critique the sport itself. After endless commentary, the man was finally called outside.

Sullivan said to Comiskey, "What name can you possibly apply to a fellow like that?"

Comiskey replied, "He is a fanatic!"

Ted Sullivan then said, "I will abbreviate that and call him a fan."

Sullivan and the Browns spent the better part of the summer fighting Philadelphia for the flag, but Ted had a far more formidable opponent in owner Chris Von der Ahe. Forever meddling in St. Louis and Association baseball affairs, Von der Ahe's relationship with Sullivan grew more strained with the pressures of the pennant chase.

One example of Chris' meddling occurred during late June. After a Saturday loss at home, Von der Ahe met with upset fans who explained that umpire John Kelly was mad at the Browns and their irascible owner. Convinced Kelly was responsible for the St. Louis defeat, Von der Ahe went to work. Without telling manager Ted Sullivan, he flashed off a telegram to Association secretary Jimmy Williams, demanding that Kelly be sent to Louisville in exchange for umpire Charlie Daniels. Kelly was to leave on a night train from St. Louis to Louisville. Daniels was to pack his bags and ride west to St. Louis. Secretary Williams then telegrammed both umpires. The great umpire trade was underway.

Without fanfare, John Kelly boarded his train and headed east. Daniels, on the other hand, managed to miss the last train out of Louisville that evening. Without drastic action, Daniels would have no chance of arriving in St. Louis for the Sunday afternoon game. After a flurry of telegrams, Von der Ahe was informed of the problem. Knowing the Sunday crowd would be enormous, Von der Ahe wired the Louisville and Nashville (L&N) railroad line. Getting Daniels to St. Louis on a special engine would cost $300! Without compunction, Von der Ahe agreed to pay for this "umpire special." Von der Ahe then decided to tell manager Sullivan.

Flabbergasted at his employer's actions but unaware of the $300 special train, Sullivan said, "Kelly was all right, why did you not speak to me about it?"

The haughty Chris could not bring himself to tell Sullivan about Daniel's personal train. Just then, an agent from the L&N railroad walked into the office.

The agent proclaimed, "Well, Chris, I just got a telegram from Louisville. Your umpire left at 10:40 on a special. Three hundred dollars is pretty stiff, Chris, for changing umpires."

Sullivan could only sigh. The ridiculousness of the extravagance etched lines on Von der Ahe's face.

"Ted, we will get it back at the gate tomorrow, as it will be a great ad, to see an umpire that was on a special train that costs $300 and it shows my power in the Association."

The umpire swap may have proven Von der Ahe's power, but his players lost to Philadelphia the next day.

In addition to managing the Browns, Ted Sullivan was also busy chronicling the Browns' owner's funny English. Von der Ahe was becoming a master of the malaprop. Once, during a manager-owner chat, Von der Ahe was speaking highly of a ballplayer whom he thought could help the Browns. Sullivan calmly reminded Chris that the player had already been released two or three times. Appearing to agree with his manager, Chris said, "That is right, a rolling moss never catches a stone." Inverted proverbs were part of the Von der Ahe lexicon. Chris offered a new twist on the phrase, "Everything comes to him who waits." Instead, Von der Ahe managed to blurt out, with perfect seriousness, "He that waits gets nothing."

Sullivan wasn't alone. Dave Reed, the St. Louis publicist fond of liquor and Latin phrasings, also noticed Chris' curious English. Reed liked to tell the story of Von der Ahe's reaction to the Browns losing three straight exhibition games. Von der Ahe called Comiskey and the players into his hotel room and said:

> Comiskey and fellers, you lost three straight to Golumpus. As Dave Reet, my secretary used to say, "a friend in neet is a friend what has got money."
>
> Vell, I've got the money, and I'm your friend. If you don't play ball as a lot of dubs play it. Und I understand dot some of you fellers took some classes of beer ven I vasn't looking last night. Now if I fint any of you fellers boosing, I vill fine effery one vich booses ten dollars. Ond as my old secretary Dave Reet used to say, "if the show fits, vear it."

Known for his excellent rapport with newsmen, Reed suffered the ignominy of being fired every few days by Von der Ahe. To Comiskey, Von der Ahe spoke of Reed: "Dot dem Dafe Reet is out again bainting der down. He can't keep sober two days in a bunch already." Comiskey replied slyly that he knew of a intemperate, out-of-work writer who'd do wonders for the team. When asked, Comiskey replied that his name was Shakespeare. "Dot Shagespeare you schpeak uf, Commy, may be a goot writer but I don'd gif a dem if he wrote 'As You Like It,' 'Catch As Catch Can,' or 'Vere You Dem Please.' He can't write goot schtories as Dafe Reet. If Dafe ain't sober tomorrow, you can schend Shagespeare arount to der office und I vill gif him a trial."

However, the race for the flag wasn't so funny. By late August, pennant stress was having devastating effects on the Von der Ahe-Sullivan relationship. On their last eastern swing, the Browns were playing New York, in a virtual tie with Philadelphia. Von der Ahe ordered Sullivan to change pitcher Mullane in the middle of a game. Sullivan disagreed and the feud intensified.

Von der Ahe was furious that his boys had lost games to the inferior New York club. That evening, he made an unannounced inspection at the hotel. Nearly all his players were out enjoying the town. Immediately, Von der Ahe lashed out at Sullivan and blamed his manager for the Browns' indiscretions. During the hotel-room spat, Sullivan hurled his gift watch back at Von der Ahe. With that act, Ted Sullivan's tenure with the St. Louis Browns ended.

To replace Sullivan, Von der Ahe named Charlie Comiskey to the post. The 24-year-old Comiskey was without managerial experience. The St. Louis *Missouri Republican* sniped, "Mr. Von der Ahe thinks that he, with the assistance of Comiskey, can successfully manage the affairs of the club." St. Louis still had nineteen games to play.

It didn't take long for Comiskey to fit right in. The next day, the new manager organized a special morning practice to teach pitchers to cover first base. A New York sportswriter remarked that "the amazed spectators jeered and hooted the tall, gawky, lanky youngster who dared to make such an innovation." Comiskey's innovations and positive attitude kept St. Louis in the race.

By September 21, the Browns trailed Philadelphia by only two and one-half games. There were seven contests remaining. Despite the deficit, St. Louis ball fans remained in a frenzy. Philadelphia was at Sportsman's Park, beginning a crucial three-game weekend series, and a clean sweep for St. Louis would mean first place.

Amid swirling winds, 10,000 crammed their way into the ballpark. Anxious to show his importance, Von der Ahe invited Congressman John J. O'Neill and the governor of Missouri to his private box. Both teams trotted out their ace pitchers: Bobby Matthews took the mound for Philadelphia, and Tony Mullane carried the St. Louis hopes. Charles Daniels officiated; the same man whom Von der Ahe had sent for earlier in the season.

What followed was one of the wildest tilts ever to take place on a diamond in St. Louis.

After winning the coin toss, St. Louis manager Comiskey requested that the visitors bat first. Left fielder Jud Birchal opened with a sharp single off St. Louis shortstop Bill Gleason's shin. First baseman Harry Stovey singled to left. After right fielder Alonzo Knight's weak bouncer to the infield, Stovey was forced at second base. The next batter was shortstop Mike Moynahan, who rapped to Gleason. In an attempt to cut off Birchal, Gleason threw home. Unfortunately, the ball sailed high over the outstretched hands of catcher Tom Deasley. It was 1–0, Philadelphia.

Mullane's start was shaky, but his nervous fielders certainly weren't helping.

Batting with two men on base, center fielder Jack O'Brien punched a grasscutter toward shortstop Gleason. He scooped up the sphere and made a soft toss to second baseman Joe Quest, to force Moynahan. Quest wasn't cooperating. Joe dropped the ball and then allowed it to squirt away. Error, Quest. Knight, meanwhile, picked up steam and raced for home. Quest recovered in time to make a sharp peg to catcher Deasley. Knight was the second out. Moynahan, straining to hear his coach, bolted for third. Tom Deasley threw wild to third baseman Latham, and the ball squirted away again. Error, Deasley. Alertly backing up the play, Gleason recovered the ball and tried to get O'Brien at second base. Quest was set for the throw, but dropped it. Error, Quest. Moynahan, who began the play on first base, raced for home. Miraculously, Quest fired a strike to catcher Deasley. O'Brien was out. The inning was over. Philadelphia still led, 1–0. St. Louis ball cranks were aghast. Many finally realized that no runs had scored and broke into an uncertain cheer. On one play, Joe Quest had been responsible for two errors and two assists. The Sportsman's Park faithful had just witnessed a double play with three errors! Ball cranks attempting to score the game muddied up their scorecards.

It is unknown whether the Governor or Congressman attempted to explain the play to Von der Ahe.

The visitors tallied four times on two hits in the third, thanks to Arlie Latham's three-error inning. Philadelphia added one more in the fourth for a 6–0 lead. By now, Von der Ahe and his guests realized that the St. Louis pennant hopes were blowing in the wind. In the bottom of the fourth, however, the Browns rallied. First baseman Harry Stovey sprained his ankle on a harmless pop foul. Philadelphia's stellar batsman departed, to be replaced by pitcher and utility man George Washington "Grin" Bradley. St. Louis' outfield combination of Hugh Nicol and Fred Lewis keyed the uprising with their bats and base running. Bradley hurt Philadelphia by botching his first play in the field. Philadelphia led, 6–3.

Both clubs added three more in the fifth. The Browns managed to kick the ball all over the lot, giving Philadelphia a 9–3 bulge. In their half, St. Louis cranks were thrilled when Fred Lewis deposited a Matthews pitch over the right field fence. The Browns trailed, 9–6. St. Louis tightened matters with two tallies in the home seventh. Dusk was gradually creeping over Sportsman's, but nobody was leaving the park. It was 9–8, Philadelphia.

In the eighth, third baseman Latham changed positions with catcher Deasley. St. Louis' regular backstop was having a devil of a time catching the swift slants of Tony Mullane. Latham did no better, and the Athletics scored four more runs on three hits, two errors, a wild pitch, and three passed balls. At this stage, the Browns trailed 13–8, and fans may have ordered a schooner to drown their sorrows. Somehow, St. Louis rallied again. Due to Gleason and Nicol's base running and the lamentable work of catcher Rowan (eight errors) and outfielder Bradley, the Browns pulled to 13–11. Philadelphia manager Lew Simmons had Bradley switch positions with center fielder Jack O'Brien. Unfortunately, Bradley's outfield play was dreadful, and he made two errors in the inning. At the conclusion of the eighth, umpire Daniels threw up his hands and called the game due to darkness. With the help of catcalls from the crowd, the Browns bullied Daniels into changing his mind.

The Athletics went quietly in the ninth. Deasley departed and was replaced by Tom Dolan. Arlie Latham took his five errors back to third base. Needing two for a tie, the Browns came up for their final at bats. Second baseman George Strief popped up to right field, but Alonzo Knight muffed the ball for the sixteenth Philadelphia error of the day. Dolan was scheduled next, but, the Browns sent up better-hitting Tony Mullane. Umpire Daniels apparently did not notice, perhaps dreaming of a nice shower. Mullane popped to the shortstop. One out. Bill Gleason smashed the ball deep to center field and Strief streaked around the bases. Center fielder Bradley, with four errors at first and in the outfield, made a frantic dash to get the ball. Like an early day Willie Mays, Bradley made a miraculous over-the-shoulder catch. The heroics quieted the screaming faithful straining to see amid darkening skies. When Comiskey meekly grounded out, the game was over. The Athletics were the 13–11 victors.

All told, there were twenty-eight errors committed (sixteen by the visitors) and twenty-four hits in the game. Both pitchers managed to stay in all the way. Only five of the twenty-four runs were earned. Mullane's ugly pitching line read nine innings, thirteen hits, thirteen runs, one earned run, one base on balls, and seven strikeouts.

The Browns bounced back on Saturday to squeeze out a 9–8 win.

On Sunday, the massive throng threatened the foundation of Sportsman's Park. A reported 16,800 jammed in to see their heroes take on the Athletics. The entire male population of St. Louis had seemingly converged at Grand and Sullivan Avenues. Comiskey called his ace, Mullane, to the mound. Lew Simmons surprised everyone by naming St. Louis native George Bradley as his starter. Bradley, a nonsmoking, teetotaler, would later recall, "I remember how the Browns smiled when they heard I was going to pitch . . . When I got in the square, however, it was though I was born again . . . Well, I went in and you know the rest."

For the still hopeful Browns, the rest wasn't so good. Bradley shut down Comiskey's men on three hits to win 9–2. Philadelphia eventually won the pennant by one game over St. Louis. Ten years later, Bradley would admit his secret. When he could get away with it, Bradley liked to steam the ball in boiling water, place it in a vice, and press the sphere "until it was as mellow as a ripe pear."

Losing to Philadelphia affected the Browns players. Following the campaign, the squad took out their frustrations by scheduling no fewer than twenty fistfights with their peppery third baseman, Arlie Latham. The St. Louis players were mostly upset because Latham had an extraordinary talent for baiting the opposition and umpires while upsetting his own teammates. One by one, the St. Louis Browns lined up to take their swings at Arlie. The scrappy Latham fought well. Some Browns knocked Latham out cold, but he boxed his share of men to the turf.

At the conclusion of the 1883 season, Harry Oberbeck, a promising outfielder, decided to sue the St. Louis Browns. Oberbeck had played in just four games and gone hitless. The lawsuit charged that Von der Ahe had unfairly released the player and challenged the whole idea of American Association contracts.

At the beginning of the campaign, Oberbeck was signed by the Alleghenys. He then appeared in a couple of games with Peoria of the Northwestern League without a contract. According to Oberbeck, Von der Ahe persuaded him to play ball for the Browns while promising to iron out any problems with Peoria. Von der Ahe, noting that Harry's bat couldn't even produce a loud foul in fourteen tries, released Oberbeck. Peoria then expelled Oberbeck for leaving their club. Now young Harry was without a job and, pending reinstatement, could not chase or bat baseballs as a profession.

Ballplayers around the country awaited the results of Oberbeck's suit. Believed to be the first of its kind, the suit argued that American Association clubs could not retain ball players for a season and expel anyone who broke their contract. Association clubs could also not release players at their whim and without notice, which seemed unfair. A decisive win by Oberbeck could have meant that all baseball contracts were not binding.

During the trial, the St. Louis Browns weren't exactly represented in the best light. Von der Ahe's attorney, Tom Cornelius, a baseball illiterate, was questioning St. Louis' ex-manager Ted Sullivan. Cornelius "asked him [Sullivan] if this ball they were talking about had a string tied to it and what the devil the players meant when they said Oberbeck was 'a wind hitter.' " The reference to Oberbeck's inability to bat was lost on Cornelius. Oberbeck's attorneys made their case and won a $400 judgment for their client. Despite the victory and Oberbeck's attorney's comments on "well-determined rights" by players, the owners retained their power over their employees.

Although he may have looked silly in the Oberbeck case, Von der Ahe didn't seem to mind. In front of the Sportsman's Park Club and Association, the Browns magnate joyfully claimed that he cleared an enormous profit for the season. With the tight pennant race, nearly 300,000 attended 1883 games at Sportsman's Park. Despite his ignorance of the game, Von der Ahe was serving on several American Association committees. His local political background was serving him quite well.

As a result of the National Agreement, the 1883 season was a rather prosperous venture. Profit margins for the Association showed Philadelphia $75,000 ahead, St. Louis $50,000, Cincinnati $25,000, and Baltimore $10,000.

6

"The Strongest Nine"

Fierce opposition to the reserve rule was the basis for a territorial challenge to the National League and American Association. On September 12, 1883, delegates from eight cities met in Pittsburgh to discuss plans for a brand-new baseball organization to be called the Union Association of Professional Baseball Clubs. The Unions then proceeded to pattern their organization after the National League and American Association. For starters, they adopted the American Association constitution and agreed to the validity of all League and Association contracts. Receipts were to be divided, as in the National League, through a percentage plan, with a $75 guarantee for all visiting clubs. The linchpin, though, was the Union Association's abolition of the reserve rule. Players would no longer be bound to clubs beyond completion of their contracts.

Among the financial backers of the Union Association was Henry V. Lucas, a St. Louis real-estate tycoon. Two of Lucas' relatives were past presidents of St. Louis Browns clubs in the league. Adolphus Busch, an extremely wealthy St. Louis brewer, was a Lucas partner. Lucas was fond of quoting Busch. "Don't stop until you have secured the strongest nine that ever represented St. Louis, no matter what it costs." Like their American Association rivals, four Union magnates were connected to the brewing industry.

Union magnates, foreseeing big profits, were optimistic. In 1883, baseball attendance was on the rise. Because of the reserve rule, competition for players was kept low. The Union secretary gushed, "We are certain to succeed. Our refusal to be bound by the eleven-man reserve rule assures us the good will of every player in the country."

In the middle of the St. Louis winter, the ambitious Lucas proclaimed, "I wish the season were here now. I am impatient to see the boys at work and the balls flying about." Lucas' St. Louis team had been practicing at a handball alley in the city.

Union naysayers wrote that baseball already had two major leagues.

Almost no large city was without a team. St. Louis, Cincinnati, Baltimore, Washington, and Philadelphia already had clubs in the American Association. Boston and Chicago sported clubs in the National League.

By December 1883, the powerful Lucas bullied his way into the presidency of the Union Association. The Union Association upset the existing baseball organizations. Chris Von der Ahe saw their dealings as major-league competition and a direct run at his St. Louis dollars. The St. Louis Unions' formation was similar to that of the American Association. Lucas had befriended players over drinks, listening to their "slave" stories. Exactly who was this Henry Lucas setting up shop in Von der Ahe's St. Louis? Von der Ahe must have wondered about his own foray into baseball just a few years earlier. Would Lucas be to the Unions what Von der Ahe was to the Association?

Henry Lucas certainly seemed serious about the venture. He built Lucas Park on his own land, with a capacity for 10,000 fans. Lucas believed in comfort and aesthetics. Features included a huge grandstand, upholstered folding opera chairs, and leisure facilities. Patrons entering were serenaded by a cage full of canaries. With such amenities, the park was dubbed "The Palace Park of America." Fans weren't the only pampered guests. The grounds housed a dressing room and reception area. One room was for reading and lectures. Another was designed for hygiene. The washroom had no less than nine bathtubs. For the fifty-six-game home schedule, ball cranks could purchase a reserved season ticket for $22. Bleacher season tickets sold for $11.00.

Competition for players among the three organizations intensified. Ted Sullivan, only months removed as the Browns' manager, searched across America for players to fill Union uniforms. With higher salaries, two- and three-year deals, and the abolition of the reserve rule, Union contracts seemed enticing. A. G. Mills, president of the National League, proclaimed, "The Unions are making efforts to debauch our players."

The League and the Association responded to the challenge. Both set up "reserve teams," squads of semipro and amateur players who would participate in exhibition games and be ready in case of emergency. Reserve team players were not permitted to sign with the Unions. The idea was to prevent as many men as possible from signing with the neophyte league. Reserve games would be contested on home grounds and cost a quarter. Von der Ahe saw the reserves as talent farms and an incentive for Browns' players. "If you don't do well you will be dropped to the reserve crowd." Quipped *Sporting Life,* "The ballplayer who fails to get employment . . . had better give up all idea of ever going into the business."

In November 1883, John Day of the National League wrote legislation that blacklisted players who had ignored the reserve rule. One month later, the American Association voted to expand from eight clubs to twelve attempting to tie up territory and further decrease the pool of players from going Union. Brooklyn, Indianapolis, Toledo, and Washington were added to the Association. The Association also adopted a modified version of the Day

Resolution, with a caveat that Association deserters could be accepted back, provided they didn't play in a Union game.

The first salvo in the war was fired in the winter of 1883. Anthony J. Mullane, a talented 24-year-old pitcher, would be the center of the storm. After pitching sensational ball for the Browns in 1883, Mullane jumped his contract. Promised an advance and $2,500, Mullane signed with Lucas' Unions. Realizing the gravity of the situation, Von der Ahe strong-armed several magnates in the Association to pool money for the upstart Toledo franchise. Toledo would then entice Mullane away from the St. Louis Unions. Von der Ahe understood that Toledo would not threaten the Browns' pennant chances. Before the first pitch of the St. Louis Unions' season, Mullane jumped the Lucas entry to sign with Toledo. *Sporting Life* reported that Lucas was offering Mullane $3,000 for two years but that Tony would settle only for $3,000 in advance. The Cleveland *Herald* gave details of the jump: "These are facts and show Mullane to be a man of a most sordid nature. He will bear watching."

With these events, the Von der Ahe and Lucas feud intensified. Von der Ahe refused to meet the St. Louis Unions in exhibitions. Chris was busy preparing Sportsman's Park for the new season. In April, he purchased a set of turnstiles originally used at the Philadelphia Centennial celebration. He also opened a press to print score sheets so avid cranks could track the games. That same month, an exhibition between the Browns and their reserves drew more than 7,000. The parent club won, 8–6.

On April 20, 1884, the Union Association began play. The St. Louis Unions defeated Chicago 7–2 in a steady, cold drizzle. Al Spink reported that 10,000 were present to sit, get wet, and watch a ball game. Though most of the Union clubs were comprised of experienced minor-league men, Lucas stocked his club with major-league veterans, enticed by bonus money. Ted Sullivan managed. The Maroons, as they were called, were led by second baseman Fred Dunlap, right fielder Orator Shaffer, left fielder Buttercup Dickerson, center fielder Dave Rowe, and pitching sensation Billy Taylor. Homegrown St. Louis infielders Jack Gleason and Joe Quinn manned the corners. The Maroons were head and shoulders above other Union clubs, winning twenty of their first twenty-one games.

With the overwhelming success of the St. Louis club, the Union pennant race and fan interest fizzled. Union clubs eventually began to drop out, citing financial difficulties. Despite the absence of a competitive Union race, Mullane, Von der Ahe, and Lucas kept the summer interesting. An early May debut in St. Louis by Mullane in Toledo flannels brought jeers from the Browns faithful. When Mullane stepped up to bat, he raised his cap in a derisive gesture. To counter the near hysteria created by Mullane's return, Lucas hatched his plan. One day after Tony appeared in St. Louis, Lucas' attorneys obtained a court order restraining Mullane from playing in the city. Lucas' lawyer then proceeded to follow Mullane's Toledo club to Cincinnati to obtain more injunctions.

After less than two months, Ted Sullivan departed as field boss of the

Maroons. Perhaps Sullivan didn't want to be mixed up in the Mullane mess. Ted probably felt more comfortable doing what he did best—scouting players. The way the Maroons played, they didn't need a manager.

Notwithstanding the fierce competition for sporting dollars, there were some light moments. During the spring, the Browns' reserves were away on a road trip. Von der Ahe wanted to keep tabs on his men, so he told his manager to telegram results of the game. The manager thought that Von der Ahe wanted a pitch-by-pitch account. A day after the contest, a telegraph boy came into Von der Ahe's office with a large, bulky envelope.

"This is a telegram for you, Mr. Von der Ahe, and there are $27 charges on it."

Von der Ahe eyed the boy nervously.

"What! Did someone telegraph me his will from across the ocean?"

"No, Mr. Von der Ahe, it is an account of the ball game, sent by your manager, from Terre Haute, Indiana."

Von der leapt out of his chair.

"Why didn't he telegraph me a history of his life?"

Von der Ahe took the message, paid the lad, and read the telegram. Sure enough, it was an account of the game he had ordered. Immediately, Von der Ahe repaired himself to the telegraph office to wire his manager.

"For God's sake, don't send any more telegrams."

The row between Von der Ahe and Lucas was further exacerbated by the feuding of Browns' catchers Tom Dolan and Pat Deasley. Dolan, furious over Deasley's higher salary, arranged with a teammate to rough up his rival. Later, Dolan was called into the president's office. Von der Ahe explained to Dolan that his behavior would no longer be tolerated. Backup catcher Dolan had been a constant thorn in the side of manager Jimmy Williams. Von der Ahe also commented that Dolan's batting, throwing, and base running were not up to standard. When Dolan vehemently disagreed, Chris told his catcher to put on his uniform and get ready for the game. Following his boss' orders, Dolan donned Browns flannels. However, the game that Dolan would play in was not at Sportsman's Park. Instead, Dolan telephoned Western Union. Soon after, a telegram flashed to Henry Lucas.

"Dolan has jumped the Browns and he is on his way," read the message.

"I'll let him catch Sweeney this afternoon," was Lucas' reply.

In an instant, Dolan headed a dozen blocks to the grounds of the St. Louis Maroons. Word of the defection spread through town like wildfire. A host of fans and reporters, including Al Spink, were on hand as Dolan stepped off his cab to cheers. Dolan was late for the ball game, but he caught for the Maroons that day.

The town was abuzz with the story. St. Louis papers carried extras about the jump and printed a rash of tales about further jumps of St. Louis Browns to teams around the Union Association. All later proved false.

Dolan's surprise left egg on the face of Von der Ahe, Lucas, and Pat Deasley. For allowing Dolan to walk, Von der Ahe looked like an insensitive owner. Henry Lucas looked foolish for repeatedly being quoted saying that he wanted no contract breakers on his nine. Yet, owing to the Maroons' weakness behind the plate and Dolan's assertions to Lucas that Von der Ahe expelled him, Dolan was received with open arms.

Pat Deasley had to endure a series of negative articles in the press that were concocted by Thomas Dolan. In September, Deasley published his retort in *Sporting Life*. Deasley called Dolan's assertions concerning Deasley's drinking and their salary dispute a pack of lies. It probably didn't help when the Browns' salaries were printed in *Sporting Life* in July.

Another Browns versus Maroons row occurred when a Browns player sauntered over to Union Park one day to challenge manager Fred Dunlap. The St. Louis player started the fisticuffs, shouting at his rival that the upstart Maroons were stealing their fans and money. The fight didn't last long. Dunlap beat Comiskey's boy so badly that the latter needed assistance getting home.

In August, two more Union clubs faltered due to financial difficulties. Meanwhile, as the Association was closing its season, the Toledo Blue Stockings were suffering severe monetary reverses. Desperate to recoup losses, Toledo sold Tony Mullane, Curt Welch, Sam Barkley, and others to the Browns for $3,500. The owners of Toledo were to collect $2,500 cash up front. Von der Ahe cleverly added a proviso for refunds. When all the players' signatures were affixed to contracts, the balance would be paid. This unscrupulous dealing by Von der Ahe was no doubt directed at Mullane.

Exactly ten days after Toledo officially disbanded, Von der Ahe and manager Charlie Morton signed the agreement. Morton, Barkley, and Welch attended the signing, but conspicuously absent was Tony Mullane. Feigning sickness, Mullane was actually sneaking away with Cincinnati representatives. To spite Von der Ahe, Mullane refused to report to the Browns. Instead, Tony signed a $5,000 deal with the Reds, with half the money to be paid in advance. This was the second time Mullane had stiffed Von der Ahe in 1884.

By September, with the Union Association in complete disarray, reports surfaced that their top two teams, the Maroons and Cincinnati, were interested in joining the National League. Before their schedules could be completed, the entire Union Association shut down. Only five of the original eight teams finished out the season. Henry Lucas barely broke even and claimed $17,000 in arrears for trying to bolster other clubs to keep the organization afloat. The Unions lost heavily due to player jumps, unrealistic contracts, and a lack of attendance.

Contract warfare also impacted the National League and the American Association. Due to player raids, the National League was forced to subsidize some clubs. Expansion in the Association, designed to keep players away from the Unions, produced a watered-down product and financial losses.

The St. Louis Maroons ended 94–19, still the best won-lost record in the history of major-league baseball. St. Louis paced the Union Association in nearly all the batting, pitching, and fielding departments. In so doing, Lucas' powerful Maroons led to the downfall of the Union Association. The words of Adolphus Busch had proved oddly prophetic.

In a state of near collapse, only four Union representatives gathered for a meeting in December 1884. Henry Lucas was reelected president. However, within days, newspapers were again reporting that Lucas was negotiating with the National League. One month later, sans Lucas, the remnants of the Union Association met in Milwaukee. Only two clubs showed, and the Union Association disbanded.

Two critical issues concerned the League and Association upon the conclusion of the campaign; the suspension of Tony Mullane and the absorption of the St. Louis Maroons into the National League. Upset at a second spurning from Mullane, Von der Ahe pressed hard for his suspension. In December 1884, the Association held its annual gathering in New York City. The Association's board convened and staged a mock trail. Representing St. Louis was Browns' Vice President John J. O'Neill. In defense of Cincinnati was O. P. Caylor. Tony Mullane was in the city and called as a witness, but did not attend. In a unanimous decision, the Board voted to suspend Mullane for the entire 1885 season and forced him to repay the Cincinnati team $1,000. According to the board, Mullane had brought "discredit on the base ball profession, causing discontent and insubordination among all professional players and setting an example of sharp practice equivalent to actual dishonesty."

No formal charges were ever brought against St. Louis or Cincinnati. The pitcher took the ruling in stride and promised to return the money. Mullane also vowed there would be tough games ahead for his opponents. While not formally stated, the ruling made Mullane Cincinnati property for 1886. Cincinnati promised to stand by their suspended pitcher and made their ball grounds available to him for practice.

The ruling surprised many. *Sporting Life* wrote that Mullane committed no illegality and that the contracts he signed were not worth the paper they were printed on. Nonetheless, the case revealed the high-stakes nature of professional baseball. Mullane had been suspended, but Von der Ahe's conduct wasn't exactly pristine. Suspension of the powerful owner could have collapsed the entire American Association.

With the conclusion of the Mullane case, the Association voted to pare down to eight teams. Rules were written to formally charge umpires, managers, or players with disgraceful or drunken conduct. Tellingly, there were no such rules for owners.

In January the National League met for its annual fete. Discussions centered on Lucas' bid to place his franchise in the League. As Lucas presented his case, the League wired Von der Ahe for his consent to waive the portion of the reserve clause that dealt with territoriality. The League also stipulated that upon Von der Ahe's acceptance, a meeting between the two men should be scheduled. Von der Ahe, however, wanted nothing to do with Lucas. The Browns' owner flashed a telegram back to New York, opposing Lucas from entering the League. Chris demanded $10,000 to pay for losses the Browns incurred while Lucas ran the Unions in St. Louis. Declining the preposterous fee, Lucas met in secret session with the National League. The senior circuit insisted Lucas abide by the rules of the reserve clause. Lucas would have to agree to denounce the very foundation of the failed Union Association. He would also have to pay $6,000 to retain several of his old players.

After nearly two weeks, Association boss Denny McKnight joined the League in talks about the Maroons franchise. The Association was informed by the League that they had broken the National Agreement by the absorption of the Cleveland team by the Brooklyn franchise. In the costly three-way war during the summer of 1884, the Cleveland League club was in a state of collapse. Charlie Hackett, who was to manage the Association's Brooklyn team in 1885, visited Cleveland players in their homes, enticing them with Association contracts. Hackett somehow managed to spirit away several players at a Cleveland hotel. In effect, Hackett was involved in a kidnapping plot to obtain players for the Brooklyns. To ratchet up the stakes, the League demanded expulsion of the Brooklyn team by the Association or admittance of the St. Louis club to the League. Von der Ahe telegrammed Association leaders to end the disagreement and conditionally accept the Maroons. In return, the Association could place one of its clubs in League territory in an emergency. The League agreed, and the Brooklyn-Cleveland controversy was dropped.

The crucial showdown over the Lucas affair loomed. Once again, John J. O'Neill served as Von der Ahe's point man. Meeting behind closed doors, O'Neill and Lucas reached a tentative compromise. So desperate was Lucas to gain entry to the League that he was willing to charge fifty cents for spectators, have no Sunday games, and sell no beer in his park. But still, no solution was reached.

On the return train trip to St. Louis, a confident O'Neill and Lucas again discussed the matter. The men agreed to meet again at Tony Faust's seafood restaurant in St. Louis. Lucas finally agreed to pay $2,500 damages to the Browns. The St. Louis baseball turf war, conducted largely in newsprint, was coming to an end. Von der Ahe, sanguine in the knowledge that the Maroons would charge twice the admission, play no Sunday ball, nor sell foamy refreshments, knew his St. Louis profits were safe.

On the field, the Browns' 1884 season was mostly forgettable. Expected to compete for the Association pennant, St. Louis instead finished in fourth place, eight games behind New York. The season full of distraction likely hurt the club. Characterized by high salaries, the Browns played with a patchwork squad all summer. St. Louis didn't hit well, and several of their pitchers were crippled early on. The team's best player was pitcher George McGinnis, who worked to a 24–16 campaign, punctuated by back-to-back one-hit shutouts against Brooklyn.

The season's big highlight occurred at Sportsman's Park in mid-July. Before a large throng, the Browns met the Philadelphia Athletics. President Von der Ahe watched comfortably from his front-row box. Early in the contest, Athletics' slugger Harry Stovey lifted a deep fly into the right-field corner. As the crowd arose to determine whether the ball was fair or foul, Stovey circled the bases at a trot, convinced the hit was a home run. The umpire wasn't so sure. There was no foul pole to aid in his decision. With the arbiter slow to rule, first baseman Comiskey vigorously demanded that Stovey return to second base. The Browns' captain cited a park rule that all balls hit over the short right-field fence were two-base hits. Unfortunately, Comiskey hadn't bothered to tell the Athletics about the rule that day. While both teams howled, the Sportsman's Park faithful let loose a barrage of catcalls.

Von der Ahe didn't understand the rhubarb and jumped over the rail onto the field. Addressing his manager, the Browns' owner said, "Vot's the matter here, Commie; vy don't you blay?"

"Oh, Stovey hit the ball over the fence and he wants to take a home run. I want him to live up to the ground rule and go back to second. What will we do about it?" said the Browns' captain.

"Vell, I tell you," Von der Ahe postured. The Browns' owner hitched up his pants, stuck out his chest, and proclaimed in a soliloquy for all the gathering to hear, "Look here Mr. Umpire, vot's knocked is knocked, und vot's over de fence is ofer de fence. Go ahead mit der game."

As a compromise, Stovey was awarded a double. Von der Ahe's curious lack of knowledge about baseball was actually perceived as knowledge. His "unwittingly logical" comment left an imprint on the Association and became the "accepted ruling for such a situation."

In 1884, Von der Ahe and captain Comiskey made some crucial adjustments to revamp the Browns. Among them was the release of deadwood. Catcher Pat Deasley, whom Von der Ahe viewed as a troublemaker, was dispatched to New York for $400. Second baseman Joe Quest departed to make room for Sam Barkley. Outfielder Fred Lewis defected to the Unions late in the year, but not until his September drinking binge led to manager Williams' resignation. About Williams, a contemporary newspaper wrote: [He] ". . . would rather tackle a hundred angry water works customers than a solitary St. Louis base baller—especially when the slugger is drunk and in possession of the idea that it is his solemn duty to slug the manager of the nine." Four Browns players—Tip O'Neill, Arlie Latham, Dave Foutz, and Bob Caruthers—shared successful, if unspectacular campaigns. Crowd favorites at Sportsman's Park, these players helped provide St. Louis a foundation of sustained, winning baseball.

Tip O'Neill had converted from pitcher to full-time fly chaser. By no small coincidence, after O'Neill had been formally released to the New York club following the 1883 season, Association secretary Jimmy Williams voided the deal. Though O'Neill didn't care much for pitching or outfield play, his batting was too valuable to lose. At first, O'Neill's transition had fans muttering that he was "slothful" in chasing fly balls. In time, however, O'Neill learned to enjoy the position. Talkative third baseman Arlie Latham gave St. Louis a much-needed spark. However, versatile pitchers Dave Foutz and Bob

Caruthers outshone them all. Both men could also play the outfield due to their strong bats. By a stroke of good fortune, the Northwestern minor league collapsed during 1884. Chris Von der Ahe seized the opportunity. In July, Von der Ahe purchased the entire disbanded Bay City (Michigan) club to acquire the sidearming 25-year-old sensation Foutz. Outbidding all other clubs, the Browns bought Foutz's contract for a record $2,000 and then paid the slender hurler $1,600 for the balance of the season. On Foutz's signing, Von der Ahe cryptically remarked: ". . . he is a bewilder and make no mistake." The Foutz signing paid off instantly. Though troubled by a three-week bout of malarial fever, Foutz still finished with fifteen wins in twenty-one decisions.

Two months later, 20-year-old Bobby Caruthers was signed from the failed Northwestern League's Minneapolis squad. Caruthers' signature was worth $250 a month. Debuting on September 7, 1884, Caruthers four-hit the Athletics to win 6–2.

7

"All's Fair in Love, War, and Baseball"

By 1885, the 25-year-old Comiskey's astute ballplaying and managerial philosophy had turned the Browns into pennant winners. Von der Ahe's naming of Comiskey as full-time manager was the master stroke. Or luck. Unlike the previous three seasons, this squad was handled by Comiskey from day one. Ted Sullivan would write of Comiskey, "He had a volcano fire burning inside him to make himself famous." Von der Ahe's previous managers lacked the necessary skills to pilot championship teams. Ned Cuthbert was a player, but hardly a leader of men. Ted Sullivan, a roughhouser, could handle his malcontents but couldn't deal with Von der Ahe. Jimmy Williams possessed executive and managerial skills but lacked patience with the roughhousers. Hiring Comiskey solved all of Von der Ahe's managerial problems.

After three seasons of also-rans, Von der Ahe desperately wanted a championship banner to fly at Sportsman's Park. Opening up his checkbook, Von der Ahe signed better players. Many of the new blood were recommended by ex-manager Ted Sullivan, who traveled thousands of miles in railroad smoker cars. The peripatetic Sullivan spent so much time on trains that some cars became known as "Ted Sullivan specials."

As extra incentive, Von der Ahe promised (and threatened) his men in the spring of 1885: "See here now, I don't vant some foolishness from you fellows. I vant you to stop dis slushing and play ball. If you vin de 'scampionship,' I gif you a suit of clothes and a benefit game extra, and if you don't you vill have to eat snowballs all winter."

The infusion of young talent, a steady everyday lineup, and vast improvements in the St. Louis batteries made the difference. Offensively, the Browns were extremely efficient. They won numerous low-scoring games. St. Louis pitching led the Association in earned run average, fewest walks, and shutouts. The Browns' fielding was the best in the Association. Most astonishing was their ability to win home games. Sportsman's Park faithful rarely went home muttering about a loss. For the season, St. Louis compiled a 44–11 record. During one stretch they captured twenty-seven consecutive home contests. St. Louis won only six of their first eleven games. Then Comiskey's gang hit their stride, winning twenty in a row and later seventeen consecutive games. These long skeins propelled the Browns to their first Association pennant. St. Louis won the flag by a margin of sixteen games. *The New York Clipper* wrote of their success, ". . . they pranced from bag to bag as if they were monarchs of the diamond, treating the weak attempts to stop them . . . with a lofty air of disdain and contempt."

The Browns were a reflection of their versatile manager, Comiskey, a combination of brains and brawn. Comiskey, now the player manager and captain, based his philosophies on his own ballplaying skills. He believed in tight pitching, good fielding, heady base running, discipline, and teamwork. This combination deemphasized batting prowess in favor of fundamentals. Comiskey believed that inactive players fuss and fume and hurt a ball club. St. Louis' young manager was proving himself to be an excellent judge of player talent.

Though Comiskey stressed speed, his pitchers needn't be overpowering, only effective. St. Louis aces Bob Caruthers and Dave Foutz perfectly fit Comiskey's plans. Together, they formed the best pitching duo in the Association. Caruthers, a smallish, sinewy, muscular 21-year-old, simply sized up a batter's weaknesses and let his fielders do the rest. A contemporary paper described Caruthers' pitching as "steady, careful, unphenomenal." Dave Foutz joined the Browns after lying about his age and probably his 40–1 pitching record at Leadville, Colorado. Possessor of a razor physique and nicknames "Scissors" and "His Needles," Foutz led the Browns quietly by example. "Curves, speed, and strategy" described his pitching success, according to one scribe. Foutz could spell Comiskey at first base, and, like Caruthers, he could also man the outfield. Both Caruthers and Foutz could boast of devastating bats.

The third St. Louis starter, George McGinnis, had been relegated to spot duty. In 1885, McGinnis pitched a one-hitter against Baltimore, but with the emergence of Caruthers and Foutz, McGinnis' days were numbered with the team.

To catch St. Louis pitchers, Von der Ahe employed the graceful, rifle-armed, and courageous Doc Bushong. A practicing dentist in the off-season, Bushong pioneered the art of one-handed catching to preserve his right arm and hand. Though Bushong was protected by a rubber device placed in his mouth for foul tips, he once had a foul tip bounce off his head into the pitcher's glove for an out. Catching in those days was a perilous business. Bushong's contribution to the club was based solely on his catching skills. He was a weak hitter.

In the field, Comiskey preached teamwork. St. Louis players practiced their defense endlessly. Their quick anticipation and proficiency resulted in a club that relied more on each other and less on signals. By studying batters' tendencies, the Browns learned to position their fielders. Comiskey's club committed errors, but also took chances.

The Browns' captain firmly believed that winning clubs were comprised of players that would "turn tricks." One trick involved storing balls on ice before home games, and then secretly injecting them into the game when the visitors batted. Other popular tricks were throwing at batters, tripping and blocking runners, and knocking down fielders. The entire St. Louis infield was comprised of tricksters.

Second baseman-utility man Yank Robinson played infield, outfield, and even catcher. Performing gloveless at second base, Robinson was known for his range, accurate throwing arm, and double-play acrobatics. Ambidextrous, Robinson sometimes startled the opposition with lefthanded throws across his chest to nail base runners heading to third. Though Robinson was a mediocre opposite field hitter, he earned Comiskey's respect with his bunting and base running abilities. Comiskey also recognized Robinson's unique clubhouse demeanor. When the Browns engaged in petty bickering, Robinson would act as mediator. A heavy drinker, Robinson often incurred the wrath of Von der Ahe. The St. Louis owner hired a detective to tail Robinson and confirm his drinking. When confronted about the indiscretion, the clever Robinson avoided a $100 fine by explaining to the magnate that he was taking medicine for what he called "hydrophobia." Explained Robinson, ". . . [the medicine] is so strong it makes me weak." The Browns' owner felt sorry for Robinson and advanced him $25 for more medicine. Hydrophobia is fear of water! Besides drink, Robinson had another weakness: He was frightfully afraid of railroad wrecks and of dying in his sleep on a train. Figuring that his survival depended on his being awake, Robinson spent many a night forsaking slumber by chatting with anyone who would listen.

Shortstop Bill Gleason was transformed from an upright citizen firefighter to a scrappy, nasty ballplayer once he stepped between the white lines. Gleason, a consistent batter, thought nothing of tripping runners, flashing his spikes, and leaning into pitches to go to first base on a hit by pitch. With Arlie Latham, Gleason was an expert at practical jokes and drinking escapades. The jokes were often at the expense of the gullible Chris Von der Ahe.

Third baseman Arlie Latham was entirely another kind of trickster. An original one-man anecdote factory, Latham was an unbridled and unpredictable free spirit, determined to use baseball as his personal stage. Everybody in St. Louis was compelled to watch. Some thought "The Freshest Man on Earth" was wound a bit too tight for incorporating gymnastics into ball games. Rare Latham home runs were punctuated by cartwheel flips down the third-base line. Latham, a continual chatterbox, entertained, amused, and celebrated with fans by telling stories, giving speeches, and singing at his position. He gave everybody else gray hair. When not entertaining the masses, he heckled umpires and opposition alike, greatly encouraging St. Louis cranks to spew invectives at their enemies. To protest unpopular umpires' decisions, Latham faked fainting spells.

In the off-season, Arlie took his act on the road, performing in Broadway shows. Chicago's Cap Anson employed the crowd pleaser in a production called *The Runaway Colt*. One evening, Latham was supposed to slide into a base on the stage. However, the enthusiastic Arlie managed to overshoot the footlights and went right into the bass drum.

Latham wasn't just a comedian; he was a genuinely talented Browns spark plug. Opposition pitchers cursed the fact that Latham led off ball games, often with a single, a stolen base, a few laughs, and another St. Louis run. Latham was as quick on his feet as he was with his mouth. Arlie loved to slide home and kick up chalk in a blaze of dust and glory. He really enjoyed foisting practical jokes on the St. Louis owner, and he tried everything to irritate his boss. Arlie ridiculed Von der Ahe by speaking with a thick German accent. Latham had enough nerve to throw buckets of water on Von der Ahe and then run away. During a rather uninteresting affair at Sportsman's Park, Latham was coaching first base. Suddenly, Latham's body began to writhe unexpectedly. Arlie begged the umpire for time. With thousands looking on, Arlie twitched and stammered like a man possessed. He ran in circles. He stomped his feet. He tore across the infield into the outfield grass. Then Latham ran back to the coaching area. By this time, players, officials, and police were crowding around him to find out what was the matter. Arlie pretended not to notice at first and then announced,"Oh nothing, my feet just went to sleep."

With the exception of Curt Welch, St. Louis outfielders were nowhere near as colorful as their infield counterparts. Left fielder Tip O'Neill was only an adequate fielder and poor base runner, yet his smallish but potent bat kept him in the game. O'Neill had an uncanny ability to foul off good pitchers until selecting one to his liking. When he did, he'd embarrass the hurler by blasting the ball to the furthest reaches of the yard. O'Neill was the idol of St. Louis youngsters, who begged to carry his bat bag to the park.

Right fielder Hugh Nicol didn't quite fit the Browns mold. A graceful fielder, Nicol's light hitting displeased Comiskey, but Nicol somehow endeared himself to St. Louis fans. Nicol seemed the antithesis of the hard-nosed, intense St. Louis fraternity. In time, his gentlemanly behavior probably helped remove him from the team.

Center fielder Curt Welch, a largely uneducated and ill-mannered man, spent far too much time hanging around saloons. His drinking wasn't confined to the bar, however. He kept a ready supply of beer behind the outfield billboards at Sportsman's Park. Presumably, as the clubs were changing positions, Welch would sneak a drink. This fact certainly helped Welch as a virulent member of Comiskey's umpire-baiting club. Welch's talents shone in his outfield play. At the crack of the bat, the speedy, shallow-fielding Welch would place his head down and tear to the spot of the ball's descending parabola. Astonishing the crowd, Welch invariably settled under the sphere. Often he covered O'Neill's area in left field. A natural athlete, Welch was an expert on diving catches on sinking liners. Welch also possessed a fine throwing arm, comparable to any of his peers. As a batsman, Welch was a consistent team player, honing his bunting skills and his ability to be hit by a pitch.

The St. Louis Browns became synonymous as the "bad boys" of the Association. Cursed and reviled by the opposition, the Browns were also envied and respected. While the Browns batted, Comiskey and Bill Gleason worked the coaching lines. Both men stood just a few feet away from home plate to offer their sarcastic views on the opposition catcher or umpire. The catcher and umpire's breeding and personal habits were brought to their attention. Comiskey also would pretend to converse with a player within the umpire's hearing range. All the while, the Browns' captain was insulting the arbiter, though not directly to his face. When Comiskey wished to show his extreme displeasure, he crowded the umpire and stood with hands on hips, screaming like a drill sergeant at a hapless private. "You're a peach!" Comiskey would say, or "How's that, Mr. Umpire?" These verbal barbs unnerved opponents and caused mistakes. Umpires thought twice about questionable calls against St. Louis, especially in games at Sportsman's Park. Most umpires would just as soon stay away from St. Louis altogether.

Comiskey's pestering eventually led to the chalk lines and the implementation of the coaching box. Boston manager Jim Hart would recall that the box was created "for the sake of not unduly increasing the population of the insane asylums or encouraging justifiable homicide . . . This helped out the catcher, but the pitcher and the other players . . . were still at the mercy of Comiskey . . . no man was in command of more biting sarcasm . . . or quicker at repartee."

So intimidating were the Browns that they once induced the Brooklyn club to lose 18–5 and commit twenty-eight errors in one game. For their troubles, owner-manager Charles Byrne fined each player $50.

Quoting Comiskey himself:

> All is fair in love and war, and the same may be said of baseball. . . . A player [may] acquire the reputation of being a gentleman both on and off the field . . . I go on the field to win a game of ball by hook or crook. It is the game we are after, not reputations as society dudes . . . I do not endorse leg-breakers, brutes and ruffians, who expect to win by injuring some one or indulging in profanity . . . The St. Louis team never yet sent any players to the hospital. I do not endorse work of that kind.

Yet Comiskey, a foul-mouthed ruffian by anyone's definition, would also remark, "I believe that kicking is half the game."

To further encourage this rowdy behavior, Von der Ahe endorsed umpire baiting by his men. He happily paid fines levied by arbiters, believing that on-field tirades were part of baseball theater, entertaining the masses and increasing profits.

During one such row with Philadelphia, *The Sporting News* described, somewhat tongue-in-cheek, "The full gist of the Athletic charges simply state that Comiskey said 'Dammitt.' Judging by the language heard on amateur fields, and simply from an amateur standpoint, leaving all professionalisms aside, we, if the judge, should pronounce Comiskey guilty and fine him one cent."

Playing Louisville at Sportsman's Park one day, Dave Foutz was pitching and Pete Browning was taking a lead off first base. Comiskey was playing behind the Louisville runner. The other infielders were prancing around trying to confuse Browning. *The Sporting News* picks up the description: ". . . and suddenly Bushong [the catcher] signaled; and Foutz dashed over towards first base with the ball in hand, touching Browning before the latter knew what happened. Such a play was never before seen, and the spectators howled with delight .. . ."

Smart, aggressive base running was also a hallmark under Comiskey. Quickness afoot was paramount. In baseball's early days, sliding was considered rather risky, especially since diamonds were often strewn with rocks and pebbles. To combat the problem, Comiskey taught his men the headfirst slide, which technique helped the runner see the play in front of him and eliminated painful leg bruises. Arlie Latham and Curt Welch practiced the hook slide, a method whereby a "runner tucks one leg under his body and uses the other to catch, or hook, the side or one corner of the bag as he passes it." This slide gave fielders a smaller tag target. Comiskey said that sliding changed "as the bruises on our bodies dictated. It was much like broiling a steak. If rare on one side turn it over." Later, sliding pads did much to alleviate these bruises.

As manager, Charlie Comiskey fidgeted on the bench. Always on top of game action, Comiskey constantly glided from one end of the pine to the other. St. Louis players caught on to this mannerism. Sometimes, the faithful at Sportsman's Park would be puzzled by Comiskey's sudden jumping and screaming from his seat. Captain Charlie did not appear to be urging on his cohorts. The fans were seeing the results of a well-placed nail.

Comiskey was a sore loser, hating especially to lose to poor teams. These defeats weighed on his brain like a ton of bricks. He ranted and raved but, more importantly, he observed. It wasn't uncommon for the detail-oriented Comiskey to memorize the on-field actions of players from years before. Naturally, this knowledge was used to the Browns' advantage. Every weakness was exploited. In Comiskey's eyes, a ball club could never score enough runs during a game.

In addition to his on-the-field duties, Comiskey also recruited players, negotiated contracts, set up train schedules, secured the grounds and equipment, paid hotel bills, and kept the financial books. With these multifaceted duties, Charles Comiskey earned every penny paid him by Von der Ahe.

Ecstatic over winning the 1885 American Association pennant, the city of St. Louis staged a nighttime parade. The streets were jammed with people. Many leaned out of windows or peered from balconies to watch their conquering heroes. The procession was led by mounted police, the United States Cavalry Band, and the state militia. Local St. Louis amateur clubs marched in the gala, as well as the Cincinnati and New York Giants major-league outfits.

Next came the Browns' entourage. A pretty young belle sat atop a Sportsman's Park float that contained pictures of the Browns' players. Von der Ahe rode just behind in a carriage with his VIP guests. Trailing the procession, on foot, were the Browns players. The music of the band was drowned out by continuous applause and the reports of firecrackers and explosives. The Atchison Flambeau Club provided a wagonload of ammunition and fireworks. Paraders carried live bombs, torches, Roman candles, and pinwheels. On cue from a bugler, the fireworks took center stage. Shotgun blasts from upstairs windows punctuated the night air. It wasn't a victorious war celebration, but it sure seemed like one. Afterwards, a grand banquet took place.

Unfortunately, the event was marred by a series of injuries. A tin mortar-launching pad blew up, sending pieces into the calf of the operator and a few spectators. The mortar operator thought the event too important to leave, and he stayed on until a stretcher took him away. One man's face was ripped open by a stray shell; another suffered injuries to his thigh. A third man watched his hand being split open by an eight-inch piece of tin. A lady's dress caught on fire. Despite these mishaps, the parade continued to conclusion.

The *Missouri Republican* considered the pageant a smashing success.

The day following the pennant celebration, a baseball exhibition took place at Sportsman's Park between the Cincinnati Reds and the Browns. On the mound for the Reds was suspended pitcher Tony Mullane. Buffalo Bill's Wild West Show performed after the ball game.

Across town, the play of the St. Louis National League entry could hardly be compared to their dominance in the Union Association. Henry Lucas' Maroons foundered. Managed by Lucas, the Maroons sleepwalked through the season. Lucas did retain five of his Union stars—second baseman Fred Dunlap, utility man Joe Quinn, outfielder Orator Shaffer, and two pitchers—but all five suffered severe dropoffs in production. The poor seasons were understandable; all League players who jumped to the Unions were blacklisted. The League reinstated the jumpers, but each violator had to pay a $500-$1,000 fine. Lucas emptied his pockets to pay, even paying for a couple of Cleveland jumpers. The out-of-shape, dissention-plagued Maroons finished dead last in the League. In an understatement, critics wrote that the Maroons were greatly damaged by charging fifty cents to see their games.

Von der Ahe could not help but notice the irony. The 1884 St. Louis Unions destroyed the Association by winning too many games. On the other hand, the 1885 team was a pathetic lot; certainly no local competition for the Browns. What self-respecting ball crank would attend losing Maroons' games when they could see baseball's newest sensation at Sportsman's Park for a quarter? And have beer and Sunday ball to boot? In reality, the Maroons would not have drawn if they'd charged a nickel. One clever *Sporting Life* writer reasoned that the play of the Maroons was due to "slack fever," "sore arms," "stiff knees," "a fear of being hit by fly balls," and "the evident aversion to . . . hitting a ball with sticks or pieces of wood."

Another Von der Ahe run-in with a player had profound consequences for the Association. Unable to get along with manager Comiskey, second baseman Sam Barkley wanted to be traded. Barkley made his displeasure known to the owner. To comply with the dissatisfied player's wishes, Von der Ahe made Barkley available for $1,000. Two Association clubs were interested, Baltimore and Pittsburgh. At first, Barkley verbally committed himself to Pittsburgh, however Baltimore convinced the second baseman to sign as soon as Von der Ahe released him from his contract. After Baltimore obtained a signature from Barkley, they sent Von der Ahe a check by registered mail. In the interim Von der Ahe had agreed to Pittsburgh's offer and shipped Barkley to the Smokey City. Confused by these events and perhaps afraid of Von der Ahe's Association powers, Barkley then signed with Pittsburgh.

Barkley's flip-flop sent shock waves throughout the Association. Baltimore appealed and the Association's board of directors was compelled to take up the matter. The Board's findings were severe: Barkley was guilty of "dishonorable conduct." The Board recommended a $1,000 fine and suspension for the entire 1886 season. After completion of the penalty, Barkley would be Pittsburgh property. When Association President Denny McKnight read the report, he rejected it. McKnight was overruled. As a result of mishandling the Barkley affair, the Association's board asked McKnight to resign. Eventually, McKnight did resign, but not before locking himself in his office. Wheeler Wyckoff then took over as Association president.

The dispute spilled into the courts. Barkley's threatened to sue the Association. The matter was finally settled out of court, Barkley's fine was reduced to $500, and his suspension lifted.

Needless to say, the affair pleased no one and caused a polarization among Association owners. In time, the Pittsburgh franchise would move its entire club into the National League and as a result, the American Association charged the National League with tampering and trying to destroy its organization.

Organizationally, the other big news was a controversy surrounding the New York entry. It was discovered that the New York franchises in both the American Association and the National League were owned by the same interest. Both clubs played through the entire season, however, in December 1885 the Association canceled their New York club for being subservient to the National League club. A team representing Washington was set to take the place of the banished Association New Yorkers. What the Association did not realize was that a wealthy financier named Erastus Wiman had stepped in and bought the Association club for $25,000. Faced with a lawsuit from Wiman and the loss of thousands in revenues from largely populated New York, the Association readmitted the New York club. To smooth over the situation, Wiman paid for and donated a trophy to be given to the Association's champions.

8

Von der Ahe Challenges Spalding

At the conclusion of the 1885 campaign, Chris Von der Ahe challenged Al Spalding's National League Chicago White Stockings to a series of games. Von der Ahe craved recognition as owner of the best baseball team in America. In 1882 and 1884, National League and American Association teams had squared off for postseason matches. However, never before had there been a "World Championship Series." Far from being sanctioned by their respective baseball organizations, the contests were unofficial. The arrangements concerning the number of games, sites, prize money, and umpires were decided by the two clubs. Thinking big, both owners believed the time was right for a twelve-game, seven-city barnstorming series. Plans called for the opening game in Chicago, three games in St. Louis, and the rest in Pittsburgh, Cincinnati, Baltimore, Philadelphia, and Brooklyn. With the exception of Chicago, all parks were part of the Association circuit. Most of the games would be played under Association rules. Cranks in these cities could enjoy beer and whiskey while watching Anson and Comiskey's men fight it out. To make it interesting, both clubs put up $500 as a purse. The money was secured by an editor of a magazine called *The Mirror of American Sports*.

These arrangements were advantageous to the upstart Browns. Chicago was daring St. Louis to beat them. In retrospect, Spalding didn't take the affair seriously. In contrast, Von der Ahe may have viewed the series as an opportunity to promote his team, give the Association credibility, enhance his national reputation, and stroke his ego.

"Confident" was the word to describe the Chicago White Stockings managed by Cap Anson. In the pennant race, the powerhouse Chicagos (87–25) edged the New York Giants by two games. The White Stockings were led by their astonishing pitching. Rookie John Clarkson won 25 of 27 games en route to a 53-win season. Jim McCormick captured 20 of 24 decisions and 14 in a row. Home runs, unusual for the day, also played a part in the success of the team. The White Stockings hit one-third of all League circuit clouts. Four of the top six sluggers in the League wore Chicago uniforms. Left fielder Abner Dalrymple led with eleven homers, right fielder Mike "King" Kelly had nine, and shortstop Tom Burns and first baseman Cap Anson cracked seven. The Chicago team was so strong they were able to overcome their enormous weakness: fielding. The White Stockings had troubles afield, especially in the infield, committing nearly 500 errors. Baseball historian Jerry Lansche described their fielding: "To say the Chicago infield was a sieve would be an insult to the sieve." So bad were Anson, Fred Pfeffer, Burns, and Ned Williamson that they were nicknamed "The Stone Wall Infield."

Despite the best-laid plans, the series played itself out as a chaotic and disorganized mess. The games in Chicago and St. Louis were competitive enough but beset by squabbles over the umpires. The final games featured competent umpiring but were one-sided. Constant haranguing by the combatants kept controversy swirling throughout the series.

Before game one at Chicago's Congress Street Grounds, individual athletic competitions took place between ballplayers. By the time umpire David L. Sullivan signaled for the game to begin, it was already 3:15 p.m. Curiously, Sullivan hadn't even officiated a contest in 1885. St. Louis staked their pitcher Bob Caruthers to 5–1 lead after seven innings over Chicago hurler John Clarkson. However, in the eighth inning, with darkness fast approaching, Caruthers hurried his motion in hopes of completing the game. The results were disastrous. After Chicago closed to 5–2, Pfeffer unloaded with a three-run homer over the short porch in left field. The Browns completed their swings in the bottom of the eighth without scoring. Then umpire Sullivan declared there was not enough daylight to continue. Game one ended in a 5–5 tie. Chicago manager Cap Anson may have averted a loss, but he was furious at center fielder George Gore, whom he accused of lushing. Gore was suspended for the remainder of the series. Taking Gore's place was Billy Sunday, who would later become a well-known evangelist.

After a 280-mile rail trip, the series shifted to St. Louis' Sportsman's Park for game two. Three thousand rabid partisans were on hand to cheer Von der Ahe's heroes. Dave Foutz was picked to pitch for the Browns and Jim McCormick for Chicago. In the first inning, St. Louis scored three times and enjoyed a 4–2 lead after five innings. The spectators were enjoying the advantage but were getting rather vocal over umpire Sullivan's work. Two early close calls riled the crowd. In the second inning, Foutz knocked a ball a foot to the left of the right-field line. When right fielder Clarkson bobbled the ball, Foutz reached second base. Sullivan then ruled foul, and partisans howled. After Foutz struck out, more catcalls filled the air. One inning later, Browns' second baseman Sam Barkley took a pitch over his head for strike three. Many cranks were now bellowing, "Get a new umpire!"

In the sixth, Billy Sunday doubled to right and was wild pitched to third. King Kelly rolled to shortstop Gleason, who apparently threw out his man. However, umpire Sullivan had his eyes on Sunday coming in to score and called Kelly safe at first. Comiskey was livid. Several Browns rushed Sullivan, including St. Louis vice president John J. O'Neill, who was watching from his private box. Comiskey strode over to Sullivan and threatened to walk off the field. For fifteen minutes, the Browns kicked up dirt and howled like banshees. Sullivan then reached into his pocket, pulled out his watch, and began a two-minute countdown. The umpire would forfeit the game if the Browns didn't return to their positions. Comiskey motioned his charges back to their places. While a bemused Anson came to bat, Kelly stole second and Cap singled to center to tie the score. Pfeffer popped to right fielder Nicol, who muffed the ball but was fortunate to force Anson at second. Pfeffer then stole second and raced to third on a passed ball. The next batter was Ned Williamson. After a succession of foul balls, Ned grounded one into foul territory behind first base. The ball kicked up a clump of grass and spun back into fair territory. Comiskey calmly went through the motions and tossed the ball to second baseman Barkley, covering first base. While Williamson hustled down the line to beat the throw, Pfeffer scored the lead run. It was 5–4 Chicago. Comiskey then got right into Sullivan's face. The Browns' first baseman argued that Sullivan had shouted "foul ball," nullifying the hit, the run, and Chicago's lead. Anson had actually blurted out the words. Comiskey threatened to produce a rule to prove the play foul. Sullivan caved in to Comiskey and was about to send the runner back to third and Williamson to bat. Meanwhile, Kelly and Anson of Chicago demanded to see the rule book. Since the Browns' captain was bluffing, Sullivan ruled the hit fair. The antsy St. Louis crowd hooted, but Sullivan agreed with Chicago. With the 5–4 lead restored, Comiskey pulled his men off the diamond. Two hundred angry fans stormed the field to make a beeline at Sullivan. Alert police restrained the crowd, but when a second wave of enraged fans milled onto the turf, Chicago players picked up bats in defense. St. Louis' finest then hustled the Chicago players off the field. Sullivan was spared from the mob and escorted into a carriage by park superintendent Gus Solari. That night, Sullivan pronounced the game forfeited to Chicago from the confines of his hotel room. Sullivan would later acknowledge his error, but the forfeit stood. Now two championship contests had been played, neither to a logical conclusion.

The umpiring controversy continued for the next two ball games in St. Louis. Umpire David Sullivan was fired by the Browns before the start of game three. In his place was a local man named Harry McCaffrey. Chicago manager Cap Anson may have disapproved had he realized McCaffrey was only two years removed from being a Browns outfielder. The umpire's calls didn't seem to make a difference. St. Louis rattled Chicago starter John Clarkson for five runs in the first inning. Behind Bob Caruthers, St. Louis coasted, 7–4. The series was now tied at one win apiece with one tie.

The next affair, game four, was delayed forty-five minutes because White Stockings player-manager Cap Anson refused to let McCaffrey work. Anson had probably discovered McCaffrey's past affiliation with the Browns. After much jawing with Charles Comiskey, Anson finally agreed to allow McCaffrey on the field. However, when the arbiter was approached at his seat in the grandstand, he said, "I wasn't good enough for Chicago last night, and you can't have me today for any price." St. Louis Maroons player Fred Dunlap also declined an invitation to officiate, and the job fell to a handlebar-mustached treasurer of a local pulley company named William Medart. A National League umpire in 1876–1877, Medart had since turned his attentions to the Browns, becoming an ardent supporter. Medart wasn't the only man a little green around the ears. Seventeen-year-old "Bug" Holliday, a local amateur who played the game for free, substituted for outfielder Clarkson.

The game turned into a splendid pitcher's duel between Chicago's Jim McCormick and St. Louis' Dave Foutz. The real story, though, was Medart's biased umpiring. After an Abner Dalrymple home run in the fifth, the White Stockings led, 2–1. In the same frame, Medart suspiciously called Chicago's Tom Burns out on a pickoff play. Still trailing by a run, the Browns batted in the bottom of the eighth. St. Louis tied the game on Caruthers' single and went ahead as Bill Gleason raced from second on Curt Welch's ground out to third base. St. Louis led, 3–2. In the ninth with one out, St. Louis second baseman Sam Barkley allowed Tom Burns to reach on an error. McCormick then popped up weakly behind first base. Comiskey drew a bead on the ball but let it slip through his hands. The frustrated Comiskey then picked up the baseball and playfully tapped McCormick, standing with one foot on first base. Umpire Medart, possibly dreaming of a St. Louis championship, called McCormick out. Disgusted by the unabashed favoritism, Browns' fans began to scream. Chicago players went into full-scale revolt. McCormick charged Medart, but Anson raced in from the bench to hold his pitcher off the umpire. Billy Sunday entered the fray with fists flying and called Medart somewhat less than an honest man. Kelly intervened to restrain Sunday. After matters settled down, Holliday fouled to Browns' third baseman Latham. St. Louis squeezed out a 3–2 win.

The Browns stayed in St. Louis for the next several days, playing exhibitions against their crosstown rival Maroons. After a long train trek east, the series resumed in Pittsburgh for game five. Neither David Sullivan, Harry McCaffrey, nor William Medart would be allowed to officiate. Instead, Cap Anson called on "Honest John" Kelly to work the rest of the series. In front of only 500 chilly fans, Chicago won easily, 9–2. John Clarkson bested Dave Foutz. Game six, played in Cincinnati, was more of the same for St. Louis. About the only highlight of the day was a pregame announcement by umpire Kelly. Standing near home plate and facing the grandstand, Kelly proclaimed that by agreement of Spalding and Von der Ahe, game seven would be the finale. Contests originally scheduled in Baltimore, Philadelphia, and Brooklyn were called off. Weatherwise and financially, the series had been an enormous bust. The Browns may have not realized that they were scheduled to play a game that day, securing only two hits off Chicago pitcher McCormick.

The White Stockings probably didn't either, committing ten errors to St. Louis' eight. The fifteen hundred fans in attendance probably felt cheated. This brand of baseball wasn't worth a plug nickel. As in game five, Chicago easily romped 9–2. That evening, Comiskey and Anson met to resolve the "hotel room" forfeit in St. Louis. With twin blowout victories behind him, Anson exuded confidence. He said, "We will not even claim the forfeited game. We each have two victories and the winner of today's game will be the winner of the series."

Cap Anson should have eaten his words. The final game in Cincinnati, attended by 1,200, was even more of a joke than the previous games. John Clarkson was slated to pitch for Chicago but showed up tardy by five minutes. Anson wasted no time and gave the ball to game-six hero McCormick. Dave Foutz twirled for St. Louis. Fan interest dwindled early. This time the Browns hit McCormick hard, calling for low balls instead of fanning at the pitcher's high tosses. Overall, twenty-seven errors were committed by the lethargic ball teams; Chicago had seventeen miscues as first baseman Anson messed up four himself. St. Louis won easily, 13–4. When the dust settled, reports surfaced that Anson had challenged the Browns to one more game at $1,500 each club, winner take all. It never happened.

Albert Spalding reintroduced himself to the press by declaring, "Does anyone suppose that if there had been so much as that at stake that I should have consented to the games being played in American Association cities, upon their grounds, and under the authority of their umpires?" Spalding was also quick to deny the agreement that the seventh game would be decisive.

In the aftermath, a great debate raged over who was champion. The general public saw the series as a tie. The baseball world regarded the Browns as the best. Von der Ahe and his players were certainly convinced. Mindful not to upset the powerful Spalding, Von der Ahe agreed with the Chicago magnate that the series was a draw. Von der Ahe's public acknowledgment cost his players their share of the $1,000 purse. *The Mirror of American Sports* returned Von der Ahe's and Spalding's wagered money. The 1885 Series was somewhat less than a success. Only seven of the scheduled twelve games were contested. Only 14,200 fans attended the games. Game receipts totaled $3,000. Unlike future sports classics where fans were sorry to see one team lose, this series was so sordid that neither team deserved victory. The Chicago infield lived up to its reputation by averaging an error per game per man. If play on the field was indifferent, the attitude of the participants was despicable. The arrogant White Stockings hardly respected their American Association rivals. As for the Browns, the partisan umpiring in St. Louis bordered on criminal.

Perhaps Spalding got the last laugh. At the conclusion of the games, he telegrammed Von der Ahe with events of the World Series. Spalding's telegram said that Anson and Comiskey had exchanged punches that precipitated a riot in Sportsman's Park. Although Comiskey was the worst for wear, both men landed in jail. Outside an angry mob awaited, ready to lynch

Anson. Von der Ahe, unaware of the joke, reacted oddly. His face turned ashen "and afforded much amusement to all in on the secret."

For Von der Ahe, a better series took place between the Browns and the St. Louis Maroons. Beginning on October 19 and continuing until after the conclusion of the games with Chicago, Von der Ahe's Browns bested the Lucas entry in four straight games. The results were hardly surprising, considering the Maroons' lowly stature. The first game, won by Bob Caruthers 5–2, drew 10,000 paying customers at Sportsman's Park. The Browns were again victorious in the second game, a 6–0 shutout by Caruthers on October 25. Two days later, Von der Ahe smiled again with his boys winning 11–1. In the finale, the Browns sneaked by the Maroons 1–0. The Browns held the Maroons to eleven hits and three runs in the series. For the disgusted owner of the National League St. Louis entry, Henry Lucas, the final shellacking would be his last.

"Well you can count me out of this baseball business. This game has sickened me."

Perhaps, more accurately, Lucas' pathetic club and lack of profits had sickened him. The Maroons ended the season with no fewer than four regulars hitting under .200.

So humiliated was Lucas that he sold his club before the start of the 1886 season. Lucas' baseball calamity was only the beginning in a series of financial reverses. Having lost an estimated $100,000 in the game, Lucas saw his fleet of barges sunk in a heavy storm. The one-time champion owner would never recover from these disasters. He died at fifty-three, a $75-a-month city street-department employee.

Following the 1885 championship, pitcher Bob Caruthers and catcher Doc Bushong held out for the upcoming season. Greatly dissatisfied over the National Agreement's $2,000 salary maximum, they threatened a trip to Europe and Australia if their salaries weren't increased. When Von der Ahe refused their overtures, Caruthers cabled Von der Ahe from Paris, France. The message stated that he was with Bushong and that they wouldn't be returning stateside until April 1. Von der Ahe wasn't quite convinced the threat was real. To make sure, the Browns owner checked the ship's manifest for transatlantic voyages. After numerous telegrams passed between the combatants, Bushong signed. Caruthers eventually inked a deal for $3,200 for the 1886 season. The cables earned the Browns' pitcher the nickname "Parisian Bob." Meanwhile, pitcher Nat Hudson also held out, positively ruining Von der Ahe's off-season.

9

"The Browns Are Here!"

Despite the player holdouts and the inconclusive 1885 Championship Series, Von der Ahe and his Browns entered the new campaign with extremely high expectations. The Boss President seemingly spent the entire season boasting about and celebrating with his team. Another year's experience for player-manager Charles Comiskey paid handsome dividends.

In the spring, Von der Ahe scheduled a series of exhibitions between the rival St. Louis teams. To promote the affairs, Von der Ahe hired boys to pass out handbills proclaiming "The Great Games: Browns versus Maroons at Sportsman's Park. March 28, April 3 and at Union Park March 27, April 1." The players looked swell in their spanking white uniforms with brown trim and hose. Emblazoned on their chest were the words "St. Louis."

Opening Day's fanfare began with a parade to the ballpark, complete with ballplayers, brass bands, and Von der Ahe himself leading the procession. Quite often, Arlie Latham would don a fake nose and a flattened derby hat. Waddling behind the Browns' leader, Latham broke up everyone watching the parade. Chris never understood what the laughter was all about. A sizable crowd awaited the teams' arrival at Sportsman's Park. Von der Ahe dutifully marched onto the field dressed in striped spats, silk top hat, Prince Albert coat, maroon-colored kid gloves, and a gold-headed cane. His two trusty greyhounds were at his side. Von der Ahe was most proud of his gold watch and fob. Inside was an album containing pictures of the Browns. As Von der Ahe settled into his private box, the band would strike up a tune. With warm applause cascading into the St. Louis air, the Browns jogged onto the field and began to fling their baseballs. As they practiced, Von der Ahe glanced around his park, sized up the gathering, and smiled broadly. A frothy mug was in order.

The baseball game seemed an afterthought.

At the conclusion of the athletic affair, Von der Ahe lit a victory cigar while the satisfied crowd filed noisily out of Sportsman's Park. Then, the stocky Browns' owner would take part in a smaller but more profitable parade. Flanked by rifle-armed security guards, Von der Ahe transported the game's cash receipts in a wheelbarrow to his Grand Avenue bank. Von der Ahe would traipse into the bank to deposit the money. Speaking of his patrons, Von der Ahe loved to say, "Five tousand tamn fools, und one wise man. Und dat wise man iss me—Chris Von der Ahe."

St. Louis was loaded with talent. Few observers could deny that the Browns were an extraordinary baseball team. They overwhelmed their opposition with their batting, pitching, and fielding prowess. At Sportsman's Park, St. Louis rarely lost. This fact kept the patronage happy, but they were doubly pleased by the availability of suds. Von der Ahe's beer sales soared. St. Louis certainly entertained the home faithful. Pitcher-outfielders Dave Foutz and Bob Caruthers completed two of the more remarkable seasons in history. "Scissors" Foutz won forty-one games while leading the loop in ERA. Foutz pitched in nearly sixty games and manned the outfield for more than forty. Bob Caruthers captured thirty victories, was second in ERA and fourth in the Association in batting. With Nat Hudson winning sixteen games, longtime veteran George McGinnis was expendable. In midseason, "Jumbo" went to Baltimore. The catching corps hit poorly, as predicted, but Doc Bushong and his understudy Rudy Kemmler handled the Browns' staff well. The infield was a marvel. Leadoff hitter Arlie Latham scored a ton of runs. Yank Robinson coaxed bases on balls. The other stalwarts, Comiskey and Gleason, also contributed by getting on base, scoring runs, and fielding their positions with flair. In the outfield, only Hugh Nicol couldn't pull his weight, but, the tandem of Foutz and Caruthers more than made up for Nicol's weak stick. When center fielder Curt Welch wasn't imbibing, he was a demon on the diamond. Welch simply destroyed teams with his base running, miraculous fielding, and hitting. Left fielder Tip O'Neill blossomed as a hitter in 1886, leading the club in base hits and batting average.

Several summer imbroglios did little to derail the Browns. Three controversies erupted concerning Von der Ahe and his enemies in the Association. They included the late payment of fines and a fight in Baltimore. In all of them, Arlie Latham was involved. At an Association meeting, Brooklyn owner Charles Byrne pointed out that Comiskey and Latham had not paid fines. Immediately, Von der Ahe handed over $260 to President Wyckoff, as if to show his respect to the Association and flaunt his wealth. When Baltimore President Billie Barnie was called to speak by President Wyckoff, he told of a near riot in his city, brought on by the "vile language plainly heard in the grandstand." Barnie called for stiff fines and suspensions for the instigators Latham and Bushong. Von der Ahe quickly defended his charges by saying they had been disciplined. He haughtily threatened to quit the Association. Owner Phelps of Louisville jumped to the aid of Von der Ahe and threatened to pull his team out also. The matter was resolved with a promise of written apologies from the players and $100 fines.

Browns opponents tried virtually everything to slow down the team. The pettiness reached a nadir in Philadelphia when Manager Simmons sanded areas around first and second base before a crucial Saturday doubleheader. Comiskey reported that the sand around first base was one foot deep. An explanation that the grounds belonged to the Athletic club did not satisfy Comiskey. The Browns captain tersely informed Athletics' captain Stovey and threatened to boycott the game if the sand was not removed. Stovey was unmoved, but when umpire George Bradley ordered the silliness to stop, a groundskeeper trotted in with a wheelbarrow and shovels. After one load was hauled away from first base, Comiskey told the groundskeeper to bring a bigger cart. While a few Athletics players milled onto the field, Comiskey grabbed a shovel and began to work. Arlie Latham also picked up a shovel, and soon the removal of sand began in full force. Without enough tools for everyone, some players used their hands to toss sand into the wheelbarrow. A big Decoration Day crowd was gathering at the park, and there was pressure to play the games. Fans wondered about the commotion. This theater of the absurd encouraged crowd whispers and then hysterical laughter. When Comiskey was satisfied, the game began—fifteen minutes late.

The sand plan backfired on the Athletics. St. Louis simply ran wild, collecting 22 hits and nine steals in the first game alone. Catcher O'Brien was ineffective at stopping St. Louis speedsters and was replaced. Browns runs were so plentiful that they barely had time to rest at second base. Comiskey decided to leave a sand pile in the middle of the diamond. St. Louis rolled over Philadelphia 18–1 and 11–3 behind Bob Caruthers and Nat Hudson.

It would be an understatement to say the St. Louis squad was confident of winning the 1886 pennant. A banquet toasting their success was held on July 13—three months before the conclusion of the season. Chris Von der Ahe paid for the whole affair. All the players were invited, along with team officials and members of the press. Tables were "loaded down with good things" and "wine flowed like water." The festivities took place in right field of Sportsman's Park. Von der Ahe waxed rhapsodic about his club's esprit de corps and Charlie Comiskey, who was presented one share of stock in the Browns. "I want you always to remain an honor to St. Louis and the Association. I also want you to win or try to win every game, no matter what club opposes you, or no matter what lead you hold in the race." Chris also boasted that the St. Louis Rowing Club had asked to name a new boat after him.

For winning the American Association championship for 1886, New York sportsman Erastus Wiman presented the Browns with a 20-inch-tall, solid silver trophy of a batsman and a floral arrangement shaped like a baseball diamond. Known as the "Wiman Trophy," the St. Louis prize was modeled on Chief Roseman, the New York catcher. It was reportedly worth $2,000.

On March 17, 1886, Al Spink invested some of his gambling monies and launched the first issue of his publishing dream, *The Sporting News*. A weekly publication, the magazine would be western competition for the eastern-based *Sporting Life*, formed three years earlier. The publication was copied in long-hand and set to type at a nickel a copy. A subscription was $2 a year, postage paid.

Al worked tirelessly to write and promote his enterprise, consumed by his roles as writer, editor, and circulation and advertising manager. Spink's writing experience and his contacts in St. Louis' sporting, barroom, theater, and political fraternities were essential.

The first issue featured local and national baseball items, with news from the diverse worlds of cycling, hunting, and boxing. There was also a special section simply called The Theater. To help defray costs, the magazine advertised with St. Louis business dollars. Readers were introduced to products ranging from footwear to firearms to beer. Local theaters were only too happy to advertise, given Al's interest in that art form.

Despite the diversity, baseball news was paramount. *The Sporting News* covered the National League, the American Association, local clubs, and everything in-between. The magazine doted on local ballplayers as St. Louis developed a reputation for turning out crack talent.

An early ad symbolized baseball's impact in St. Louis. Von der Ahe's Golden Lion Saloon, operated by John Peckington of the Sportsman's Park Club and Association, was located only two blocks from the ballpark. Inside, waiters wore brown caps and shirts to help publicize the Browns. Outside the saloon, a huge golden ball proudly displayed a sign that read "Game Today." When a flag was raised, it signified that the Browns were out of town. Thanks to the telegraph, the Golden Lion, among others, posted inning-by-inning ball scores. These reports fostered betting on ball games, right in the saloons. To top off the merriment, an outfit called "Whistling Julius" Lehman's Manhattan Quartet sang lullabies in the bars.

Unfortunately, Al Spink's enterprise struggled financially. Considering his multiple duties, Al was barely able to keep the weekly afloat. Spink wasn't keen on the "inside" duties of copyediting and dealing with advertisers, preferring to scope out and report stories. Desperate for a business manager, Al persuaded his brother Charles to take the $50-a-week job. Charles learned fast. Despite not having any sports or newspaper experience, Al's brother quickly fit right in, eagerly soaking up knowledge and displaying rare business acumen. The partnership seemed perfect. *The Sporting News* could boast of an expert "outside" man and a developing "inside" man. Though the brothers' personalities sometimes clashed, the magazine began to prosper. Extrovert Al was a risk-taking free spender. By contrast, Charles wanted no part of the hustle and bustle of reporting. He was content with pinching pennies and running the daily affairs of the shop.

For Von der Ahe and his juggernaut Browns, the existence of *The Sporting News* proved a godsend. Both organizations thrived on each other. Von der Ahe wished his friend well in the inaugural issue. Al Spink, meanwhile, spent countless hours promoting the Browns. On May 10, 1886, Spink wrote of the club, "Nothing can stop them in their wild career short of a hurricane." Four months later, as the Browns were habitually wiping out Association teams, the magazine wrote, "Von der Ahe never looked so happy. He makes life a regular picnic." Spink was plugging his paper and adding no small measure of pride to the city itself. Browns' secretary George Munson also wrote for the weekly as St. Louis correspondent. Critics charged that Von der Ahe had stock in the company and that the magazine should be printed in brown ink.

No one understood how to deal with Chris Von der Ahe better than Charles Comiskey. Von der Ahe's wife, Emma, had resigned herself to the fact that her husband wasn't going to change. Von der Ahe's teenage son, Eddie, who was regularly taken to the ballpark, didn't quite understand his father's outlandishness. Chris' political friends and drinking buddies had discovered that Von der Ahe required constant praise to satisfy his enormous ego.

Manager Comiskey fully comprehended this and several other facets of Von der Ahe's personality. The "Boss President" wanted to be known as a "baseball man," though he understood little of the game. When the Browns won, Von der Ahe reveled in taking credit for their success. Conversely, if the Browns lost a game or two, Von der Ahe habitually damned his players, the local papers, or anyone else. Chris Von der Ahe's disposition was uneven, at best. His was a moody existence, fluctuating from extreme joy to unbridled anger. Von der Ahe's cheery smile signaled either a Browns' victory or that Chris had realized big profits. To celebrate, Von der Ahe often acted as if he owned the whole town; wearing fancy clothes and strutting around like a proud peacock. Unfortunately, losing money and ball games didn't suit Von der Ahe. Even his closest associates didn't want to be around Chris after a galling loss.

During the Browns' first few seasons, Von der Ahe seemed content to let his managers run the show. In time, however, Von der Ahe developed a penchant for interfering in club affairs. To placate his boss, Comiskey became an expert at listening sympathetically to Chris' tirades. After the Browns' president issued Comiskey his daily instructions, the manager did just the opposite. Comiskey realized that his handling of the team led to their success. However, like all trusty lieutenants, Comiskey understood that generals are always responsible for winning battles. When Von der Ahe suffered criticism from the Association, newsmen, or players, Comiskey deflected the remarks onto himself, serving as Chris' buffer. So adept was Comiskey at this that *Sporting Life* reported the Browns' success was due to Von der Ahe's pleasant personality and management skills.

Comiskey's relationship with Von der Ahe was unique. Although Comiskey kept himself in good graces with his boss, other players strayed from the straight and narrow. After a loss, a drinking episode, or disrespect from his players, Von der Ahe was quick to fine his men. To quote Von der Ahe's philosophy, "If a player is drunk or disobedient, he should be fined . . . this is but just and proper. Surely, no good business man will permit his employees to shirk their duties without exacting the proper penalties from them . . . the same rules . . . apply in the base-ball line."

Comiskey, however, handled an impending fine as an opportunity to explain to Chris the extra work a ballplayer was doing. Often, at Comiskey's suggestion, fines actually became bonuses. After being fined $100 for some indiscretion, Arlie Latham met Chris in a bar to plead his case. Chris listened and agreed to reduce the fine to $50. Cleverly, spendthrift Latham then asked for and received a $50 loan, explaining to Von der Ahe that they would then be even-steven. Latham estimated that Von der Ahe must have levied him a million dollars in fines. The Boss President rarely collected, because he'd forget the next day.

In St. Louis, the Browns were so popular that everything Von der Ahe or his players said or did made news. When outfielder Hugh Nicol commented on the efficacy of two umpires instead of one, *The Sporting News* jokingly interjected, "It is a wonder he does not think it would be a health and comfort of the players to have nine beautiful ladies on the field to face the players." American Association batting champion Tip O'Neill was so revered that his portrait was placed on a large banner and displayed on the Browns' train. At bat, O'Neill was serenaded by "a dozen maidens in flowing robes [that] sounded a fanfare on silver trumpets." Baby boys with the surname of O'Neill were proudly named Tip by their parents. A reporter poked fun at Von der Ahe by writing about a German named "Onderdunker," who was obsessed with the attention he was getting in the society columns. Browns' followers delighted at word of Arlie Latham's exploits with the fairer sex. In a Pittsburgh hotel, Latham supposedly cuddled up to a young lady at dinner and politely asked if she wanted syrup on her hotcakes. When she dutifully responded, Latham took the jug and said, "Will you have it, ah, zig zag or take it in a puddle?" At the comment, the lady fainted, as perhaps did many of the readers.

As the Browns' fame spread, Von der Ahe stayed busy keeping himself and his team's name in the papers. He promoted St. Louis with pioneering advertising maneuvers. Chris' biggest supporter was *The Sporting News,* which zealously indulged its readers with details of Von der Ahe's professional and private life and stories about the players. The *Globe-Democrat* and the *Post-Dispatch*, local newspapers, also helped by printing theater-style game announcements. St. Louis' German-language newspaper, *Anzeiger des Westens,* also advertised the club. A Cincinnati-based German paper advertised the Browns in that city.

"Nothing is too goot for my poys!" Von der Ahe loved to say.

One full-page newspaper ad paid for by Von der Ahe correctly prophesied, "The Browns Are Here! The Hardest Hitters, the Finest Fielders, the Best Base Runners, the Coming Champions!" The confident Browns owner delighted in proclaiming "Ve lick der stuffings out of every team in baseball."

Local merchants quickly understood Von der Ahe's flair for publicity and practically lined up to advertise their products. Other ball teams were content with streetcar billing, handbills, and small boys handing out flyers to passersby on the street. Von der Ahe realized a small fortune on sales of lithographs, posters, cigars, snake oil, beer mug crockery, imitation pennants, and sporting goods. With the success of the team, St. Louis was fairly saturated with Browns' memorabilia.

Von der Ahe also had illustrations made of himself to be sold by various firms. The pictures portrayed a glorified image of Von der Ahe, deemphasizing his portly features and big nose. However, Von der Ahe's grandest example of his burgeoning ego was his statue. At the age of thirty-four, the St. Louis magnate commissioned a relative in Germany to sculpt his life-sized image. Erected in 1885, the stylized statue wasn't quite Michelangelo's *David*, but it was nattily dressed in Von der Ahe's trademark frock coat. The statue stood for many years outside Sportsman's Park, welcoming St. Louis baseball fanatics and serving as ridicule for visiting ball teams.

The Browns' owner further capitalized by naming a group of apartment houses after his players. On each corner of the houses was, appropriately, a saloon. The fine print in Browns' player contracts was a clever way to recoup monies. Many were forced to room at Chris' boardinghouse, thereby relinquishing a portion of their salary right back to Von der Ahe!

Von der Ahe's zeal for publicity and promotion paid off handsomely. He was reportedly earning some $75,000 a year in the 1880s. St. Louis was the best money-making organization in the game.

At a time when it was unheard of for a woman to attend a ball game, Von der Ahe installed a ladies' room at the ballpark and then offered ladies their own special seating sections and souvenirs. An early baseball publication wrote, "Women's attendance purifies the moral atmosphere of a base ball gathering, repressing . . . outbursts of intemperate language."

The Sporting News stated, "Every lady who attended . . . would be presented with a cake of soap. This was something of a libel to the fair patrons [who] have seen many a pretty girl . . . and to one who seemed in need of soap. Von der Ahe . . . is too gallant a man to allow his fair patrons to be libeled either by soap dealer, druggist, of any other manner of men."

The Sporting News also intoned, "Each lady who attends Sportsmen's Park next Thursday will be presented with a beautiful breastpin souvenir. . . . The souvenir represents a bat with a ball and cap and glove and mask attached to the ends."

Von der Ahe mass-produced a satin kerchief especially for Ladies Day. Flanking a flattering drawing of owner Von der Ahe were his beloved players. Imagine, the women of St. Louis, having just washed themselves with soap passed out at Sportsman's Park, walking the streets fully accessorized with baseball breastpins and Browns' kerchiefs!

The Browns had a secret for their astounding success. Von der Ahe claimed that, "The reason my boys play such a great game is that they drink Phos-Ferrone." The new flavored carbonated beverage cost $1 for twenty-four bottles, delivered. Phos-Ferrone was manufactured in St. Louis but many players imbibed in other, more spirited beverages. If Phos-Ferrone was so great (the Chicagos were drinking it and winning), how come other nines weren't enjoying it as well? Von der Ahe's comments served as an endorsement and unintended self-parody. Von der Ahe also appeared with Latham and Comiskey in advertisements for a cigar firm.

Thanks to *The Sporting News* and the St. Louis dailies, all of the city knew Von der Ahe. With each new success, Von der Ahe's ego increased incrementally. He loved to portray himself as a one-time poor immigrant who braved a perilous sea voyage to come to America. Arriving in the United States alone and near penniless, Von der Ahe started out as a grocery clerk. Within the space of fifteen years, he became a store proprietor, saloon owner, real estate holder, landlord, and baseball magnate. Von der Ahe also cultivated the image of a happy immigrant. He often referred to himself as the "Lucky Dutchman."

Von der Ahe embodied the traits of the German immigrants of the period. He was industrious, earnest, and orderly, and he also had an ingrained respect for authority. Like most Germans, Von der Ahe understood the need for relaxation. He enjoyed dividing his time "between hard work and hard guzzling." With Von der Ahe's increasing financial gains, his personality changed.

With his new fortune, Chris made a spectacle of himself and his team. If reporters were ever in need of a story, they would simply call on Chris. To his detractors, Chris was a pompous example of a gentleman of means. He always wanted to act rich, but often acted the fool, due to his robust drinking and a wandering eye for the ladyfolk. Von der Ahe was merely *nouveau riche.*

While the Browns were easily winning the Association pennant, Von der Ahe decided to stage extra events at the ball yard. A Sunday–morning benefit featured local amateur teams. While fans focused on the actions on the field, a renegade ticket seller escaped with the game's receipts. Von der Ahe, soured over the experience, decided that charity baseball games might be ideas of the past. For-profit attractions were better suited for his pocketbook. A handsome Buffalo Bill Cody made a stop at Sportsman's Park with his Wild West Show.

The entirety of the 1886 campaign seemed predicated on one fact: The St. Louis Browns and the Chicago White Stockings would again meet for the championship. From the start of the season to the long, hot summer of wool flannel uniform sweat, on-field tirades, hotel hijinks, drunken train rides, and the back-slapping camaraderie of men—these two teams were destined to meet on the ball field. Poems were written and songs were sung proclaiming the contests to be. This time, one team would emerge victorious. The Chicagos were a dynasty, having won pennants in 1876, 1880, 1881, 1882, and 1885. St. Louis was building for greatness. The contrasts didn't end there. The ownership of the clubs matched bartender Von der Ahe with sporting goods manufacturer Albert Spalding. On the managerial front, Charlie Comiskey led by example; Cap Anson of Chicago was mentor to his players. In the respective cities, civic pride swelled to a fever pitch. As early as July, stories about spectator betting started circulating. Despite rules to the contrary, rumors flew about bets among owners and players.

10

The Undisputed Champions

The hype surrounding the 1886 Series was nearly as good as the action on the field. Chris Von der Ahe, Al Spalding, Cap Anson, manager Watkins of Detroit, and the respective merchants and fans of both cities kept the pot boiling. Chicago manager Anson stated that the Browns would finish last in the Association! Detroit manager Watkins announced that neither his club nor Chicago would play unless the series was winner-take-all and the games were contested on neutral grounds. Watkins then upset Von der Ahe and Spalding by declaring that the White Stockings were drunk during the 1885 championship. Meanwhile, Von der Ahe kept insisting that his Browns were the superior club.

All the posturing and bravado came to a head with incessant wagering taking place among interested parties. Browns pitcher Dave Foutz was reportedly wagering on his team to win. Fans of Chicago and St. Louis were betting on their local heroes. Two trade institutions, the St. Louis Exchange and the Chicago Board of Trade, were quoted as backing their respective teams. Another report intimated that Spalding himself would wager $5,000 on his club defeating the Browns. Von der Ahe countered by saying Spalding never "made such a proposition for the rules of the National League and American Association forbid the betting of money on games." Von der Ahe proclaimed in the *Post-Dispatch* that Spalding discouraged "betting on baseball on general principles, and yet he offers to bet and bet largely himself." The paper also cited Von der Ahe as saying that he would never bet on baseball games. Al Spink's newspaper cleverly printed two poems foreshadowing the fall event. This doggerel, entitled "Gloria De Brownis" and "Browns and Chicagos" was supposed to resemble Greek mythic poetry.

As the 1886 season came to a close, Von der Ahe telegrammed Chicago owner Albert Spalding to play "a series of contests to be known as the World's

Championship Series." Von der Ahe also proposed that the games take place on the two home grounds. One day later Spalding conditionally agreed to Von der Ahe's challenge. The series would last nine games with four in Chicago, four in St. Louis, and the finale played at a neutral site. The Chicago games would use National League rules, while the St. Louis affairs would be contested under American Association guidelines. For the final game, the clubs would agree on the rules just before the contest. Umpires would be selected by a special board. The arbiters would be authorized to inflict fines (with monies going to charity), and all their decisions would be final. If necessary, a board of arbitration would settle disputes between the clubs. St. Louis and Chicago would pay their own expenses. Finally, Spalding proposed that the winner of the series be rewarded with all gross gate receipts.

Von der Ahe's reaction to Spalding was reportedly, "Sure, we will take them up and teach those fellers a lesson. No club is goot enough to beat the Browns."

The key stipulation was Spalding's winner-take-all proposal. Since the American Association had challenged the established National League, a back down by Spalding would appear cowardly. Nearly all the conditions were met, except for the nine-game provision. Von der Ahe cited the Browns' previous engagements with the St. Louis Maroons. Instead, the series would be the best of seven games with the first three played in Chicago.

However, the maneuvering wasn't finished. On the eve of the opener, to much fanfare, the Browns boarded a special train at Union Depot. A large banner on the side of the train read "St. Louis Browns, Champions of 1885 and 1886." Inside the train sat a large delegation, including several reporters and Von der Ahe. Not to be outdone, Al Spalding wrote to his manager, Anson, urging victory and promising not only a suit of clothes for each man but one-half of the gate. Spalding also offered bonuses to his players for abstaining from drink during the contests. "We don't intend to . . . insult ladies and gentlemen in this city or any other by allowing men who are full of beer and whiskey to go upon the diamond in the uniform of the Chicago club." *The Sporting News* reported a wild story about Von der Ahe having purchased the contract of pitcher Toad Ramsey specifically for the purpose of defeating Chicago for a fee of $100 a game. Von der Ahe called the story a fairy tale.

The White Stockings appeared poised, having compiled an astonishing 90–34 won-lost record. They boasted the National League's best offense. Slugging first baseman Cap Anson and catcher/utility man Mike "King" Kelly wielded big sticks. Most of the time, they were driving in run-scoring machine and leadoff hitter George Gore. Despite a weak defense, Chicago served up a trio of devastating hurlers: John Clarkson, Jim McCormick, and newcomer Jocko Flynn.

None of the first three games played in Chicago's Congress Street Grounds were tightly contested. As promised in the Von der Ahe-Spalding agreement, partisan umpiring would not be an ugly element in 1886, as it had been the previous year. Jim McQuaid worked the first game and "Honest John" Kelly worked game three. However, in the second game an experiment was tried. Three umpires were on the Chicago grounds, and each team was allowed to pick one umpire. Chicago drew McQuaid; the Browns selected Joe Quest. In effect, the plan was a two-man rotation. Kelly, who umpired behind the plate when the bases were empty, was the "referee" whose decisions would be final in any argument. The umpire plans must have worked, because very little was heard from the arbiters throughout the series.

Chicago's Jack Clarkson shut down the Browns in games one and three by 6–0 and 11–4. Clarkson beat Foutz and Caruthers. In game two, the Browns won handily, 12–0, behind Caruthers' one-hitter. In the Chicago victories, local reporters egged on fans who unmercifully booed the Browns. Cheering sections became jeering sections. One fan made such a spectacle that umpire McQuaid had him removed from the grounds. The best highlight occurred in game two, when St. Louis outfielder Tip O'Neill walloped a McCormick toss down the left field line along the parked carriages. By the time Abner Dalyrymple could retrieve it, presumably working his way underneath horses and their droppings, O'Neill had rounded the bases for an inside-the-park home run.

The real story of this series would be the behavior of the players *off* the field.

Following the St. Louis victory in game two, several newspapers reported that Chicago players were drinking after their opening game victory. The papers intimated that the lushing contributed to Chicago's lackluster play. Rumors also surfaced that Chicago was "hippodroming," or deliberately losing games to prolong the series and hype gate receipts. The charges intimated that Chicago may have been party to gamblers and that the games were staged. As the clubs departed Chicago for St. Louis on an evening train, Al Spalding stayed behind in Chicago for business. Cap Anson, meanwhile, took two extra players to St. Louis. One was pitcher Mark Baldwin, a minor league 39-game winner in 1886. Baldwin, already signed for 1887, had yet to appear in a major-league game. He would be Jim McCormick's replacement. Cap Anson had reported that McCormick had rheumatism and would be lost for the series. Another new player was reserve catcher Lew Hardie, insurance for catcher Mike Kelly, who'd been spiked by the Browns' Yank Robinson. When a *Post-Dispatch* reporter asked Anson about hippodroming, he responded, "I can tell you now positively that these games are for blood." Von der Ahe was in no mood for Anson's Baldwin ploy, forbidding the youngster from appearing in the games.

Buoyed with confidence, Anson's White Stockings acted as though the series was a foregone conclusion. Just two more victories and a championship banner would float in the Windy City breeze. According to news accounts, several of the players had morning rendezvouses at gambling halls in St. Louis. Chicago's White Stockings weren't betting on the locals. Much of the wagering was done at Wiseman's Pool Room. The Browns had other ideas.

Sporting a 52–18 record at Sportsman's Park, the Browns were confident, believing their cranks were the best in baseball.

Games four and five, attended by uproarious gatherings of about 10,000 a contest, prompted more hippodrome speculation. St. Louis won in the fourth game 8–5, with Dave Foutz defeating John Clarkson. St. Louis also won the controversial game five the next day, 10–3, behind Nat Hudson. After the fourth game, many Chicago players joked with reporters at the hotel. Despite his loss, Clarkson appeared in fine spirits. Mike Kelly told stories. Shortstop Williamson, whose dropped pop-up let in the game-winning run, said "Yes, sir, they beat us today on the level." The Chicago team secretary stupidly boasted to reporters that thousands of dollars rode on the series. Chicago manager Anson wanted no part of these proceedings. When a newsman asked how Anson's superior Chicago squad could lose to Association upstarts, Anson shot back, "Didn't you see it yourself? Wasn't you there?" The Chicago manager was extremely upset for the fifth contest. Before the game, he penciled in Mark Baldwin's name at pitcher. When Comiskey discovered Baldwin, he raised quite a ruckus, properly argueing that Baldwin hadn't been a member of the 1886 Chicago squad. Umpire McQuaid concurred, but only after a coin flip decided matters. To counter the snub, Anson then picked shortstop Williamson to pitch, since The White Stockings' third pitcher, Jocko Flynn, nursed a sore arm. Catcher Kelly went to shortstop. Later in the contest, outfielder Jimmy Ryan took the mound, sending Williamson to the green garden. With the farcical replacements and their ridiculous errors and wild pitches, even St. Louis fans shuddered. This wasn't championship baseball; it was vaudeville. The *Chicago News,* citing talk at pool halls and betting parlors, joined in the hippodrome suspicion. The "pins have been set up awkwardly and the wires have worked bunglingly."

If St. Louis ball cranks were excited and unable to sleep after game five, Saturday's game six brought them no relief whatsoever. All through the morning, town talk centered on Von der Ahe's Browns. Sportsman's Park was a festive place that warm afternoon. Baseball fever gripped the city.

Those fortunate enough to secure a ticket crammed inside the ball yard, anticipating a glorious victory. There were over 10,000 such fans. Christian Frederick Wilhelm Von der Ahe and Albert Goodwill Spalding settled into their private boxes. As the men settled into their seats, shouts to beer vendors filled the air. Ladies and children were also present among the throng, fully prepared to offer up screams for their heroes. When the Browns marched into Sportsman's Park, the band struck up a lively tune. Comiskey's men whipped the ball around for all they were worth. St. Louis fans went wild. Glasses chinked. Hurrahs were shouted. Women and children squealed with delight.

At 2 :00 P.M. the visitors from Chicago arrived in two horse-drawn carriages. The White Stockings jumped onto the grass and were cheered by the partisan St. Louis crowd. To acknowledge the welcome, the Chicagos doffed their caps.

Among the many horse and buggies debarking at the park was a vehicle owned by Oliver Wiseman. Proprietor of a rather busy establishment, Wiseman would say that the Browns *had* to win this game to disprove the hippodrome. Baseball wagers of twenty-five cents and above were commonplace at his business.

Gracie Pearce worked the game alone. Clarkson, starting his fourth game in six days, pitched for Chicago, and Caruthers, working on two days rest, hurled for St. Louis. Chicago put their best lineup on the field, as did the Browns. The business on the ball field began.

Neither team scored in the first stanza. In the second, Caruthers walked Chicago's Fred Pfeffer, who promptly stole second and went to third on Doc Bushong's passed ball. Both Williamson and Tom Burns fanned. Then Jimmy Ryan came through with a clutch two-out single. Chicago led, 1–0. With this, a crank in the left field bleachers, dressed in a stovepipe hat, jumped from his seat. He boldly shouted, "Hurrah for Chicago." St. Louis fans would not tolerate the interloper; he was knocked down and dragged out of Sportsman's Park. In the bottom half, Ryan excelled again. Right fielder Dave Foutz hit a long drive to the outfield. Ryan outran the ball and made a fabulous catch. Pfeffer knocked a fourth inning Caruthers' pitch into the right-field bleachers. Anson's men enjoyed a 2–0 advantage. Chicago threatened further, but the Browns' Curt Welch snared Clarkson's dangerous outfield drive to end the rally.

A light rain halted play in the fifth inning; and some rowdy fans milled onto the field. St. Louis, trailing by two runs and hitless against Clarkson, tried to convince umpire Pearce to call the game. Pearce did not acquiesce. Instead, police escorted several fans away. Fearing a riot, the Browns temporarily left the field. However, a frantic Von der Ahe called his charges back onto the field, and when the rain subsided, play resumed.

In the sixth inning, restless St. Louis rooters hooted Yank Robinson and Dave Foutz. Fred Pfeffer, becoming a real thorn, grounded a ball through second baseman Robinson's legs. Pfeffer kept running and ended up on third when Foutz bobbled the ball in right field. The Browns had bungled their way into a two-error, three-base play. Ned Williamson's sacrifice fly scored Pfeffer. Clarkson continued his mastery over St. Louis. At the end of six complete frames, no St. Louis player had a hit.

Tip O'Neill frustrated the faithful in the seventh. O'Neill timed a Clarkson pitch for a double to center. George Gore recovered quickly and threw out O'Neill, who was trying to stretch his hit into three bases. As the seventh inning ended, Chicago still led 3–0.

Caruthers bore down in the eighth stanza. Chicago failed to score. Trailing by three, the Browns came to bat in the bottom of the eighth. Captain Comiskey started a rally with a clean single, only the second hit off Clarkson. Curt Welch hit a slow roller to third baseman Tom Burns. In an effort to get the Browns' speedy center fielder, Burns threw the ball wild. The sphere darted past Anson and caromed into right field. With runners on second and third and none out, Foutz lifted a deep sacrifice fly to the outfield. Comiskey scored the first run. Welch tagged and took third. The St. Louis patronage woke up and began to dream of delicious possibilities. Their hollering didn't abate, delaying the game several minutes. Yank Robinson then disappointed the throng by popping out. Two were down. Doc Bushong worked Clarkson for a base on balls. With runners on first and third, clown prince Arlie Latham stepped in. White Stockings' catcher King Kelly wasted no time, complaining to umpire Pearce that Latham was carrying an illegal bat. One side of the wood had been whittled flat. Pearce agreed and ordered Arlie to change his bat. As Latham took his practice swings, Cap Anson guyed Arlie from his first base position. The Chicago manager had spent the afternoon mimicking Latham's comical coaching style. "Knock it down here. This is our puddin'! This is the weak spot!" Latham was ready, with a response right out of fiction. As the mighty Casey would later do, Latham addressed the multitude. "Don't get nervous folks, I'll tie it up." Arlie's chutzpa caused many in the crowd to sputter beer. On Clarkson's next pitch, Latham roped a line drive to left field. Abner Dalrymple froze momentarily, then watched as the ball flew over his head and rolled to the wall. Welch and Bushong scored. Latham ended up on third. The score was tied! Sportsman's Park was a madhouse. The crowd threatened to shake the building to its foundation. Coins showered the field. Cranks were so excited they flung their pool tickets in the air, some of which were worth hundreds of dollars. When a semblance of order returned, Caruthers grounded out to end the inning.

As he entered the ninth, Caruthers seemed to work on pure adrenalin. Chicago did not score, despite a one-out double by Tom Burns. Dalrymple struck out to end the rally. Clarkson set down St. Louis in the home half. Swift right fielder Jimmy Ryan helped Clarkson by making a sensational leaping grab on a long drive by Tip O'Neill. The game entered extra innings.

The tenth inning was easy for Caruthers. Bobby struck out his opposite number Clarkson, then Gore and Kelly lifted easy flies to the outfield. Only one St. Louis run was needed for the championship. St. Louis' Curt Welch was so determined to get on base that he led off by leaning into a Clarkson pitch. Signaled by umpire Pearce to take his base, Welch trotted to first. Anson shot Welch a dirty look and protested that Welch had made no attempt to avoid the toss. Pearce, intimidated by Anson and trying to avoid a row this late in the series, relented to Chicago. Welch returned to the plate and lined Clarkson's next delivery to center field for a base hit. As Curt pulled up at first base, he sneered at first baseman Anson. Dave Foutz grounded to shortstop Williamson. Thinking double play, Williamson hurried, and bobbled the ball. All hands were safe. An outfield hit would win. Yank Robinson was next. The Browns' second baseman stared at Clarkson, then looked down at third-base coach Comiskey. Following orders, Robinson successfully bunted both runners along. The game, and the series, rested on the legs of Curt Welch at third base. With Bushong batting, Welch pranced down the third-base line, hoping to rattle Clarkson. He was so far from third that catcher Kelly had a legitimate chance for a pickoff throw. Anticipating a high-inside pitch-out, Welch broke for home. Clarkson tried to quick pitch Bushong, but instead fooled his own catcher. The delivery came in tight, near Bushong's shirt, and bounced high off a lunging Kelly's glove. Welch raced home like a demon. The ball rolled about ten feet from Kelly, who made no attempt to retrieve it. In the excitement Comiskey raced down the line from his coaching box. Thinking fast, the Browns' manager reached down and stuck the ball in his pocket. The Browns were the undisputed champions of baseball. St. Louis won it 4–3.

Reactions to the dramatic finish were completely unbridled. As Welch flashed home, Chicago catcher Kelly angrily flung his glove and mask. Hats and cushions were flung in joy. The crowd offered up three cheers for their champion Browns. The band struck up. Men leapt into the grass and gleefully hoisted their heroes off the field. A private box, containing about thirty ladies, engaged in a mass embrace. Von der Ahe beamed and then let out a hearty belly laugh. In his typical fashion, Von der Ahe ordered champagne for everyone in sight. Thousands of delirious ball fans stayed to see the Browns off the field. Others offered congratulations when their heroes emerged from the dressing room in civilian clothes.

Most of the Chicago club, led by Anson, quietly boarded their carriages for the hotel. A rowdy gathering awaited the losers. A policeman was assigned to keep fans away. Ned Williamson was gentleman enough to walk over to the Browns' dressing room and offer his congratulations.

Al Spalding was reportedly so miffed over the loss that he neglected to book rail arrangements on the return trip to Chicago. When hippodrome rumors surfaced yet again, a livid Spalding said, "Do you suppose for a minute that any men of standing in the business community like Von der Ahe and myself are going to hazard our good name by going into a scheme like this?" Spalding may have been doubly embarrassed. Von der Ahe was said to have helped a few Chicago players who went broke betting on their own team.

The *St. Louis Republican* gloated, "Chicago should confine itself to the slaughter of hogs as a popular amusement" because "baseball seems to require more headwork."

Whether Welch slid into home or merely raced across is conjecture. At any rate, the play came to be known as "Welch's $15,000 Slide," the monetary figure referring to the winning gate. The total was actually $13,920.10. Von der Ahe kept half the money and paid the rest to his players. Each member of the Browns, including secretary Munson, received $580. Several St. Louis players also earned money from personal bets. An estimated $100,000 changed hands during the series. In all, over 43,000 spectators attended the games.

That same evening, Von der Ahe, ever the promoter, wrote a short note to "Friend Spalding." It read, "What do you say if we play that game in Cincinnati, on Tuesday, anyhow?" Spalding responded with "Friend Von der Ahe, We must decline with our compliments. We know when we have had enough."

Von der Ahe's crosstown rival St. Louis Maroons were also no match. Chris' charges easily won the city series, five games to one. After the final game, the last game ever played by the Maroons, a newspaper intoned that the Browns "are now champions of the city, of the American Association, and of the world."

In the days following, a series of banquets was given in St. Louis to toast the victorious Browns. The "Wiman Trophy" was displayed at Mermod and Jaccard's Jewelry. To celebrate, Von der Ahe doused himself and his jubilant friends in beer. At one such gathering hosted by the St. Louis Exchange, Von der Ahe spoke. "Gentlemen, I am glad of this opportunity to thank you for the way you have stood by me and my club. We have always tried our best to win, and when we did win, it was always done fairly and squarely."

The cover of *The Sporting News* featured drawings of the conquering heroes with a proud headline, "St. Louis Browns, Champions of the World." Another company illustration featured a drawing of a Browns' batter next to a globe, captioned "Monarchs of the Sphere."

As the 1887 campaign loomed, Von der Ahe managed to secure a new pitcher. A St. Louis native named Charles Koenig signed in the off-season. Koenig had recently played on a semi-amateur team named the Peach Pies. Among his teammates were Patsy Tebeau, Jack O'Connor, Joe Herr, and Perry Werden. When playing ball locally wasn't enough, Koenig snuck off in the middle of the night to board a train, against his parents' objections. The Browns owner noted that the strapping youngster was German, strong, and determined.

11

"As Sure as the Sun Shines"

It can be argued that the 1887 edition of the St. Louis Browns were the finest team ever placed on a ball diamond. The Browns had the look of champions, winning 95 of 135 contests. They were led by a tremendous rotation of rookie ace Silver King, Bob Caruthers, and Dave Foutz. All won twenty-five games or more, despite a malarial attack on Caruthers and a late-season injury to Foutz. Player-manager Charles Comiskey anchored the infield with Yank Robinson, Bill Gleason, and the incomparable Arlie Latham. Collectively, these stalwarts batted .311 and scored over 530 runs. The outfield was also most impressive. Tip O'Neill hit a miraculous .492, leading the league in doubles, triples, home runs, and batting average. Center fielder Curt Welch caught everything in sight. When Caruthers and Foutz weren't destroying opponents on the mound with their precise pitching, they were slugging away in the outfield. Both hit .357. During a July 4 doubleheader in St. Louis, Foutz hit a home run in the morning game and then went five for six with two more circuit clouts and nine runs batted in for the afternoon game. The catching, still weak at bat, was solid with newcomer Jack Boyle and the able Doc Bushong. The Browns boasted four men with more than 100 runs batted in, six players who scored 100 or more runs, and a seventh (Welch) with 98. Many critics described their on-field behavior as excessively rowdy. Riots followed them as they toured the circuit. However, St. Louis backed down from no team. Like owner Chris Von der Ahe, Browns' fans loved every attention-getting minute.

At Sportsman's Park, the team was virtually unbeatable, winning 79 percent of the time. On the road, the Browns were the Association's best drawing card. St. Louis romped to the pennant by fourteen games, in part due to an early season stretch in which they won twenty-nine of thirty-one games. St. Louis led or was near the top in every team category, scoring more than eight runs per game and possessing the deepest pitching staff in the Association. St. Louis fielders paced all of their rivals. So confident was the local *Sporting News* that it proclaimed in March, "The Browns will be champions again, as sure as the sun shines, and the wind blows."

As a result of the Browns' 1886 championship, several players held out before the 1887 season. While Von der Ahe complained of high salaries, Comiskey was concerned about his men becoming prima donnas. Pitchers Nat Hudson, Dave Foutz, and Bob Caruthers refused to sign contracts. So did third baseman Arlie Latham, shortstop Bill Gleason, and center fielder Curt Welch. By the end of March, though, nearly all the men had affixed signatures, including Caruthers and Foutz, who signed for $3,000 each. Nat Hudson wanted $2,500, but when Von der Ahe agreed to give him only $2,000, Nat remained unsigned. Chicago manager Cap Anson made overtures to Hudson, but American Association President Wyckoff released a statement that Chicago could not tamper with the National Agreement's Reserve List. Von der Ahe set an asking price of $6,000 for the release of the young right hander. In the meantime, Hudson returned home to tend to his sickly mother, finally reporting in late May.

The addition of 19-year-old St. Louis native Charles Frederick Koenig was a bonanza for Von der Ahe's Browns. He was quickly named "Silver" for his premature shock of white hair and "King" to make his German name easier for reporters. After a brief trial with the financially strapped 1886 Kansas City National Leaguers, King signed for $2,000. However, the club folded two weeks later and King had problems collecting his pay. He was approached by George Munson in the winter of 1886 and offered a contract. A physically imposing specimen of manhood, the six-foot-tall King presented himself with a barrel chest, long arms, and huge hands that helped him nearly hide the baseball. Throwing "crossfire" without a windup, King mixed his pitches, throwing fastballs, curves, and change ups alike with the same motion. He also possessed incredible control. King's instant success (he won his first seven games) prompted opponents to complain that he was out of the pitching box. King's pitching abilities precipitated another contract squabble. Threatening to work with his father as a bricklayer, King demanded his salary be doubled from $1,800 to $3,600 after the season. Von der Ahe compromised, and King did receive a considerable raise.

Yet, for all this glory and great play, the Browns (and the Association) were victims of their own success. Von der Ahe would describe the season as his most frustrating because of player holdouts and fines, dickering with Charles Byrne and the Association, secret dealings with the National League, and rumors of a Browns' sale. Von der Ahe stayed in the limelight during a mid-season courtroom baseball trial and a controversy involving an exhibition game.

Rumors swirled throughout the season concerning the National League, which was desperate to pry the Browns from the American Association. With its own revenues decreasing, the League figured the Browns would increase gate receipts, balance the competition, and provide a star attraction. American Association clubs were more profitable, even with lower admission prices. However, inherent in a switch of the Browns from the American Association to the National League were a host of problems, foremost being the legality of the move. Many believed the Browns rowdy playing style would not be tolerated in the more sedate National League, nor would the meddling of Von der Ahe. The timing seemed perfect, though. Von der Ahe was becoming disgusted with the leadership of American Association President Wyckoff, whom he felt favored Brooklyn in decisions and did not furnish official umpires to many St. Louis games. Von der Ahe also feuded with Brooklyn President Byrne. Von der Ahe's opinion of Byrne, "if published in adjoining columns, would scorch the space line between." Byrne called Von der Ahe a "mentally small man" and said that "He seems to be impressed with the idea that no other club has any right to defeat his men, and the result has been to make him very arbitrary in his methods and language." A wild rumor circulated in the New York papers concerning the sale of the Browns to *New York World* publisher Joseph Pulitzer for $100,000. Pulitzer, who merged the St. Louis newspapers, the *Evening Post* and the bankrupt *St. Louis Dispatch,* had been in New York City just a few years. Browns' secretary Munson quickly discredited the story. Von der Ahe screamed, "The St. Louis Browns will stay in St. Louis until baseball ceases to be the national game. I have never for a moment thought of selling them to New York parties, nor would I sell them for twice a hundred thousand dollars." Another story concerned Von der Ahe's proposal to buy two-thirds interest in the Association's Philadelphia Athletics baseball club. The deal was quickly rebuffed by Philadelphia brass. Von der Ahe would reportedly give $35,000 to two of the three Philadelphia owners and thus own a majority of the stock with Billy Sharsig. However, when two of the Philadelphia owners reportedly asked for $100,000, the deal was off.

The one-upmanship war between Von der Ahe and Brooklyn owner-manager Charles Byrne intensified after a series of July incidents. In a game at Brooklyn, St. Louis second baseman Yank Robinson scored the winning run by cutting third base. Brooklyn players argued that Robinson missed the bag. Brooklyn fans screamed bloody murder. After the argument seemed lost, a still-irate Byrne went and sat down on the Browns' bench. Byrne then found the miscreant Robinson and lectured him for cheating. Von der Ahe popped up from his box seat to order Byrne away. The second game of the series was no better. Again a row took place, prompting Association President Wheeler Wyckoff to ask Baltimore manager Barnie to board a train for Brooklyn to umpire the series' final contest.

Von der Ahe secretly arranged a late July meeting to dump Wyckoff. Though Von der Ahe publicly railed against Wyckoff as a poor handler of umpires, Chris' real problem was Wyckoff's anti-St. Louis bias. Von der Ahe was prepared to nominate St. Louis writer Joe Pritchard as Association President. By no coincidence, neither the Brooklyn nor Cincinnati representatives were invited. Von der Ahe's plan might have succeeded, except that Billy

Barnie, representing Baltimore (and Philadelphia by proxy), failed to show. With only four voting parties, Von der Ahe was one vote shy of a majority to depose Wyckoff. Upset with the turn of events, Von der Ahe was reported to have offered to meet with John Day of the New York Giants. The purpose of this strange bedfellows meeting was Von der Ahe's proposal to transfer the Browns to the National League.

Byrne's next move trumped Von der Ahe, who was embroiled with petty bickering over his own club. In front of the entire Association, Byrne proposed a new National Agreement. Byrne's ideas focused on a fairer salary system, a self-sustaining reserve corps of players, a new draft, and more equitable contracts. Moreover, Byrne addressed the growing inequity of teams that promoted unhealthy competition. New gate receipt divisions were also proposed along with a free Ladies Day once a week. Finally, Brooklyn's owner suggested a $1500 fine for teams exiting the playing field before the conclusion of games. Comiskey had pulled the Browns off the field in a losing game at Louisville. Byrne's ideas fit under the guise of promoting the game, but nearly all the proposals were aimed at Von der Ahe's business operation.

Unlike the previous season, where the Browns gulped down Phos-Ferrone, this season's magic elixir was an oil. A pharmaceutical company, promoting a nostrum called Merrell's Penetrating Oil, designed a booklet to advertise its product in 1887. The oil cured everything from aches and pains to colds, "penetrating to the bone" of sufferers of various maladies. Inside the booklet were drawings of the entire Browns starting lineup and Von der Ahe, all offering stirring testimonials to the power of the oil. One example was center fielder Curt Welch, who (supposedly) said: "Ramsey, Louisville's great left-handed pitcher, sent in one of his red-hot inshoots, which caught me on the hip, in the game played in St. Louis on May 4, and left a black and blue trade mark. Merrell's Penetrating Oil was recommended to me. I used a bottle of it, and it did me a world of good."

On occasion, Comiskey's Browns played ball so viciously they had to police themselves. During a June game, St. Louis center fielder Curt Welch assaulted Philadelphia pitcher Gus Weyhing after a violent basepath collision. Comiskey cursed Weyhing and ran out on the field to stick up for Welch. The Athletics would eventually protest to Association President Wyckoff. A week later, in Baltimore, Welch upended the hometown second baseman while trying to steal. Baltimore management Billie Barnie and Oyster Burns watched from the stands in street clothes. They rushed the field to get at Welch. Meanwhile, howling spectators forced a policeman to arrest Welch. Von der Ahe had to bail his fly chaser out of jail with $200. *The Sporting News,* sympathetic to the Browns, wrote; "The Baltimore audience displayed little of the instincts of human beings, but on the contrary conducted themselves like idiots." A few weeks later, Welch may have received his comeuppance. While he waited to bat, Tip O'Neill's lumber "accidentally" struck Welch in the face, knocking him down.

In mid-July, the Browns were swept into a highly publicized Sunday baseball controversy this resulting in a speedy trial at the St. Louis Court of Criminal Correction. The defendant was Chris Von der Ahe.

On Sunday, July 10, St. Louis was abuzz over morning newspaper stories announcing the recently passed ban on Sunday ball playing. Missouri's blue laws forbid baseball on the Sabbath, calling the sport "labor." Nonetheless, a large crowd showed up at Sportsman's Park for a Sunday match between the Browns and the Baltimore Orioles. Patrons understood the game was in doubt, but most came anyway to see if the new ban would hold. The Browns' management was ready also, handing out "sun checks" just in case. "I shall order my men on the field . . . and if they are arrested I shall give bond for them, and see the matter thoroughly tested in a court of justice. Our schedule was made before the Sunday law was put in force and visiting clubs will require us to play on days scheduled or forfeit the games. This might result in my club losing the championship."

The *Missouri Republican* quoted Von der Ahe: "I do not oppose the law merely because it deprives me of money but because I do not believe the law is just." The contest started promptly with no less than twenty-five mounted policemen on the grounds. As the affair was getting underway, Sergeant Phillip Florreich approached Von der Ahe, who was comfortably seated in his grandstand box. The officer promptly arrested the Browns owner with the crowd yelling "Play Ball!" Von der Ahe was taken by carriage to a local station and booked for breaking the Sunday law. Wrote *The Sporting News,* the "final score was 9–0 in favor of the police."

Judge Noonan, who initiated the controversy with his court ruling, set bond at $100, twice the normal amount for this type of misdemeanor. Instantly, William Medart, a St. Louis manufacturer, posted bond for Von der Ahe. The Browns owner went right back to Sportsman's Park to tell excited fans that he was calling off the game. His reasoning? To keep his players from being arrested.

The State of Missouri vs. Chris Von der Ahe took place the following Friday on an oppressively hot day. The principals were Von der Ahe and his attorneys, Mssrs. Lodge and Scott, Judge Noonan, Prosecuting Attorney Colonel J. R. Claiborne, Congressman O'Neill, Secretary George Munson, and Sergeant Florreich, who gave an account of the arrest. Von der Ahe entered a plea of not guilty. As the lawyers prepared their legal briefs, some baseball cranks in the audience rose and stretched, mocking the legal proceedings.

Most of the testimony was mundane. Sergeant Florreich, a fan of the Browns, testified on Von der Ahe's behalf. He described the conduct of the park as orderly. Sergeant Florreich made the arrest on the orders of his supervisors. Two nearby St. Louis property owners said the ball games were not a nuisance. Charles Turner, a long-time St. Louis citizen, real estate agent, property owner, and baseball fan, also testified. He had helped build Grand Avenue Park. Turner stated that he did not consider the actions on the field "labor." When Prosecuting Attorney Claiborne asked if the game was not harder than driving a team [of horses] along a shady road, Turner stated that baseball required more exercise but that it was not so irksome.

By far the most compelling oratory was delivered by Congressman John J. O'Neill. According to the *St. Louis Globe-Democrat,* O'Neill presented a "eulogy of the national game," speaking of baseball as "the most entertaining and exhilarating sport any person could witness." He called baseball a "godsend" for the laborer. O'Neill spoke of the glories of free air and Sunday baseball for the working classes to spend their hard-earned money for a natural diversion at the ball yard. O'Neill explained how ministers had told him of the positive influence of baseball on the Sabbath, since it kept men away from far worse places, such as saloons. To a hushed courtroom, O'Neill claimed that in all of 1887, he never noticed one man drunk or one negative demonstration at the park. Ladies also enjoyed the games, according to O'Neill. When Lodge called O'Neill's testimony "the opinion of an expert, and not a crank," the courtroom burst into laughter. Judge Noonan had to slam his gavel to restore order.

At the conclusion of the testimony, Prosecutor Claiborne read the state law concerning the prohibition of labor on Sunday. Claiborne emphasized that the players were servants of the defendant and paid by Von der Ahe. They had worked on that day, and had not been there for recreation. Had the players been amateurs, there would be no problem, stated Clairborne. Von der Ahe's attorney rebutted by reading the law again, this time emphasizing that the character of the law applied to manual labor and not recreation of any kind. Von der Ahe's Attorney Lodge questioned the exact meaning of *labor*. A lecturer would have to use mental work to think, read, and study, Lodge reasoned. According to Lodge, the law was clearly written to protect laborers, servants and craftsmen from the imposition of their masters.

Attorney Lodge and Congressman O'Neill's arguments won the day. Judge Noonan ruled that baseball was not labor. The sport was recreation, and legal games were allowed in St. Louis. In effect, the judge overruled his own opinion. Judge Noonan issued the following statement (in part):

> *Our Supreme Court in 1876 decided that hunting game on Sunday was not work or labor within the statute, and discharged the defendant, who had been convicted hunting under the Sunday laws. (State vs. Carpenter.) Since that case was decided our Legislature has made hunting game a violation of the Sunday law. But they have not prohibited, either expressly or by construction, base ball carried on decently, orderly and quietly on Sunday. I might say in addition to this that the game was a reasonable sport and use of nature's powers. And while the evidence showed that money was taken and money paid to the players, it, in my mind, is not without the meaning of this statute any more than the playing of any piano player or singer that might come into the home of a citizen on Sunday to contribute to his entertainment. I therefore find the defendant, under the laws and evidence, not guilty, and discharge him.*

Despite fearsome opposition from temperance groups, the Browns were allowed to continue to play baseball on the Sabbath. Judge Noonan's reversal became critical in Von der Ahe sustaining a profitable operation in St. Louis.

A late-season game typified what it was like to play for Von der Ahe's Browns. On an early September Sunday, St. Louis met the New York Metropolitans at Weehawken's Monitor Grounds in New Jersey. The park was smallish, with accommodations for only 500. However, 6,000 people showed, anxious to get a rare glimpse of the St. Louis Browns. The throng delighted Mets' owner John Day but caused much consternation to the ticket takers. As the teams attempted to enter the grounds in horse-drawn carriages, the crowd became an unruly mob. Some of their number actually tried to tip the Browns' carriage. Others rushed to the ticket counter to demand refunds. Local police then stepped in. The masses entered the park and nearly caused the dilapidated grandstand to collapse. When order was restored, ball cranks lined the outfield, forming a human fence. After a time, the players finally entered the field. The Browns won a dangerous, abbreviated six-inning affair, probably in great fear for their lives.

Von der Ahe and the Browns endured another controversy in mid-September. The Browns were scheduled for a Sunday exhibition in West Farms, New York against the Cuban Giants. The affair was expected to draw 15,000 paying customers. The opposition Giants were neither Cuban nor a major or minor league outfit. In fact, they were a New Jersey-based team comprised of highly skilled black ballplayers. Toiling for meager \$12–\$18 a week salaries, the crack Giants had already defeated Indianapolis of the National League and Cincinnati of the American Association. Detroit's powerhouse Wolverines edged the Giants by only 6–4.

The night before the game, as Von der Ahe was enjoying his meal at a hotel in Philadelphia, Tip O'Neill stopped by to place a letter on the owner's table and then hustle away from the scene. The letter read:

> *Philadelphia, September 10, 1887.—Chris Von der Ahe, Esq.: Dear Sir—We, the undersigned members of the St. Louis Base-ball Club, do not agree to play against negroes to-morrow. We will cheerfully play against white people at any time, and think by refusing to play we are only doing what is right, taking everything into consideration and the shape the team is in at the present.*
> *Signed—W.A. Latham, John Boyle, J.E. O'Neill, R.L. Caruthers, W. Gleason, W.H. Robinson, Chas. King and Curt Welch.*

Chris never finished his food. Instead, Von der Ahe repaired himself to a downstairs corridor to confront his team. The Browns were talking among themselves, but as soon as the owner arrived, they all became speechless. In a rare loss for words, Von der Ahe said: "As it seems to be a matter of principle with you, you need not play tomorrow." The incident embarrassed Von der Ahe, who was apologetic to ball fans and the management of the Giants, claiming that his club never missed its engagements. More likely, Von der Ahe was more concerned with the loss of his share of the gate receipts. He later estimated that the debacle cost him $1,000.

Charles Comiskey tried his best to smooth over the situation. "I think some of the boys wanted a day to themselves. They have played against colored clubs before without a murmur, and I think they are sorry for their action already." Arlie Latham spoke, as well. "We played everyday last week, and one day we played two games, and had to get up at 3 o'clock in the morning to catch a train. And then look at the team we've got. It's like a third-class amateur club. We did not want to go over there on Sunday, especially to play a nigger club, and we didn't go."

The owner of the Cuban Giants, Walter Cook, didn't buy Von der Ahe's explanation. He threatened to sue the Browns' owner in a telegram, claiming that 7,000 fans showed to see the Giants play ball with St. Louis. Many spectators departed when they noticed that the Browns' team was not on the field.

Von der Ahe also was forced to endure another season with the colorful Arlie Latham. Like Von der Ahe, Latham kept himself busy enjoying the notoriety that the Browns were receiving across America. However, Von der Ahe found Latham's clowning distracting. When the frustrated Browns' magnate could think of no other reason for punishing his volatile third baseman, he fined Latham in early July for "singing and otherwise acting up."

So powerful were the Browns that they won the pennant despite having their ace Dave Foutz sidelined for nine weeks due to injury. During a Sunday game with Cincinnati, Foutz was pitching at Sportsman's Park. A ball was hit down the first-base line. Comiskey fielded the ball, but his throw caught Foutz on the thumb of his throwing hand. The star yelled in pain. Von der Ahe rushed onto the field with a veterinary horse doctor friend named Albrandt. The good doctor handled Foutz's thumb "about as gently as he caressed the hoof of a draft horse." The injured Foutz responded "with colloquial embellishments." In the dressing room, Von der Ahe asked Dr. Albrandt about Foutz's condition. The doctor responded that the pitcher would be as good as new in three days. Unfortunately for all parties, especially the pitcher, the thumb swelled to the size of a grapefruit, keeping the hurler out of action. Frustrated by the events, Von der Ahe approached Foutz. "That bum thumb of yours has been der cause of der Prowns losing fife or six games of ball, Dafe, and I must charge it against your salary." Countered Foutz later, "I'm no horse, and a veterinary surgeon is not competent to mind my thumb." With that, Von der Ahe minded his own business.

12

"Vanity and Vexation"

Buoyed by the financial success of the 1886 Series, the 1887 World Series between the Browns and the Detroit Wolverines was the most ambitious, ballyhooed, and ceremonial barnstorming baseball event of its time. Parades, brass bands, and dignitaries were seemingly everywhere. A special trophy called the Dauvrey Cup was minted by Tiffany's and named after the wife of the New York Giants' John Montgomery Ward. The cup would be presented to the first team to win three straight World Series. Dauvrey also commissioned gold medallions for each winning member. For Von der Ahe, the 1887 Series was another chance to publicize his squad and exhibit his own showmanship.

Unfortunately, the games were also a gigantic bust, a competitive and financial disaster.

The series dragged on for fifteen games in seventeen days in ten cities, resembling a geography lesson more than anything else. Game sites included St. Louis, Detroit, Pittsburgh, Brooklyn, New York, Philadelphia, Boston, Washington D.C., Baltimore, and Chicago. The weather could charitably have been called cold. Total rail mileage topped 3,500. However, because of poor conditions and outlandish ticket prices, fan support was sparse. The owners jacked general admission prices from a quarter to a dollar. Reserved seating went for a buck fifty. All manner of weather prevailed except the kind suited for baseball. Steady drizzles, swirling winds, damp mud, frozen earth, and perilously chilly conditions greeted players and fans. The players sometimes resorted to flannel underwear or cardigan warm-up jackets. Arlie Latham once got on base, stole second, and then scored on an infield hit, presumably to get out of the cold. During one frostbitten twenty-degree day, after the players had refused to report to the field, Von der Ahe insisted the game be played for the "fans' sake." Only 378 shivering fanatics braved the chill that day. On another occasion, the *St. Louis Post-Dispatch* declared in Brooklyn: "The wind was blowing a hundred miles an hour and from forty different directions." Brass bands working the series certainly earned their money. The games went on until October 26 and were called off due to, as one paper called it, "rapidly advancing winter."

Detroit certainly had tremendous incentive to win. After a narrow miss for the 1886 flag, the Wolverines started 1887 with 19 wins in 21 games. Their arch-rival Chicago White Stockings pulled even in mid-August, but Detroit pitcher Charlie Getzein secured three victories in a five-day span to clinch the pennant. The Wolverines were led by the hard hitting of Dan Brouthers and Sam Thompson. Brothers was injured and would miss nearly all the series.

On the mound, Detroit boasted a trio of highly effective hurlers. Curve-balling "Pretzels" Getzein (29–13) was a German-born right–hander noted for pitching well on the hottest of days. His moniker was due to his confounding breaking pitches and the opposition batter's resulting ungainly position in trying to hit him.

Southpaw Charles "Lady" Baldwin was the National League's biggest winner in 1886, but the new pitcher's box rule of 1887 bothered his stride. Baldwin had a difficult time adjusting to the rule that made hurlers keep one foot on the back line of the box before taking a one-step delivery. After compiling a 6–9 record deep into July, Baldwin was sent home without pay. When Baldwin returned, he won seven of his next eight decisions. Baldwin's unusual nickname stemmed not from feminine characteristics, but from his nonsmoking, nondrinking, noncursing habits, all rare for ballplayers. Finally, there was big right-hander Larry Twitchell. A part-time slugging outfielder, Twitchell won 11 of his 12 1887 decisions.

A special rail car had been fitted up for the Detroit team directors and the press to attend the games. Among the St. Louis contingent were reporters from *The Republican, Globe-Democrat, Post-Dispatch,* and *The Sporting News.*

The Detroit owner was Frederick Sterns, a pharmaceutical magnate with no small share of Von der Ahe-style bravado. Sterns outdid Von der Ahe at every turn in this series. Wrote Sterns to Von der Ahe, "Dear Sir, I take this occasion on behalf of the Detroit club to challenge you to a series of contests for supremacy, and for the title of World's Champions." Von der Ahe agreed that the gate be divided 75–25 in favor of the winners after each contest, minus travel and hotel fees. The magnates each put up $600 for the winning club. Von der Ahe set aside $100 for each player in the event of a St. Louis victory, however, Sterns promised the Detroit victors $400 extra per man as an incentive. Two weeks before the start of the series, Sterns predicted that Detroit would win ten of the games.

Unfortunately for St. Louis, several of their players were injured. The trying season had not exactly healed their wounds. Dave Foutz' lingering thumb problem affected his curveball. Comiskey was also nursing a sore thumb. Von der Ahe remarked that he'd rather lose $1000 than lose his valuable captain.

Pitcher Bob Caruthers' hand was banged up. Catcher Doc Bushong complained of sore hands. Second baseman Yank Robinson suffered numerous aches and pains.

The 1887 Series would be played under American Association rules. However, two umpires, in the persons of "Honest John" Kelly and John Gaffney, were selected to officiate. They were to alternate behind home plate each half inning. Kelly and Gaffney would receive $200 apiece plus expenses. This umpire arrangement must have worked. Barely a mention was made of them the entire series.

The games themselves were mostly noncompetitive and, as in 1886, decided largely by actions *off the field.* When St. Louis fell behind early in the series, Von der Ahe concerned himself with lambasting his players in the press; Foutz and Gleason in particular. Gleason was benched following game six after batting .080 with no runs batted in and 10 errors in 21 chances at shortstop. Foutz had been demonstrably terrible in his base running, fielding, pitching, and batting. In game two, Foutz drove a ball into right field in Sportsman's Park. He stopped at second base. However, under the "blocked ball rule," Foutz could have kept running. The rules stipulated that balls hit into the overflow crowd had to be relayed back to the pitcher before the base runner could be put out. Foutz' base running gaffe was all the more galling since St. Louis partisans would have little incentive to help the Detroit outfielder locate the ball. In game three, Foutz and Comiskey couldn't quite get to a pop-up that allowed the winning run to score. In game six, Foutz was shelled 9–0 by the Wolverines.

The real reasons for the losses were uncovered by the *St. Louis Post-Dispatch.* After St. Louis bungled its way to a game three home loss, the players amused themselves on the train with a late night poker game. With beer flowing and tempers flaring, Browns' second baseman Yank Robinson punched center fielder Curt Welch in the nose. The Detroit players, meanwhile, were retiring early to their sleeper cars, "as sober as judges." The next night, the St. Louis card games continued. This time the games went on all night amid puffs of cigar smoke and bravado. After falling behind 6–2 in games, the *Post-Dispatch* wrote that the club "shows itself in weak, nervous, sulky dispositions and poor eyes when they begin to play ball." Team captain Charles Comiskey, supposed to be setting a positive example, preferred poker playing and drinking with his men.

Two peculiar incidents exemplified the series. Before game six began in New York, one unfortunate spectator, a manager of a local Spalding sporting goods house, was demonstrating a revolver. He somehow proceeded to hold his left hand over the business end of the gun. Startled patrons gasped as the gentleman blew one of his fingers off. An ambulance rushed him to the hospital. He was later heard to say (what else) "I did not know it was loaded." The same could be said of the Browns, who never recognized that Detroit was loaded, either. The Wolverines' resolve was forged by the heroic catching of Charlie Bennett. The catcher's hands were observed bleeding from the early stages of the contest; and he spent the afternoon with rags tied around three fingers. Unlike the spectator with the revolver, Bennett stayed the whole game.

In the aftermath, the series was largely decided as a result of the actions of Von der Ahe and Sterns. Sterns' prediction of Detroit winning ten games proved prophetic. Arguably, Chris Von der Ahe lost the 1887 World Series for his Browns. Von der Ahe's petty one-upmanship battle with Sterns may have been the difference. During the series, Von der Ahe cursed his players. As a result, the Browns took to careless playing, gambling, carousing, and fighting. Charles Comiskey threatened to slit his own throat if Von der Ahe did not consider returning a portion of his profit to his players. A bitter Dave Foutz said, "If we won the series from the best baseball club in the world outside ourselves, we would get our little hundred dollars. If we lost it, we wouldn't get a black cent." Von der Ahe bitterly complained that umpire "Honest John" Kelly had bet large sums on the Wolverines. Though each club realized $12,000 after expenses, the annoyed Von der Ahe refused to share any of the money with his players. Counting an exhibition versus the Brooklyn Bridegrooms, the Browns had played sixteen postseason games for nothing.

Sterns, on the other hand, exuded confidence. He promised his men bonus money for their success. He challenged the American Association's Cincinnati club to a one-game, winner-take-all gate during an off day in the 1887 Series. The Reds were the only club to post a winning record against the Browns during the season. Most importantly, Sterns also made sure that his manager, Watkins, kept his men away from negative distractions. The Wolverines were baseball's newest champions.

The Sporting News offered no excuses, writing that the Browns' defeat was due to poor base running and that the club batted like "wooden men." Arlie Latham did manage to hit .293 and swipe fifteen bases. Yank Robinson hit .326 with ten bases on balls. However, top Association slugger Tip O'Neill was dreadful, batting a paltry .200. Charlie Comiskey posted a .306, with only two runs batted in. In the pitching department, Caruthers was creditable, but he was overworked. Dave Foutz, in Von der Ahe's doghouse, was barely used. Silver King was effective (though unlucky) in his four games. The play of the rest of the Browns resembled the performance of drunken men.

All told, only 51,000 attended the games with a gate of just over $41,000. The winners share was $500 a man.

Immediately following the series, in early November 1887, a suspicious blaze occurred at Sportsman's Park and environs. The player's dressing room was destroyed. The fire damaged the handball court, gymnasium, and team clubhouse. The conflagration spread nearby to Von der Ahe's nearby Golden Lion Saloon. Some of Von der Ahe's critics implied arson by Von der Ahe to collect insurance; however, the matter never made it to court.

As 1887 came to a close, a reporter asked Von der Ahe, "What truth is there to the report just published that had you won the world's championship from Detroit this fall you would have transferred the St. Louis Browns to New York, lock, stock, and barrel?" Without batting an eye, Von der Ahe said, "There is more truth than poetry in the statement." Von der Ahe went on to explain that the Browns in New York City would be a money-making machine and would turn $100,000 a year in profit, far more than in St. Louis. Since Von der Ahe was in New York City at the time of the League meetings, speculation ran rampant that the Browns were transferring. *Sporting Life* didn't agree with the report, calling Von der Ahe's presence "vanity and vexation."

Near the end of November, Von der Ahe stunned the baseball world. Within a ten-day period, he sold pitchers Bobby Caruthers and Dave Foutz, starting catcher Doc Bushong, shortstop Bill Gleason, and center fielder Curt Welch. On November 21, Welch and Gleason were sold to Philadelphia. Welch commanded $3,000. Gleason's value had been reduced to $1,000, owing to his poor showing in the 1887 series. In return, the Browns received catcher Jocko Milligan, shortstop Chippy McGarr, and outfielder Fred Mann. Four days later, the Brooklyn Trolley Dodgers paid an astronomical $9,000 to Von der Ahe for the services of Caruthers. Owner Von der Ahe had refused to pay Caruthers the money he wanted. Quipped *The Sporting News*, "Caruthers wants $5,000 a year. Most ballplayers do." That same day, Doc Bushong was sent packing to Brooklyn for $4,500. One week later, Von der Ahe completed the blockbuster sales by dealing Dave Foutz to Brooklyn for $5,500. Both Caruthers and Foutz had become so disgusted with Von der Ahe that they requested trades. In total, these transactions involved $23,000.

Manager Charles Comiskey was livid. So were St. Louis ball fans. Von der Ahe had supreme confidence in Comiskey's talents to develop young players. In turn, Von der Ahe could pay the new recruits less money. But wouldn't Comiskey feel betrayed? Wouldn't Comiskey want to leave the Browns? The answers to both questions was yes. However, Comiskey stayed on due to his enormous salary and his loyalty to the city of St. Louis. Within days of the deals, Von der Ahe was stating that he expected the Browns to win the American Association championship again in 1888.

Newspaper speculation abounded about the sales. Some stories dealt with Von der Ahe's simple greed to recoup losses from the World Series. Others focused on his ego. Shortly before, Chicago magnate Albert Spalding had sold Michael "King" Kelly to Boston for the unheard-of fee of $10,000, the biggest deal in baseball. The *St. Louis Globe-Democrat* postulated that Von der Ahe was deliberately weakening his club. The daily theorized that St. Louis was too strong for the Association. By the end of the campaign, with no pennant race, Sportsman's Park crowds were dwindling. Balancing the competition would send fans flocking back to baseball. By Von der Ahe's reasoning, the whole Association would benefit and, at the same time, bring more fans to the park to see old favorites. Von der Ahe said that there was no money in pennants and that competition and uncertainty drove fans to the ball yard. He cited the champion Detroit Wolverines as a barometer. For all their greatness, the Wolverines couldn't average 1,200 spectators for home games. In hindsight, all the above may have been correct.

Sporting Life offered a different angle. "Very few people know that the sale of Welch, Foutz and Caruthers was made more at Comiskey's request than at Von der Ahe's desire. Comiskey wants no man on his team that will not obey him." In effect, the Philadelphia paper hinted at a mutinous climate among the prima donna ballplayers on the Browns.

By the late 1880s, the St. Louis Browns were unquestionably the most famous baseball team in America. Chris Von der Ahe seized the opportunity to showcase his team all over the United States. Baseball fanatics in smaller towns would have their chance to see the Browns in person. *The Sporting News* and *Sporting Life* printed schedules and stories about the St. Louis Browns postseason barnstorming tours. These November–February journeys took place across the Midwest, South, and Western United States. Often the Browns were accompanied by other major-league squads. Not only did the Browns play with their professional counterparts, they also took on minor-league and town teams.

As incentive, Von der Ahe offered his players gate receipt shares and promised they would be treated like kings. The latter promise proved true. In most locations, the crowds attending were warm and receptive. These "new" audiences allowed the men to strut around and play without the pressure of a pennant race. Von der Ahe also promoted the tours to broaden baseball interest around the country.

The first barnstorming tour took place following the grueling 1887 World Series. Beginning in early November, the Browns defeated the Chicago National League team in St. Louis. Afterward, the teams met on the platform at Union Depot to board two Pullman Palace cars. Von der Ahe's players happily showed off their finery at the station. The players dressed in suits with gold chains, diamonds, and derbies. Puffs of cigar smoke mixed with the hissing of the steam train. Secretary Munson optimistically expected profits of $1,000 per man for the trip. The teams then boarded for two games in Charleston, South Carolina, during the middle of that city's Gala Week celebration. Ballplaying stops in Memphis, Nashville, New Orleans, and Texas towns followed. From the Lone Star State, the Browns and Chicagos ventured to balmy San Francisco. There they were greeted by fanatics jamming the streets in an old-fashioned baseball parade, complete with brass band and the Philadelphia and New York teams. A three-month series of exhibitions was arranged with Browns rivals and teams from the California League. Ten to fifteen thousand squeezed into a ball yard in San Francisco for the first game. Several boys risked tree climbing for a glimpse of their idols. A boy hawking programs was said to have yelled "murder" for patrons refusing to buy. When the Browns returned to St. Louis in February 1888, critics explained the trip as a financial failure. Von der Ahe philosophized that despite the losses, the tour was a rousing success in promoting the sport in faraway places.

There was a lot of baseball on the tour, but there was a lot of fun, too. At Yuma, in Arizona territory, Arlie Latham stepped off the train at a whistle-stop. The platform was filled with Indians. While his teammates hooted from the windows, Latham proceeded to grab an Indian girl and dance with her against her will. That silliness completed, Latham spied a squaw carrying her baby. Gesturing wildly, Latham tried to communicate to her that he would trade her some fruit for the infant. The Indian handed Latham the child as Arlie gave the lady the fruit. Just then, the train started to move. Frantic, Latham could not get the Indian to take back the infant so that he could hop on the exiting train. Finally, Latham just dropped the child, and jumped on the iron horse. Luckily, the baby landed on its rear end and was not injured. As the train pulled out of the station, the Indians on the platform raised quite a commotion.

13

Four-Time Winners

To escape the pressures of business and satisfy his wanderlust, Von der Ahe and his wife departed the United States for Europe on a steamship. During his absence, Von der Ahe left the club in Comiskey's hands. As the ship was pulling away, a reporter asked, "Where will Brooklyn finish in 1888?" The owner replied, "Why, behind St. Louis."

Chris wasn't long in London before he was scheming to arrange a series of baseball games for Britons. Von der Ahe told astonished natives of a game that sometimes drew 30,000 spectators for a single match. Von der Ahe even fantasized about a world barnstorming tour to begin after the season. The tour would begin in the southern United States, then wind into Mexico and San Francisco. The players would then board a steamer to Australia, taking advantage of the seasonal weather patterns in each country. In 1874, Al Spalding had financed a disastrous baseball trip to England. In less than one month, the Boston and Athletic teams returned home. The British, with Victorian sensibilities, had no interest in a game they found unfathomable. Von der Ahe still believed that baseball could make a go of it in England. He said, "Your cricket is a slow game compared to our baseball, and I think seriously of bringing my boys over here and showing you just what America's National Game is."

In Chris' native Germany, the Von der Ahe's spent some pleasant hours visiting Von der Ahe's mother. Most probably, Von der Ahe whiled away the time bragging about his American-made fortune. And yet, like his tour in England, Von der Ahe could not help but to speak on baseball. "Wherever you go in the old country, some kind of sport or other flourishes. I found that baseball had penetrated Germany. On the college fields at Heidelberg and Berlin, there are good diamonds but there was no playing on them when I was there, for the reason that the snow was several inches thick on the ground and skating and sleighing were the only pastimes."

Perhaps Von der Ahe was merely dreaming. Perhaps he had drank a little too much beer. What indication would there be on a field covered with snow that a baseball diamond lay underneath? Was this a publicity ploy to poke fun at America's gullibility?

If Von der Ahe's physical being was in Europe, his heart was back home in America. While in London, Von der Ahe saw the Prince of Wales and commented that the prince was not as great a man as Buffalo Bill or boxer John L. Sullivan. He also attended a rugby game and a meeting of the Associated Cricketers and spoke on fighting as proving one's manhood. The British laws on assault were severe, and the reserved British acted accordingly. Name calling was common, but fighting was infrequent. The Germans, Chris observed, were a different story. "Men who did not fight there were made so miserable that they usually fell into a decline and died." Instead of fighting, Von der Ahe seemed content with throwing around his money, as opposed to his fists.

When Von der Ahe returned to St. Louis in mid-February, he looked better than ever and was filled with stories for friends and admirers. His tales revolved around his grand plans for the Grand Old Game away from American shores. Von der Ahe also remarked on the personalities of the British and Germans.

St. Louis' exhibition successes served as a harbinger. In the spring, Comiskey's new charges defeated the champion Detroit club five straight times. After the Browns dreadful defeat to the Wolverines only six months earlier, Von der Ahe was nearly giddy over this sudden turn of events.

To help transport fans to Sportsman's more efficiently, Von der Ahe arranged for a cable car called the Cannon Ball Train. The special would make the east-west ride in St. Louis directly to the ball yard. The conductors on the Cannon Ball took tickets for the train and ball game. Comfortable intracity rail travel for his players also occupied the owner's time.

The St. Louis Browns entered the 1888 American Association campaign a drastically changed team. Gone were Dave Foutz, Bob Caruthers, Bill Gleason, Curt Welch, and Doc Bushong. Nearly all the sportswriters conceded the flag to Brooklyn, with an outside chance for Philadelphia. For all the changes, St. Louis ball cranks thought Von der Ahe a madman. In an effort to placate readers, *The Sporting News* offered celluloid pictures of the old Browns for yearly subscribers. Von der Ahe hired a firm to print giant-sized posters of the departed Browns. Their images were then pasted around the city to promote St. Louis games against their ex-players.

Everyone underestimated the genius of Charlie Comiskey. The player holes left by Von der Ahe's restructuring seemed impossible to fill, yet, somehow Comiskey worked the miracle. The new men, in fact, were often better than the originals. Spring was a time for testing new players. Talented rookie "Bug" Holliday was pencilled in at Welch's position, but, he bolted to Des Moines in a contract dispute. Outfielder Fred Mann was tried in center, but didn't make the ball club. Harry Lyons had a trial at shortstop but eventually became a light-hitting center fielder. The remarkable Tommy McCarthy took over in right field. After a tryout with Oshkosh, Comiskey was impressed enough with McCarthy's defensive wizardry that he signed the youngster. McCarthy was expert at the inside baseball Comiskey cultivated. McCarthy juggled fly balls to fool base runners, stole signs, and worked the hit-and-run.

Originally, Yank Robinson was to move to shortstop, but with the failure of oversized rookie Parson Nicholson, Yank returned to second base. Ed Herr also took a turn at shortstop but was replaced by defensive specialist Bill White. Like Lyons, White was a poor hitter, but he didn't shirk at balls knocked his way.

Pitchers Silver King and Nat Hudson filled the void left by Foutz and Caruthers. King stepped up and won 45 games while tossing nearly 600 regular-season innings. King's talents stayed strong despite the fact that he detested large crowds. When King wasn't tossing baseballs, he fought with Von der Ahe over his salary. Threatening to quit baseball to work with his bricklayer father, King demanded a 100 percent increase to $3,500. The two men eventually compromised. The diminutive Nat Hudson chalked up 25 victories. Besides these men, Comiskey hoped that young hurlers Ed Knouff, Jim Devlin, and Joe Murphy would win a few games. Only Knouff and Devlin proved to be finds.

Holdover outfielder Tip O'Neill hit exactly 100 points less than in 1887, and still won the batting crown. Arlie Latham anchored the slick fielding infield and drove opponents nuts with his coaching banter. To help fill player voids, Von der Ahe formed the St. Louis Whites in the Western Association. Unfortunately, due to the popularity of the Browns, the Whites didn't draw flies. In fact, Von der Ahe couldn't give away tickets! For his graciousness, Von der Ahe was assailed with questions on why he didn't give ball cranks tickets to see the Browns. By the middle of the season, Von der Ahe was desperately trying to unload the club. Offers were made to transfer the St. Louis Whites to Denver and Lincoln, Nebraska.

In many ways, Von der Ahe's 1888 ownership of the Browns was typical, despite the player shake ups. The Browns continued to win while Von der Ahe managed the financial affairs with a firm hand, involved in all negotiations for securing players. One of the new men, acquired from Philadelphia, was catcher Jocko Milligan. When Milligan first met Von der Ahe for contract talks, he pleaded for his release and offered to pay the Browns owner $600! However, since Milligan didn't have the cash, Von der Ahe kept him under contract. To secure pitching for the St. Louis stretch drive, Von der Ahe signed Addison Gumbert for $3,000. Gumbert was the Tri-State League's best pitcher, hurling for Zanesville, Ohio. Von der Ahe had been struck with the lad after his low-hit performances; however, Gumbert never pitched for the Browns. Von der Ahe sent a telegraph to the Hamilton, Canada, club for the release of pitcher Pete Wood. When Hamilton asked for $8,000, the Browns owner balked, and no deal was made. A third pitcher, the tempestuous Louisville hurler "Icebox" Chamberlain, was acquired for $4,000. So confident was Von der Ahe on Chamberlain's signing that he measured his men for new suits of clothes to be worn for travel during the worlds championship series. Chamberlain calmly produced 11 wins in 13 decisions.

Comiskey's superb generalship guided the Browns into contention. His desire to win and his sarcasm were often transferred directly to his players. Woe be the man who didn't obey. To illustrate Comiskey's ambitions, he sometimes ordered players to sacrifice in a close game. Comiskey relayed the instructions while standing on third base. If a player didn't comply, Comiskey would have no problem walking down the line and punching his man right in the mouth.

St. Louis was off and running early in April. The Browns continued to be criticized for their dirty play and abuse of umpires. Bob Ferguson was singled out for his less-than-honest work against St. Louis. Betting-parlor patrons always wagered against St. Louis when Ferguson was known to be umpiring. Once, in St. Louis, while Von der Ahe was sitting on the Browns' bench, he jokingly told Baltimore captain Blondy Purcell that he (Purcell) had been put out fairly and squarely. Said Purcell, "I know that, but Ferguson's umpiring is so rotten, I thought I would kick anyhow."

In early July, the Browns sported a half-game lead on Brooklyn and only three games on Philadelphia. To get Brooklyn owner Byrne's goat in St. Louis, Von der Ahe staged a parade and dinner reception. Unfortunately, St. Louis lost the series. Von der Ahe bitterly complained to the Association that his former catcher Bushong, now with Brooklyn, had tried to bribe St. Louis' Tip O'Neill to deliberately throw games. For his poor play, O'Neill was suspended for a few contests, despite his pleas that he had dysentery. Silver King's effort, or lack thereof, did not please Von der Ahe, either. King lost a home game after a 4–1 ninth-inning lead evaporated. Thanks to two extra-inning errors by Arlie Latham and a Bobby Caruthers short porch home run, the Browns lost another game to Brooklyn. The next day, Ed Knouff allowed a two-run, ninth-inning double, to lose 4–3. In the space of a few more days, Brooklyn increased its lead to four and one-half games. Von der Ahe threatened mass murder of his entire ball club. The scare tactic worked. Within a span of six weeks, Brooklyn collapsed. The Browns played like madmen, capturing eighteen of twenty-one games during one stretch.

Infielder Ed Herr's inexplicable hitting also bolstered St. Louis' pennant run. Within the space of a few weeks, Herr homered three times over the left-field fence at Sportsman's Park. Herr's blows, accomplished in official games and exhibitions, had spectators aghast. In nearly 600 total games at the yard, only three others had registered the feat. All of the men were feared sluggers: Harry Stovey of the Athletics, Davey Orr of the Mets, and the Browns' Tip O'Neill. Curiously, Herr's fabulous slugging lasted but a brief time. By 1890, he was out of the major leagues.

Von der Ahe's paying customers also kept things lively. During a game at Sportsman's Park, a foul ball went flying into the stands, striking a gentleman patron in the chest. Instead of a thud, the man's chest reverberated with the sound of broken glass. Startled, the man reached into his shirt pocket and pulled out the neck of a whiskey bottle. No precious fluid remained inside. The man threatened to sue Von der Ahe, but Chris probably laughed, only to blame the spectator for bringing alcohol into his park.

A key element of the pennant chase was an enterprising 17-year-old named Rudy Hahn who stowed away on Browns' trains and became a mascot. Hahn aspired to be a ballplayer, but had lost three fingers in a buzz-saw accident. Instead, he watched over the bats at the games. After Hahn was noticed hiding between the seats, he was befriended by St. Louis players, who gave him some money and meals. Superstitious that they might lose if Rudy were sent packing, the Browns kept him for awhile. When Chris Von der Ahe was finally told about Rudy, the owner ordered a suit of clothes for him in New York City.

The season's pivotal game occurred on August 3 at Brooklyn's Washington Park. The Browns entered the affair with a slender one-half-game lead over the Trolley Dodgers. Brooklyn had already manhandled St. Louis much of the season, winning seven of eight games, including four by Bob Caruthers. Brooklyn cranks smelled blood. Silver King started for St. Louis against Caruthers. Doc Bushong and first baseman Dave Foutz were also in the lineup for Brooklyn. The two sides traded runs, and the score was tied at six after nine innings. In the tenth, Yank Robinson tripled and was brought home by the trusty bat of Tip O'Neill. The latter's sacrifice fly gave the Browns the lead. In the bottom of the inning, Silver King held together. He struck out Dodger shortstop Germany Smith to end the game. Attending the affair was a beaming Chris Von der Ahe. Brooklyn owner Charles Byrne wasn't so happy. The loss was bad enough, but Byrne also had to suspend his captain, Dave Orr, who feigned illness and took the afternoon off. Orr wasn't really sick, having been seen at the amusement park at Coney Island.

With the Browns firmly in command of the race, the irrepressible Arlie Latham telegrammed his boss the following comment: "I am full of ginger and I hope your family is the same."

Outpacing Brooklyn by six and one-half games and Philadelphia by ten, St. Louis easily sailed to its fourth consecutive pennant. The difference was St. Louis' ability to ride the honorable baseball formula of tight pitching and defense.

Strangely, all five of the old Browns weren't as successful with their new teams. The Brooklyn-based battery of Foutz–Bushong and Caruthers–Bushong fell off dramatically in pitching and hitting. Philly's Bill Gleason's hitting tumbled .064 points. Curt Welch held the line.

For the final month, St. Louis regulars rested, preparing for the upcoming World Series. For his effort, Comiskey received constant praise. His leadership abilities and discipline were compared to that of great generals. Often the praise was in the form of money. Washington offered Von der Ahe $10,000 for Comiskey's services. The National League Boston club was prepared to give Von der Ahe $15,000 to secure Comiskey. Boston pitched $10,000 for Yank Robinson. The most astonishing offer, though, was from jealous Brooklyn owner Charles Byrne, who reportedly offered Von der Ahe $100,000 and the Brooklyn team in exchange for Comiskey and the Browns. Von der Ahe politely declined all these overtures.

Following the season, the Browns posed for an unusual team photograph. Included in the studio pose was the four-year-old son of Arlie Latham, in full Browns' uniform. Also in the picture were two greyhound dogs. In no time, Latham's son endeared himself to the players. The boy walked, talked, and acted just like his famous father. Years earlier, Von der Ahe had purchased the two greyhounds after a night of drinking at Tony Faust's oyster house. The dogs' original owner was a ballplayer named Egyptian Healy. Von der Ahe quickly named the dogs "Fly" and "Prince." The latter dog was later given to Louisville owner John Botto. After their purchase, the two dogs followed Von der Ahe everywhere, including the saloons. On occasion, when Chris was attempting to catch his players drinking, he'd open the swinging saloon doors and with a flourish announce that he was there. Browns' transgressors weren't that stupid, however. As the boys hoisted their brews, they kept one eye on the saloon's swinging doors. When the players noticed the dogs from under the door, they'd duck into a back room.

A big American Association squabble in 1888 was the fifty cents versus twenty-five cents tariff. For the season, the Association experimented with 50-cent baseball. As a result of politicking by Von der Ahe, the magnates reasoned that the idea was a necessity due to increasing club payrolls. Despite protests by Baltimore and Philadelphia, the season began with clubs charging the 50-cent fee. Unfortunately, the doubling of admission fees deeply hurt attendance and revenues. Much of the Association's appeal revolved around 25-cent baseball. In early July, the National League's Philadelphia club slashed its prices to twenty-five cents. Unable to compete with their territorial rival, the Association allowed its Philadelphia club to reduce to a quarter. Soon the Association's Baltimore entry was charging a quarter before a plan was ratified to reinstitute the lower admission fees. By August 25, all of the Association's clubs had reverted back to quarter baseball. To compensate, the directors readjusted the guarantee to visiting clubs to $100. They also tried to limit player salaries. In the fall, the St. Louis club offered a proposal to reaffect the 50-cent fee. The measure failed.

Another financial battle concerned the division of gate receipts. At issue was the percentage plan versus the guarantee system. From the organization's beginning, the guarantee receipt plan had been in effect. Under the guarantee, owners of the visiting team were guaranteed $65 of the gate receipts for all games. The take would be split 50–50 for holidays.

As early as 1884, the percentage plan had been discussed at Association meetings. To take advantage of baseball's prosperity and combat the Union Association, the Association expanded to twelve clubs that year. Of the twelve, only five clubs (New York, St. Louis, Cincinnati, Baltimore, and Philadelphia) were financially secure. The seven others, in the voting majority, were reported to favor the percentage plan. The issue created much controversy within the ranks, but the guarantee system remained.

By 1887, Von der Ahe firmly believed that the percentage plan, in force for years in the National League, would mean bigger profits for his Browns. He was right. Von der Ahe threatened to transfer his franchise to the National League if the percentage plan was not adopted. Some fellow magnates believed Von der Ahe's latest threat of a League jump was a bluff going so far as to call him "Von der Gall." Others were genuinely concerned, realizing that St. Louis' participation was vital to the organization's well-being. After all, the St. Louis franchise was the most profitable in baseball. Naturally, the sporting press espoused lengthy editorials on the subject. Some praised Von der Ahe's politicking; others condemned him for his persistent threats against the Association. All of the papers seemed to agree that Von der Ahe was under tremendous pressure.

Mathematically, the percentage plan was a boon for Association teams that played to large houses. Profits under the percentage were tied directly to gate receipts. More people in the ball yard meant more money for the owners. However, for less-fortunate teams that struggled with home and road attendance, the guarantee plan kept them afloat financially.

In 1885, Von der Ahe was rather satisfied with the guarantee when the Browns captured their first Association pennant. St. Louis played to large throngs at Sportsman's Park. However, when his pets evolved into an even bigger draw on the road, Von der Ahe began to realize the profit potential of the percentage plan. Everyone wanted to witness Comiskey's umpire baiting and teamwork tactics, Latham's lively coaching and acrobatics, O'Neill's timely slugging, and Welch's spectacular play afield. Perhaps lucky ball cranks could even catch a glimpse of the mercurial Von der Ahe himself, who enjoyed traveling with the club.

By chance, Von der Ahe and Charles Byrne bumped into each other in a New York saloon. After other members of the fraternity swaggered into the bar, the din was louder than normal. The beer was flowing, cigar smoke hung thick, and all of the magnates were posturing about their finances. Finally, after some lively debate, Von der Ahe listened and agreed to Byrne's compromise. Byrne proposed that visiting clubs receive 30 percent of all receipts, with a minimum of $130 guaranteed. Shortly after, the magnates met at the Fifth Avenue Hotel. Here, rancorous debate continued. When the smoke had cleared, the American Association owners passed the Byrne percentage plan.

In June 1888, as Von der Ahe was returning with his club from a highly successful trip in the east, he was posed a question by *The Sporting News:* "You rather like the percentage system then?" "Well I should say so. Take the Brooklyn games for example. Last season when the Browns were there they got nothing but a $65 guarantee. On Sunday last we received nearly $1,500 as our share of the receipts and Monday we got $475 as our share."

14

Von der Ahe's Last Hurrah

Fresh off the financial white elephant of the 1887 Series, Chris Von der Ahe and John Day of the New York Giants managed to create a controversy. In the 1888 World Series, both owners wanted to charge exorbitant prices for seating. However, the public created such a hue and cry that $1.50 was charged for choice reserved seating, $1.00 for grandstand, and fifty cents for the hoi polloi. Von der Ahe and Day also agreed to a 60–40 percent share of the gate receipts for the winners and losers. Seven thousand dollars would be set aside to be divided among the players. Win or lose, the ball tossers on each team would receive $200 apiece. Two umpires would work the games, "Honest John" Kelly and John Gaffney.

The first club to capture six games would be declared the winner. The first five games would be contested in New York City. Game six would be played in Philadelphia. The final five contests would take place in St. Louis. After the 1885 debacle, Chris understood the public relations power of ending the series in his hometown. Most likely, he envisioned himself leading downtown parades with the streets lined with adoring fans cheering their conquering heroes.

In preparation for the spectacle, Von der Ahe sent a September 30 letter to Al Spink. The missive detailed Von der Ahe's audacious plans for the trip to New York. Von der Ahe requested Spink to arrange a special train decorated with giant banners proclaiming "St. Louis Browns. Four-Time Pennant Winners!" In addition, Spink was to ask friends in St. Louis to accompany the club on the long journey. Transportation, sleeping car, buffet, and hotel accommodations would all be paid by the Browns' magnanimous magnate! Von der Ahe also requested Spink to arrange for representatives of each of the St. Louis newspapers to make the trip at Von der Ahe's expense. Upon reading the letter, Al Spink contacted Mr. Wetherell, a local train agent. Wetherell was stunned by the instructions, saying that such a deal would cost nearly

$20,000. When Spink wrote back to Von der Ahe, the owner replied, "Tell Wetherell to mind his own business and fix that train up as I want it." If the all-expense-paid train excursion to New York wasn't enough, Von der Ahe reached deeper into his pockets to buy suits of clothes for all his guests. In all, two hundred "fans" took advantage of the suit offer. In total, the special cost Von der Ahe nearly $30,000.

The National League champion Giants, who defeated Anson's Chicago nine, boasted a dominant pitching staff with adequate hitting. "Truthful Jim" Mutrie managed the squad. No fewer than six future Hall of Famers populated their ranks. The nearly unhittable "Sir Timothy" Keefe anchored the staff with "Smiling Mickey" Welch and two Cannonball pitchers, Titcomb and Crane. The former was a wild left-hander named for the speed of his pitches. The latter, Cannonball Crane, acquired his moniker from his eating proclivities. "Buck" Ewing, the toughest backstop in the game, caught the slants of his pitchers. The infield was sparked by "Dear Old Roger" Connor at first and John Montgomery Ward at shortstop. "Orator Jim" O'Rourke and "Silent Mike" Tiernan starred in the outfield. On paper, the series looked evenly matched.

The games began in New York's Polo Grounds, despite a muddy field. St. Louis, led by manager Charlie Comiskey, arrayed themselves in spanking new Rawlings Brothers uniforms with white pants, brown belts and stockings, and brown caps with white stripes. The Giants, under Jim Mutrie, were heavily cheered by the partisans and showed off their black jerseys with white trim. The stands were packed with rabid patrons sporting shrill tin horns, and a host of baseball dignitaries. Von der Ahe's friends arrived in fine fashion as well. Curveballer Tim Keefe of the Giants opposed the Browns' 45-win phenom Silver King. A pitchers' duel materialized, and the game was decided in the late innings on St. Louis catcher Boyle's throwing error and center fielder Harry Lyons' subsequent muff on the same play. New York prevailed, 2–1.

St. Louis evened matters the next day, 3–0 behind Icebox Chamberlain and some old-fashioned hustling. Browns' outfielder Tommy McCarthy tried to score from second base by bypassing third base and sneaking through the infield. However, Tommy was called out because of the two-umpire scheme. The series actually took a nasty turn for St. Louis following the game. That evening, St. Louis players and their fan entourage hoisted beer, wine, and champagne at the Grand Central Hotel bar. Von der Ahe himself celebrated, ordering each of his players to buy a suit of clothes and send him the bill. The party lasted until the wee hours of the morning.

From this point forward, the series shifted dramatically. St. Louis played as if they were still congratulating themselves for their game-two shutout. A host of Browns' goats emerged. Catcher Boyle let Giants' base runners steal at will. Third baseman Arlie Latham failed in bases-loaded batting situations. Shortstop Bill White bobbled nearly everything that came his way. St. Louis pitching was stretched thin with Silver King and Icebox Chamberlain being forced to split the duties. Browns' starter Nat Hudson had refused to partake in the series. Instead, Hudson spent his time vacationing in Hot Springs,

Arkansas, ignoring Von der Ahe's telegrams. By the time St. Louis departed New York, they trailed four games to one.

Game five was especially painful. In front of 9,000 screaming fans, many of them delirious Irish immigrants seated in the "Burkeville" bleachers, the Browns bowed, 6–4. St. Louis blew a 4–1 lead in the eighth inning. With the score tied, Browns' centerfielder Harry Lyons and second baseman Yank Robinson collided on a pop fly. Lyons was the victim of a stomach injury and would not play again in the series. Robinson groggily returned.

St. Louis may have been thrilled to leave New York, but their treatment by the Giants in Philadelphia was downright rude. The Browns again blew an early lead as the Giants hammered Chamberlain 12–5. New York's prohibitive lead reached five games to one. St. Louis would need to capture the next five to win the series.

A nasty controversy ensued on the train ride back to St. Louis. Making a routine stop in Pittsburgh, the Browns were met at the station by their former-center fielder Curt Welch, who intimated that umpire Kelly was showing favoritism by betting on the Giants. Welch likely had read the earlier *St. Louis Post-Dispatch* comments concerning Kelly. "It is a fact that [John] Kelly is going to open a restaurant and saloon in New York, with Mike Kelly as a partner. As he will depend on the base-ball patrons for his trade it is not likely he will antagonize them by giving a decision against their pets."

Welch may have been searching for a scapegoat. According to former teammates, Curt had bet large sums on St. Louis. Chris Von der Ahe then put his foot in his mouth by publicly agreeing with Welch and remarking that umpires Kelly and Gaffney were wagering on the New Yorkers. Newsmen did not miss the opportunity to reveal Von der Ahe's idiotic comments. Before the train arrived in St. Louis, a wire had flashed to the umpires. Both men responded.

"I don't care about anyone's opinion of my work. But, I do object to being called crooked, and I will quit the business before I take anymore of that," said Gaffney.

Kelly reiterated, "If Gaffney won't umpire any more games, I won't either."

The umpires also explained that unless Von der Ahe offered a public apology, they would not work any more of the games.[3]

As the players debarked, Von der Ahe called an impromptu press conference at Union Depot. With reporters swarming, Von der Ahe explained that he had been misquoted and that Kelly and Gaffney were doing a swell job. Satisfied with Von der Ahe's explanation, both umpires agreed to resume work.

The games in St. Louis went largely in favor of the Browns, but for all the wrong reasons. The Browns won game seven with 4,800 raucous St. Louisians in support. Unfortunately, St. Louis was shelled in the eighth affair, 11–3, behind ace hurler Tim Keefe. The curveballing right-hander continually baffled the Browns, winning his fourth game. The series was over. The *New York Times* wrote, "All the game lacked to make it a first-class funeral was the music. The corpse was there, for no well-conducted funeral is without a corpse."

Immediately after the game, Giants' shortstop Monte Ward and pitcher Cannonball Crane headed for San Francisco to join Al Spalding's baseball tour of Australia. Catchers Buck Ewing and Willard Brown had more mundane destinations in mind; they simply went home.

Despite the ending of the competitive series, John Day and Von der Ahe agreed to play on. The final three games would be contested at Sportsman's Park, conducted solely for exhibition and profit. Players were promised portions of the gate.

Exhibitions, yes; profits, no. Only several hundred fans showed for the next three affairs, all won by St. Louis by the ugly scores of 14–11, 18–7, and 6–0. Mysteriously, umpire "Honest John" Kelly had returned to his native New York. John Gaffney worked the remaining games alone. Both clubs played simply to entertain. New York's lineup had been so depleted that manager Mutrie seemingly placed players in random positions. The results were predictable.

Despite St. Louis' winning streak, they lost the series. Von der Ahe was so upset he pocketed all of the 1888 Association pennant money ($12,000) for himself and withheld all Browns' benefit monies. To add insult to injury, Von der Ahe called his men "chumps" for their efforts. Counting the 1887 debacle against Detroit and two exhibitions, the Browns had played their last *twenty-seven* postseason games without pay. Browns' secretary George Munson reported that St. Louis had realized $24,000 altogether for the series. With total expenses reaching $8,000 for travel and advertisement, the Browns cleared $16,000, every penny for Chris Von der Ahe. Just over 42,000 spectators attended the eleven games.

The *St. Louis Post-Dispatch* blamed White. "The weakness of the Browns in the shortstop's position was simply appalling, and the loss of no less than three games in the series can be directly attributed to his poor work. Had the Browns had a strong man in his place the result of the series might have been entirely different."

Indeed, White was made goat of the series, committing nine errors and batting .143. He never played in the major leagues again. However, White had company. Due to Nat Hudson's absence and the lack of pitching depth, Chamberlain was 2–3 with a 5.32 ERA. Silver King worked in tough luck against Tim Keefe and won only one game. Yank Robinson struck out twelve times and made four errors.

The New York Giants' shares were much better. To a man, they received $200 apiece for winning, $28 for game ten, and $100 for the final game.

The Giants also received the silver and ebony trophy called the "Hall Championship Cup of 1888." Presented by the manufacturer of Between the Acts cigarettes, the elaborate Tiffany trophy featured miniatures of players in game action: the pitcher, batsman and catcher, and the four infielders.

Winning New York manager Mutrie was upset that St. Louis had won the last three games, saying, "If we ever engage in another World Series, the ball will stop rolling just as soon as the series is decided."

15

The Most Calamitous Race

For four straight years, St. Louis ball cranks could strut up and down the streets of their city and boast of their champions. They could thank owner Chris Von der Ahe, Captain Charlie Comiskey, and the wonderful players. However, for fans tired of successive first-place finishes, the 1889 season was a dandy. Baseball's great drama, the sustained pennant race, heated up that summer in St. Louis and Brooklyn. The predicted chase was all the more dramatic since three of the Brooklyn principals were ex-Browns' war horses—first baseman Dave Foutz, catcher Doc Bushong, and pitcher Bob Caruthers. What could not have been predicted was the fearsome circumstances of the battle. Within the span of six months, Von der Ahe had to deal with a player revolt (May), monies loaned to down-and-out ballplayers (June), a gambling scandal (July), a bribery controversy (August), Comiskey's season-long haranguing, and forfeited games in Brooklyn (September). Juxtaposed in this mess was Von der Ahe's bitter battle with Brooklyn's Charles Byrne over control of the American Association.

Charles Byrne's baseball star was on the rise in 1889. Born in New York City, Byrne was a graduate of St. Francis Xavier College. After working as a sportswriter and studying law, Byrne amassed his fortune in real estate. Contemporaries described Byrne as "a nervous little man, full of life and grit, a good talker, very earnest and aggressive." In 1883, after his polka-dot-stockinged minor-league club had won the Interstate League pennant, Byrne recruited brother-in-law Joseph Doyle and Ferdinand Abell to help finance a major-league team. Doyle and Abell were gambling house proprietors. In the spring of 1884, the group purchased both the disbanded Cleveland National League franchise and Brooklyn of the American Association. From Cleveland came third baseman George Pinckney and shortstop George "Germany" Smith.

With Abell supplying the cash and a young Charles Ebbets selling tickets, Byrne worked tirelessly to provide Brooklyn with better ballplayers. It took several trying years. During this time, Doyle and Byrne managed the club. In the 1887 season, Byrne met with Von der Ahe to discuss the sale of some of St. Louis' star players to restore competition in the Association. Von der Ahe would later comply, yielding Byrne a bumper crop of talent. At the end of the 1887 season, Byrne's group purchased the New York Mets from Erastus Wiman. The franchise was later sold to Kansas City, but a promising young player named Darby O'Brien was retained. Three other acquisitions solidified the club: utility man Thomas "Oyster" Burns, outfielder "Pop" Corkhill, and second baseman Hub Collins. The next season, Byrne hired the innovative Bill McGunnigle, a four-time pennant-winning manager in the minor leagues.

With Caruthers, the wonderfully named Adonis Terry, Tom Lovett, and Mickey Hughes, Brooklyn possessed a formidable starting rotation.

The four-time champion Browns and Brooklyn's Dodgers entered the campaign with high hopes. Brooklyn's vocal fans anticipated an exciting season and rewarded Byrne by showing up in record numbers. New York City residents were excited by the possibility of a Giants-Dodgers showdown in the postseason. The Browns' guiding light, Charles Comiskey, expressed guarded optimism. He was satisfied that his two new regulars, shortstop Shorty Fuller and outfielder Charlie Duffee, would perform well. Comiskey believed that Robinson, McCarthy, Latham, and O'Neill would produce big seasons. The pitching batteries were outstanding, making the Browns' chances "rosy." While St. Louis players dickered over salaries, the Dodgers trained in earnest. Brooklyn's serious workout methods promoted the fraternal nature of their club.

Many Brooklyn players rode bicycles for two hours in the morning. At first, there were a few "scraped faces and noses," as a result of inexperience. Brooklyn's stalwarts practiced catching, batting, and stretching at Washington Park. Manager Bill McGunnigle firmly believed in a full-day workout.

To help alleviate the rigors of training, a Brooklyn policemen presented the club with a "puny monkey" mascot. However, after a few boisterous trips to Flatbush watering holes, the monkey was having a problem holding his liquor. Club management then ordered the players to chew gum on road trips and avoid the vagaries of the saloon.

Brooklyn's exhibition season was marred by sore arms and colds. Bob Caruthers and Mickey Hughes experienced tightness after warming up in the chill of Newark. However, few considered these problems serious. To show his determination, McGunnigle promised to jump off the Brooklyn Bridge if his team lost the pennant. McGunnigle was supported by baseball writer Henry Chadwick, a Brooklyn native working for *Sporting Life*.

In St. Louis, poor relations between Von der Ahe and his employees had been simmering for years. Following the 1887 season, Von der Ahe sold three of his stars to Brooklyn. The Browns' owner then blamed the 1887 Series loss on, among other things, Bobby Caruthers' "carousing." The Browns were mad at Von der Ahe over his lavish spending habits in the 1888 World Series. During the battles with New York, Von der Ahe spent money like water and then lambasted his players for losing. Due to these actions and Von der Ahe's capricious fines, there were a host of holdouts. Only one week before the exhibition season, seven St. Louis regulars were demanding more pay. Von der Ahe was upset with Arlie Latham for the player's nonpayment of a $1,500 loan. Latham didn't appreciate Von der Ahe's salary garnishment. With the holdouts came silence. Nobody wanted to speak with Von der Ahe's 19-year-old son Eddie. Quite often, Chris sent Eddie to talks involving contract negotiations. The situation worsened when Von der Ahe issued a decree stating that unsigned players' salaries would be deducted and they would not be allowed at the park.

The Sporting News sided with Von der Ahe, who was buying the players suits, hats, shoes, and paying for banquets every season. Yet the players were ungrateful. Many of the men demanded more money and refused exhibitions. The matter was finally straightened out when Comiskey asked Von der Ahe's permission to talk to the transgressors. Following an exhibition game, Comiskey compromised with everyone except pitcher Silver King. Comiskey then publicly stated that his club was content and ready to play its best. Despite outward appearances, the Browns were anything but content. Three days later, only a week before the season opener, King signed for $3,200.

Both clubs opened on the road. Brooklyn traveled to Philadelphia and Baltimore. Comiskey's Browns played in Cincinnati and Louisville. Despite the rigorous training and seriousness of purpose, McGunnigle's men acted as if they'd never seen a baseball. The Dodgers committed a ghastly forty-four errors in the first seven games, losing six. Conversely, the Browns played sharp baseball, winning six of seven. St. Louis was greeted by 10,000 cranks and a brass band playing "The Conquering Heroes Come" in the home opener. Eddie Von der Ahe was thrilled to be part of the festivities, publishing a twenty-four-page scorebook. Eighteen thousand copies were sold within the first couple of weeks of the season. Their only blemish occurred when sore-armed Nat Hudson was bombed for seventeen tallies in Louisville. Hudson wouldn't pitch again until June. Off the field, the Browns probably shared a few laughs at Brooklyn's expense. Entering May, the Browns were 11–2. The agate type of the standings belied the turmoil within.

The boys of Brooklyn shook off their doldrums and began to win due to a deep pitching staff and McGunnigle's masterful managing. McGunnigle had developed elaborate signals using hats. In plain view of the spectators, the Brooklyn manager would take the hats on and off, cock them to the side, and even wear two at once. McGunnigle's hat act caused some ridicule but Brooklyn opponents weren't laughing.

On Sunday, May 5, a nasty incident occurred at Ridgewood Park, the Dodgers' Sunday home. (Baseball playing on the Sabbath had been outlawed in Brooklyn and was technically legal in Ridgewood, which was just over the line in Queens.) Next to St. Louis, the Brooklyn crazies were the worst in the Association, constantly hurling invectives at the enemy and the umpires. Brooklyn cranks had every reason to act this way. In New York City, saloons outnumbered churches forty to one. Sportswriters, located directly below the grandstand, had to survive the filthy debris of tobacco juice and cigar stumps routinely tossed from above. Before 12,000 inebriated cranks, Brooklyn forfeited to the visitors when fans poured onto the field. American Association rules stipulated that home teams were responsible for crowd control. Byrne vociferously disagreed and blamed Philadelphia center fielder Curt Welch for inciting the riot. Nothing was ever proven, and Welch was not disciplined by the Association. As a result, Byrne built a barbed-wire fence around the outfield at Ridgewood.

The 1889 St. Louis player revolt against Von der Ahe began over a pair of pants. On May 2, second baseman Yank Robinson warmed up before a game at Sportsman's Park. Comiskey told Robinson that his pants were too small. After a few minutes, Robinson sent a young boy to retrieve a pair of padded trousers from Robinson's room across from the ball yard. The boy did so, but would not be readmitted to the park without a ticket. The gate attendant, a Mr. Niehaus, told the boy that he was following strict orders from President Von der Ahe not to let anyone in the park without a ticket. Robinson claimed that the boy was given a handwritten note explaining the situation. When Robinson found out about the incident, he flew into a rage at Niehaus and made references to the latter's parentage. Niehaus then went to Von der Ahe in tears to tell his version of the story.

Von der Ahe, protecting his attendant, headed to the players' bench. He yelled at Robinson, embarrassing his second baseman in plain view of the players and spectators. Robinson was told that his conduct was unbecoming a gentleman. Robinson replied that Von der Ahe was no gentleman, either—in so many words. The president left the scene and imposed a $25 fine on Robinson. The second baseman started in the 5–1 victory over the Louisville Colonels, but went hitless with an error afield.

Robinson quickly admitted that his temper toward Niehaus was a bit out of control. However, Von der Ahe's bench-clearing bawl really offended Yank, and he refused to play ball until Von der Ahe rescinded the fine.

Some time later, everyone on the St. Louis team met at the train depot. Chris Von der Ahe, son Eddie, Comiskey, and Charlie Duffee boarded for Kansas City. The rest of the team stayed behind in sympathy with Robinson. The platform was a wild scene filled with bad blood commentary from both sides. The Browns were striking. After several hours, secretary George Munson bravely persuaded the team to catch the Missouri Pacific to Kansas City. Considering that two separate trains were being used, the strike was costing Von der Ahe money. He later vowed that for the next trip to Kansas City, the Browns would pay their own fares. Except Yank Robinson. For the next few days, Yank marshaled his forces against Von der Ahe. Munson told Robinson that Von der Ahe was going to fine him $25 for every day missed. Von der Ahe also threatened Robinson with blacklisting and salary forfeiture if he did not join the team in four days.

The two St. Louis dailies, the *Post-Dispatch* and the *Globe-Democrat* had differing opinions on Von der Ahe's handling of the strike.

"If Mr. Von der Ahe gives in the players would do as they pleased hereafter," wrote the *Post-Dispatch.*

The Globe-Democrat thought otherwise. "Von der Ahe, by one absurd error, has turned the team topsy-turvy. If [he] intends to fine his men for every error. . . he will wind up about sixth."

The champion St. Louis performance for four games in Kansas City was so poor that the *Post-Dispatch* speculated the games were lost by design. Naturally, Von der Ahe and Comiskey rejected this notion, but the owner promised a full investigation after the club returned home. Umpire Gaffney said, "I want it distinctly understood that I would not have been a party to any burlesque or throwing of games on a ball field. The games could not have been thrown without my detecting it. Had I suspected, I would have left the field." For the series, the Browns lost three of four games. If the defeats to the lowly Cow Boys weren't shocking enough, the scores of the contests were. On Friday, the Browns arrived late, trailed 10–0 after two innings, committed 8 errors, and lost 16–3. Chamberlain and Hudson were the unfortunate pitchers. To replace Robinson at second base, Comiskey used both Tommy McCarthy and himself. The next day, behind Silver King, St. Louis lost 16–9, booting the ball all over Exposition Park for 13 errors. On Sunday, a throng of 10,000 enthusiasts jammed the park to witness the strangest game of the series. Trailing 11–7 into the ninth inning, Kansas City erupted for 11 runs off King to hand Comiskey and his mates a crushing 18–12 defeat. Somehow, St. Louis escaped Kansas City with the finale 11–9. Icebox Chamberlain pitched.

At series end, *Sporting Life* commented:

> *[The Browns] . . . to a man looked tired and worn out. . . . the three outfielders—Duffee, O'Neill and McCarthy—chased more hog hide while in Kansas City than they will during any other four games this season. O'Neill is still suffering with a split tongue, which was caused by its hanging out of his mouth while he was hunting leather on the alkali field. Duffee's feet were so sore that he can hardly walk. Every move that he made in the outfield his feet came in contact with a brick or a portion of a roof blown from a neighboring house. McCarthy's eyes are weak, because he was forced to stare at the setting sun four days in succession . . . [One fly ball] struck the ground and rolled into a coyote hole.*

In aftermath, George Munson was a very worried man. Arlie Latham denied rumors of a sellout. Charlie Comiskey was mum. But Chris Von der Ahe was happy over the gate receipt check he received from the Kansas City treasurer. Von der Ahe dropped the Robinson fine and re-instated his second baseman. Behind the scenes, Comiskey had intervened for Robinson. To add closure, Von der Ahe proclaimed, "I am still der boss of der club, and I intend to run it my own way."

The next day, in Baltimore, Robinson was back at his familiar position as the Browns won, 21–0, behind Silver King. Yank cracked four hits in his return. Somehow, the lopsided victory validated the hippodrome charge in Kansas City. Over the next several weeks, the Browns continued to deny reports they had deliberately lost games in Kansas City.

By the time Brooklyn met St. Louis in mid-May, the Browns were leading the Association with a 20–6 slate. Brooklyn lagged 4.5 games behind at 13–8. Louisville pitcher-first baseman Guy Hecker marveled at the Browns' fast start: ". . . Commy could take a nine of farmers and win the pennant." Over the course of the next three weeks, St. Louis played Brooklyn seven times. The first four were contested in Sportsman's Park. St. Louis defeated Brooklyn 9–7 in the opener behind Icebox Chamberlain. The next day, Browns' slugger Tip O'Neill was injured by a foul tip on his head. He missed two games. Dodger catcher Doc Bushong would also be hurt in the series, splitting a finger. Nonetheless, St. Louis beat up on Brooklyn hurler Tom Lovett, 11–2, to stretch their lead to 6.5 games. With Brooklyn badly in need of a victory, pitcher Adonis Terry delivered—barely. Brooklyn trailed into the ninth inning, tied the score, and won the game in eleven innings. The *New York Times,* obviously partial, called it "one of the greatest games ever played in St. Louis."

For the Sunday finale, 14,000 crammed into Sportsman's Park, the biggest St. Louis crowd in six years. Brooklyn's Bobby Caruthers received a nice ovation and then proceeded to squeeze by his former teammates and Silver King, 2–1. Though umpire Bob Ferguson's work was called into question by Comiskey, the game appeared to have been fairly played. *Sporting Life*'s Francis Richter wrote of Comiskey and the umpires, "No man knows how to work them better, either by palaver or browbeating and no club gets more close decisions . . . than the Browns." Said Comiskey, "I do not protest an umpire's decision [to reverse it] . . . but simply for the effect it will have on him in succeeding games." As the Browns and Bridegrooms battled in St. Louis, Brooklyn's Washington Park grandstand was consumed by flames. Though Byrne's losses amounted to $18,000, he promised a new grandstand in time for the Browns' Memorial Day doubleheader.

Both Byrne and Von der Ahe were sanguine for the three-game series in Brooklyn. Byrne kept his promise, refitting Washington Park and attiring his men in spanking new uniforms. Byrne could afford financial losses, but not the ones on the field. The teams split a wild Friday doubleheader. The first game, played in the morning, was witnessed by 8,000. The Browns won 8–4. In the afternoon, it seemed as if the entire borough of Brooklyn dodged trolley cars, rode horses, or walked to Washington Park. A record 22,000, including "throng ten deep" in the outfield, cheered their Flatbush heroes to a 9–7 win. Again, Bobby Caruthers bested his old mates. The crowds were especially boisterous since umpire Goldsmith spent most of the day fining players.

No less than ten $5 fines were administered. Although Chris Von der Ahe wasn't too excited about the loss, he was ecstatic over the take. One newspaper reported that he cleared $2,000 for the day. On Saturday, heavy rains pelted Brooklyn, postponing that game until mid-June.

On Sunday, the two clubs rode omnibuses to nearby Ridgewood. In front of 11,000 enthusiasts, Silver King tossed a one-hitter to edge Bobby Caruthers 2–1. A reporter for *Sporting Life* wrote that the game was worth walking twenty miles to see. Unlike the Philadelphia forfeit, this Ridgewood gathering was without incident. Even animals were catching pennant fever; Arlie Latham was forced to carry a stray goat from the field. However, despite winning the series, Charles Comiskey fretted over sore-armed pitchers Chamberlain, King, and Nat Hudson. The Browns still led Brooklyn by five games.

Meanwhile, in Louisville, the Colonels and their owner Mordecai Davidson were at odds. Disgusted over their pathetic 8–40 won-lost record, Davidson began to fine his men. The fines covered errors, stupid base running, not sliding, abusive language, drinking, and other problems. He even withheld the Louisville meal money. On June 14, his club refused to take the field unless the fines were rescinded. Davidson said that each man would lose an additional $100 for not participating and a $25 penalty if they lost the game. Player-manager Chicken Wolf pleaded in vain with Davidson for a solution to the stalemate. In all, six players struck on June 14 and 15.

Without compunction, Davidson called a meeting to hand out the monthly Louisville pay checks. At the gathering, he told his men that because of the fines, their salaries had already been garnished. Seventeen hundred dollars had been subtracted from the players' salaries. Some players actually owed the Louisville treasury!

According to *The Sporting News,* the Louisville players wired St. Louis owner Chris Von der Ahe with their desperate grievances. In sympathy, Von der Ahe helped pay off the Louisville salaries.

Von der Ahe's reputation for helping players was well known. Quite often, when players were down on their luck, Von der Ahe loaned them money. When American Association teams were suffering financially, Von der Ahe willingly offered his cash. Chris reasoned that the strength of the Association depended on financial stability, but he was funneling money to Louisville players. Von der Ahe's own players seethed. Eventually, a settlement was worked out by Association President Wyckoff and other magnates. Davidson sold his club at the beginning of July.

Four days after the Louisville debacle, St. Louis' Silver King bested Brooklyn's Adonis Terry 5–4 in a makeup game.

Heavy rains followed the Browns on their June road trip in the east. En route to Baltimore, the St. Louis train was delayed in Harper's Ferry, West Virginia. By the time St. Louis reached their destination, umpire Gaffney had forfeited the game to the Orioles. Comiskey argued that the Browns had spent an extra day in Columbus due to heavy rain. The Baltimore and Ohio Railroad had given assurances, but no one had counted on the monsoon in West Virginia. The Browns arrived in Baltimore's Union Station at 4:45 p.m. They commenced a brisk warmup while Comiskey argued with Gaffney, and then defeated the Orioles in a fast game, 5–1. Virtually no one watched. Most ball cranks were at home eating supper.

In Philadelphia, 10,000 cranks showed up at Athletics Park, but Mother Nature wouldn't cooperate. As the fans settled into their seats, a frightening storm whipped up, prompting a virtual stampede. Some fans rushed onto the swampy field. Others tramped to the ticket counter for rain checks. Unfortunately, the Philadelphia management apparently was too busy counting the take. St. Louis secretary George Munson explained, "When the people were in line after the game had been called, I tried to get Mr. Whitaker to get his rain checks out at once but he was in no hurry, and I hammered at him for half an hour before he finally gave them to his gate men."

Von der Ahe wasn't too pleased, either. "In St. Louis we give out rain checks when the people come in the gate, and I believe they follow the same plan in Brooklyn . . . and at the next meeting of the Association I shall endeavor to have some legislation enacted which will compel all the clubs to follow our plan."

Near the end of June, the lowly Colonels snapped a 26-game losing streak at the expense of St. Louis. An embarrassed Charles Comiskey, who was again complaining about the umpiring, committed four errors in the game. The Cincinnati Reds then defeated St. Louis in two of three games. During this time, a strapping, 21-year-old league right-hander named Jack Stivetts was signed to bolster the St. Louis pitching staff. Right-hander Nat Hudson, who had appeared in only a handful of games, was suspended for "insubordination." Hudson had refused to practice at Sportsman's Park.

As June closed, Brooklyn still trailed St. Louis by 4.5 games.

Von der Ahe and the Association had other worries. *Sporting Life* editorialized that the Browns should be ashamed of their home attendance. St. Louis drew only 2,000 for a home contest with Cincinnati. To deflect criticism, Von der Ahe again threatened to pack up and jump to the National League. After the Browns exacted revenge by sweeping Louisville to small home crowds, a local ball crank explained that cranks were still fuming over Von der Ahe's fire sale following the 1887 season. The temporary 50-cent admission also alienated patrons who did not appreciate the rotting grandstand, the clouds of tobacco smoke, or the stench of beer.

Von der Ahe responded by comically saying that many improvements had been made at his ball yard. Seat cushions were free. The Browns' magnate erroneously claimed that he'd not realized much money from his baseball business, only "some."

Another *Sporting Life* writer accounted for the drop-off by writing that many would-be fans simply checked the "1,001 saloons and pool rooms" rather than attend in person. *Sporting Life* also wrote that baseball gambling should be abolished. Betting on one's own team, a common practice, was condemned but not illegal. Although he gambled on baseball and horses, Von der Ahe often voiced his opposition to baseball pool rooms. Chris didn't seem to be against gambling per se, as it generated interest in baseball. However, he was concerned that baseball gambling in St. Louis' numerous watering holes and pool rooms cut into his business.

That summer, the city of St. Louis was alive with entertainment and relaxing activities. Trotters and thoroughbreds raced at Forest Park. There was opera and open-air concerts in the park. Swimming contests were in vogue. An historical recreation called "The Fall of Paris" was staged. The five-club St. Louis Baseball League contested games at Kensington Park and the St. Louis Amateur Grounds. Left-hander Ted Breitenstein pitched his Home Comforts to the championship over the Sultan Bitters. Though the league lasted only one season, President Joe Flood was fond of boasting that 20,000 rabid cranks once attended a game. Admission for the semipros was only fifteen cents. All of these events kept Von der Ahe's profits down.

Nonetheless, Von der Ahe realized big money on his club away from home. One lady from an eastern city gave her reasons for attending. "The Browns are all good looking but that man O'Neill is the handsomest man on the team, and he is shaped like a Samson." *The Sporting News* offered its own analysis. "Wherever Captain Comiskey and his merry men go, sunshine and boodle follow."

Further evidence of St. Louis' popularity concerns the story of an intelligent 16-year-old Browns fan. In early July 1889, two letters passed between Von der Ahe and Louis Pausch. Pausch was a baseball crank and supporter of the St. Louis Browns. In his letter Pausch declared himself a mascot and sent along a tintype portrait of himself in a Browns uniform. He certainly knew how to stroke Von der Ahe's ego. He complimented the president on his handling of the club. However, the importance of the letter was to underscore Louis' capture of a black cat that he saw in Cincinnati wearing an ominous ribbon. On the ribbon was written the following: "Hoodoo of the St. Louis B. B. C." The lad also warned, "do not let any black moving object cross your home plate and you will be successful." In brief response, Chris thanked the lad. The boy sent off a quick reply saying that he hoped to see Von der Ahe in Cincinnati because of "several important things to tell you." A grateful Von der Ahe responded by allowing Pausch to "continue as Browns mascot."

Rumors began to circulate that Brooklyn and Cincinnati would join the National League. The civic leaders in both cities didn't want ballplaying on the Sabbath. Cincinnati's President A. S. Stern griped about 25-cent weekday ball. Byrne believed that bigger crowds awaited the Dodgers in the National League.

Brooklyn invaded St. Louis for a three-game series to celebrate America's Independence. On July 3, Brooklyn's Caruthers whipped Silver King, 7–4. St. Louis cranks greeted umpire Gaffney with a host of hisses and catcalls, especially over his handling of balls and strikes. On the holiday, the clubs squared off for a morning-afternoon doubleheader. The Browns won the morning tilt as Chamberlain beat Terry, 4–3. Brooklyn catcher Joe Visner, starting for the injured Doc Bushong, had a miserable day. Visner was unable to throw out the speedy St. Louis base runners. In the nightcap, Brooklyn won, 12–10. Lovett started for the visitors, but Caruthers nailed down the win. Arlie Latham made three ridiculous errors. Both Von der Ahe and Byrne remained puzzled over the relatively small crowds in St. Louis. Brooklyn management realized only $600 for the July 4 doubleheader. Though St. Louis destroyed Columbus and Baltimore in succeeding games by 14–0 and 25–5, something wasn't quite right.

By mid-July, Comiskey began to suspect strange doings on his ballclub. After Comiskey alerted Von der Ahe, Chris hired a detective to investigate. The *New York Times* reported ". . . letters [were] said to have been received from Omaha and Kansas City with regard to peculiar bets offered against the Browns on days when King [pitched] and when Latham was doing some of the bad playing which he has exhibited on a number of recent occasions." Yank Robinson was also caught in the web of suspicion. Comiskey and Von der Ahe suspected Latham, King, and Robinson of crooked playing. Arlie Latham's case received the most attention. Latham explained to Comiskey that he had hurt his arm. All three denied charges of dishonesty.

Latham jokingly explained what he believed to be the genesis of the charges: "The other day a young fellow whom I did not know left Chris Von der Ahe's side and walked up to me with the question 'How's this report Arlie, about your selling games.' Supposing him to be one of the full-blooded cranks you meet in every ball town, I laughingly replied, 'Well, ole man, they say so, I guess it's so!' and then walked on. If I had any idea he was a reporter, I'd kick the pants off him."

Over the next six weeks, battle lines were drawn in the Latham case. Charges against pitcher Silver King and second baseman Yank Robinson faded. Walter Arlington Latham was becoming a scapegoat for all the sins of the St. Louis Browns.

Francis Richter, the editor of *Sporting Life,* sided with Latham, but added that Von der Ahe was within his rights to investigate. Richter urged both Latham and King to sue the *Post-Dispatch* for libel. The Philadelphia weekly believed in the honesty of the players. Throwing ball games, especially under these circumstances, was far too risky.

Brooklyn's Charles Byrne, making money from gambling interests and baseball, was careful to side with the players. Byrne didn't want more attention drawn to first baseman Dave Foutz and ace pitcher Bobby Caruthers, who regularly wagered on their own team. Without any hard evidence from his detective, Von der Ahe allowed Latham to play. Comiskey daily penciled in the loudmouth third baseman on the lineup card. Latham's teammates grew more wary of Arlie with each passing day.

While the Browns were dealing with the Latham controversy, Brooklyn was trying to deal with the weather. In Cincinnati on July 14, the Trolley Dodgers and Reds were caught up in heavy rains and cyclonic winds. A 150-foot section of fence was lifted off the grounds and hurled into nearby horses, causing a frightening stampede onto the field. Part of the grandstand roof collapsed. Though no spectators or players were harmed, many were scared silly.

While the Browns were enjoying a full five-game lead on July 17, a telegram was sent by the new Louisville owner to Von der Ahe. The communication revealed an offer to trade Louisville's Toad Ramsey for the Browns' suspended Nat Hudson. Despite Ramsey's horrendous 1–16 record and his reputation for drinking, Von der Ahe agreed to the deal, ecstatic to part with the disgruntled Hudson. Hudson had also been suspended for a month in the spring for complaining of a sore arm in chilly conditions. Both teams were tired of their respective men.

The Sporting News wrote that Ramsey would improve with Comiskey's handling. Shortly after arriving in St. Louis, Von der Ahe lectured Ramsey on intemperance. Chris explained that a continuance would lead to Ramsey's blacklisting. If Ramsey could lay off the booze, he'd reap the benefits of St. Louis pitching glory. Sheepishly, Ramsey admitted that he had fallen into the wrong crowd at Louisville. A bit leery over the trade, Comiskey introduced Toad to the bench.

Brooklyn's cyclonic experience in Cincinnati apparently galvanized the Dodgers. When they returned home, they were greeted by their rabid fans and more rainy weather. Displaying a newfound vigor, Brooklyn won nine of their next eleven on friendly grounds. Several games were contested in the rain. Byrne had insisted the games be played, rain or shine. The Browns, meanwhile, were reeling from the Latham revelations and the Ramsey-Hudson trade. Barely winning half their games in the east, the St. Louis lead shrunk to a mere two games.

August 1 typified St. Louis' frustration and Brooklyn's determination. In wet Philadelphia, a crabby Comiskey insisted his men stay off the field due to hazardous conditions. The Athletics claimed forfeiture. With no game being played, Comiskey proceeded to blast the umpires and Byrne in the press. He raged that the umpires hated the Browns and that Byrne was controlling their salaries. In the preseason, American Association President Wheeler Wyckoff met with his umpires in Byrne's office to explain new playing rules. As a member of the Association's committee to revise their constitution, Byrne had judiciously studied the rules governing the game. Growing tired of Comiskey's whining, some newspapers censured the St. Louis captain for roughhouse play and using profanities in front of the ladies.

In Brooklyn, the Dodgers took a doubleheader from the pathetic Louisvilles. Both games were contested in steady rain. Sawdust covered huge mud puddles on the field. Dave Foutz won the opener 8–6 after his teammates rallied in the late innings. With ten Louisville errors in the second game, Tom Lovett won, 14–1. Brooklyn captain Darby O'Brien convulsed the hometown patrons by playing in the mud. Byrne had said he didn't want to disappoint the Brooklyn cranks by not playing. Louisville was no match for his steady Dodgers.

Von der Ahe and his player relations were further exacerbated by the case involving Harry Lyons. At the end of the 1888 season, Lyons' share of the pennant money was refused by Von der Ahe. The outfielder, who'd been injured and missed half of the 1888 World Series, sued for $71.40. In a Philadelphia courtroom in early August 1889, Von der Ahe testified that Lyons didn't earn his money. The Browns' magnate did have a point, judging by the type of season Lyons had. However, several of Lyons' ex-teammates spoke in court. The judge decided for Lyons. Von der Ahe was indignant and appealed.

Ted Sullivan had been summoned by Von der Ahe from Washington to briefly manage the affairs of the Browns in Brooklyn. Sullivan's appearance prompted a host of rumors. Von der Ahe dismissed stories that his Browns were moving to Washington or Chicago or Philadelphia. A tale that Charles Comiskey was leaving for Cincinnati for $10,000 or Brooklyn for $12,000 wasn't worth the paper it was printed on.

Over the next eleven days (August 2–12), the Browns battled Brooklyn in two weekend series. Before large, boisterous throngs in Brooklyn, Byrne's men bested Von der Ahe's fading St. Louis boys. Byrne had promised his men special victory cigars for beating the Browns. The grounds were still wet on August 2 when St. Louis' Icebox Chamberlain defeated Caruthers 6–2. The next day, however, Brooklyn evened the series with a 13–6 triumph. Neither Toad Ramsey nor Jack Stivetts were effective. For the Sunday finale, the clubs traveled to Ridgewood. Before 17,000 rowdy cranks who stayed behind the barbed-wire fence, Brooklyn won again, 7–2. Dodger workhorse Bobby Caruthers took extra pleasure in beating Silver King, who'd put a pretzel in his pocket for good luck. The pretzel was not nearly as salty as Comiskey, who again complained about his sore-armed hurlers.

Despite the recent setbacks, Comiskey was confident for the showdown in St. Louis. The Browns lead was a precarious half game. On Saturday, August 10, the Browns squeezed 4–2 in ten innings. Their outfield play was brilliant, with Charlie Duffee, Tip O'Neill, and Tommy McCarthy making sterling catches. Bob Caruthers took the loss.

Arlie Latham didn't play on Sunday. He was suspended for the balance of the season for "recent poor work." Von der Ahe's investigation of Latham revealed "facts which for the good of the game must be kept quiet." Latham's Brooklyn efforts were also called into question. Charlie Comiskey had demanded suspension, claiming that Latham had been responsible for 16 of the Browns' 31 losses. Eleven of those losses had come in the previous five weeks. There might have been another revolt on the ball club had Latham not been reprimanded. Comiskey insisted that Von der Ahe would need a new manager and first baseman if Latham was allowed to continue. After a closed-door session at Von der Ahe's residence, attended by Von der Ahe, Comiskey, Latham, and Munson, *The Sporting News* reported the sketchy details. Latham admitted that he'd been in the company of a known gambler named Lynch. However, Latham denied ever betting against his team. Latham also admitted to his poor play. According to Arlie, he would be careful about his associations and would no longer consort with Lynch. Von der Ahe told Latham the suspension was Comiskey's doing and only the Browns manager could reinstate Latham. Comiskey's own position was tenuous, considering that he was wagering heavily on his own club.

Before the largest home crowd of the season, 15,000, the Browns pummeled the Bridegrooms 14–4. Pete Sweeney, a third baseman recently acquired from the hapless Washington Senators, took Latham's place. Comiskey acted typically by not allowing injured Brooklyn catcher Bob Clark to leave the game. Comiskey's belligerence usurped the diagnosis of three physicians who examined Clark at the scene. During the medical time-out, hundreds of St. Louis cranks swarmed the field.

On Monday, August 12, Icebox Chamberlain embarrassed Bob Caruthers and the visitors 12–0. The defeat was devastating to Brooklyn manager McGunnigle, who stayed on the bench and wept. Von der Ahe wasn't crying, being too busy patting everyone on the back and buying them beers and cigars. Byrne resigned himself to the St. Louis sweep and agreed with Henry Chadwick that the Brooklyn batting must improve.

Incredibly, the Latham case would not die. Quite bitter over his suspension, Latham traveled to Louisville to meet with Byrne. A telegram by Byrne to Von der Ahe stated, "What is the lowest price you will take for Latham's release?" Von der Ahe suspected Byrne of plotting with Louisville directors to finance the sale of Latham to the Colonels. The Browns' owner knew that the struggling Louisville treasury had been depleted. To end all speculation, Von der Ahe responded that his suspended third baseman would not be released for $100,000. On Comiskey's suggestion, Von der Ahe met twice in early September with the Athletics over the proposed trade of Latham and center fielder Duffee for outfielder Curt Welch and slugger Denny Lyons. The meetings lasted for hours, but no trade was made. Von der Ahe also tried to buy pitcher Sadie McMahon of Baltimore, but the asking price was too high.

The course of the pennant chase changed dramatically over the next three weeks. St. Louis began to pitch badly and lose. Both King and Chamberlain complained about being overworked. Silver King lost twice in Baltimore. Observers were tempted to ask the whereabouts of Jack Stivetts and Toad Ramsey. Arlie Latham was reinstated by a desperate Comiskey after the former agreed to behave himself. The move was doubly curious since Latham's replacement, Pete Sweeney, was knocking the cover off the ball. Latham returned just in time to watch a hard shot go by him for a double. Arlie made no effort to catch it, thinking the ball would roll foul. The play drew the ire of Comiskey, and Latham's teammates continued to distrust the third baseman. Captain Comiskey was the butt of jokes in the newspapers during the losing streak.

The Brooklyns, meanwhile, were winning, infuriating Comiskey, Von der Ahe, and the Browns. On August 25, the Reds and Dodgers played a Sunday game in Hamilton, Ohio. Cincinnati President Stern was forced to move the game due to the recent decision of the Cincinnati Superintendent of Police to suspend Sunday baseball. The Cincinnati mayor backed the plan. However, in the fourth inning, with an impromptu crowd of 1,500, Hamilton police swooped into the park, arrested the players, and fined them $159.30. An angry Stern paid the fines and thought more seriously about moving to the National League.

If ball cranks thought nothing could match the repugnance of the Browns' play at Kansas City in May, they were sadly mistaken. New dispatches surfaced, accusing Byrne of unsportsmanlike influence on Association teams, umpires, and players. The Cow Boys of Kansas City lost six straight games to Brooklyn. That wasn't unusual. It was the way the Cow Boys appeared to roll over and die; their pitchers looked easy and their fielders booted error after error. The games in Brooklyn appeared to be anything but fair. When no American Association umpires showed up for the contests, injured Brooklyn catcher Doc Bushong was called to officiate. No objection was raised by Kansas City manager Bill Watkins. The American Association Constitution stated that three substitute arbiters' names were to be furnished to President Wyckoff by each team before the beginning of the season. Byrne's three substitutes were "in a neighboring graveyard and were dead to the world." Both *The Sporting News* and *Sporting Times* of New York agreed that Byrne was guilty of foul play. To add to the suspicion, Bushong reportedly offered a job to Browns' slugger Tip O'Neill, provided O'Neill "played for his release." In other words, if Tip deliberately played poorly, Byrne would secure him. Something was rotten in the state of New York, and it was Byrne's baseball team.

Naturally, Chris Von der Ahe formally protested to the Association's Board of Directors citing a collusion scheme against his Browns. Von der Ahe demanded a replay of the games or a rebuke of Byrne and his Brooklyns, with the contests counting as Brooklyn losses. Chris also protested the game played in Hamilton, Ohio. Byrne also transferred a Columbus game to Brooklyn without a majority of the Association clubs' approval. The Trolley Dodgers won that rescheduled game. Von der Ahe wasn't finished. Three other games were cited by the Browns' owner, all under the influence of Byrne's bribery. Umpire John Kerins related: "Captain O'Brien, of the Brooklyns, came to me and told me it would be worth $100 to me and the chance to umpire in the World's Series of games if Brooklyn got there." Von der Ahe was sure that he had his proof. As battle lines were drawn, a flurry of attacks were made on the principals. Charles Byrne, Kansas City manager Watkins, and Von der Ahe were all roasted. For the most part, newspapers sided with their native teams. *The Kansas City Times* accused Von der Ahe and Comiskey of whining and resurfaced rumors of the Browns throwing games at Kansas City in May. *The Sporting News* stuck by its Browns and wrote of the "Brooklyn Black Legs."

To add incentive to the pennant chase, two St. Louis businessmen, Otto

Steifel of Steifel Brewing and John Peckington of the Golden Lion Saloon, initiated a benefit fund. A total of $1,000 had been raised by early September toward a goal of $6,000. Three thousand dollars were for St. Louis if they could capture their fifth consecutive Association flag. Three thousand more dollars would be available if they won the world title.

Von der Ahe was busy making an order to a St. Louis printer for a special lithograph. The artwork would depict a hand with five fingers and an inscription "Five Time Winners." Chris made a late-season trip to the printer to see how his brainchild was coming along. With St. Louis falling behind in the race, Von der Ahe said to the printer, "We have not won that other finger yet, could you keep it off until we see if we can win it? And if we don't win, couldn't you make that hand with four fingers?"

The final six weeks of the 1889 pennant race between St. Louis and Brooklyn were nothing less than all-out war. Scribes wrote of the action in nearly Biblical proportions. City newspapers screamed sports headlines about their favorite teams. With the excitement came analysis about winners and losers and tensions by ballplayers and fans alike.

In early September, Brooklyn took the lead as the Dodgers beat Cincinnati while the Browns were being swept by seventh-place Columbus. Pitcher Mark Baldwin fashioned two wins against Comiskey's boys. The losses were doubly embarrassing to Comiskey, since he had predicted a perfect record against the first-year team. It didn't help when Comiskey was picked off first base by 20-year-old catcher Jack O'Connor. Making the out call was Browns' umpire nemesis Bob Ferguson. In disbelief, Comiskey straddled the white chalk baseline and walked "pigeon-toed" to home plate to greet Ferguson. "Why, you poor, blind chucklehead, alleged umpire . . . your purpose seems to be to rob the St. Louis team. . . . You are in a combination to assist Brooklyn to take the pennant, and you can't deny it."

Ferguson threatened Comiskey with a $100 fine and forfeit if he didn't repair himself immediately to the bench. Commy did walk, but Dave Orr trotted around the bases after his tenth-inning blast defeated the Browns.

Baseball sportsmanship reached a nadir in Brooklyn on Saturday, September 7. The St. Louis Browns traveled to Washington Park for a series with the Association-leading Brooklyn Trolley Dodgers. St. Louis trailed by two and one-half games. Brooklyn manager McGunnigle gave the ball to ace Bobby Caruthers, and Comiskey went with Icebox Chamberlain. The 15,000 in attendance that day, many of whom were behind a rope boundary in the outfield, would never forget it.

The Brooklyn *Eagle* described the crowd:

> *The bleacherites were black with people and . . . jammed together in one immovable mass, and the only time they could gather themselves together was when the excitement got the best of them and everybody was forced to throw up their hands and were compelled to sway about like a wave on the ocean from the irresistible and frenzied throng. The banks back of the field-*

ers were littered with a multitude, and even on the high fence venturesome enthusiasts perched themselves on a precarious and dangerous footing. The rays of the sun, when not obscured by the threatening clouds, poured down on the sweltering mass with terrible intensity, and the crowd shed their coats and vests, but the perspiration still poured from them like small rivers. The excitement as the game progressed, made it worse for them, for they shouted, yelled, stamped and acted in a general way like mad men until they were utterly exhausted.

Comiskey's boys entered the grounds to catcalls and hisses. Brooklyn's beloved Dodgers were greeted with resounding applause. At 4:00 P.M., umpire Goldsmith called the game to begin.

The Bridegrooms jumped out in front with two first-inning runs against the nervous Chamberlain. Icebox surrendered two doubles into the standing-room-only crowd. The Browns committed two errors. St. Louis hardly had a monopoly on errors, however. One vendor, hawking beer from a tray filled with glasses, dropped his inventory as Brooklyn scored. Disgusted with Brooklyn's early advantage, Von der Ahe exited his private box and stormed to the St. Louis bench armed with his field glasses. As the Browns' owner spewed forth invectives at his men, Comiskey unloaded on umpire Goldsmith. *Sporting Life* referred to the scared umpire as a "shuttlecock in a cyclone." The cyclone was Charlie Comiskey's mouth. Not to be outdone, the partisan Brooklyn crowd jeered and hurled beer bottles, glasses, and epithets at the St. Louis men. With every pitch, the air seemed filled with shouts of bravado and pent-up masculine emotions. In the St. Louis half, Latham, who had been spiked at third base, reached first and was tossed out trying to steal. The partisan crowd jeered Arlie mercilessly. As McCarthy batted, he was serenaded with a chorus of boos. To counter, McCarthy doffed his cap in mock approval. The Browns did not score, and after four innings, Brooklyn still led 2–0.

In the fifth frame, Brooklyn realized the dimming of the sun's rays and began to stall. McGunnigle and his mates hoped the game would be called for darkness. However, Goldsmith held fast. Above the din of the throng, the Browns scored once in the fifth on Milligan's single and twice in the sixth inning on hits by Yank Robinson and Shorty Fuller. As the tying run crossed the plate for St. Louis, third-base coach Latham cartwheeled in the box and rolled in the grass. The crowd was both delighted and worried by this display. Now leading 3–2, Comiskey copied McGunnigle's tactic. The Browns' motivations seemed obvious to the thousands of witnesses. St. Louis took turns talking strategy with pitcher Chamberlain. Catcher Milligan went out to talk to his pitcher. Then, the entire St. Louis infield followed, one by one. Even O'Neill and McCarthy offered their views, jogging in from the outfield to converse with Chamberlain. To further slow the game, Comiskey screamed that the contest be called after every pitch. St. Louis also stalled at bat. Exhorted by the Brooklyn cranks, Goldsmith began to fine each of the Browns, including instigator Comiskey. Much to the chagrin of Goldsmith and everyone else, St. Louis promptly paid off all fines, nullifying their effect. Incredibly, the Browns tried fire and water to convince Goldsmith to end the game. Von der Ahe, yelling from his box, could not tolerate the situation any longer. He sent a small boy out of the park on an errand. The lad returned with several candles. Chris then lit the candles in front of the Browns' bench. The spectators were hardly amused. They began to throw beer glasses in an attempt to douse to flames. Unfortunately, a stray piece of paper was blown into the candles, nearly setting the grandstand on fire. At the end of the eighth inning, with the score 4–2, St. Louis, McCarthy grabbed the ball and dropped it into a bucket of water. The soggy baseball would now be much harder to hit. Perhaps, reasoned McCarthy, if the ball could not be seen, batters could at least swing at the splash. McCarthy's ball-dousing greatly upset Comiskey.

Two innings earlier, umpire Goldsmith had admitted to Comiskey that it was too dark to play. However, as the Browns had the lead on hostile grounds, the umpire let the game continue. Goldsmith did not know that the Philadelphia at New York game had already been called some forty minutes earlier.

By the ninth inning, there wasn't enough light for Goldsmith to see that Brooklyn catcher Bob Clark had struck out swinging! Eventually, Chamberlain walked Clark to first. From his first base position, Comiskey hollered at Goldsmith to call the game. Goldsmith could either not hear above the din or ignored Comiskey for fear of the mob. Browns' catcher Jocko Milligan could only stick out his glove on the next two pitches —and pray. The next batter couldn't locate the ball. The catcher couldn't catch it, and Goldsmith was shaking in his boots. Comiskey came toward home plate and again asked the arbiter to call the game on account of darkness. Brooklyn's frenzied crowd was witnessing pennant-race baseball—in the dark. After Clark was called safe at second base, proud Comiskey motioned his men off the field. It was 6:25 P.M.

The Browns had "outbatted, outfielded, and outran" the home team. Now the St. Louis club had to contend with the mob. The Brooklyn nasties pelted the enemy with bottles and fruit. McCarthy, Robinson, and Comiskey were all hit with projectiles. McCarthy received a nice gash on the mouth. Milligan's cheek was grabbed. Latham was hit with a bottle. Charlie Duffee said he'd rather hoe cotton for $10 a month than play at Washington Park. Even Von der Ahe narrowly escaped a beer glass thrown at him. Once inside the dressing room, the barrage continued. Stones came crashing through the windows. Several St. Louis players huddled into a corner for safety. The Brooklyn police finally arrived. Instead of protecting the visitors, the sergeant-at-arms and his boys heaped more abuse on the Browns. Comiskey would comment that it was a miracle that the Browns left Washington Park alive.

On the following afternoon, Sunday, September 8, a huge crowd gathered at Ridgewood Park. As the masses entered the yard, cranks were jabbering about Saturday's game in the dark and the riot that ensued. Among the spectators was Henry Chadwick, official scorekeeper. The gathering was unaware of wire dispatches flying around the American Association. Outraged at the treatment of his players, Von der Ahe sent a terse telegram to Charles Byrne: "I refuse to allow my club to play any more games in Brooklyn."Byrne wired Association President Wyckoff to protest. The Trolley Dodgers arrived for warmups. The Browns stayed fast in their hotel. Scribes at the *New York Sun* joked in a hypothetical conversation between a ball fan and Byrne. Said the fan, speaking about the St. Louis club, "Here they come!" An anxious Byrne asked, "Where are they?" "In that balloon," was the reply.

Wyckoff's reaction was to notify Von der Ahe and the other clubs that the Browns were fined $1,500 for leaving the field in Brooklyn on Saturday and $1,500 for not showing up in Ridgewood on Sunday. In effect, these were both forfeited games. Quipped *The Sporting News,* "Von der Ahe will, of course, pay these fines, when the pigs begin to fly." When the angry Byrne called on the fuming Von der Ahe to reconsider, the Browns' president requested that the Saturday game be replayed. Byrne refused, citing the American Association constitution: ". . . I shall never rest until the American Association metes out to this man the punishment provided by the constitution for his insolent defiance of its provisions. . . . The Association must either expel the St. Louis club or go out of business. . . . I mean to push this matter to the end, because the integrity of our national game demands it."

Wheeler Wyckoff, caught in the middle of the controversy, ordered an emergency American Association meeting for September 14 in Philadelphia.

Von der Ahe stated his position:

> *If, with their police protection arrangements at Washington Park on Saturday, they could not protect us, how would they do it at Ridgewood without police? I was stoned at Ridgewood last year, and I don't want any more of it. My players add that they would not go to Ridgewood for $5,000 each . . . The crowd assaulted McCarthy, Robinson and Comiskey on Saturday, and things looked dangerous for me at one time. If I had a pistol I might have been tempted to use it. Goldsmith acknowledged to our men that he knew it was too dark to play that game on Saturday. I cannot blame [Goldsmith]..The umpire was ready to call the game in the sixth inning, when the Brooklyns were ahead, but as soon as the Browns took the lead that ended all desire to stop the game . . . Why, when Goldsmith took out his bog watch after my men had left the field, the electric lights on Third Street had been lighted ..I am unable to stand it any longer, and would much rather go out of the business.*

The sporting press had a field day. There was speculation that Von der Ahe would sell his players and his team over the incident. In poor taste, *The Sporting News* published the Browns' salaries and selling prices, totaling $43,000. Von der Ahe was reported to have said he wouldn't part with his club for $200,000. The St. Louis weekly openly accused Byrne of manipulation and called the Dodgers "The Kilrains of the Baseball World." The *New York Clipper* also sided with St. Louis, condemning Brooklyn's overzealous fans and recommending that the Goldsmith forfeits be overturned. Veteran scribe Henry Chadwick took a different tact, calling Comiskey "dirty" and "overrated." Chadwick wrote that Byrne's charge of expulsion against St. Louis should be considered. *Sporting Life*'s Francis Richter couldn't understand Comiskey's decision to exit the diamond with a lead. Richter thought expelling St. Louis from the Association would be nonsense.

Far from resolving their differences, Von der Ahe and Byrne agreed to play the remainder of the series on Tuesday and Wednesday, September 11–12. Byrne promised police protection. The respective presidents were convinced that the upcoming American Association meeting would solve the stalemate. Both were confident of victory on the field and in the boardroom.

On Tuesday, the St. Louis team arrived at Washington Park in miserable weather. Seeing the steady rain and soggy grounds, Comiskey and McGunnigle agreed not to play. The next day was more of the same. Downpours washed out the intense competition between Brooklyn and St. Louis. Both contests were postponed to a later date. While the rain washed away the games, it did nothing to dampen the hard feelings.

Byrne stated that the reason he could not provide police protection was that Ridgewood was outside Brooklyn's corporate city limits.

Comiskey said, "Byrne is a shoe string gambler, a con man and ought to be thrown out of baseball." The rest of the Browns agreed. The Browns' captain also related this character study of Byrne.

> *While in New York at the Polo Grounds I saw Byrne surrounded by local reporters . . . loud enough for anyone to hear I heard him say: "This man Comiskey so bulldozed the umpires in the recent Brooklyn-St. Louis games at St. Louis that they gave our players all the worst of it. This so disheartened my men that they lost the three games in succession. And now what do you think? Why he has the audacity to come here and attempt to repeat the same tactic on our grounds." Before he got any further he spied me and closed his trap.*

Comiskey also criticized Association umpires Ferguson and Goldsmith. He called Wyckoff incompetent and "a tool of Byrne."

A few days after the controversy, Von der Ahe still had not paid the Wyckoff-imposed fines. To compensate, Wyckoff instructed all Association clubs to withhold money from the Browns until $3,000 was reached. The Philadelphia team disregarded Wyckoff's instructions. The *Philadelphia Press* heaped praise on Von der Ahe. "[His] true and manly characteristics showed last Sunday when the Browns refused to play the Brooklyn Club at Ridgewood, a borough entirely without police protection. He could have played his team, secured his share of the gate receipts, which would surely have amounted to all of $5,000, and come away from the grounds unharmed, but he sacrificed his own personal interest for the welfare of his men." Wyckoff's latest salvo puzzled Von der Ahe, since the Browns' president had paid Wyckoff's expenses to attend all St. Louis' World Series games.

While the parties marshaled their forces for the special Association meeting, the affair was rescheduled for September 23. This time, the meeting would be held in Cincinnati. The extra week of preparation gave the combatants and commentators plenty of time to air their dirty laundry.

On the diamonds, wet conditions played havoc with the pennant contenders. Heavy rains pelted the East Coast. In Philadelphia, the Browns and Athletics were inundated with downshowers for four straight days. Von der Ahe and Comiskey were none too pleased that their charges lost twice in three tries. Tip O'Neill departed the club for a few days due to a death in the family. Von der Ahe was trying to get three of the washed-out games rescheduled after the end of the season. The Bridegrooms, meanwhile, slogged their way to back-to-back doubleheader wins over the Louisville Colonels at Washington Park. When the Browns returned home, they were seven games in arrears. It would only get worse.

On September 21, St. Louis endured a 17–6 shellacking by the Reds at Sportsman's Park. The next day, O'Neill's replacement, Tom Gettinger, committed a costly ninth-inning error to lose another game for Silver King. Jack Stivetts finally secured a Browns' victory, but the Reds left town with two wins over the fading champions.

Finally, the day to settle the dispute arrived. Brooklyn was represented by Joe Doyle, Ferdinand Abell, and Byrne. Batting for the Browns were Von der Ahe, Comiskey, and John J. O'Neill, who so eloquently spoke for Chris at the 1887 Sunday games trial. The rest of the Association's clubs were also represented.

By a twist of fate, Von der Ahe, Byrne, and Abell met in the lobby of the hotel for check-in. The two presidents ignored each other. Abell, however, approached Von der Ahe with an old-fashioned, back-slapping, "How are you, Chris? I am glad to see you old fellow." Von der Ahe simply nodded. If this was a ploy by Byrne to unnerve Chris, it failed miserably.

Several hours of testimony followed. Comiskey spoke of catcher Milligan's bruises for lack of being able to see the ball. The Browns' captain was rebuked when he asked if he could comment on President Byrne. Wyckoff told Comiskey to stick to the facts. Byrne had Brooklyn newspapermen and police verify that it was not dark. O'Neill was allowed five minutes for his say. Of the decision, *The Sporting News* wrote, "Of all the dishes of crow ever served up to mortal man, that crammed down Byrne's throat yesterday by the American Association was the worst. Byrne and his partners Doyle and Abel came here for the purpose of annihilating Von der Ahe. Instead, Von der Ahe annihilated them." By a vote of 6–2, the board determined that Brooklyn's forfeit was unfair in the September 7 game. The game officially reverted to the end of the eighth inning, with the Browns a 3–2 winner. Umpire Goldsmith was censured and dismissed. The reversal was a clear victory for Von der Ahe. Comiskey was justified for leaving the field, under the circumstances. Browns' and Dodgers' players were reprimanded for their poor conduct. The Ridgewood forfeit was upheld. Von der Ahe was ordered to pay a $1,500 fine to Brooklyn for refusing to show at the Sunday game. All other charges and accusations were dropped. The nattily dressed Von der Ahe was delighted with the Association's actions. Byrne, who was totally confident of double victory, was stunned and angry over the first game result. Though Byrne wanted sympathy, the behavior of his own rowdy fans hurt his cause.

It may have been politically calculated, but the split decision rendered by the board of directors caused a chasm of disagreements between American Association owners. Cincinnati President A. S. Stern said that the Association lacked a head.

Despite Von der Ahe's moral victory, the Browns' season spiraled out of control. On September 25, with St. Louis trailing Brooklyn by four and one-half games, Von der Ahe called a meeting of the St. Louis board of directors. In a veritable rage, Von der Ahe fined a broke Arlie Latham $200 and suspended him indefinitely. He fined pitcher Silver King for poor pitching and contract violations. Both Latham and King "played not to win," according to the ranting Von der Ahe. Pitcher Icebox Chamberlain was suspended and had to fork over $100. Second baseman Yank Robinson was reprimanded for "trying to swallow a brewery" in Kansas City. Thirteen games remained.

Miraculously, the Browns won their next eleven in a row. The streak featured Comiskey's adept alternating of Stivetts and Ramsey at pitcher and Von der Ahe's daily dressing down of his manager and players on the bench. A week after his suspension, Chamberlain was reinstated, but Von der Ahe ordered Comiskey to replace Icebox with Toad Ramsey. In a final defiant act against Von der Ahe, Yank Robinson showed up late at the park on October 2, exactly five months after prompting St. Louis' early season revolt. Von der Ahe related to Robinson that his tardiness would mean a fine. Robinson balked to pay or play. Von der Ahe then upped the ante to $200 and threatened Robinson with blacklisting. Twice suspended Arlie Latham, working in a hotel billiard room, was also busy attending all St. Louis home games. Latham's presence at the park was a bit odd; onlookers said that he was rooting for the opposition. Arlie must have looked at his teammates with a mixture of marvel and regret.

To counter St. Louis' surprising run of prosperity, Brooklyn manager McGunnigle repeatedly gave the ball to pitching ace Bobby Caruthers. Responding to the pennant challenge, Caruthers won five times in the final two weeks. Four of his victories were shutouts in mosquito-infested Columbus, Baltimore, and twice against the hard-hitting Athletics. Caruthers' late-season heroics wrapped up Brooklyn's first American Association flag. The victory was especially satisfying to Byrne, who defeated the hated Browns with one of their old men. To celebrate, the Brooklyn owner passed out cigars.

Browns' followers had to contend with a winter of frustrations. Von der Ahe manfully admitted that his error of refusing to play ball at Ridgewood had cost St. Louis the flag. In addition, Von der Ahe estimated his monetary losses during the Brooklyn imbroglio at some $4,000, accounting for the Sunday forfeit, the rain outs, and the fine. Byrne didn't escape easy; Chris hinted that $10,000 in lost revenue would be a fair estimate for the Brooklyn organization.

When the season ended, the Browns fell short by two games. Von der Ahe's three makeup games with Philadelphia, which would have been played after the season had officially ended, required Association board approval. Byrne was fully prepared to contest any decision for Von der Ahe in the matter. President Wyckoff somehow averted the potential Philadelphia controversy. Board members envisioned only more chaos if the issue of the September Brooklyn-St. Louis rain outs were challenged. The embattled Association was thankful for the end of this most trying of seasons.

An investigation into the whole sordid affair never happened. Neither Byrne nor Von der Ahe requested one. Such a probe likely would have yielded more bitter recriminations. Questions involving Comiskey, Latham, Byrne, Von der Ahe, Bushong, and Watkins were never answered.

Many followers of the game saw the campaign as dishonorable manipulations of managers, players, fans, and umpires. Both Von der Ahe and Byrne were vilified in the sporting press. Despite the exaggerations of the principals, the truth remained elusive. It is likely that the Browns deliberately lost those May affairs in Kansas City to protect Yank Robinson. Brooklyn's Byrne, in his insane pursuit of the championship, probably committed despicable and unsportsmanlike acts.

Incredibly, into the winter, *The Sporting News* scooped out more fantastic stories. The paper wrote of games involving the Browns against Louisville and Cincinnati, in which bribes of suits, overcoats, and money were offered as extra incentive to defeat St. Louis. Another detective tale related to Columbus shortstop Lefty Marr, who suspiciously made four errors to help the Trolley Dodgers win a game. Money was said to be involved. Von der Ahe's comments: "We have lost but it was scheming and not ball playing which beat us. The Browns won every series including that with the Brooklyns . . . the club which got the pennant did not earn it. Byrne had Bushong remain at Cincinnati and watch the games there. Bushong did not leave until the games were all played. What do you think of that? What a howl Byrne would raise if I sent a man to watch the play of other clubs against his team."

The Sporting News again speculated that the season was so traumatic that Von der Ahe would sell out and leave the game.

While the Browns squared off against Kansas City for bragging rights for the State of Missouri, the Trolley Dodgers entertained the New York Giants in the World Series. Players on both clubs bet heavily, and Giants owner John Day complained about Brooklyn using crooked methods to win the series. New York won anyway, six games to three.

At season's end, Latham curiously telegraphed Von der Ahe with the last word: "Mister Von der Ahe, come home and blame it on me."

The rancor created by the 1889 pennant race fractured and polarized the American Association. Two camps formed. One was a "combine" comprised of St. Louis, Louisville, Columbus, and Philadelphia. The other camp featured the clubs of Brooklyn, Cincinnati, Kansas City, and Baltimore. At issue was the forfeiture of games made against the noncombine clubs. Feelings ran extremely high on both sides. Francis Richter reported that the decisions concerning the disputed Dodgers-Browns games in Brooklyn were vital to the future of the Association.

On November 11-12, 1889, Association magnates met in New York in an attempt to iron out their differences and replace departed president Wyckoff. Two men vied for the position: Zach Phelps and L. C. Krauthof. Phelps was the "combine" candidate, while Krauthof represented the interests of the noncombine group. After two days of heated discussions, a deadlock remained. More than forty ballots were cast, all a 4–4 tie for the candidates. With the Association in need of bold action, the Brooklyn Trolley Dodgers and the Cincinnati Reds provided just that. Aware that the National League was conducting their meeting in a nearby hotel, Brooklyn and Cincinnati exited the Association's fete, walked down the street, and applied for admission into the National League. Eager to crush their competition, the National League accepted the teams. A few days later, the Kansas City club jumped to the Western Association. The Baltimore club shed its Association ties and jumped to the Eastern League. Now the Association was left with only the four "combine" teams. These losses were especially damaging in light of recent seasons. After the 1886 season, the Pittsburgh club was lured into the rival National League. Pittsburgh's replacement was weak Cleveland. At the close of the 1887 campaign, the New York team withdrew to be replaced by Kansas City. Also that year, the National League St. Louis Maroons departed for Kansas City. In 1888, the Cleveland Association club bought out the collapsing Detroit National League team and then defected to the National League. Association magnates replaced Cleveland with Columbus. In all the franchise transactions, the National League fared better than the American Association.

On the verge of collapse, the Association somehow managed to scrape together four new teams, three based in New York. A entirely new Brooklyn outfit, composed of minor leaguers, was awarded a franchise, along with Rochester and Syracuse. The Brooklyns were financed in part by Von der Ahe as a foil for Byrne's new National League franchise. Two clubs in Brooklyn was a clear violation of the territorial provisions of the National Agreement. A club from Toledo, Ohio, was the Association's fourth entry. The Rochester, Syracuse, and Toledo entries were all admitted from the International Association. All four Association clubs seemed doomed from the start. Rochester, Syracuse, and Toledo had much smaller population bases than their predecessors, little baseball tradition and, most importantly, a lack of operating capital. Of the exiting clubs, Cincinnati and Baltimore were original Association members. The Trolley Dodgers entered in 1884. Kansas City had been in the Association in 1888–1889. Into the midst of this new baseball war entered a third party. The major leagues were in peril.

Despite the bitter pennant race and baseball's coming turmoil, Von der Ahe and Charlie Comiskey organized a 10,000-mile Western tour. This marathon travel extravaganza was comprised of an All-Star team of Browns (O'Neill, King, Boyle) and National League players (Pat Tebeau, Jimmy Ryan, and Mark Baldwin). Jack Crooks admitted that he was touring to learn Comiskey's methods of handling men. Crooks wasn't alone as an apprentice. Von der Ahe's 19-year-old son, Eddie, toured as financial manager with George Munson as his mentor. Not surprisingly, several of Von der Ahe's men were involved in contract disputes and were prepared to leave the team. Other players quit in mid-tour. Arlie Latham departed at Tacoma to join an opera company. Icebox Chamberlain lasted one week. Silver King departed at New Orleans. Darby O'Brien left at Portland. A promising pitcher named Mark Baldwin pitched for the barnstormers. Despite inclement weather, this Browns hybrid team piled up a sensational 36–1 won-lost record. Only the Boston League team defeated them. The highlight of the trip were the games in San Francisco. Arlie Latham bantered with Boston star King Kelly. Latham kept up his incessant chatter while chasing after balls. On one occasion, Kelly hit a liner past Latham at third. "The Dude" just gave the ball his patented wave of the glove to put the crowd in stitches. Overall, though, the trip was a financial disaster. Net receipts amounted to less than $1,300. The Sporting News could not resist crowing about their Browns. "The fact is the Browns play ball in its scientific form; they do it aesthetically; they give the game the poetry of motion, the logic of success. They make it a symphony. They dash it with bits of color, as it were, and a glimpse of sunshine, a very painting with purple mountain tops, blue flecks of sky green sward and wooded glens. They are artists and the Texas league club fade into the insignificant."

At Kansas City, a well-known German comedian named Max Arnold endeavored to play right field in a game. *The Sporting News* scouting report wrote of Arnold that "he went right in avoiding all the balls batted toward him. Barring that and a trifling peculiarity in striking at the ball after it had landed in the catcher's hands, he is a great ball player."

Charlie Comiskey's son Louis, serving as mascot, was "arrested" with his buddy in Mexico for riding a donkey across a church graveyard. The arresting Mexican officials shared a great laugh. Both lads were given presents for their trouble.

At the conclusion, *The Sporting News* told of secretary George Munson's Chinatown gifts to his friends. The magazine also joked that the players had trouble "keeping dry," a double entendre on the weather conditions and their drinking propensities.

16

A Player's Rebellion

More than any other reason, the Player's League cut deeply into Von der Ahe's empire of profit. The organization, called the Brotherhood, was formed in 1885 as a charitable fraternity. It was founded by New York Giants' shortstop John Montgomery Ward. With owners and players constantly dickering over salaries, the players also wanted a voice concerning their movements. Ballplayers hated the idea of being shipped from one team to another at the owner's discretion. Indeed, owners were playing the part of robber barons, interested in maximizing profits with a stable, inexpensive workforce.

Ward was an outstanding player and articulate spokesman for the Brotherhood. He began his major-league career as an 18-year-old pitcher in 1878 for the National League Providence Grays. Ward won 22, 47, and 38 games in his first three seasons. He also tossed the major league's second perfect game in 1880. After blowing his arm out, Ward made a transition to outfielder and middle infielder. By 1883, he was a jack-of-all-trades, expert in the defensive and base-running arts. Ward would eventually author a book entitled *Baseball: How to Become a Player.* But, for all of his athletic ability, Ward was best described as brainy and ambitious. He strongly believed in championing players' rights by providing written statements and provocative speeches. Ward graduated with a law degree from Columbia University, a nearly unheard-of feat for a ballplayer.

As a foil for Monte Ward's liberal ideas, the magnates offered Albert Goodwill Spalding, owner of the Chicago club. Ten years Ward's senior, Spalding was part of the prevailing establishment, helping to found and star in the inaugural National League season of 1876. As a right-handed pitcher for pennant-winning Chicago, Spalding also managed the club while winning forty-six of the team's fifty-two games. Before that, Spalding was the best player on the nearly unbeatable Boston Red Stockings of the ill-fated National Association, which died after the 1875 campaign, beset by scheduling and player behavior problems. Especially disgusted by his ballplaying brethren,

Spalding believed they spent too much time cavorting about saloons and brothels. Ballplaying, though, was merely a springboard for his business. A pioneer of mass-produced sporting goods, Spalding supplied the league with balls and equipment. By the age of forty, Spalding had become a millionaire.

Within a year after the formation of the Brotherhood, 107 players had been enlisted from National League and American Association teams. Two prominent baseball scribes sided with the Brotherhood: Tim Murnane of Boston and Ren Mulford of Cincinnati. Both men informed their reading public of Brotherhood affairs. However, it was Ward's 1887 article in *Lippincott Magazine*, "Is the Base Ball Player Chattel?" that galvanized the players. Citing the reserve clause, standard in player contracts, Ward offered evidence that ballplayers were little more than slaves. Ward also crystallized the idea of the reserve clause for the general public. The clause bound ballplayers to their clubs as long as their services were desired. Releases could occur at any time, depending on the whim of the magnates. Ward and the Brotherhood were opposed to the buying and selling of players and blacklisting men who refused salary offers. Ward illustrated the problem with the high-profile sale of Mike "King" Kelly, sold from Spalding's Chicagos to Boston for the fantastic sum of $10,000. On the reserve clause, Ward wrote, "It inaugurated a species of serfdom which gave one set of men a life-estate in the labor of another, and withheld from the latter any corresponding claim."

Albert Spalding would say that magnates were ". . . responsible for making professional baseball a dignified, honest business that guaranteed ballplayers the dignity of profession and . . . munificent salary."

Begrudgingly, the National League accepted the Brotherhood. In a joint conference in 1888, the Brotherhood attempted to negotiate the abolition of reserving players at less than the previous year's salary. The National League postponed the request and waited until most men were signed for the 1889 season.

The case involving shortstop Jack Rowe and third baseman Deacon White further exacerbated tensions between the League and the Brotherhood. Rowe and White, members of the 1888 Detroit Wolverines, were sold to Pittsburgh prior to the 1889 season. However, the men had other plans, as partners in purchasing and playing for the Buffalo minor-league team. Said Pittsburgh magnate and former employer of Rowe and White at Detroit, Frederick Sterns, "White may have been elected president of the Buffalo club . . . but that won't allow him to play ball in Buffalo. He'll play in Pittsburgh or he'll get off the earth." Though Monte Ward understood that the case threatened to spark a legal challenge to the reserve clause, he quietly persuaded the erstwhile owners to play in Pittsburgh instead. National League player sympathies were with Rowe and White, and there was talk of a strike; but a far grander plan was shaping up in the Brotherhood.

During the summer of 1889, Pittsburgh outfielder Ned Hanlon interested Cleveland trolley-car magnate Al Johnson in the idea of a "player's league." Johnson, the brother of Cleveland mayor Tom Johnson, was an inveterate ball fan, known to play poker with the players. Over cards, Johnson was told stories of player injustices suffered at the hands of their employers. With interests in Cleveland, St. Louis, and elsewhere, Al Johnson may have envisioned teeming crowds of fans transported to the park on his trolley lines. Johnson spent the rest of the summer locating financial backers for the league.

That fall, Al Spalding financed a global barnstorming baseball tour to promote the game. The tour made stops in Honolulu, Sydney, the Indian subcontinent, Rome, Paris, Cairo, and England. Among the members of Spalding's entourage was Monte Ward. While baseball was being showcased abroad, big trouble brewed for the game at home. Cincinnati owner John Brush was busy devising a classification plan, sanctioned by Spalding and the National League. The plan called for a five-level pay schedule from $1,500-$2,500 that categorized players based on their "habits," "earnestness," and "special qualifications." The first two categories were concerned with player's off-field exploits, especially boozing. The latter category dealt with a players' ability on the diamond. Brush's plan outraged the Brotherhood. As Ward was debarking in New York City returning from the world tour, other Brotherhood members greeted him at the dock to tell him the news. Within days, the Brotherhood met and made public their plans for a Player's League. This new, independent baseball organization would begin play in 1890. The Player's League would challenge existing National League territories by placing seven of their eight teams in League cities. Also challenged were long-standing League policies concerning player contracts and the distribution of profits. Provisions for profit sharing were established. Two- and three-year deals would be offered to Brotherhood players, with salaries at least equal to those of 1889. No player could be released until the end of the season and not without a vote by a board of directors that included fellow ballplayers. The reserve clause would be abolished. As written in "The Brotherhood Manifesto" addressed "to the public:"

> *Players have been bought, sold, and exchanged as though they were sheep instead of American citizens. "Reservation" became for them another name for property rights in the player. By a combination among themselves, stronger than the strongest trust, they were able to enforce the most arbitrary measures, and the player either had to submit or get out of the profession in which he had spent years in attaining a proficiency.*

Most notable was the provision that players could move from team to team during the season, pending board approval. Blacklists would not be tolerated. The Brotherhood also established penalties for drunkenness and other unsavory behavior.

Recognizing their collective interest in fighting the National League, representatives of the Player's League and the American Association met in the fall of 1889. The Association grimly noted its organization's disintegration from within. The Player's League may have been hoping to strengthen its organization with Association clubs while taking advantage of Chris Von der

Ahe's money, but any amalgamation plans were doomed from the start. Monte Ward attended the December 1889 Association meeting in Rochester, New York. At that gathering Von der Ahe threatened to place a whole new Brooklyn club in Ridgewood Park to contest Sunday games there. The blustery Chris acknowledged a violation of the National Agreement but "violations of that kind have taken place before. The League put a club in St. Louis in opposition to the Browns and then asked what I was going to do about it. Now what is to prevent us from placing a club in Brooklyn?"

Less than two weeks later, Von der Ahe was busy shaking hands at the Player's League conference. Unsure of which side to take, Von der Ahe originally supported "capitalists" against labor. After all, Von der Ahe himself was a capitalist who had fought many contractual battles with his players. Al Spink, supporting the Brotherhood, tried to convince Von der Ahe to change his mind. Within a month, Von der Ahe favored the Player's League, wishing them every success. Rumors flew that Chris would move his franchise into the Player's League. In effect, Von der Ahe's changing positions made him look the part of a fool. Monte Ward quickly dropped any idea of incorporating Von der Ahe or any Association teams into the Brotherhood. Though Ward agreed that the Player's League would benefit from Von der Ahe's finances, he was quoted as saying that Chris would "injure our cause" because "he talks too much."

Legal challenges to the Player's League began in the waning days of 1889. Brotherhood members were advised not to sign National League contracts for the 1890 season. Attorneys representing the League advised their clients that the reserve clause would bind players to their teams. After Monte Ward was notified he was still a New York Giant, a round of lawsuits began. In January 1890, the Giants were denied an injunction against Ward. The ruling cited that the reserve clause lacked fairness and mutuality.

The floodgates opened.

After more legal skirmishes, the defections commenced. Nearly 80 percent of the starting players in the National League jumped to the Player's League. Buck Ewing, Roger Connor, and Dan Brouthers were among the stars that deserted the National League. The Association lost more than twenty men, including Charlie Comiskey and Pete Browning. League owners tried to tempt their men with huge salary increases, bribes, and long-term deals. King Kelly was offered an astronomical $10,000 bonus and a blank-check three-year contract. The proud Kelly said, "I can't go back on the boys."

When the smoke cleared, the Player's League had cornered the market on talented ballplayers.

With the inherent problems concerning the formation of the Player's League, contract squabbles for top-notchers affected fan loyalties. The 1890 campaign was a three-way war among leagues—only worse.

Just before the season began, the National League and Player's League ran a dirty game of franchise bluff. One league would announce the formation of a franchise in a certain city and then wait to see the rival league's response. This ploy may have satiated magnates' egos, but it played havoc with prospective fans. In mid-March, the National League announced ten franchises, making scheduling difficult. The League wanted their two weakest teams, Washington and Indianapolis, to exit the organization. The Washington club, going nowhere at the box office, decided to fold. The persistent John Brush, owner of the Indianapolis club, had no intentions of disbanding. Pleading with the League, Brush claimed $12,000 worth of season tickets sold. Eventually, the League paid Brush $60,000 to *not* field a club for 1890. Indianapolis was allowed to remain in the League as a sort of ghost team. The Player's League kept its secretary a very busy man. At Ward's instructions, the Brotherhood placed its clubs in direct competition with the National League. The only two noncompeting cities were Cincinnati in the National League and Buffalo in the Brotherhood. The Player's League boldly sent its rivals their schedule. ". . . the National League can, should it so chose, avoid conflicting dates with our clubs in the cities of Boston, New York, Brooklyn, Philadelphia, Pittsburgh, Cleveland, and Chicago. May I also suggest that the National League adopt a resolution permitting its clubs to play against those of the Player's League, before and after the championship season of both leagues."

The National League countered with a circular. ". . . Managers are asked to avoid using the trains and hotels patronized by the Player's League clubs at the same time."

At the ball yard, action was sometimes too close for comfort. In New York, the Player's League built a ballpark under the Coogan's Bluff rock cliffs. The Player's League outfield jutted right up against the National League's outfield at Manhattan Field. On May 12, New York Giant Mike Tiernan homered over the canvas wall that separated the ball yards. The ball landed in the Player's League Park. Confused at first, fans from both parks cheered.

Over the summer, the National League battled the Player's League for supremacy, territoriality, and most importantly, fan interest. Considering the infighting in the Association, League powers chose to engage their attentions on Monte Ward's Brotherhood. As fan interest equated directly to attendance and money, the battle was fearsome.

Baseball's saturation resulted in disenfranchised and disinterested fans. After a month, attendance fell off sharply. The game on the field became secondary to the battles being fought by the magnates. Avid fans noticed a strangeness about baseball. The National League began to schedule dates to conflict with the games of the Player's League. Almost overnight, it became easy to acquire free passes to ball games. The National League and Player's League handed out tickets to barbershops and charities. There were numerous special-day promotions wherein one class of patrons (actors, for example) entered the grounds for free. To cover embarrassing League attendance figures, Spalding hired men to stand outside Player's League gates to check in on crowds. As his henchmen acquired information from the press, Spalding then published his own figures. League crowd sizes were hyped as high as 150 percent, with Player's League crowds always underestimated. However, reporters soon caught on to Spalding's game. While the magnates became concerned over baseball's future, Spalding thought the game might perish. Monte Ward simply said that the "game would live if both leagues die."

As the season dragged on, National League magnates realized the high cost of their war. In order to keep the League afloat, various owners bought stock in other clubs. It seemed a conflict of interest, but it was a matter of survival. Spalding, Arthur Soden, Al Reach, and John Brush all bought stock in the New York Giants. With losses mounting, Player's League magnates were ready to quit. A few couldn't meet their payroll. With inclement September weather, Player's League pennant races fizzled. As the season ended, so did the Player's League. The National League had crushed the upstarts. Some Player's League owners tried to merge their holdings with clubs in the National League or American Association. The New York Player's League club was absorbed by the New York Giants. The Pittsburgh Player's League club merged with their League rivals, as did the Brooklyn Player's League team. Both Boston and Philadelphia of the Player's League entered the Association. Al Spalding bought out Comiskey's Chicago Player's League squad for $18,000. Incredibly, Cincinnati's Aaron Stern sold his interests to a group led by Al Johnson. However, the National League declared that franchise forfeited and awarded Cincinnati territory to John Brush.

Spalding would later comment that the war used "printers ink and bluff" as weapons. Writing in his baseball history *American's National Game,* Spalding penned, "If either party of this controversy ever furnished to the press one solitary truthful statement . . . a monument should be erected in his memory. I have no candidates to recommend for the distinction."

In a New York City saloon to toast the demise of the Player's League, Ward referred to the experiment as "quasi-socialism." Ward also commented that "Baseball is a business, not simply a sport."

The aftermath showed National League, Player's League, and American Association ledgers awash in debt. The League estimated losses at $300,000. The Player's League reported $125,000 in arrears. However, the unintended victim of the war was the American Association. Though figures are unavailable, the Association was heavily damaged by its 25-cent admittance fee. Syracuse, Rochester, and Toledo all exited the Association in financial ruin. New Association squads were added in Boston, Washington, and Cincinnati. The 1890 Boston Player's League club had been the most financially successful in the game. Boston was transferred directly into the Association for 1891. The Cincinnati team, financed in part by Von der Ahe and led by Mike "King" Kelly, would be in direct competition with the National League Cincinnati in 1891.

Peace negotiations aimed at ending the conflict between the surviving baseball organizations lasted into the fall of 1890. The talks involved franchise viability and player repatriations. All contract jumpers were restored without penalty to their 1889 clubs. A new National Agreement was signed between the National League, the American Association, and the Western Association. Nearly all the "extra" ballplayers found themselves looking for new lines of work.

In spite of a short life span, the Player's League was responsible for several innovations. All clubs wore white uniforms at home; several donned colored togs for road games. For the first time, two umpires worked the diamond. Team pennant flags were flown at all ballparks to help announce the day's games.

Fan interest in the 1890 World Series mirrored the apathy of the season. Keeping with tradition, the Association met with the League. The Brooklyn Leaguers were led by Oyster Burns, Germany Smith, Dave Foutz, and Bob Caruthers. Opposing them were the revitalized Louisville Colonels, the same squad that had suffered so miserably in 1889. This time, by virtue of having lost the fewest players to the Brotherhood, Louisville thrived. Oddly, a tragic tornado may have helped to spur on the Colonels. Louisville swept into first place by mid-season and were never headed. Chicken Wolf batted .363; Scott Stratton improved from three wins to thirty-four; Red Ehret ballooned from ten wins to twenty-five. Despite the intrigue, the series ended in a tie.

The Association's Brooklyn team played so poorly they earned the sobriquet, the Castaways. By late June, Brooklyn's ballplayers were playing the game without pay. The Brooklyn treasury went broke. The club folded up shop in August and was replaced by the reformed Baltimore Atlantic Association club. After acquiring all the rights to the ex-Brooklyn players, the Baltimores decided that no former Brooklyn player was worth retaining.

17

A Fine Mess

Upon the commencement of the difficult 1889 season, Chris Von der Ahe and ex-manager Charles Comiskey engaged in verbal sniping. At issue was credit for St. Louis' success. A Von der Ahe tirade began the hostilities. In an interview with *The Sporting News,* Chris suggested that he himself made Comiskey's reputation. Comiskey was a good enough captain, Chris related, but with a $5,000 annual salary (and part interest in the team), Comiskey acted ungrateful. Von der Ahe also claimed that Comiskey had only signed one man for the Browns. Over the years, Comiskey had been given undeserved accolades by the sportswriters for his managerial skills. Said Von der Ahe, Comiskey always found himself in scrapes and possessed an "ugly disposition." "He raised a number of rows in Brooklyn, Baltimore, Cincinnati, and Philadelphia and always kept me in hot water." Finally, Von der Ahe claimed that Comiskey was not respected by his players.

Sour grapes.

After a reporter showed Comiskey the interview with Von der Ahe, Comiskey fought back. He'd been reluctant to comment earlier, but now Comiskey was protecting his character. Comiskey disagreed that he was a disorganizer. Instead, Comiskey said that Von der Ahe and his son Eddie were experts at destroying club morale. ". . . the two came near to driving me and all the players crazy." Comiskey resented Von der Ahe's young son Eddie doing his father's dirty work, especially at contract time. Comiskey had turned down a lucrative offer in the middle of the 1889 season. Comiskey related how Eddie had asked him in "an apologetic way" to sign. When Comiskey refused, the elder Von der Ahe stepped in. Comiskey then shocked Chris Von der Ahe by refusing to re-sign. Von der Ahe made his own manager miserable by guying Comiskey during St. Louis' crucial games with Brooklyn!

Comiskey also had this to say about Von der Ahe:

> *. . . Pete Sweeney, who played with the Browns last year, showed me a*

> *letter from young Von der Ahe telling him that it was me that had fired him from the team. The letter stated that Von der Ahe wanted Sweeney to play first base and left the impression that Von der Ahe . . . intended to sell me to a one horse club or another. I had intended to call Von der Ahe . . . but on hearing of the way he had treated Munson, I resolved not to have anything more to do with him. The people of St. Louis, for whom I have a reverence and affection, know whether I earned my money with Von der Ahe or not. I fought his battles always . . . As to my being a disorganizer, the team work I got out of the Browns gives lie to that statement.*

Von der Ahe's battles with Comiskey were hardly unique. The Browns' owner endured a whirlwind 1889 off-season that involved squabbles with his men, their eventual defections, the near collapse of the Association and not, coincidentally, the restructuring of all of professional baseball. In hindsight, Browns' player dissatisfactions served as a microcosm for the Association and the League.

One by one, several key St. Louis players deserted and then bad-mouthed Von der Ahe on the way. Tip O'Neill fired off some verbal shots at his old boss. Silver King complained bitterly of Von der Ahe cheating him out of part of his 1889 salary. King said that he would not play for Von der Ahe for "a million dollars a minute." Arlie Latham responded, "Will I play ball in St. Louis again? Not unless you put a chain around me and lock me up in your park." Latham had spent his off-season signing and then balking with several clubs. Latham bantered with reporters about Eddie Von der Ahe, who was sent to sign Arlie for 1890. When Eddie stated that Latham was desperate for money, Arlie calmly grinned and whipped out some large bills and a check for $500. An upset Eddie then left the hotel.

Determined to seek revenge for his mistreatment, Comiskey organized several of the Browns to jump ship. Von der Ahe retaliated by saying that Comiskey would not be released from the Browns for $20,000. When the smoke cleared, Comiskey, Latham, O'Neill, King, and catcher Boyle had all signed with the new Chicago Player's League club. Yank Robinson ended up in Pittsburgh. Catcher Jocko Milligan was signed by Philadelphia. In all, five starting players from 1889 were gone. Von der Ahe retained only shortstop Shorty Fuller, center fielder Charlie Duffee, right fielder Tommy McCarthy, and second-year pitcher Jack Stivetts. After Comiskey reportedly offered pitcher Icebox Chamberlain an $800 increase to sign with Chicago, Von der Ahe again summoned his son. Chamberlain greatly resented the fact that Eddie was two years younger than he was, but eventually, signed with the 1890 Browns.

By the start of 1890, *The Sporting News* began to editorialize on Von der Ahe's crumbling empire. The weekly had supported Chris throughout his baseball career, including the bitter 1889 pennant feud with Brooklyn's Byrne. Now, with the Browns faltering and Von der Ahe fining his players, the paper took a different angle. The troubles escalated upon the formation of the Player's League. When *The Sporting News* supported the Player's

League and a rival team in St. Louis, Von der Ahe fumed. It is probable that the magazine was trying to make more money by promoting more baseball. After all, *The Sporting News* had scooped the story of the Player's League when St. Louis native and ballplayer Joe Quinn spilled the beans. Writing sarcastically, the weekly also claimed that nearly all of Von der Ahe's player signings were due to "luck" and his associations with Ted Sullivan, Charlie Comiskey, and Ned Cuthbert. Pitchers Foutz, Caruthers, King, and Stivetts had been secured for next to nothing. Nat Hudson was a Chicago amateur. Catchers Doc Bushong, Jocko Milligan, and Jack Boyle were all acquired by trade. On Comiskey's advice, Tip O'Neill was converted from pitcher to hard-hitting outfielder. Shorty Fuller came recommended by Ted Sullivan. Yank Robinson was plucked from the Baltimore Unions after rave reviews by Comiskey and Cuthbert.

Tensions between *The Sporting News* and Von der Ahe continued to surface.

Without his powerful mouthpiece, Von der Ahe gallantly fought the hard fight. Taking a cue from St. Louis dailies, newspapers around the country started to report unflattering tales of Chris' personal life. Rumors swirled of Von der Ahe's retirement from baseball, his jump to the National League, the unjust fines, and his heavy-handed management tactics. Von der Ahe supposedly threatened to go into the minstrel business and open up theater events at night in Sportsman's Park. Another story concerned Von de Ahe's comments to a young player who had played a bad game. "Did you never see a base ball until you came to St. Louis?" Thanks to *The Sporting News,* the Browns were saddled with a host of unceremonious new names such as the St. Louis Boozers and the St. Louis Kickers. Von der Ahe himself was lampooned as Vonderhaha. His trademark signature, "Christ. Von der Ahe," was also debased by the weekly, which made veiled references to Von der Ahe's ego by comparing him to Jesus. The St. Louis Browns were called the laughing stocks of baseball. One biting commentary said, "Our advice for the St. Louis Boozers, who are now in Louisville: Do not come home and all will be forgiven." Fighting back, Von der Ahe attempted to boycott *The Sporting News* with the help of John J. O'Neill, printer George Stone, and saloon proprietor Peckington. Acting on a plan conceived in a bar, the men sent letters and postcards to *Sporting News* advertisers, urging them not to do business with the weekly. Supporting the St. Louis Browns was a matter of civic duty, read Von der Ahe's propaganda. In response, *The Sporting News* referred to O'Neill as Chon Chay O'Neill and John Jackass O'Neill. The paper countered that despite the boycott, circulation was increasing. *The Sporting News* started a rumor about a Player's League team right in St. Louis. The venture took wing when Browns' ex-secretary George Munson was supposedly offered $50,000 by "leading businessmen" of the city. Though *The Sporting News* was urged to cease their attacks by friends of Von der Ahe, they would only reconsider when Von der Ahe "called off his skunks." Chris' son Eddie was also attacked for alienating his father from old friends and making dumb remarks.

For Von der Ahe, it wasn't so much that *The Sporting News* supported the new Player's League; it was the *way* they did it. *The Sporting News* trumpeted the Player's League as having the best pitchers. In March 1890, exhibition games were arranged between the Chicago and Cleveland Player's League teams. The contests would take place right under Chris' nose, in hometown St. Louis. The Player's League couldn't immediately finance a team in the city. With great spirit, a new ballpark was quickly erected and named Brotherhood Park. Financed with help from the Olympic Athletic Club, the grandstands took only two weeks to assemble. A cinder path was added for track events. The exhibitions were calculated to drive Von der Ahe from his St. Louis perch. "Baseball and athletics in St. Louis have been at the mercy of one man," wrote *The Sporting News*. The newspaper offered "testimonials" from Browns' pitcher Elton Chamberlain and Sportsman's Park designer Gus Solari on the virtues of the new park. Von der Ahe himself was supposed to have visited the rival ball yard. It would have been easier to slap Von der Ahe in his face.

A grand reception was afforded the Chicago and Cleveland teams at the train depot. A Fife and Drum Corps was on hand to greet the arrivals. *The Sporting News* invited all local baseball professionals to the festivities. A mob scene, described as a "monstrous reptile," surged to see the new heroes. A diamond-studded Arlie Latham took off his hat, danced a little jig, and said, "Ah, there boys." The band played the familiar tune "When 'Arlie' Comes Marching Home." The crowd went wild with cheering. The new Chicagoans—Comiskey, King O'Neill, Boyle, and Latham—all boarded carriages with four white horses and a banner proclaiming, "We are the people. Come see us at Brotherhood Park tomorrow." An impromptu evening parade followed through the city streets. To add salt to Von der Ahe's wounds, *The Sporting News* reported that Arlie Latham telegrammed his ex-boss; "A little German band would not be out of place."

By a quirk of fate, heavy snow fell on the city for the next several days, postponing the games. However, after a week of practice in the cold powder, the games began. Once again, an "Auld Lang Syne" parade took place downtown. The ballplayers marched into the park to a packed house rigged with flags and bunting. The Saturday game was attended by nearly 5,000 people, each paying twenty-five cents. On Sunday, a larger throng appeared, estimated at 10,000 to 20,000, taxing streetcars and horse traffic in the city. For the next week, members of the Brotherhood in St. Louis were treated like royalty, attending opera, comedy, theater, and banquets.

The Player's League, triumphant in its gloating, had taken a page right out of Von der Ahe's book.

Unbowed by the criticism of *The Sporting News,* player losses, and the challenge of a rival league, Von der Ahe vowed to recapture the pennant in a weakened Association. In an effort to attract fans, Von der Ahe shelled out $50,000 to refurbish Sportsman's Park. Chris also announced a gargantuan raise in Sportsman's Park stock, from $5,000 to $50,000. Von der Ahe's detractors remained skeptical, especially when the Browns' owner postulated on a new ten-year lease for the park. To train for the season, Von der Ahe practiced his men indoors during inclement weather. One of the exercises involved a vaulting horse. Chief Roseman, new to the Browns, wasn't too thrilled with the apparatus. Reluctantly, he jumped over the horse just as Von der Ahe walked into a session. Von der Ahe spied Roseman's half-hearted jump. Roseman protested, complaining that he just wanted to play ball. "If I want to jump over a horse, I'll sign with a circus."

Unfortunately, Browns' fans weren't buying. With an unrecognizable, patchwork squad, interest in the club sunk to an all-time low. Spring exhibition games at Sportsman's Park were financial flops. Only ten people reportedly showed for an exhibition loss to Evansville. During a game with Omaha, Von der Ahe pulled pitcher Chamberlain off the field and suspended him for six weeks without pay for deliberately trying to lose. Chamberlain would relate that the players were nervous because "the boss manager" kept peering at them through a telescope. During a particularly argumentative series with Columbus, Tommy McCarthy wiped out opposition pitcher Jack Easton, who was backing up third base. With clenched fist, McCarthy barreled into the diminutive Easton, who got up and charged McCarthy. With St. Louis fans howling, Easton's teammates corralled their enraged pitcher and prevented further fisticuffs. Von der Ahe screamed an epithet at Easton, saying that he should be blacklisted. The Columbus team answered back in chorus that McCarthy was the instigator and he should be blacklisted.

When the minor-league Detroit club folded in late June, Von der Ahe signed six of its players—catcher Jake Wells, first baseman Jake Virtue, second baseman Bill Higgins, outfielder Count Campau, shortstop Bobby Wheelock, and third baseman Jimmy Donely. With this new blood, Von der Ahe vowed to win the pennant. Two men, Virtue and Wheelock, never donned St. Louis flannels. Of the other four, only Campau contributed.

The Virtue, Higgins, Wheelock transactions led directly to a lawsuit against Chris Von der Ahe. Detroit manager William Gray had agreed to release three of the men to the Browns for cash. However, the deals stalled when Higgins balked at the sale and refused to take up residence in St. Louis. Von der Ahe then agreed to pay Detroit $1,666 for Virtue and Wheelock, provided they suit up for the Browns for the balance of the season. Unfortunately, the entire transaction fell through when Virtue and Wheelock refused to call Von der Ahe their employer. The Detroit club then sued Von der Ahe for the cash, claiming that the Browns' owner had reneged. Chris remained in hot water with the Association for the failed deal. The affair again focused attention on baseball's slavery issue.

In early July, pitcher Toad Ramsey was accused by Von der Ahe of being drunk. Ramsey denied the accusation. During a Sunday game, Ramsey was on first base. Coach Campau, perhaps on orders by Von der Ahe to test Ramsey's sobriety, ordered his runner to steal second base. The Toad made a half-hearted attempt, hesitated, and was thrown out easily. As he returned to the bench, Von der Ahe cursed at Ramsey in German. The partisan St. Louis crowd responded with some English for Von der Ahe. Ramsey retaliated with a few four-letter phrasings for his employer. For his trouble, Ramsey was ordered off the grounds by Von der Ahe and suspended without pay. Less than two weeks later, Ramsey was reinstated and pitched a strong game against Syracuse.

Unhappy pitcher Icebox Chamberlain's 1890 season with St. Louis was short-lived. After only four games, Chamberlain's whining prompted a Von der Ahe suspension for one month. During the player's benching, the Association's Brooklyn club offered Von der Ahe $6,500 for Chamberlain's release. Von der Ahe declined. Cincinnati then upped the ante to $6,800. Von der Ahe stuck to his guns. Not wanting to help St. Louis' chief rivals, Von der Ahe kept the hurler on the bench. When reinstated, Chamberlain responded by being blasted in his return game. Von der Ahe's next move was to suspend Chamberlain again. This time the penalty was indefinite and without pay. After frequenting poolrooms in Buffalo, Chamberlain finally ended up in Columbus, a team without any real pennant aspirations.

Through the summer, Von der Ahe also had to compete with the Barnum and Bailey Circus, the great St. Louis Fair, and a new triweekly program of horse racing matinees. Ex-secretary George Munson was busy planning more summer exhibitions of Brotherhood teams in St. Louis. Meanwhile, *The Sporting News* continued its assault of Von der Ahe by commissioning portraits of the Chicago Brotherhood team for sale to subscribers.

Despite Von der Ahe's personal indiscretions, Chris fancied himself as a champion of fair play. At a fourth of July morning-afternoon doubleheader in St. Louis, Von der Ahe was forced to make a difficult decision concerning Brooklyn manager Jim Kennedy.

To celebrate his team's morning victory, the greenhorn manager of the Gladiators was offered a table with Von der Ahe under the grandstand at Sportsman's Park. Von der Ahe wanted to meet with Kennedy to offer advice. A table was spread with food, and several Brooklyn players joined in the festivities. Kennedy confided to Von der Ahe that it was a hot day and that his men deserved more fun. In an instant, a keg of ice-cold beer was ordered. Two Browns' players wandered over to the party. After a while, the St. Louis men were consuming more liquid refreshment than sustenance.

At noon, firecrackers and pistol reports announced the start of the afternoon contest. St. Louis and Brooklyn took the field. In front of a large crowd, the home-standing Browns again lost the game. To the many imbibing beer, the loss didn't really matter. Noticeable in defeat, however, was the play of the Browns who had quaffed at Von der Ahe's impromptu picnic. Heady with cold beer and the rays of the scorching sun, the drunken Browns stumbled off the field to the clubhouse. Someone informed the St. Louis president of the intoxicating play. Furious, Von der Ahe arose from his box and headed toward the Brooklyn bench. When Chris spotted Kennedy, he immediately lectured the manager on the high standards of the National Game.

"Jim, on account of our old acquaintance, it cuts my heart to my feet, but for the good of the game, you are expelled for life," said Von der Ahe.

Familiar with Von der Ahe's antics, Kennedy didn't take Chris too seriously. That night, Von der Ahe and Kennedy boarded a train for an Association meeting in Louisville. Feeling morose over his weighty decision, Von der Ahe summoned Kennedy to chat about the expulsion. Kennedy decided that such a solemn occasion would require refreshment. Ringing a train porter, the wily Kennedy returned Von der Ahe's magnanimous gesture from the previous day.

"Jim, tonight I would give one thousand dollars if I could change places with you," the Browns' president lamented.

"Have courage, Chris, be like the Roman father who had to sentence to death his own son to satisfy justice."

By this time, Kennedy was doing his best to console Von der Ahe and keep himself from laughter. All the while, the porter kept hustling Kennedy and Von der Ahe more alcohol. Kennedy was doing his level best to stay sober. Slurring his speech, Von der Ahe wasn't faring as well. Kennedy's expulsion was unbearable for Chris. After some time, the two men finally decided to turn in for the evening. Kennedy accompanied Von der Ahe to his berth, but Chris needed help from the porter to make it into bed. As Chris rolled into his Pullman sleeper, he made one last comment to Kennedy. "I was thinking it over, Jim. I will not expel you. Now, Jim, I will sleep happy."

Kennedy could have predicted the softhearted Von der Ahe's response. "Thank you, Chris. It will save you a lot of pain,"

In late July, Von der Ahe advertised an exciting new event at Sportsman's Park. A hot-air balloon ascension, complete with a pretty lady, would take place at the park. The event, of course, wasn't free. One St. Louis weekly suggested that Von der Ahe get himself in the balloon, fly away, and not come back.

Desperate for another Association flag, Von der Ahe promised each of his players a $100 bonus for a first-place finish. Unfortunately, the Browns were hardly in a mood to cooperate, especially in light of their owner's treatment. The season also took a toll on St. Louis managers. No fewer than five men attempted on-field decision making. Tommy McCarthy began the campaign and finished a short stint later. Chief Roseman, John Kerins, Joe Gerhardt, and Count Campau reminded no one of Charlie Comiskey. Few respected Roseman's ability to control his men. However, if players snickered at Roseman's half-hearted admonitions, they fairly howled at Von der Ahe's. During one particular team meeting, Von der Ahe questioned his manager as to the whereabouts of young pitcher Jack Stivetts. Von der Ahe suspected boozing. Roseman answered that Jack was home with lumbago. Realizing that several Italian saloon keepers ran their businesses in the vicinity of the ballpark, Von der Ahe boomed, "I told you, Chief, dot I don'd vant any of my blayers to associate mid dos dago saloon men. Shust you fine Chack Stiwetts $10 for keeping gombany mit dot feller Lumbago."

In late August, Von der Ahe managed to acquire suspended Philadelphia slugger Denny Lyons. Certain the signing would revitalize the club, Chris shot off his mouth once more. Von der Ahe's remarks so upset Lyons that he refused to recognize his new employer and sat out the rest of the season.

The wildest donnybrook of the season took place at Sportsman's Park on August 16. The visitors were the Philadelphias. Browns' manager Count Campau handed the ball to Jack Stivetts. Philadelphia pitched Ed Seward. Two thousand anxious midwest ball fans showed up for the spectacle. Bob Emslie umpired, but perhaps wished he had stayed in bed.

Early on, Philadelphia scored a barrage of runs against young Stivetts. When the Phils weren't hitting, they were being hit by pitched balls. In the second, with the hometowners in arrears 9–0, Campau replaced an embarrassed Stivetts with Toad Ramsey. The pitching change somehow woke up the lifeless bats of the Browns. While Ramsey held down Philadelphia, St. Louis pecked away for two single-inning scores. In the fifth, St. Louis tallied five times after two men were out. The rally produced a walk, a double, a single, a double, a single, a double, and a single in succession. St. Louis cranks began to yell themselves hoarse with joy. The Browns trailed 9–7.

In the seventh, Philly captain Curt Welch tried to replace pitcher Seward with Sadie McMahon. However, umpire Emslie steadfastly disagreed. Citing a new substitution rule, Emslie explained to Welch that two designated subs had to be listed on the lineup card before the start of the game. McMahon was not one of them. Welch was having none of it. Welch and McMahon loudly protested their case to Emslie. While the Browns joined in the fray, the uncouth Welch kept up his verbal assault. By this time, St. Louis cranks were in a lather and yelled for the game to go on. Finally, Emslie agreed to placate the unruly Welch by allowing McMahon to pitch. As a reward for his sore ears, Emslie then received a few choice words from St. Louis manager Campau, who would now play the game under protest.

In the top of the eighth, St. Louis still trailed. Catcher Jack Munyan coaxed a base on balls from McMahon. Shortstop Fuller singled Munyan to third. Boston-bred Tommy McCarthy was the next batter. McCarthy backed down to no man. McMahon fooled Tommy with a pitch, and the outfielder punched a slow roller along first base. McMahon charged the ball but collided fearfully with McCarthy running down the line. Munyan scored and Emslie ruled McCarthy safe. The visiting Athletics screamed in chorus. Emslie then endured another round of unpleasant barbs. With Sportsman's Park a cacophony of catcalls, Emslie pulled out his watch. Threatening Philadelphia with forfeiture, Emslie tried to yell above the din. More cursing ensued. After an extremely long delay, the Athletics returned to their positions. The Browns scored four times and now led 12–10.

In the bottom of the eighth, Welch decided to take matters into his own hands. Curt singled, stole second, went to third on a wild pitch, and scored on a base hit. Pitcher Toad Ramsey clung to a 12–11 lead.

Welch began the ninth inning in a rage. He seethed. He ranted. He raved.

All Welch's anger was directed at umpire Emslie. The arbiter appeared clearly rattled by the display, but summoned the courage to order the demon Welch off the field. Emslie again pulled out his watch. For ten full minutes, Welch refused to leave. Finally, amid much howling from the St. Louis faithful, Welch departed the Sportsman's Park grounds. Philadelphia went out meekly against Ramsey, and the game was over. St. Louis won 12–11. For his behavior, the unbridled Welch was fined $50. Pitcher Sadie McMahon and outfielder Blondie Purcell were also fined.

The season's main theme was fines, fines, and more fines. Von der Ahe was frustrated with his lack of earning capital. Less than two months into the season, St. Louis players were complaining of being fined for little or no reason. Outfielder Chief Roseman, who owned two saloons in Brooklyn, said he didn't need baseball and threatened to quit if his fines were not rescinded. An indiscretion usually involved a tongue-lashing from Chris or Eddie Von der Ahe, a $50 fine, and a promise that if the player improved, the fine would be remitted at the end of the season. For suspensions due to drinking, Chris Von der Ahe sent full accounts to the newspapers.

Backup catcher Billy Earle was a particular thorn in Von der Ahe's side, playing only twenty-two games due to various spats with the owner. Four Browns, including Earle, Tommy McCarthy, Chief Roseman, and Pat Hartnett spent an elongated May evening at a military-style ball complete with polkas and square dancing. When the group finally returned the morning after, owner Von der Ahe read his men the riot act and reiterated the club's 11:00 P.M. curfew. All were fined except Hartnett, who was simply released. A few weeks later, Earle fought with Von der Ahe over money. The feud led to Earle returning home to Cincinnati. After being talked back to the Browns, Earle refused to play ball one Sunday. Von der Ahe leveled the catcher with another stiff fine. A strict Baptist, Earle had promised his mother never to violate the Sabbath. Ironically, the St. Louis Christian Association agreed to pay Earle's penalty. However, the proud backstop would not allow the benevolent gesture. Von der Ahe then sold Earle to Sioux City.[6] Billy Earle wasn't finished with Von der Ahe. By the end of June, Earle told reporters that $575 in fines were levied against him. Earle also related that circulars were sent to Browns players warning them of a $10 or $25 fine for not winning the afternoon's game.

Erratic pitcher Toad Ramsey didn't endear himself to Von der Ahe either. Ramsey was a hard-core drinker with a bad reputation. He was said to be the inventor of the Toad Ramsey cocktail: a pint of whiskey poured into a pitcher full of beer. The concoction was reportedly consumed by the inventor three times per day. Von der Ahe eventually told a reporter that he'd release Ramsey for a nickel. There were no takers.

Near the end of the campaign, Von der Ahe's players were out of control. Several were known to stay out all night drinking. In Baltimore one evening, Captain McCarthy, Toad Ramsey, and Bill Higgins had still not returned to their hotel rooms past midnight. Von der Ahe patiently waited for the night owls at the head of the stairway. When his charges arrived in a disheveled appearance, Chris was armed with a few choice words. Pitcher Ramsey was told to pack his bags and not return. Bill Higgins was suspended. Captain McCarthy, supposed to set an example, received a stern lecture.

The St. Louis winter of 1890–1891 could have been time for Von der Ahe to swallow his pride. Realizing the crippling effects of the Player's League on the American Association, Von der Ahe probably spent much of his time licking his wounds. However, the feelings of self-pity didn't last long. In early November, at Tony Faust's seafood house, Von der Ahe met with Charles Comiskey and the two men buried the hatchet. The conversation centered on the demise of the Player's League and Comiskey's possible repatriation to the Browns. Comiskey had turned down a three-year $30,000 deal from the Philadelphia club. After a round of drinks at the restaurant, Von der Ahe, Comiskey, and George Munson visited Sportsman's Park to reminisce some more. For hopeful St. Louis baseball cranks, the meeting signaled a return to glory.

Ex-Browns Tip O'Neill, Yank Robinson, Jack Boyle, and Silver King all called on Von der Ahe at his private residence. *The Sporting News* reported the story with vigor, treating Comiskey's return as the revival of baseball in St. Louis.

To solidify the new friendship, Von der Ahe, saloon pal John Peckington, Comiskey, O'Neill, and Yank Robinson all went on a hunting and fishing expedition at a nearby swamp. Reportedly, the men caught only colds. However, for Von der Ahe, this time the biggest fish did not get away. Charlie Comiskey would again manage the Browns in 1891.

18

The End of the American Association

President Von der Ahe, secretary Munson, and captain-manager Comiskey entered 1891 with a heavy dose of optimism. All fairly gushed about St. Louis' chances. The optimism was fueled by an outstanding collection of players. On the mound, St. Louis boasted Jack Stivetts and Clark Griffith. Jack Boyle was the catcher. The infield was comprised of Comiskey at first and Bad Bill Eagan at second. Shorty Fuller would play short, and the hard-hitting Denny Lyons would man third base. In the outfield garden, St. Louis featured right fielder Tommy McCarthy, left fielder Tip O'Neill, and a diminutive deaf-mute named Dummy Hoy. The latter was signed by Ted Sullivan, who communicated with the talented fly chaser with paper and pencil.

The opening game of the season between the Cincinnati Reds and the St. Louis Browns was as eventful as any played at Sportsman's Park. It began normally enough—the usual baseball parade, led by a brass band, inaugurated the beginning of the campaign. The Reds traipsed into the park in their blue uniforms with pea green stockings. The St. Louis faithful wildly applauded the Reds' new catcher, King Kelly. As the Cincinnati players sat down on their benches, the Browns followed, to even bigger applause. Jack Stivetts pitched for the Browns against the Reds' 17-year-old Willie McGill.

The umpire, though, was a bit odd. He was none other than Bill Gleason, the shortstop sold by Von der Ahe after the 1887 season.

The Reds jumped to a quick 3–0 lead after three innings, the first tally scored by ex-Brown Yank Robinson on a Stivetts wild pitch. In the fourth frame, the Browns secured the lead. Umpire Gleason's ball and strike calls resulted in four bases on balls for the Browns and five runs. Catcher King Kelly, with a good view of McGill's pitches, became so irate with Gleason that he ripped off his catching gloves, shouted some invectives, and departed the grounds. Young McGill was none too pleased either. After four innings, St. Louis led 5–3.

In the fifth, Kelly reconsidered and returned to the ball yard. As he stepped in to bat, Gleason reminded him that he was no longer in the contest. Kelly argued that he hadn't really left the action. As the crowd jeered, the two men turned up the volume on their vocal chords. Gleason probably figured that Kelly's loss would disappoint home cranks. Kelly was allowed to hit. The Reds tallied four more off Stivetts and led 7–5. In the bottom of the frame, as Kelly squatted down at catcher, Gleason again reminded Kelly that he wasn't in the game. More jawing followed between Gleason and Kelly. Then, realizing his predicament, Kelly again walked off the field. As Kelly exited he said [about Gleason] to the crowd, "He is too strong for my game." The exiled Red took a seat on the pine. New catcher Jerry Hurley watched helplessly as the Browns sliced the lead to 7–6 with two more walks. Darkness was fast approaching.

St. Louis tied the score at seven in the eighth. Sportsman's Park was filled with obnoxious shouts. The faithful were riled over Gleason's obvious impartiality and the gathering gloom of evening. Few could figure how the umpire could see the ball. The resourceful McCarthy took full advantage by walking, swiping two bases, and scoring when catcher Hurley had trouble locating a McGill pitch.

By the ninth inning, the baseball assumed the mannerisms of a ghostlike sphere, the Browns couldn't see it, the Reds couldn't see it. The fans couldn't see it and yelled themselves hoarse about it. Neither could umpire Gleason. The Reds failed to score in the ninth. In the home half, Kelly ordered his players to stall, hoping to get the game called a tie. McGill fidgeted on the mound. He wiped his brow, stretched his arms, and kicked at the dirt. Umpire Gleason sensed he was being had. In one last dig at Kelly, Gleason threw up his hands and called the game forfeited to St. Louis. The final was 9–0. The Browns had made only three hits off McGill against fourteen for the Reds.

Von der Ahe, sitting in his private box, was also incensed over Gleason's decision. He protested to the American Association that the Browns would win games on their own merits.

The next day, Sunday, a huge throng of nearly 15,000 enthusiasts showed to witness another Reds versus Browns spectacle. The boys of St. Louis won handily, prompting talk of another pennant. The enthusiasm extended to the sandlots, where St. Louis youths gleefully played ball in record numbers.

Despite an overworked pitching staff, St. Louis' excellent play continued into the summer. O'Neill, Lyons, and McCarthy all batted over .300, and the infield was bolstered by the slick gloves of Comiskey, Eagan, and Fuller. In a May game, Hoy made a sensational catch after tracking down a tough liner. On their way back to the bench, the Browns all applauded the little hero. In congratulations, Shorty Fuller touched Hoy's cap. Embarrassed, Hoy's face turned beet red, and he pulled his cap down over his head. The players laughed. Von der Ahe offered this cryptic witticism: "That little man can't hear, but George, can't he see." That same week, pitcher McGill was acquired from the Reds to help Jack Stivetts and Clark Griffith.

The St. Louis Browns stayed in the thick of the race, battling the tough Boston squad. In early July, St. Louis took the pennant lead with a 4–3 victory in Beantown. Von der Ahe, happily viewing from his box, "almost fell out of the grandstand in the exuberance of his joy, and was ready to give each player a lot in the business corner in St. Louis."

Like a saloon.

By week's end, both Jack Boyle and Denny Lyons disappeared for a few days. Rumors flew that the men had jumped to the Pittsburgh National League club after meeting with a certain Mark Baldwin. Lyons and Boyle later admitted to startled teammates that they were in Atlantic City on a drinking spree. Both transgressors expected heavy punishment from Von der Ahe. Inexplicably, at the beginning of August, Von der Ahe released pitcher Clark Griffith. The Browns' pennant competitor, the Boston club, snatched up the right-hander. Days later, Willie McGill quit the club to tend to his recently widowed mother. Von der Ahe sadly consented to McGill's wishes and signed left-hander Ted Breitenstein. A former factory worker, Breitenstein was plucked from the disbanded Grand Rapids club. The Boyle, Lyons, and McGill situations demoralized the Browns. After infielders Eagan and Fuller pulled up lame, the Browns disintegrated, losing game after game in the east.

A young infield hopeful named Jim Wild tried to make the club. On Von der Ahe's advice, Comiskey agreed to test Wild's skills by having him handle a few hot smashes from Tip O'Neill's bat. After O'Neill's grounders bounded off every conceivable part of Wild's body, the rookie agreed to sit down. For his troubles, Wild earned a hot tub bath and fairly begged Comiskey to be let go. The Browns' manager obliged. One year later, Comiskey received an oddly worded letter, full of misspellings and containing references to farm animals. The letter was from Jim Wild, who thanked Comiskey for giving him a chance. Wild was anxious to repay the manager. Amused by the communication, Comiskey replied "send them." After a few days, Comiskey was greeted by a postal worker who presented him with a large crate. Inside was a pig and a sheep, courtesy of Jim Wild. Comiskey may have guffawed, but Von der Ahe probably found the package none too funny. The Browns' owner had no use for pigs and sheep on his ball club.

Von der Ahe then suspended pitching ace Jack Stivetts and Denny Lyons for excessive boozing. Lyons would not play again, his suspension being for the remainder of the season. Willie McGill, absent for two weeks, returned to the club and was promptly fined $50. Thanks to Von der Ahe's meddling, Comiskey no longer had control of the Browns. To replace Eagan, who was also reportedly drinking, Tommy McCarthy was summoned from the outfield.

With the team sliding, the Sportsman's Park faithful stayed away—in droves. The loss of revenue hurt the upkeep of the ball yard, which was rapidly becoming decrepit and decayed, with a dingy clubhouse. A series of baseball exhibitions did little to improve the park's image. In June 1891, a Fat Man's game was played at the park. Two teams of girth met, representing Chicago and St. Louis. Proceeds for the contest were to go to a religious mission called the Fresh Air Fund. Adolphus Busch promptly invited all the men to his brewery with the "promise that they shall not leave this place with any dust in their throats." A month earlier, Sportsman's was the scene of a curious baseball exhibition between clubs composed of armless, legless, and blind men. The papers did not note who won or lost.

By early September, McCarthy and Stivetts had to deny their signing with the Boston National League club. With the season hopelessly unraveled, the suspended Lyons found a Philadelphia barroom to his liking. Lyons wasn't content to drown his sorrows alone; he took Stivetts and McGill with him. Von der Ahe was livid, fining all the men and suspending Stivetts for the remainder of the season. Then Von der Ahe blacklisted Lyons and publicly blamed the out-of-work third baseman for the loss of the pennant. The Browns concluded the campaign with a host of amateurs in their lineup. The Boston Reds, with Dan Brouthers, Hugh Duffy, and Tom Brown, won the pennant by eight games over St. Louis.

Somehow, young Ted Breitenstein, making his first start, tossed an 8–0 no-hitter on the season's final day. Using a drop curve and a rising fastball, "Red" baffled the Louisville club. Breitenstein wasn't even aware of the no-hitter until catcher Boyle congratulated him and the St. Louis players carried him on their shoulders to the clubhouse. The youngster was simply following the advice of manager Comiskey. "Let 'em hit and trust to heaven and the outfield," said Comiskey.

Outfielder Tommy McCarthy added; "Bear down on the first man, kid. Get him away each inning and you won't have to worry."

The myriad suspensions enabled twenty-nine men to wear the St. Louis uniform in 1891, including one game for a washed-up Yank Robinson.

Incredibly, the situation worsened. Von der Ahe bragged that he had signed Cy Young and Arlie Latham for 1892. He released outfielder Dummy Hoy, who had grown to detest Chris, and backup catcher John Munyan. Of Munyan, Von der Ahe said, "He could not catch a string of sausages, nor hit a dead elephant with a club." Bad Bill Eagan became so drunk on the train during a barnstorming tour to Sioux City that he tweaked Von der Ahe on his nose. Eagan asked, "Say, Chris, how much did it cost you to color that?" The stunt cost Eagan his job. At Chris' insistence, the conductor deposited Bad Bill fifty miles west of Chicago in the dead of night. Ted Sullivan, who had spent the summer scouting for the Browns, had supposedly penned a new play entitled *Mr. Von der Grab of St. Louis*. The play parodied a certain local citizen. One by one, the players spoke out against their owner, declaring they would not play in St. Louis again. Comiskey, O'Neill, and McCarthy were the most notable. Von der Ahe blamed Comiskey for the poor showing and for letting his men get out of control. Upon the conclusion of the 1891 season, a full-scale desertion of Von der Ahe's Browns commenced. By the end of the winter, only pitchers Ted Breitenstein and Jack Easton would be signed for the 1892 Browns.

As bad as it was for the St. Louis Browns in 1891, the American Association was teetering on the brink of collapse. In February 1891, following the disintegration of the Player's League, the National League recognized that its only competition was the weakened American Association. The peace was fragile, but holding.

Then came a case that strained relations once again. During the difficult repatriation of players, the National League decided to raise its reserved lists from fourteen to twenty-five men. Two Association men from the 1889 Philadelphia team ended up with National League teams. Louis Bierbauer was a .320 hitting second baseman with Player's League Brooklyn. Bierbauer would eventually sign with Pittsburgh of the National League. Harry Stovey inked his deal with Boston of the National League. The American Association cried foul. As decided earlier, the National Board convened. The stakes of the decision were exceedingly high. A vote against the Association would undermine the entire repatriation process and start the war anew. Incredibly, Association President Alan "White Wings" Thurman cast the deciding vote *against* the Association's best interest. The National Board ruled that Bierbauer and Stovey had not been reserved by their clubs. With Pennsylvania newspapers fanning the flames, the Pittsburgh club became known as the "Pirates." Decimated by the vote, the Association met to fire Thurman and inform National League President Nick Young that they were dropping out of the National Agreement. This move would prove fatal.

In effect, all Association players were then available to the highest bidder. The Association steadfastly believed that baseball owners were gentlemen and that the jumble of players left over from the Brotherhood would return to the Association out of respect. The assumption was false. The Association underestimated the power of the National League and its own lack of fan support. All attempts to divide gate receipts to reduce franchise disparity would eventually fail.

Enter Christian Frederick Wilhelm Von der Ahe.

Waging territorial war with the National League, the Association's directors placed an 1891 team in Cincinnati under player-manager Michael "King" Kelly. In 1890, Kelly played with Boston of the Player's League. Von der Ahe believed Kelly to be a savior. Largely with Von der Ahe's money, the Association lured Kelly into its league and financed a ball ground in Cincinnati known as Pendleton Park. The Association's Cincinnati club was in direct competition with John Brush's National League Cincinnatis.

"Kelly's Killers," as they were ironically known, were a complete disaster. Cincinnati cranks did not patronize Pendleton Park. By August, Von der Ahe turned the club over to Association headquarters, and the team moved to Milwaukee. Trying to better the situation, Von der Ahe authorized Kelly to resign with any Association club and the King promptly signed on with his hometown club, the red-hot Boston Red Stockings. Kelly was there one week. Incredibly, the National League Bostons enticed Kelly with a $25,000 contract. The King packed his catcher's gear and jumped to the Beaneaters. Boston ball fans took Kelly's flip-flop in stride and remained loyal to their native son. Von der Ahe and the Association had other ideas since Kelly's move impacted negatively on Association finances and credibility.

King Kelly didn't let Cincinnati's situation bother him. Realizing his players lacked the talent to compete, Kelly chose to poke fun at Von der Ahe to retain his sanity. The clever Kelly focused on Von der Ahe's personality, his wardrobe, his drinking propensity, and the magnate's pocketbook.

During a trip to New York City, Von der Ahe purchased a Stanley Sash, a trendy flaming-red waistband. Eager to flaunt his new wardrobe, Chris showed up at Pendleton Park one afternoon. When King Kelly noticed Chris' grand entrance, he couldn't believe his eyes. Von der Ahe arrived gussied-up in duck pants, tanned shoes, an "anarchistic necktie," a blue sack coat, and the red sash. Kelly let out a roar and then said, "With that makeup you look like a cross between a barber's pole, a pousse-cafe and the Star Spangled Banner." The comment so embarrassed Von der Ahe that he went back to a local hotel to change his outfit. Like a glutton for punishment, Chris returned to the park, this time wearing something more subdued. Again, Kelly spied Von der Ahe and said, "You're alright now, Chris. That charge of disturbing the peace with your clothes I made against you is dismissed."

On another occasion, Kelly and Frank Bancroft conspired to fool Chris into believing that a nearby event was cutting into his profits. Hosting a gathering of St. Louis dignitaries in Cincinnati, Von der Ahe was perplexed by the lack of patronage. To Bancroft, Von der Ahe lamented, "Vot t'ell is der madder? Ver is der crowd?" Bancroft couldn't resist. After making eye contact with his co-conspirator Kelly, Bancroft replied, "Oh, they've gone to a dogfight about a mile up the road." Infuriated, the Browns owner bellowed, "I vill haf dot guy arrested who is pulling off dogfights near my grounds. Now I know vy ve ain't doing business. I vill haf der legals after dot dogfighting bunch." Immediately, Bancroft and Kelly faked conversations with policemen to have the dog men run out of town. During the process, Bancroft asked Von der Ahe, "Do you want warrants for the dogs, too, Chris?" Still fuming, the Browns' owner barked "Yes, for der whole dem business." Barely able to contain themselves, Bancroft and Kelly finally let Chris in on the secret. There were no dogfights, though the spectacle would certainly have raked in more money than the sad-sack Cincinnati team. To atone for his gullibility, Von der Ahe ordered drinks for everyone in the party.

As rumors flew of the impending Cincinnati move to Milwaukee, Kelly's boys showed up in St. Louis. Unsure of their futures, Cincinnati simply went through the motions, fairly begging the Browns to beat them. St. Louis complied.

Chris Von der Ahe was conspicuous by his absence.

To illustrate his team's tenuous job security and add some levity, King Kelly sauntered onto the field. Hardly dressed for baseball, Kelly wore green socks under his patent leather shoes. In place of his ball cap was a straw hat. Nonetheless, the game commenced. After every at bat, the King exited the park and walked straight over to Von der Ahe's nearby saloon. Perhaps unable to face his second club's extinction, Von der Ahe himself poured libations. To ease Chris' pain, the thoughtful Kelly offered to pick up the tab. The two men talked over better times to drown their sorrows.

The Cincinnati experiment was only one of Von der Ahe's desperate moves to strengthen the American Association. Secretly, he was funneling capital to the Louisville, Indianapolis, and the nascent Milwaukee organizations. The Association's foundering was helped by several players jumping to National League clubs in the middle of the season. The writing was on the wall. Other Association magnates were attempting to cut their losses.

In early August 1891, Von der Ahe and John Brush called a temporary truce and met in Cincinnati to discuss a settlement. Unfortunately, the war raged on. That same month, the Association's Boston club attempted to drop ticket prices to a quarter, in violation of a territorial agreement with the Boston National League club. The effort failed.

As the season closed, both Boston clubs sported pennant winners. The American Association champions were the Boston Reds. The National League Beaneaters, five games behind Chicago's Colts when King Kelly joined them, ripped off eighteen victories in a row to secure the flag. However, there was no championship series, due to the animosity between leagues. Near the end of October, the Association tried one last gambit, admitting a club from Chicago. Except for Von der Ahe, no one really believed in the plan. While courting National League magnates, Von der Ahe was financing a club to compete with Albert Spalding's dollars. The Chicago club proved to be only a baseball team on paper.

Remembering Von der Ahe's oft-repeated comments on the viability of a twelve-team league, the League magnates negotiated to absorb the Association's four strongest franchises. The St. Louis club was among the defectors. On December 7, 1891 the American Association disbanded. In bitter irony, the National Agreement and the reserve clause had strengthened the Association in 1883 and held it together in 1890. In the end, the Association's decision to drop the National Agreement led to its demise.

A week later, in Indianapolis, the victorious National League was joined by St. Louis, Louisville, Washington, and Baltimore. The five failed Association franchises in Boston, Philadelphia, Columbus, Milwaukee, and Chicago were compensated equally for $135,000 after Chicago and Milwaukee threatened legal action if not bought out. The debt would be assumed by all twelve clubs. The new organization would be called The National League and American Association of Professional Baseball Clubs. To maintain fan interest, the League decided on a split schedule pennant chase for 1892.

In a long-winded speech to National League magnates, Von der Ahe spoke of the Association. "But schendelmens, dis veight of responsibility is so heffy dot a strong feller lige Chon L. Sullivan would get round-shoulder lifting it. And I, Chris Won der Ahe, vos der main guy in der Association for ofer 10 years. Vile de Association vus dancing, Won der Ahe was paying der feller dot blays der violin."

For years afterward, Von der Ahe enjoyed bragging about how he forced the League to sue for peace. As part of the agreement, the National League would now allow its teams to play Sunday baseball, sell liquor, and charge a quarter. Cincinnati's John Brush, Brooklyn's Charles Byrne, and Cleveland's Frank DeHaas Robison all visited Chris in Missouri.

"If you fellows want to see me, come to St. Louis," said Von der Ahe.

Once the magnates arrived, Chris sent a telegram to the Southern Hotel. "I'm busy, come out to my saloon at Grand and St. Louis Avenues."

Sadly, Chris Von der Ahe had not learned the lesson of Henry Lucas and the failure of the Union Association. The success of any baseball league depended on capital, leadership, player satisfaction, and necessity. The American Association could not be sustained without these factors. Most importantly, one man could not prop up an entire baseball league.

With the breakup of the Association, the breakup of the St. Louis Browns commenced. Charles Comiskey was reportedly signed by the Cincinnati National League club for $7,500 for each of three years with 20 percent of the net profits. The final Von der Ahe-Comiskey split left Von der Ahe especially bitter. Comiskey's departure stung Von der Ahe, but his exit to Cincinnati wounded Von der Ahe's pride. Von der Ahe had spent the last season battling John Brush for Cincinnati dollars. As Comiskey departed, so did virtually everyone else. At first, Von der Ahe planned on raiding National League rosters, but Eddie Von der Ahe objected, saying League men were too expensive. Von der Ahe was forced to spend his first National League winter securing a brand-new St. Louis team.

With the future in doubt, a series of exhibitions was planned before the 1891 season was over. This tour was to feature two teams known as the "Comiskey Combination." One team was mostly Browns players; the other squad was comprised of Chicago Colts. Starting in St. Louis, baseball exhibitions took place in Memphis, Nashville, St. Paul, Minneapolis, Texas, Denver, Iowa, and San Francisco. Very little about the tour was successful. The Browns' time in Sioux City was especially forgettable. By the time the Browns arrived at their destination, the locals were waiting. St. Louis tried an old trick. To provoke bigger crowds, they let the hometowners win the first game. However, the strategy backfired as Comiskey's boys lost the next four straight. Von der Ahe was so disgusted that he departed Sioux City after the third game. The Chicago squad fared much better. Unlike the Browns, who played in chilly conditions and were lucky to draw 200 a game, the Colts feasted by winning in front of four to five thousand. If this barnstorming tour was any indication, the Browns were no longer showcase material.

A contemporary report told of a rather dubious event. The Browns were scheduled to play an exhibition game in Moberly, Missouri. Nine Browns players were available for the contest, however, one man managed to miss the train. Comiskey faced a dilemma. With only eight players, the $500 guarantee money was in jeopardy. Noticing that his employer was on hand, Comiskey ordered Chris into flannels.

"You know, Charlie, I neffer had a uniform on in my life," said a nervous Von der Ahe.

Thinking fast, Comiskey made up an outlandish fable to coerce Von der Ahe. The half-truth took full advantage of Chris' baseball ignorance. "Put it on and get out in center field. I'll tell the pitcher not to pitch that centerfield ball at all, and you won't have anything to do," said Comiskey.

At first, the home nine didn't quite notice the ruse. With "St. Louis" boldly emblazoned across his chest, Von der Ahe took to practicing earnestly. He seemed to fit right in with the other ballplayers. By the second inning, though, Von der Ahe was beginning to question Comiskey's promise. All sorts of balls were flying out to center field, and Von der Ahe was expected to chase after them.

"Py cott, I qvit," said the exhausted Browns owner.

Later in the game,Von der Ahe actually made a miraculous, excuse-me catch of a ball knocked his way.

"If dey can effort to pay $500 to see me play ball, I can effort to spend id."

That evening, Von der Ahe treated himself and his guests to a marvelous night on the town.

The Later Years

19

Growing Pains Revisited

Chris Von der Ahe's 1892 entry into the National League was not without fanfare. No trumpet calls announced Von der Ahe's arrival for his first National League meeting, however, his rather gregarious clothes made the announcement moot. A contemporary New York paper described:

> *. . . Magnate Von der Aheful's new mackintosh . . . drowns the noise of the Fifth Avenue stages and makes people forget the recent aurora borealis . . . and it fit him much after the style of the late Julius Caesar's cloak. But the St. Louis magnate continues to grow, and he will yet fill out the mackintosh as the stuffing of a balloon fills out the silk bag. This particular mackintosh has a tail about two feet long, and when he swept through the corridors of the Fifth Avenue Hotel, a cloud of sawdust and cigar chips followed in his wake like a mist of glory. The color of the wonderful garment scared most of the street car horses, a sort of cross between a hectic flush and New Jersey clay. But it is most becoming to the St. Louis boss' maroon complexion. I may seem to be wasting much space on this garment, but it was the most striking feature of the late meeting.*

In effect, Von der Ahe's *clothes* preceded his duties. Unfortunately, Chris did not realize that despite his being a League magnate, he was very much an outsider. Al Spalding, John Brush, and Charles Byrne would see to that. The League really wanted the famous St. Louis baseball presence, but some magnates may have silently hoped that Von der Ahe would drink himself to death. Right away, an attempt was made to pacify the German. Von der Ahe was appointed a member of the rules and scheduling committees. Considering that Von der Ahe remained wholly ignorant of baseball rules, the appointment was ironic. The scheduling committee seemed a odd fit, since Von der Ahe had once chided the Association for scheduling too many rain outs in St. Louis. Nonetheless, Von der Ahe earnestly served with his fellow magnates.

Far more important than Von der Ahe's attire was the new National Agreement. To further solidify its position as baseball's premier organization in March 1892, the National League voted to rewrite the document to include a player draft provision. Unlike before, the National League now allowed minor-league teams to reserve players to sell to the highest bidder. The National League persuaded several higher minor leagues to accept their "A" and "B" classification plan in return for player reservations. "A" players could be drafted for $1,000. "B" players were worth $500. Without a union or competing major-league organizations, the low minor leagues were completely frozen out of the new agreement. The new National Agreement also offered a plan to recoup the financial losses of the previous two seasons. The owners reimposed a salary limit of $2,400 per player, initiated a $30,000 salary cap, and limited each team's payroll to a total of thirteen men.

St. Louis fans realized that Von der Ahe's days of lavish spending were over. The buzzword around St. Louis was that Von der Ahe was a cheapskate. He signed player contracts more prudently than ever. Those willing to play for Von der Ahe's compensation could sign on the dotted line. Those who didn't agree would waste their breath negotiating. As in previous years, the elder Von der Ahe sent his son to do his bidding. Hired as treasurer of the Browns, Eddie was touted in the papers as a "very bright boy." Chris had high hopes, grooming Eddie as the heir apparent to the ownership job. The youngster earned his position by studying under George Munson. To all who knew him, Eddie was a spitting image who worshiped his father. After all, Chris Von der Ahe was one of the biggest names in St. Louis. When Herr Von der Ahe wasn't being praised for his ball team, his brownstone flats, his grocery, or being the life of the party, he reveled in escorting politicians and bossing people around. Eddie liked the attention. However, one slight difference existed between Edward Von der Ahe and his father: The younger Von der Ahe knew a financial discrepancy when he saw one.

Before the season began, *The Sporting News* jabbed at Von der Ahe's changing ways. It reported that nine of the twelve League clubs would be wearing dark gray travel uniforms. With this innovation, money could be saved on laundry bills. Teams could travel the entire circuit without washing. For the second half of the campaign, St. Louis donned solid brown uniforms. Von der Ahe staunchly defended his payroll. A few years earlier, Chris had bragged about his club being the highest salaried team in the Association. He would only say now that they weren't the lowest.

Von der Ahe spent his dollars on ballpark renovations, replacing a large section of the grandstand with cushioned seats under the east-west roof. As per National League custom, Von der Ahe raised prices for these seats to fifty cents. Under the north-south wings, ticket prices rose to seventy-five cents. Ladies Day, a popular free attraction, was abolished. Von der Ahe believed that the fairer sex would keep men from the game.

Von der Ahe and his St. Louis Browns endured an encyclopedic Murphy's Law of bad luck in their first few National League campaigns. Nearly everyone who supported Von der Ahe as a winner deserted him when his fortunes turned for the worst. As the Browns began to lose with regularity, Von der Ahe's initial optimism in the League faded fast. His once vibrant personality also went south, turning the once-proud owner of the Browns into a crabby blowhard. The misfortune didn't end with Von der Ahe's team. It extended to his health, his son's health, and his professional and private life.

The play of the National League Browns could be described with the catch-phrase "a little upper Sandusky," a comment used to illustrate a man's character, a woman's looks, or an unpleasant experience. Originating in 1890, it came into use after the Brooklyn Player's League Club traveled to the Ohio town to play an exhibition. Few cranks showed up, and the club realized all of $1.75.

St. Louis fans, realizing the dilution of their product, began to roast managers, players, and Von der Ahe himself. Ball games at Sportsman's Park degenerated into ugly cursing matches. Angry fans could telephone (or bang on the door of) the Sportsman's Park Club and Association office, which was located right in the ballpark.

One of baseball's oldest saws, "You can't tell the players without a scorecard," was useful in describing the 1892 National League entry of the St. Louis Browns. A full-scale desertion had taken place. Players no longer under contract signed with other teams. Von der Ahe's Browns began with only two players from the 1891 squad. Gone were all remnants of winning St. Louis combinations: Captain Comiskey, Jack Stivetts, Jack Boyle, Tommy McCarthy, and Tip O'Neill. Bob Caruthers, late of Brooklyn, was coaxed into returning. Unfortunately, Caruthers appeared long past his prime. These Browns were a whole new cast of characters. Sadly, just before the season was about to begin, right-handed pitcher Darby O'Brien died. O'Brien, recently signed by St. Louis, was all of twenty-four years old. O'Brien's death didn't exactly boost the spirits of the new club.

Von der Ahe also signed a collection of formerly talented players. Ex-Louisville sluggers Pete Browning and Chicken Wolf were to take over outfield duties, but, the two of them lasted for only a handful of games. "Pebbly Jack" Glasscock signed on to play shortstop for the Browns. Only two years removed from back-to-back .330-plus seasons, Von der Ahe considered Glasscock a gem. Glasscock didn't quite appreciate his boss. Jack's unusual nickname was a misnomer. On hot days, he enjoyed picking up blades of grass to suck the juice from them to keep sweat off his hands. In the process of throwing away the grass, ball cranks thought he was groundskeeping pebbles.

With the massive turnover in players and the defection of Comiskey, Von der Ahe faced the daunting task of securing new talent. He fancied himself an excellent judge of ballplayer abilities, although, the facts say otherwise. Desperate for pitchers in 1892, Von der Ahe listened to the overtures of a youngster named Bill Hawke, a "slender youth of rather countrified appearance."

Hawke had simply walked up to the owner at a hotel to secure a trial. Von der Ahe was impressed with the youngster's pitching and his sincerity, especially when Hawke pulled out a handkerchief and out came a handful of hay seed. Unfortunately, Hawke's pitching was as wild as his proverbial name.

Another prospect, a Texas pitcher named Thorp, tried his hand at securing a position. Von der Ahe seemed excited about the youngster's potential for throwing the ball through a plank—when Thorp could find the plank. The youngster's tosses didn't always find the catcher. Von der Ahe kindly paid Mr. Thorp's rail fare back to Texas.

In the waning days of the American Association, Bill Gleason scouted a rather smallish lad from Cedar Rapids to play third base. Von der Ahe came out to Sportsman's Park to watch the tryout. However, after a brief look, Von der Ahe said: "Dot little feller! Take him over to the Fairgrounds track and make a 'hoss yockey' out of him." Gleason was compelled sell the third baseman to the Baltimore club. His name? John Joseph McGraw.

Yet, Von der Ahe remained optimistic, saying, "We have a team of sober men to begin with. Drunkards . . . are an intolerable nuisance to a club. I don't object to a ballplayer drinking an occasional drink between the time he leaves the ball field until the next morning. I do object to his appearing on the ball field . . . in a stupid or groggy condition."

The season began with Von der Ahe challenging his old captain and manager Charles Comiskey in the St. Louis press. "I will put up $500 for charitable purposes, against any Cincinnati man's salary (Comiskey preferred) that the Browns will beat the Reds out in the championship race. The winner to take the money to his own city and distribute it among charitable institutions."

Comiskey replied ". . . I think Von der Ahe is bluffing . . . if he means business, let him post his money with a Cincinnati man and I will cover it. . . . I have no other ideas that we will beat the St. Louis Browns out in a walk."

In the opener, Comiskey's Reds jumped off to a quick start against Von der Ahe's Browns. The Reds' lineup featured Arlie Latham at third and Tip O'Neill in leftfield. All received rousing ovations. The old favorites defeated the new Browns by a football-like score of 14–10. St. Louis shortstop Jack Glasscock was singled out as the goat, fumbling balls all over the diamond.

Opening day served as harbinger. A few days later, on Easter 1892, the first Sunday game in the history of the National League was played at Sportsman's Park. Before 15,000 rabid cranks, the revamped Cincinnatians again met the hometowners. On the mound for Cincinnati was Tony Mullane, who'd caused Von der Ahe so much trouble in 1884. Bob Caruthers pitched for St. Louis. In the second inning, Tip O'Neill batted while Arlie Latham worked the third base coaching line. Arlie bantered with the crowd with his continual chatter. Just like old times. Tip could only manage a weak groundout. Of O'Neill, Latham said to the spectators, "See, I told you he can't stand much applause." Reds' outfielder "Bug" Holliday, a St. Louis native, did relish the applause. His home run propelled Cincinnati to an easy 5–1 win.

If Von der Ahe's April was bad, his May was positively horrendous. He began to painfully realize the limitations of his team. Unable to profit away from St. Louis, Chris' finances started to suffer. He became so embittered over the horse racing issue that he enlisted Al Spalding's help and the two magnates lobbied local politicians for bills to limit the sport. St. Louis fans, unaccustomed to such poor play, stayed away from the ball yard. The St. Louis Jockey Club, an organization of horse racers, had recommended that Von der Ahe reschedule games so as not to interfere with nearby Fairgrounds horse racing! Incredibly, Von der Ahe agreed to the request. As a result, the Browns spent most of the month of May on the road.

The Tommy McCarthy affair symbolized the bitterness of Von der Ahe's players upon St. Louis' transfer into the National League. McCarthy was originally contracted for the 1892 season. His signing included a $300 advance for recruiting St. Louis players in New England. When McCarthy jumped ship and sold his services to the Boston club, it infuriated Von der Ahe, and the Browns' magnate sought revenge. In May 1892, two constables routed McCarthy from his hotel bed in St. Louis. The officials seized McCarthy's watch and chain to satisfy Chris' claim. To add insult to injury, the constables also compelled McCarthy to pay $19.50 in interest. At a Saturday Browns-Boston game, McCarthy spent the afternoon railing at Von der Ahe from his coaching box. More than two years later, Chris was sitting comfortably at Boston's South End Grounds. In the fifth inning, a constable approached the mustachioed magnate. After the police ascertained Von der Ahe's identification, he was escorted to a Boston jailhouse. Von der Ahe could only think of McCarthy and the $300 advance. The Boston owners bailed Chris out of jail.

On May 29, a Sunday exhibition game was played for the widow of Hub Collins, the veteran Brooklyn outfielder who had died of tuberculosis one week earlier. Over 7,000 crammed Eastern Park to witness the somber affair between Brooklyn and a team comprised largely of former St. Louis stars. Comiskey, Latham, O'Neill, Fuller, Foutz, and Caruthers all participated. Over $3,000 was raised for Mrs. Collins, including admission, grandstand money, and scorecard sales.

Chris Von der Ahe wasn't thinking of the widow. Instead, Chris lamented, "If I only had that team, Boston wouldn't be in the lead today. There's no use in talking, the old Browns could play ball. I can't get any such work out of my present nine."

A May 1892 Louisville Courier-Journal report was typical. "As for the play of the great Browns, the least said the better. These once-celebrated warriors seemed stricken with old age and palsy, and juggled the ball in an amateurish way that made the heart of der greatest manager on earth ache."

While the Browns played as if they were amateurs, National League magnates continued their heartless payroll deductions. To pay off debts related to the American Association absorption, the League decided to slice salaries again. In June, nearly every player suffered a significant cut. The St. Louis club was no exception. Von der Ahe chose to invite the men into his office one by one to inform them of the news. Re-signed shortstop Jack Glasscock quipped, "Excuse me, . . . I'm going into Von der Ahe's barber shop to get my salary shaved." When Glasscock departed, he was $500 poorer. Other Browns lost between $200–$400 during their office visits. Needless to say, club morale plummeted. Loss piled upon loss.

After Comiskey's departure, Von der Ahe had little luck hiring managers for the club. To compensate, he appointed himself field boss for the 1892 season. Chris split his duties between the bench and the stands, but by mid-season he had developed a rather odd habit. At both posts, Von der Ahe had taken to wearing field glasses to observe his players better. He'd bark out directions as if he knew what he was doing. Whenever he noticed a problem, he'd bellow and embarrass his charges in his inimitable mixture of German and English.

Two incidents illustrate Chris' lack of understanding of outfield play. Right fielder Frank Genins was fined after having the audacity to simply look up at a ball travelling over the fence. A perturbed Von der Ahe asked Genins why he didn't "spring mit yourself against dot fence and howl and shake your fist as dot ball vent ofer?"

Left fielder Cliff Carroll's problem was more acute. On August 17, Carroll was having a particularly tough time on the diamond, misjudging fly balls and grounders alike. Von der Ahe was busy keeping score and keeping an eye on Carroll from his private box. The batter hit a one-hop liner to Carroll, chest high. The outfielder appeared to stagger forward slightly. The ball was nowhere to be seen. Meanwhile, the batter kept churning around the bases and headed for third. After a few seconds, Carroll recovered the ball, which had miraculously lodged itself in Carroll's shirt pocket. For this unintended gaffe, a furious Von der Ahe fined Carroll $25 for "indifferent play." "How can a man lose a ball in his pocket? Surely, he must have been asleep in the field." Carroll protested the fine and was promptly suspended. He then jumped the team. Carroll had been the most productive hitter on the ball club. Von der Ahe offered to make amends with his unlucky outfielder. The Browns' owner welcomed a Carroll appeal before the club's board of directors or National League President Nick Young. The next year, the suspended fly chaser was traded to Boston for Joe Quinn.

In actuality, several of Von der Ahe's player-captains made the on-field baseball decisions, but not before probably rolling their eyes at Chris' ministrations. A local newspaper sarcastically proclaimed, "Someone is needed who can control the men and at the same time bluff the President of the club." At intervals, Jack Glasscock, Cub Stricker, Jack Crooks, George Gore, and Bob Caruthers managed the Browns—all with little success.

Adding to St. Louis woes was the play of former standout Bobby Caruthers. His pinpoint pitching skills eroded, Caruthers manned outfield for most of the season. Unfortunately, Bobby wanted desperately to play first base. He thought that in time he'd be another Charlie Comiskey. Critics described Caruthers' brief tenure on first base as awkward. For some reason, Caruthers never did learn proper foot placement. He'd put his right foot on the base and his left foot straddling the baseline. This maneuver worked fine until someone hit a ground ball to the infield. Invariably, Caruthers and the base runner managed to tangle and wind up on the ground. More than once, Von der Ahe sniped, "You nefer vus cut out fer a paseman! Ven I vunt a rough and tumble acrobat to blay dot base I'll hire a band of moosick to blay effery time he dose dose falls."

Another Von der Ahe acquisition, pitcher Kid Gleason, spent more time being fined than playing ball. Gleason somehow endured Von der Ahe's ravings to post a successful record. After one such fine, Gleason angrily entered Von der Ahe's office. "Look here, you big, fat Dutch slob. If you don't open that safe and get me the $100 you fined me, I'm going to knock your block off." Von der Ahe had no recourse but to return the money. In early August, Von der Ahe exacted some revenge when he suspended the haughty Gleason for being out of condition.

Perhaps Von der Ahe could have been forgiven for his indiscretions. His mind was clearly elsewhere. Rumors had been circulating that Von der Ahe was considering relinquishing his lease on Sportsman's Park. A family named Dunn owned the property and wanted to try other events at the facility. Because the yard was becoming dilapidated and only one-year leases could be secured, Chris decided to go elsewhere. In July 1892, Von der Ahe met with heirs of the Jesse Lindell estate to negotiate for a tract of land near the St. Louis Fairgrounds. Later that same day, Von der Ahe met with the board of directors of the Sportsman's Park Club and Association. Chris had good news. Chairing a meeting attended by attorneys and his drinking buddies, Von der Ahe was all smiles. A brief discussion ensued on cutting player salaries further. Then came Von der Ahe's announcement. Chris' meeting with the Lindell estate was a success. The smell of pungent cigar smoke filled the air.

Browns' team secretary George Munson informed the press of all the details. Groundbreaking would be in August for a new 14,500 seat Sportsman's Park. Lindell streetcar service would bring cranks right to the door. The new ball yard, financed by the Mississippi Valley Trust Company, would have a 15-year lease and cost $50,000. Architects August Beinke and his partner were just returning from a ballpark tour with all the best ideas. A beaming Chris Von der Ahe would brag that the new Sportsman's would be the finest park in America, with private boxes, a clubhouse, a pavilion, rooftop press boxes, a ladies' powder room, and concession stands galore to satisfy the inner man. A long bar would be located on the ground floor to allow fans to imbibe while viewing the game. Beer and sandwiches would cost a nickel. If that wasn't enough, there would be a fresh-air view of the Fairgrounds from the grandstand. From a distance, cranks could view the horse races and distinguish the colors of the silks. Von der Ahe himself was given a private office at the ball yard complete with bay window and entertainment area for his guests.

The Browns ended their 150 games as winners only 56 times. Due to poor conditioning and inexperience, the Browns played the 1892 campaign in a stupid, groggy condition. Despite this, St. Louis did manage to lead the League in one category; they hit 62 home runs at Sportsman's Park. Unfortunately, the opposition clubbed many more. At the conclusion of the last game of the season, all paused to remember the glories of the old Browns at Sportsman's Park. In typically ostentatious fashion, Von der Ahe helped the crowd recall Gus Solari, the beer gardens, the Four Time Winners, and Welch's $15,000 "slide." Nary a mention was made of one Charles Comiskey. That winter, Von der Ahe quit as manager.

20

A Brand New Sportsman's Park

In January 1893, Von der Ahe did a whoops-a-daisy on his snow-covered steps at his residence. The fall only bruised his shoulder, but some papers reported that Von der Ahe broke his collarbone. Twenty-two-year old Eddie Von der Ahe wasn't so lucky. One month after his father's accident, Eddie was run over and nearly killed by a cable car in St. Louis' West End. A car traveling the opposite direction fractured Eddie's collarbone. Young Von der Ahe also suffered a broken left thigh, facial lacerations, and internal injuries. Taken by carriage to his home on St. Louis Avenue, Eddie spent well over a year bedridden. The recuperation period was slowed by Eddie's delirium tremors. For some time, Chris Von der Ahe neglected his duties to be at his son's side.

At the March League meeting, Von der Ahe served on the rules committee with Brooklyn's Charlie Byrne, Cincinnati's John Brush, and Arthur Soden of Boston. The committee discussed several changes. Flat bats would be outlawed, and foul bunts would be considered strikes. The most important innovation, however, was lengthening the pitching distance to sixty feet six inches.

Representatives of the defunct Eastern League also attended the meeting. The Eastern League pleaded its case concerning its disbandment before the conclusion of the 1892 campaign. With two weeks to play, the minor league folded due to financial reasons. In short order, several League teams secured contracts on Eastern League players. The Eastern League protested, saying that the players were still under the auspices of the reserve rule. When the National League upheld the protest, Browns' management saw the action as suspicious. St. Louis had already signed a total of six men from the Eastern League: catcher Heinie Peitz, pitcher Dad Clarkson, outfielders Tom Dolan and Sandy Griffin, and two other obscurities. All the players were to be returned to their original contracts. None of the stronger old-guard National League teams had signed any of the Eastern League players. All of the four Association-transfer teams had signed Eastern men.

When Von der Ahe learned news of the player shuffle, he said, "The Eastern League has forfeited all right to these players signed by the St. Louis Club. They were not paid their salaries, and the clubs . . . have no more hold on them . . . the League practically ratified our action." Thanks to Von der Ahe's furious politicking, Peitz, Dolan, Griffin, and Clarkson did end up playing for the Browns in 1893. The National League may have felt sorry for the Browns and upheld the transactions.

For 1893, Chris hired Bill Watkins, who had guided Detroit over St. Louis in the 1887 World Series. Watkins' record was spotty, but Von der Ahe figured Watkins' value was in his connection to the defunct Eastern League. The veteran Watkins had managed Rochester in the minor league.

Watkins was determined to field a competitive squad. Given complete control to scout, secure, and train his men, Watkins took his charges to Hot Springs, Arkansas. He whipped them into shape with handball games and galvanic battery treatments for sore arms. Watkins had the Browns practice their running skills by tearing around the base paths. Swift Tommy Dowd made the circuit in 13.5 seconds. Unfortunately, most of the men preferred to practice at local watering holes. Catcher Dick Buckley took his training a bit too seriously. As a roommate of Joe Quinn during spring warmups, Buckley kept Quinn awake by exercising with dumbbells at one o'clock in the morning. After Quinn lashed into Buckley, the two men went back to sleep. However, Buckley woke up again and drove Quinn nuts by tossing baseballs against a chimney. While the perturbed Quinn complained to manager Watkins, Buckley had a big laugh.

The Sporting News, unaccustomed to a losing team in St. Louis, exercised every opportunity to write negative, poison-pen barbs about the Browns. Charles Spink's paper reported on an 1886 diamond medal that surfaced in a St. Louis pawnshop. *The Sporting News* waxed nostalgic about the glorious St. Louis teams of the 1880s. "Where are they now" was a popular feature. Spink's writers also reminisced about Charlie Comiskey's "vocal line drives" of coaching exhortation. Comiskey was famous for barking out phrases such as "Good boy, Robby," "Line 'er out, Tip," and "Now Lath." To compensate for the disastrous local ball team and build circulation, *The Sporting News* conducted a rather farcical "Most Popular Player in America" contest. The results were published weekly. Naturally, all the winners were St. Louis Browns. Joe Quinn finished first, Charlie Frank second, and Ted Breitenstein came in third.

In addition to baseball, Von der Ahe set his mind on local politics. *The Sporting News* reported in April that Chris won $1,700 betting on the St. Louis mayoral race. Despite the fact that Von der Ahe was a Democrat, he placed his faith in a Republican.

In mid-April, the struggling Southern League disbanded. Immediately, the Browns signed outfielders Charlie Frank, Bill Goodenough, and shortstop Bones Ely. Though these transactions were cause for celebration, they should have served as warnings to Von der Ahe and Watkins. St. Louis was fielding a club based on the misfortunes of dying minor leagues with money from political wagering. These players made Von der Ahe quite happy. He would only have to pay them a minimum amount to play ball.

The season opened in grand fashion with the usual downtown parade. On April 27, 1893, the paraders marched to new Sportsman's Park led by four of Adolphus Busch's black Arabian prancers. Mr. Busch himself handled the reins. Wrote the *Post-Dispatch,* Busch ". . . likes a game of base ball as much as other people like his beer." Invitations were passed to politicians of St. Louis and Louisville, businessman, and leading lights of St. Louis. Missouri's lieutenant governor gave a grand speech. Then, in ostentation only Von der Ahe could contrive, St. Louis newspapers and *The Sporting News* were buried under home plate. To help drum up interest, *The Sporting News* presented readers with a color lithograph of the spanking new yard. The picture showed the grandstand, bleachers, and diamond—all ringed by a bicycle track. Naturally, the park was filled with humanity. Every nook and cranny was occupied by springtime cranks. A large number settled into the under-the-grandstand drinking area. Some fans risked standing on the fence and scoreboard top. Others stood on housetops or climbed telephone poles. They all wanted to be there for the revival of winning baseball in St. Louis.

Not so fast.

Despite the optimism of a new ball park and Watkins' work in signing new men, the club floundered again. The season began promisingly, but degenerated into little more than a shuffling of inept ballplayers, injuries, and excessive boozing. Jack Clarkson was suspended for refusing to pitch. Left-hander Ted Breitenstein jumped the club in Chicago after hoisting a few beers. In one game, first baseman Perry Werden's pants were uncomfortable. Needing to take off his belt to readjust his shirt, Perry called time out. When play resumed, Werden's belt was off. Naturally, a ball was hit near the big first baseman. He chased it, but looked a little silly using both hands to hold up his sagging pants. Luckily, second baseman Joe Quinn made the play unassisted. Occasionally, Sportsman's Park crowds swelled to see the Browns. Huge throngs showed to see the Bostons, Anson's White Stockings, and ex-Browns players Dave Foutz of Brooklyn and Charlie Comiskey, Silver King, and Arlie Latham of the Reds. Mostly though, the faithful were few, and dwindling.

Believing he could make money with other events, Von der Ahe scheduled a bicycle tournament at Sportsman's in July. While horses were churning up turf at the Fairgrounds, bicyclists were churning up cinder and dust at Sportsman's Park. The dust hardly helped field conditions for players or patrons. By now, Von der Ahe's players were disgusted with Chris and his methods. To appease them, Von der Ahe promised his men receipts from an upcoming Civil War reenactment called "The Bombardment of Fort Sumter."

The amount could have reached $2,500. To collect, St. Louis had to win twenty of their next forty games. Instead of playing harder, the Browns embarked on a long losing skein. Meanwhile, Chris boasted to secretary George Munson that he'd be selecting 200 girls for the Sumter show. All Sumter really accomplished was the further destruction of the ball grounds. Numerous animals traipsed around the field. Spent firework casings littered the diamond, provoking an outcry among players and the sporting public. Outfielders weren't quite sure what they could trip over next in pursuit of fly balls. Routine plays turned into adventures, even for scorekeepers. Von der Ahe charged Herman Fenske with the unenviable task of ground maintenance. At night, Fenske ran Von der Ahe's saloon. With every complaint, Von der Ahe offered more promises that he was going to redecorate the grounds. Regular patrons became quite weary of Von der Ahe. The Sumter show, like nearly all the others, was a financial flop.

Von der Ahe may have been proud of the new Sportsman's Park, but his building contractors were hopping mad. A round of lawsuits arose as a result of Von der Ahe's nonpayment of hardware supplies. Lithographs and costumes also went unpaid, prompting legal action. Two other lawsuits involved failed ballpark events. The Men's Business Gymnasium gave boxing and club-swinging exhibitions for a week in August. They later sought payment in the courts after Von der Ahe refused their wages. Von der Ahe may have been upset because few patrons showed to watch this spectacle. More disastrous was the Pinkston debacle. Hired to perform "military and pyrotechnic exhibitions" to celebrate the fourth of July, the ragtag outfit failed to deliver. Perhaps the fireworks fizzled or the military marchers were out of step. At any rate, Von der Ahe and Pinkston endured a series of legal entanglements over the venture.

In the middle of the summer, Von der Ahe traded shortstop Jack Glasscock to Pittsburgh for Frank Shugart. The transaction stunned St. Louis players and fans, who realized Glasscock was one of the few bright spots on the team.

Incredibly, St. Louis still managed to play winning ball through July. Then they lost four straight to Cleveland and a 25–2 disaster in Pittsburgh. In the Pittsburgh game, infielder Jimmy Bannon and Frank Pears endeavored to pitch. Bannon's reward was a one-way ticket off the club. Sickened by this mess, Joe Quinn tried twice to resign his captaincy. Von der Ahe rejected Quinn's resignation. Two weeks later, the club was caught in a cyclone and nearly swept out to sea while taking a ferry from Washington to New York.

With losing, player frustrations mounted. During one home stand, the club blamed its poor showing on novice umpire Joe Hornung. According to St. Louis, Hornung made bad decisions, talked back to disagreeable fans, fined players willy-nilly, and had a terrible time understanding the fundamentals of the strike zone. Balls thrown over St. Louis batter's heads or in the dirt could be called strikes. A local paper quipped that Hornung "knows as much about umpiring as a pig does about grand opera."

Ted Breitenstein was one of the few players on the club worth watching. Teaming with catcher Heinie Peitz, he formed the famous "Pretzel Battery," a nickname acquired in the Golden Lion Saloon, the Browns' watering hole of choice. As Breitenstein, Peitz, and first baseman Perry Werden were sitting down to a table full of pretzels, a fan spied them and alerted other patrons to their presence. Ted's season was just as salty. The stellar left-hander became involved in twenty one-run decisions, winning eight. For Breit's fine efforts, Von der Ahe's compensation was only $1,800, one of the lowest salaries in the league for a talented pitcher. After an August argument with teammates, Breitenstein refused to board the train. Threatening to quit the game and open a saloon, Breitenstein stayed away from the club for four days. When he rejoined the club in Cincinnati, he pitched both games of a doubleheader.

Upon the conclusion of the season, the Browns simply went home after failing to make arrangements for exhibition matches. At the end, Von der Ahe was extremely disappointed. Watkins blamed injuries for the poor showing. The real reason for St. Louis' failure, however, was probably Von der Ahe. His bicycle tournament and Civil War reenactment distanced him from his players. Adding to the misery was the trade of Jack Glasscock. With this alienation, his players took to boozing. Von der Ahe admitted after the season that he paid his players with IOUs.

To counteract baseball's problem with drinkers, League magnates John Brush and Frank DeHaas Robison proposed new legislation in the winter of 1893. Stiff fines of $100, $250, and suspension were suggested. Players participating in the saloon business would be banned from the sport. The Brush-Robison proposal was never ratified. So pervasive was drinking that fines, suspensions, and bans would soon deplete nearly all baseball talent.

In St. Louis, off-season scuttlebutt centered on the formation of a new Western League. Von der Ahe was rumored to be involved along with his old manager Charlie Comiskey. There was speculation that the new league would be a perfect breeding ground for St. Louis players. The Browns surely needed better men. When Comiskey visited St. Louis in late October, rumors started to fly again. Old Sportsman's Park was vacant, with a "For Sale" sign. Comiskey would go against Von der Ahe head-to-head, wrote the pundits. However, all the rumors soon dissolved. Von der Ahe joked with reporters that his Western League St. Louis Whites (1888) were a $8,000 mistake.

With his profits shrinking, Von der Ahe spoke out in favor of the split season. "With all the clubs starting out again . . . on an equal footing, interest is revived and why should not the tailenders take heart and make one more effort? It certainly gives clubs that started out handicapped by players who were injured . . . a chance to show what they can do when in proper condition. It must be remembered that many a club has not started into play winning ball until the hot weather months rolled around."

21

Chris' "Drupples"

The 1894 season was no better. Von der Ahe endured a series of events that conspired to keep his team and himself reeling. His crumbling private life greatly affected his one-time sunny personality. This string of misfortune rubbed off on the Browns. At first, Von der Ahe vowed to manage St. Louis again, commenting, "I am determined to put a stop to a good many abuses which were costly to the St. Louis club last year. Players don't have the respect for Watkins, Comiskey or any of my managers which they have for me. They know I mean business, when I take my seat on the bench, and they are careful to play ball for all they are worth."

The bluffing Von der Ahe quickly realized he didn't possess managerial skills. Von der Ahe then set his sights on big-name personalities to guide his Browns. King Kelly rejected Von der Ahe's overtures in October 1893, still upset over the 1891 falling out with the Boss President. A few months later, the venerable Harry Wright was to meet with Von der Ahe for the St. Louis job. Wright certainly possessed managerial experience; he spent eighteen years in the majors and was a member of baseball's first professional team, the 1869 Cincinnati Red Stockings. However, at the National League meeting, other magnates trumped Von der Ahe by nominating Wright as chief of umpires. While the National League owners toasted Wright's new job, Von der Ahe fumed.

Without Kelly or Wright in tow, Von der Ahe settled on a hard-hitting, heavy-drinking outfielder named George Miller. Sporting a variety of nicknames like "Foghorn," "Doggie," and "Calliope," Miller was hired to manage without a lick of major-league experience. As with Watkins, Comiskey, and others, Von der Ahe promised Miller full control of the club. Miller promised Von der Ahe he'd swear off liquid intoxicants. Neither man was true to his word. Chris interfered, and field skipper Miller drank to excess.

Spring training wasn't good, either. Due to late signings and scant money in the treasury, the Browns practiced in St. Louis. Other National League clubs traveled south to take advantage of the warmer weather.

Even Von der Ahe's attempts to create good will backfired. Trying to endear himself to his ballplayers, Von der Ahe ordered a new suit of clothes for each man prior to the 1894 campaign. Not coincidentally, the new threads were identical to the attire worn by Von der Ahe. Shortly thereafter, many Browns frequented St. Louis' finest watering holes. To catch his boozers in the act, Von der Ahe hired a cadre of detectives to go undercover in the saloons. One detective caught up with three transgressors. Summoned to their employer's office, the players were informed by Von der Ahe of a $25 penalty.

"Boss, all you're trying to do is soak us enough in fines to get back what you spent on these suits."

The Browns' president blew his stack. Then he carefully thought over the player's comment, forgave the men, told them to behave, waived the fines, and sent them on their way.

St. Louis jumped out of the gate early. They shellacked the Pirates 11–3 on opening day at Sportsman's behind Ted Breitenstein. Deep into May, St. Louis featured a hot team with hot bats. However, as the weather warmed, St. Louis plummeted in the standings. Manager George Miller accused his old Pirate teammates of deliberately trying to spike him in late May. Browns' pitchers were belted all over National League ball yards. Von der Ahe publicly accused umpire John Gaffney of being drunk on the field. The portly magnate habitually dressed down his men for their poor play and after-hours imbibing. Releases and fines were commonplace. The *St. Louis Post-Dispatch* intimated that "thousands of dollars" were recovered in fines to recoup monetary losses, which reportedly reached $15,000 in the season's first six weeks. Outraged and forced to defend himself, Von der Ahe explained that manager George Miller had imposed all fines. "If a player is drunk or disobedient, he should be fined . . . this is but just and proper. During 1893, the fines amounted to $425, in 1892 $110, making an average of $260 per year for the last three years. If this is robbing the 'poor ball-player,' we must plead guilty."

The Sportsman's Park crowds continued to dwindle. Most patrons seemed content to quaff a few beers between sputtering over the Browns' indifferent play. When baseball wasn't the main course on the menu, a benefit was held to help the widow of baseball editor Ben Armstrong. An all-day athletic tournament was staged, featuring wrestling, boxing, track and field, bicycling, greyhound races, and a ball game.

A May 10 loss in Cincinnati illustrates the Browns' strong batting and pathetic pitching. Chris Von der Ahe and the Reds' John Brush attended the affair. Tom Parrott pitched for Cincinnati, and Pink Hawley twirled for St. Louis. As the Browns jumped out to the early lead, Von der Ahe grinned, happy as a clam. John Brush seemed none too pleased. The Browns battered Parrott for six home runs. Shortstop Frank Shugart blasted three. Catcher Heinie Peitz socked two, and outfielder Doggie Miller smoked another. The hometown rout embarrassed Brush. Then, suddenly, the Reds piled up eleven runs in the fifth inning, without the benefit of a homer. The Browns' Pink Hawley pitched like a rank amateur. With each Cincinnati hit and crowd response, Von der Ahe's face contorted, until it resembled "a ripe pear about to explode." The Reds won the game easily 18–9.

Right-hander Kid Gleason was sold early in the season to Baltimore for $2,400. Away from the meddling Von der Ahe, Gleason helped pitch the Orioles to the pennant.

Left-hander Ted Breitenstein spent his campaign terribly overworked. His pitching statistics fell off markedly. Breitenstein calmly took his turns in the rotation, fighting off control problems. By September, he must have believed his arm would literally fall off. In the first eight days of that month, Ted worked thirty-four innings. On September 9, he miraculously pitched a complete game in the opener of a doubleheader. In the second affair, Browns' hurler Dad Clarkson was knocked out of the box early. Von der Ahe called on his star southpaw to pitch the rest of the game. Breitenstein refused, citing exhaustion. The Boss President then embarrassed Breitenstein in front of the home faithful by fining him $100 and suspending him indefinitely.

Al Spink's love for theater and horse racing blossomed in 1894. Spink wrote a play called *The Derby Winner* that debuted in St. Louis and featured a live horse on a treadmill finale. Critics described the work as a racetrack farce melodrama. If anything, *The Derby Winner* was ambitious, requiring a production and acting cast of 100. Although the project played to appreciative audiences in St. Louis, it resoundingly flopped on the road. Al Spink departed *The Sporting News* to oversee the daily operations of his play. In his stead, his brother Charles took over full operation of the weekly. Despite incurring losses in Chicago, New York, and Washington, D.C., among others, Spink doggedly pressed on. He financed the play with money from his own pocket. *The Derby Winner* might as well have been an old mule racing in the Kentucky Derby. Al was eventually forced to quit. The play cost Spink and his beleaguered backers $40,000.

The Derby Winner also affected the management of the Browns. In July, Al Spink hired away the energetic St. Louis secretary George Munson to act as advance man. To replace Munson, Von der Ahe briefly appointed himself to the post.

Strangely, Munson's permanent replacement was Harry B. Martin, a cartoonist from New York City. Harry's new job was to act as the Browns' secretary and official scorer at Sportsman's Park. Martin and Von der Ahe feuded from the start. Martin believed in emphasizing St. Louis players over Von der Ahe. The St. Louis magnate, in perpetual hot water with his team, fans, creditors, his wife, his son, and nearly everyone else, didn't find it necessary to keep a low profile.

> *Mardin, you vos a good bress agendt, but Munson vos der best bress agendt. Now you magke der mistake of 'drinkin' dot der beable vish to read about dem bum ball players. Mardin, vot der American beable like to readt is aboudt me, Chris Von der Ahe. Now, Mardin, cut oudt dot bunk about dem*

sheepscrew ball players and give der bublick dots of goodt stuff aboudt vot I, Chris, am goin' to do. Dot's vot magkes circulation for der newsbabers und money for dis glub.

On another occasion, Harry Martin was working as official scorer at Sportsman's Park. Manager Calliope Miller was having a particularly tough time with Philadelphia. In one inning, the Phillies scored eight times, with four of the runs unearned, resulting from a Miller throwing error. Miller had an excuse; he seemed rather hungover from the previous evening's merriment. Thanks to the Browns' pathetic play, Martin's scorecard resembled hieroglyphs. Seeing this, Von der Ahe demanded to see Martin in the press box.

"Why didn't you go down there and kick the manager out of the game? Should I do everything around here? Is it up to me to manage those lousy low-lifers?"

Flabbergasted, Martin sheepishly said, "But I am only the official scorer, Mr. Von der Ahe. I am no manager."

"Well then, from now on you are the manager too. You go down and tell that Calliope feller (sic), that good-for-nothing bum to get the hell out of my park and you sit on the bench and tell 'em what to do."

Following instructions, Martin walked down to the players' bench and took a seat. The relieved Miller seemed all too happy to relinquish his position. Martin watched helplessly as more Philadelphia runs crossed the plate. The next day, both men returned to their regular jobs.

During 1894, after he had tired of his shortstop, Von der Ahe ordered Martin to draft a letter trading Frank Shugart to Louisville for outfielder Tom Brown. Puzzled by the request, Harry Martin drafted a telegram for the Louisville owner. After reading the text, Von der Ahe became furious because of the telegram's "plain language." The deal was off. Perhaps, Chris expected the more formal prose of his ex-secretary George Munson. Martin eventually drafted another letter. Shugart departed St. Louis, and Brown came to the Mound City.

Al Spink's return to *The Sporting News* was lukewarm, at best. Brother Charles didn't think much of *The Derby Winner*, anyway. A public fissure occurred between two of St. Louis' leading citizens. With Al on the road, Charles radically altered the concept of the magazine. In response to his dislike of the play, Charles deleted horse racing, theatrical, and boxing news. Henceforward, the magazine would concentrate exclusively on baseball. Charles also dropped patent-medicine advertisements, believing they welcomed readers with lower social class. These changes did not help. Circulation fell off dramatically.

Al moved to Chicago and soon left his brother and the magazine altogether. Charles Spink had Al working in a new subordinate role. To try to recover his pride, Al tried (and failed) to sue his brother to retain his financial interest in the paper.

To boost readership, Charles hired Alonzo Joseph Flanner, a law apprentice and former sports editor of the *St. Louis Post-Dispatch.* Flanner had signed on to *The Sporting News* in the early 1890s, but by 1895, after Al's departure, Flanner took Al's job. Charles Spink and Joe Flanner formulated a plan of action. Figuring that negative articles on Von der Ahe would attract readers, *The Sporting News* "attacked the interest." With his losing ball club, questionable business practices, sordid finances, and crumbling private life, Von der Ahe was an easy target. These anti-Von der Ahe editorials prompted Von der Ahe's comments that his team should be patronized as a "St. Louis institution." The magazine went to great lengths to uncover Von der Ahe's indiscretions. To further upset Von der Ahe, Flanner campaigned against liquor sold at the ball yard.

When the smoke cleared, the Browns found themselves buried in ninth place.

Several other 1894 events typified Von der Ahe's growing torment. In the fall, Von der Ahe purchased Buck Taylor's Wild West Show. The show was a roundup of entertainment, featuring forty cowboys and cowgirls and fifty Indians. The Indians, who were full-blooded Sioux, were each rented from the United States government for $12 a month. But cowboys and Indians weren't the only entertainers involved. George Miller, Von der Ahe's manager and star batsman, also starred in the extravaganza as payment for debts due Von der Ahe. If Miller could shoot blanks from a Winchester at stagecoach-robbing Indians, Miller and Von der Ahe would be even steven. Miller "killed" off a few Indians and erased the debt. The shows, like the Browns, were not a financial success. George Miller wasn't exactly Buffalo Bill, and neither Chief Sitting Bull nor Annie Oakley were on hand to draw crowds. After the performance, there was more bad news. As Von der Ahe vacationed at Hot Springs, a lawsuit was being readied by Clemens Whirlwind, seeking $292.50 for nonpayment to American Indians in the program. Local newspapers poked fun at the legal maneuver and gave the Indians racial slur names such as Old Man Afraid of His Mother in Law and Old Woman with Only One Sock. As *The Sporting News* reported, the reluctant justice wouldn't be available to try the case because he was busy getting a haircut.

On October 18, 1894, a secret meeting was held in Philadelphia to form a new baseball league. Thinking that the twelve-club National League needed healthy competition, the new American Association of Baseball Clubs was proposed. Among the speculators were *Sporting Life* editor Francis Richter, Al Buckenberger, and Fred Pfeffer. Buckenberger had managed the Pittsburgh club in 1894. Second baseman Pfeffer played for Louisville. Applicant cities included Pittsburgh, Chicago, Milwaukee, New York, Brooklyn, Philadelphia, Washington, and St. Louis.

The secret and the Association were short-lived.

The venture survived barely long enough to rile Chris Von der Ahe. Old managers Charles Comiskey and Ned Cuthbert upset the Boss President. Comiskey, rumored to be in charge of a new St. Louis team, stated that the town could easily support *three* baseball teams. The *St. Louis Chronicle* reported that Ned Cuthbert would manage the St. Louis club. Cuthbert proclaimed the new club would rent out the vacant old Sportsman's Park and intimated that three unnamed Browns would defect to the new Association.

The American Association platform stated it wasn't interested in fighting the National League. There would be quarter baseball and Sunday games, but no scheduling conflicts. The new Association was intent on honoring all valid contracts of National League players. However, the old guard didn't buy the plan. The National League made it clear that contracts and territory would be upheld "at any cost." The League threatened "suspension for life" for "treachery" when the names Buckenberger and Pfeffer surfaced in the newspapers. Both were suspended. Richter called the suspensions a "bluff," but the new American Association, in effect, ceased to exist then and there. In December, at a hearing to clear their names, Buckenberger signed an affidavit denying any involvement and was reinstated.

The Pfeffer case was more complicated. Instead of appearing in person, Pfeffer forwarded written arguments to the hearing. The words didn't impress League officials, and Pfeffer was blacklisted. Shortly afterward, Pfeffer signed on to coach the baseball team at Princeton University. So popular was Pfeffer in Louisville that 10,000 fans signed a petition to boycott Colonels games for 1895. With a lawsuit pending, the National League reinstated Pfeffer in February 1895, conditional to his playing only for Louisville, agreeing to the National Agreement, and paying a $500 fine. Pfeffer's friends paid the fine.

There were lessons to be learned from the experience. First, the National League was dead serious after the Player's League. Second, they owned a monopoly on major-league baseball. Finally, the National Agreement and the reserve clause were powerful documents.

The winter League meeting of 1894 showcased Von der Ahe's feud with *The Sporting News*. Five magnates, including Al Spalding, endorsed a plan to sanction that paper as the official league organ. The Spink brothers, however, neglected to tell Von der Ahe of the proposal. When the measure came before the board, Von der Ahe was furious because the Spinks' did not ask his opinion. Von der Ahe argued that *Sporting Life* would serve as a better mouthpiece for the League. In deference to Von der Ahe, the measure failed.

22

"An Affront to the Community"

It would be impossible to imagine a more disastrous family scenario than Von der Ahe's during most of the 1890s. As his baseball fortune crumbled, so did his relations with his wife, Emma, and his son, Eddie. Subsequent encounters with the opposite sex brought Von der Ahe more ruin. The tales of divorce and womanizing became so ridiculous that in 1895 the *Washington Post* printed a scathing attack on Von der Ahe's financial and personal affairs. The article enraged the St. Louis owner, and he instituted legal proceedings for $50,000 in damages against the newspaper. When the *Post* agreed to a public retraction, Chris dropped the lawsuit. Yet, all the trouble—or "drupples" as he called them—seemed to emanate from Von der Ahe. *The Sporting News* wrote that Chris was his own worst enemy. The paper started referring to the Browns as "Coochie Coochies," doubtless after one of Von der Ahe's pet names for his girlfriends. Even worse was the comment that Von der Ahe's private affairs were "an affront to the community."

The Cincinnati ball grounds were the scene of a unique wedding in September 1893. The park was packed with guests, and there were gifts from the players. After a promenade in a horse-drawn carriage, the beaming bride and handsome groom made their vows in baseball uniforms at home plate. One mischievous fan tossed a doll at the wedding party. The groom grinned while tucking the "baby" under his arm. The bride jerked the doll away, tossed it aside, and broke its neck. This prompted laughter from the crowd. This baseball wedding symbolized Chris Von der Ahe's marriage to Emma. She knew that Chris was really married to the game. The doll symbolized Chris' son, Eddie.

Chris' troubles with wife Emma and son Eddie had been brewing for years. Emma supported her husband from his days as grocer to his triumphs with the Browns to his declining days in the League. She somehow tolerated her husband's fondness for the ladies and accepted the fact that he was most susceptible to flattery. Chris was often in the company of rather wealthy individuals. When a female remarked about Chris, he took it as an open invitation to flaunt his wealth and sexual proclivity. Von der Ahe had a weakness for women.

During one sordid episode, Von der Ahe was out on the town with a woman other than his wife. Emma Von der Ahe was at home. Near the conclusion of their festivities, the couple decided to take a horse-and-buggy ride. The horse somehow managed to clip clop right to Von der Ahe's house and then suddenly stop. Emma Von der Ahe looked out the window to see her unfaithful husband with another woman. While the couple tried to get the stubborn horse to move, Emma came careening out of the house to whip the two startled passengers.

Chris made light of the affair in a conversation with Charlie Comiskey.

"Do you know, Commie, that the horse that ran away with us must have known the number of my house."

Only eighteen months after his son's near-fatal cable car accident, Von der Ahe sued Eddie for possession of his Grand Avenue property. The well-publicized disagreement developed over money. Sometime in 1894, the elder Von der Ahe borrowed $11,000 from Eddie to use in an unnamed business venture. Eddie Von der Ahe wanted security for the loan, so Chris Von der Ahe gave his son title to six stone-front houses on St. Louis Avenue. One of the properties was Von der Ahe's own residence. The titles were conveyed without record. Von der Ahe did not want to damage his credit and wanted to be able to recover the properties at a later date. Unfortunately, Eddie Von der Ahe had mortgaged some of the property to James Noonan without telling his father. Upon learning of his son's indiscretion, Chris Von der Ahe was furious. He immediately fired Eddie as Browns' treasurer and brought a lawsuit against his son and Noonan in August 1894. In the suit, Von der Ahe admitted his indebtedness and asked the court to allow him to pay off the loan for the restoration of the titles. Von der Ahe also asked that his son be compelled to give an accounting of his business with Noonan. Emma Von der Ahe sided with her son. She convinced Eddie to settle the matter by deeding back all the property to his father in exchange for the $11,000 loan. However, the dispute dragged on when the elder Von der Ahe could not uphold two considerations of the settlement: to drop the lawsuit and allow his son to visit his mother. When Eddie, who was living at a hotel, came to call on his mother, he was angrily dismissed by his father and ordered out of the house for good.

In June 1895, the senior Von der Ahe's business venture was revealed. With another German, Von der Ahe opened the Von der Ahe-Reinke grocery. Located next to his saloon on North Grand Avenue, the new establishment featured a most ostentatious opening, similar to Herr Chris' baseball parades. A steady crowd attended, keeping the manager and twenty-five clerks busy all day. On hand was Sportsman's Park bandmaster William Weil, who conducted a twelve-piece orchestra hidden behind a bank of plants in the middle of the store. Clerks passed out souvenir pins to each lady customer. Reinke, an experienced grocer, had probably never seen anything like this. Despite his troubles, Von der Ahe had two of his lady friends at the grocery for the send-off—Della Wells and Kittie Myers. In a short speech, Chris praised his bandmaster and offered him a medal for past services.

The Sporting News criticized the events by commenting crassly that Von der Ahe's relationship with Reinke was built on the transfer of deeds to Chris' mortgaged $11,000 flats on Grand Avenue.

At about this time, Von der Ahe hired a frail, fresh-faced 22-year-old German immigrant girl named Anna Kaiser. Anna, who spoke little English, was hired as Von der Ahe's housemaid. The girl had come with her parents from the old country just four years earlier.

Emma Von der Ahe remained furious with her husband over the legal action against his son. She also condemned her husband for the hiring of Miss Kaiser and Von der Ahe's threatening behavior. On January 19, 1895, the robustly built Emma filed for divorce from Chris Von der Ahe on statutory grounds. Her husband seemed unperturbed, issuing this statement from his office:

> *. . . The allegations are entirely untrue. I have liberally supported my wife and son; she leaving my residence only yesterday; my son up to July last, when he proved recreant, and I very properly, told him to get out. My son has realized through me at least $5000 each year during the past eight years, which constitutes his present fortune. This income he is now deprived of, having made a record at his attempt to retain my property. It appears that this suit is the only weapon he can, through his mother's partiality, wield, hoping thereby to prejudice the community against me personally and damage my business.*

> Von der Ahe's son Eddie responded in kind. *"She would have brought suit long ago if it had not been for me. My father abused my mother and I can prove by over eight persons that he has been guilty of adultery. He told my mother last Monday that if she did not bring suit by Thursday he would bring suit himself. In regard to that property, he conveyed it to me in order to protect himself."*

Two months later, on March 26, Emma Von der Ahe was given a judgment for $3,150. Emma's attorney argued successfully that his client was blameless. The judge granted the divorce. At the hearings, a timid Emma cited Chris' infidelity and brutal treatment, providing names and dates of Von der Ahe's rendezvouses with the fairer sex. Two of the named ladies were Kittie Myers and the flamboyant Della Wells. Mrs. Emma Von der Ahe formally charged her husband with adultery from 1893 to 1895, however, she believed that Von der Ahe had been conducting affairs prior to that time with "numerous and different women in St. Louis and elsewhere." On one occasion,

Emma was embarrassed when a gentleman visited her house to report that Chris was seeing *his* wife. Mrs. Von der Ahe also spoke of Chris' habit of not returning home when in town and calling to say that he'd return from a business trip on a certain date. Mr. Von der Ahe would then arrive two days earlier and spend that time with girlfriends. A superintendent at Sportsman's Park corroborated the assertions concerning Della Wells and Kittie Myers. Other witnesses verified other stories. Meanwhile, Von der Ahe's attorney tried to claim his client's worth at between $20,000 and $30,000. Chris sat by stoically while his worth was revealed to be $50,000. Chris Von der Ahe did not try to disprove Emma's infidelity charges. Von der Ahe's estrangement from Emma included their son, who moved in with his mother. Eddie quickly repudiated his father. The *Philadelphia Record* sniped, "Chris Von der Ahe has been released—by his wife."

In an effort to comfort his soul, Von der Ahe visited his own statue in St. Louis' Bellefontaine Cemetery. It must have seemed rather odd for passersby to see a man contemplating at the site of his own grave. The statue, erected in 1885 when Chris' fame was on the rise, stylized a standing Von der Ahe, king of all he surveyed. Now the granite served only as a reminder of the glory days. Those winning Browns teams of Comiskey and Latham and Foutz and Welch were ancient memories, but Chris could still dream of the raucous throngs at Sportsman's Park and the downtown parades for his "poys."

23

"A Damn Dutch Fool"

The Browns of 1895 further illustrated Von der Ahe's professional struggles. Chris managed to alienate his players, his fans, the National League, and just about everyone else. Fresh off the new American Association scandal, Von der Ahe hired ex-Pirate manager Al Buckenberger to handle the Browns. "Buck" spent long hours writing letters to players, devising new signs, and fixing a training regimen. The outgoing Buckenberger believed in cultivating friendships among his players and practicing with them. The Browns' new man was surrounded by fine talent. Pitcher Ted Breitenstein and catcher Heinie Peitz comprised the famous pretzel battery. Emerson "Pink" Hawley was a highly regarded pitcher. Roger Connor, Joe Quinn, Bones Ely, and Doggie Miller formed the infield from first to third. Tommy Dowd, Duff Cooley, and the recently acquired Tom Brown took over affairs in the outfield. Von der Ahe promised his new manager full reins with the team, but didn't mind that Buckenberger was also president of the Wheeling Club in the Interstate League.

Before the season could begin, turmoil ruled the once-hopeful St. Louis Browns. Tom Brown refused to report and threatened retirement. Others were slow in signing contracts for their summer employment. Heinie Peitz held out for $2,000 and received $1,600 after an angry Von der Ahe intimated that Peitz tried to boss him. Erratic pitcher Dad Clarkson, fighting trade rumors, was offered $200 extra a month if he could abstain from alcohol. A short time later, Von der Ahe traded Pink Hawley for Red Ehret and $3,000 in cash. The Browns' magnate promised that the money surplus would go to securing talent. However, when Von der Ahe showed up at the League meeting in a fancy new suit, St. Louis fans felt betrayed. Von der Ahe had long since become a nonentity in National League affairs with ridiculous proclamations that he was the head of the League.

Von der Ahe then stirred up a hornet's nest in the city, claiming that the Browns were a St. Louis institution and should be patronized accordingly.

When he bragged to reporters about the worth of St. Louis players, his figures were always much higher than he was actually paying them. Pittsburgh manager Connie Mack added insult to injury when he offered a few runs a game as handicap to the Browns. *The Sporting News* intoned that the Browns' owner would use Buckenberger's "reputation as a foil for the stupidity and incapacity of Von der Ahe."

Von der Ahe couldn't even get along with his prospective groundskeeper. After viewing the diveted Sportsman's Park grounds with Von der Ahe, a turf man named Pridie agreed to go to work. The two men discussed reseeding the grass. However, no salary was discussed during the meeting. Later that evening, Pridie asked Herr Von der Ahe what he could expect to be paid. This easily upset Von der Ahe, who told the man that he would have to work a month first without compensation. Disgusted over his treatment, Pridie never worked for Von der Ahe. In effect, Von der Ahe fired Pridie *before* he had even hired him.

On March 12, 1895, the Boss President committed a thoughtless and near murderous act that could have cost him his baseball career or significant prison time. While near Sportsman's Park, Von der Ahe spied a black man across the street. The man was George W. Stevenson. Frustrated over his recent divorce and mounting debt, Von der Ahe assaulted Stevenson. Defenseless and bewildered, Stevenson took a few fists in the face and then several shots at his feet from Von der Ahe's pistol. One of the shots struck Stevenson in the heel. Von der Ahe was arrested for felonious assault; Stevenson filed a $5,000 lawsuit for damages. A judge of the Court of Criminal Correction ruled that Stevenson committed no crime by standing on a public street. The judge ruled that Stevenson was not a willing participant to Von der Ahe's pistol practice. Von der Ahe protested the charge, claiming that Negroes had repeatedly robbed his saloons to carry away cases of alcohol. Chris' own employees, however, called that a trumped-up defense. These character witnesses related that when Von der Ahe's son Eddie was the treasurer of the saloon, cases of liquor were routinely sent to the homes of Von der Ahe's two mistresses. When Eddie took inventory and queried his father about the shortages, Von der Ahe would make bogus charges of robbery. With a $500 bond posted, the case went to the Grand Jury, only this time, the charge was assault with intent to kill. Unfortunately for George Stevenson, the suit was lost because he failed to give security for court costs.

The Stevenson matter further exposed Von der Ahe's unusual financial practices. Eddie Von der Ahe insisted on full accountability during his tenure. Unfortunately, the elder Von der Ahe freely dipped into his own treasury, taking $10, $50, and even $100 from the saloon cash register. Ballpark gate receipts were also fair game for Chris. As a result, bills for the Browns went unpaid.

The Browns' exhibition games, played in the south, were a certified flop. Only the desperate came to witness the St. Louis club. Von der Ahe lost money by the handsful. The Browns lost one game to Atlanta's mercurial German left-hander Crazy Schmit. The left-hander would eventually fail after applying for a position on the Browns. Schmit was a tad odd. He enjoyed keeping a list of opposing batters' weaknesses underneath his cap. The list wasn't too accurate; Schmit's career record in the majors was only 5–17.

As the National League campaign dawned, Von der Ahe promised a brass band to spiel at Sportsman's between innings. According to *The Sporting News,* "The Spherical Sport March" was played on opening day, but it could have been called "The Fallen Magnate" or "Where Am I At?" The fans made it clear that bands were nice, but they wanted winners. As a consequence, the Browns began with a hopeless attitude. It would only get worse. Von der Ahe continued to rant and rave. He publicly humiliated his players and threatened fines for the slightest transgressions. Reading *The Sporting News* was verboten. The Browns played the campaign under a cloud of rumor, most of which involved their imminent departure from the team. Pitcher Ted Breitenstein was particularly affected by a rash of stories that he was to be sold for $5,000, $10,000, or $20,000. "Somebody's dickering mit you," Von der Ahe liked to say to his star left-hander.

With nearly all the Browns realizing they could be traded, sold, or fired, St. Louis' play suffered. Word soon filtered from ex-Browns Latham, Comiskey, and Gleason that playing for Von der Ahe was akin to torture. It would be easier to jump in the Mississippi River than toss baseballs in St. Louis. As the team sank to the depths of the standings, injuries thinned the ranks. Denny Lyons (knee), Doggie Miller (shoulder), and Heinie Peitz (leg) ended up in the hospital. Von der Ahe not only withheld their pay but suspended them when they refused to take the field. The hard-hitting Lyons would later try to play on his busted knee, helping to wreck his career. The St. Louis *Post-Dispatch* produced a cartoon that ridiculed Chris' handling of the situation. Entitled "Von der Ahe's Baseball Exchange," the drawing depicted Chris in an apron, as a sort of baseball grocer.

In May, Von der Ahe tried a Ladies Day at Sportsman's Park. The game was advertised as free for the fairer sex. However, when the ladies arrived they were told that the free seats were in the rock-hard bleachers. Indignant about the experience, many women spouted unladylike invectives about the Browns' owner.

That same month, after George Miller had made four throwing errors in an inning at catcher, he quit his post as Browns' captain. Heinie Peitz accepted a $400 raise to take the job. In late June, the popular Buckenberger resigned when Von der Ahe ordered his manager to suspend players and cut salaries.

"Puck, you fine dot Fred Ely twenty-five tollars." said the Boss President.

"Fine him, for what?" answered back the soon-to-be ex-Browns manager.

"For drying to make a grandstand blay!" exclaimed Von der Ahe.

Second baseman Joe Quinn became Buckenberger's reluctant replacement. If Von der Ahe's players didn't have a predisposition to drink, the owner certainly drove them to drink. In a final defiant act, Buckenberger called his players into Von der Ahe's bar and paid for all the liquor they could swallow. The Browns were disorganized, demoralized, and in a state of near mutiny. Desperate to find a scapegoat, Von der Ahe kept up his threats. Quinn's gentlemanly persuasion barely held the team together. In July, a "spy" reported to Von der Ahe that he had seen Breitenstein take four beers *during* a game. A bartender confirmed the story. When questioned, Breitenstein denied partaking of drink and then admitted that it was only soda water. The loyal Quinn had no choice but to reprimand his star hurler.

Von der Ahe's spy business became a cottage industry. When Von der Ahe promised to pay men to dig up dirt on the Browns, many jumped at the chance. The idea was to follow the players around to keep an eye on their activities. Spies, or "private watchmen" as Chris called them, reported to the owner every morning with information and names. Von der Ahe described the transgressors as those with their "belly up to the bar." However, the informants themselves weren't exactly St. Louis' most upstanding citizens. Often they were men desperate for drink themselves. The spies themselves had a few problems. They would have to be able to invent good stories, watch out that others weren't spying on them, and make sure they could answer Chris' summons. Von der Ahe's outrageous temper allowed him to dismiss informants who had no sordid tales to report. As a result of this rather dubious system, players' wages were garnished in the form of fines for drinking. A swallow of beer was worth $2.00, whiskey $5.00, and those said to be partaking of gin could expect a fine of $50.00! Convinced ballplayers could not perform after a night of lushing. Von der Ahe vowed to field a temperance club. In 1880s and 1890s baseball, with violent games, long train rides, and owners that treated men like slaves, this proved impossible. Never once did Von der Ahe consider closing his own bar to help players avoid the temptation.

Spying on players wasn't the only job for Von der Ahe's private watchmen. In mid-July, one henchman went so far as to search in a man's pants for a foul ball. Standing guard at Sportsman's Park, one overzealous watchman saw a foul ball hit into the grandstand. National League baseballs weren't free, and those fouled off were routinely returned to the field of play. The incident caused quite a ruckus in the stands. The ball was not found.

At about the same time, the Trades and Labor Union began to boycott Von der Ahe for hiring nonunion scabs to work the ballpark. By hiring these employees and paying them a cheaper wage, Von der Ahe reasoned he could save money. Chris simply turned his nose up at the protest.

Meanwhile, the disintegration continued. The Browns played terribly, and few came to watch. Infielder Frank Bonner, acquired from Baltimore for pitcher Dad Clarkson, refused to play for Von der Ahe. Bonner instead would toil for Wilkes-Barre for less money. When Bonner finally did agree to don St. Louis flannels, his skills suffered demonstrably. Bonner was later sold for $500. Long-time veteran first baseman Roger Connor retired. "I am getting old now, and nervous," said Connor. To cut costs, the Browns traveled to Louisville with a total of eleven men. Von der Ahe drove his players mad by his incessant use of binoculars and blowing of a shrill whistle. He upset his managers by dictating pitching changes. On one occasion, a spectator implored Von der Ahe to grab a glove and head out to right field. After a loss by pitcher Breitenstein, a fan quizzed Von der Ahe. "Vell, you see dot bitches vot goes to der vell too often sometimes gets busted once. Don't it?" The spectator could only shake his head. In fact, much conversation attempted with the German magnate resulted in shaking heads. A local paper quipped that Von der Ahe "knows enough English to sell beer and make a fool of himself."

Von der Ahe's foolish behavior would continue. In July, the cash-strapped owner launched one of the game's strangest plans. The scheme offended baseball purists, alienated his depleted fan base, defied the constitution of the National League, and further solidified the St. Louis team as a laughingstock. In his inimitable way, Von der Ahe invited the press for a huffy announcement. The Boss President explained that portions of the Sportsman's Park left and right field bleachers would be altered and grass sod torn up in a circle around the yard. Chris Von der Ahe, saloon owner and baseball rapscallion, was building a horse racing track *inside* his ball park. The reconfigured grounds would contain another bar attachment so that patrons could enjoy a brew and a bet.

The plan was ironic, considering Von der Ahe's previous battles with the horse race crowd. Stiff competition from the nearby Fairgrounds, and the East and Madison race tracks faced Von der Ahe. Sportsman's Park racing could commence almost immediately, but only if the Fairgrounds closed.

Within moments of Von der Ahe's comments, local and national writers punched away at typewriter keys and zipped off telegrams in editorial response. Some saw the announcement as a bluff. Others deplored the gambling element and wrote that Von der Ahe's move was dangerous to baseball's well-being. Most agreed the National League should act to force Von der Ahe from the game. *The Sporting News* reported an unnamed syndicate of men ready to purchase the Browns. In the outcry, nary a man could be found who supported the race track—except Fred Foster.

Fred Foster was Chris' partner in the venture. A veteran racing promoter, Foster duped Von der Ahe into believing that money could be made in a racetrack/ballpark. Considering his credit troubles, it is likely that "money" was the only word that Chris heard and understood. The racetrack deal gave Foster use of the ball yard for $10,000 with two-year concession rights. Foster promised winning purses of $350, which would attract top horses and top-dollar crowds. Naturally, Von der Ahe would figure in the profits. Von der Ahe expected to clear $20,000 a year on the racetrack.

Von der Ahe faced intense criticism for his proposal. Eminent baseball writers Henry Chadwick, Jacob Morse, and O. P. Caylor blasted him. Local St. Louis papers were encouraging citizens to stay away from the track. Opponents cited that horse racing culture promoted riff-raff, shady characters, and increased crime due to gamblers trying to pay off debts to bookies. Baseball had survived dishonest elements in the past. Promoters, magnates, officials, and players had been upholding traditions of honesty and integrity. No backsliding into the mire of fixed games could be tolerated. Leading the list of papers promoting these positions was none other than *The Sporting News*. For those newspapers that depended largely on baseball readership, a scandal in the sport could cripple circulation.

The *St. Louis Republic* started the legal maneuvering when it wired National League President Nicholas Young for his views on the antigambling clause in the League constitution. The constitution stated: "An association club will be subject to expulsion under the following rules: Section 3. For allowing open betting or pool selling upon its grounds, or in any building owned or occupied by it."

The St. Louis Republic wrote, "When the racing commences, there will be betting on the events, and this is expressly prohibited by the constitution of the National League and American Association of Base Ball Clubs. The St. Louis franchise will be in jeopardy the moment the first race of the new track is decided." In retaliation, Von der Ahe tried to revoke the privileges of the *Republic* at the park. All Browns' advertisements were dropped. The *St. Louis Star-Sayings* was skeptical of the *Republic* story and telegrammed Young for a clarification. Young stated, ." . . . the question of opening a race track . . . necessarily would have to be adjusted by the league directors, and their findings submitted to the league, and, in case of expulsion, it would require a unanimous vote. . . . As a league official, I would have no decisive jurisdiction."

Chris Von der Ahe's combination ballpark and racetrack caught Young and the National League totally off guard. The Sportsman's Park turf was already in pathetic condition due to Wild West shows, the Fall of Fort Sumter, and other extravaganzas. Players complained of the divots. Even venerable groundskeeper Gus Solari couldn't landscape at the park any longer. Solari quit after sustaining numerous insults from Von der Ahe. What would Sportsman's be like when race horses trod the grounds? Would ballplayers succumb to gamblers and bookies? Would the park take on the stench of animals and their refuse? While the League pondered these matters, Von der Ahe argued that section 3 only applied to baseball and went full steam ahead with the plan. Von der Ahe never consulted other baseball people for their opinions. The National League now had a definite reason to exorcise Chris Von der Ahe from the sport. However, despite repeated editorial warnings, the League dragged their heels. League moguls planned an August meeting to discuss the track mess, but it was canceled due to scheduling conflicts. Cleveland magnate Frank DeHaas Robison would only remark that the track was a local affair and that Von der Ahe would eventually lose his shirt and shut down. Cincinnati's John Brush, advancing Von der Ahe money to help pay Browns' salaries, offered his paradoxical comments. Brush said there was nothing in the League Constitution to prevent racing provided the track was removed prior to the start of the 1896 baseball season. Brooklyn's Charles Byrne succinctly called Chris a "d__n Dutch fool." When reporters asked why the league had not acted, Byrne related that Von der Ahe had not done anything.

Setbacks dogged the Von der Ahe-Foster race track from the outset. As the workers began to reconfigure Sportsman's Park for the 3/8-mile track, heavy rains turned the grounds to mud, delaying the opening several weeks. Horse promoters at the Fairgrounds, keeping a watchful eye on the conversion, extended their race season into October. Foster and Von der Ahe's idea for fast horses and fast bucks washed away in the quagmire.

Two summer incidents held Von der Ahe up for further ridicule in his own ballpark. During a Sunday visit by the Cincinnati Reds, Von der Ahe was barking to his players from the Browns' bench. When a foul ball was deposited over the stands, umpire Keefe called for a new ball. The Reds' George Hogriever yelled at Von der Ahe within earshot of the grandstand, "Come on Chris, come on with that dollar and a quarter." The crowd roared, knowing Von der Ahe's reputation as a miser. Von der Ahe then attempted to order Keefe to have Hogriever removed. Hogriever sauntered over to Von der Ahe to ask what the trouble was. "Don't let him [Hogriever] talk to me!" bellowed the Browns owner to umpire Keefe. With the crowd fully enjoying this spectacle, Keefe ordered Hogriever to the bench and then ejected *Von der Ahe* from the grounds. The humiliated Boss President raved and flailed his arms for his private watchmen to remove Hogriever and deposit him on Grand Avenue. The Cincinnati players then came to the aid of Hogriever and ran the frightened Von der Ahe off the field.

Another wild incident was precipitated by the Tebeau brothers of St. Louis. Sportsman's Park nearly became the site of a riot in the stands.

The Tebeaus, Pat and George, grew up in a crowded, hardscrabble, working-class Irish neighborhood called Kerry Patch. The men in Kerry Patch earned their living as laborers, dock workers, and street cleaners. While goats and chickens roamed the streets, housewives exchanged gossip. But it was the unbridled violence that earned Kerry Patch its reputation. A contemporary guidebook describe the people's main preoccupation, relating that the "chief amusements consist of punching each other's eyes." All human activity seemed an excuse for fistfights; in fact, police often joined in the fray. Many children of Kerry Patch ran with gangs committed to mayhem. Throwing bricks, knocking hats off passersby, and disrupting street cars were Kerry Patch specialties.

During a contest against the Clevelands, Von der Ahe's greyhound Fly bolted onto the field. The dog's owner chased after the animal. On the field, Chris was met by two Cleveland toughs, Pat Tebeau and fellow Kerry Patcher Jack O'Connor. As the two pushed Von der Ahe off the playing field, Chris screamed to umpire Hank O'Day to "Trow dose men oud." O'Day refused, and the Cleveland roughnecks stayed. Later in the contest, Pat Tebeau took to making faces at the Browns' owner. To retaliate, Chris blew his shrill whistle.

"What's the matter with you now, Chris?" said Tebeau.

"I'm going to have you arrested," yelled Chris.

"Arrest nothing, you big stiff. You better keep still or I'll have to put you off the grounds. It wouldn't take much to make me hit you in the nose anyway," said the Cleveland manager.

By now, the crowd was clearly agitated (or highly amused) at what they were witnessing. St. Louis and Cleveland partisans were about to fight, right in the stands. George Tebeau took it upon himself to grab the throat of one of Chris' watchmen, who had stormed onto the playing surface. O'Day called a halt by telling Von der Ahe he could be removed. Cooler heads prevailed.

St. Louis ball cranks were sickened by these sad affairs. One "fan" sent a threatening letter to Von der Ahe, promising tarring and feathering if the team didn't win seven games on an Eastern road swing. When the Browns captured only five contests, Von der Ahe acted the part of a scared rabbit. He started to practice target shooting as part of his daily regimen. On a June morning, Von der Ahe summoned the injured George Miller and Denny Lyons to the park. The Boss President ordered the men to stand at first and third base, saying, "I shoot at you and you tell me how close I come." When a trembling Chris pulled out his pistol, Miller and Lyons disarmed Von der Ahe. The men intimated to the boss that "further illusions to pistol practice with them as targets, would result fatally to him."

As a replacement for Lyons, Von der Ahe signed J. Ryan to play third base. Ryan lasted two games and two at bats. Walter Kinlock of Denver's Sanden Electrics semipros was to be the Browns' next third baseman. Kinlock was only 17 years old, and his first game would also be his last. In Chicago, Kinlock tried to field a bunt by Bill Lange and ended up on his duff. After a few teeth-rattling hot smashes, one by Lange, young Walter feared for his life. This was big-league baseball. He approached manager Quinn saying he had a girl back in Colorado who "wouldn't look well in black," and asked to be released. Quinn, a off-season mortician, knew all about grieving widows. The Browns' manager agreed that if Kinlock finished the game, he could take the next train back to Denver. Said Kinlock, "It has always been my ambition to play ball in the National League . . . I have played ball . . . and am satisfied that I shall never put on a uniform again. I will go back to my trade of steam fitting. No more or me. Oh, no!" Thus ended the big-league career of Walter Kinlock; three at bats, one hit, two strikeouts, and near heart failure.

Baseball fans following the St. Louis soap opera began to question Herr Von der Ahe's mental health. After all, the Browns magnate was shooting at people, fining players, spying on his own charges with detectives, and hiring and firing managers right and left. Von der Ahe's personal life wasn't much better. The local papers postulated that Von der Ahe had been "lucky" with his championships. Comiskey had been the brains behind St. Louis, making stars of previously unproven mediocrities. The Browns' ex-manager commented that players sold by Von der Ahe in the 1890s could have made the club contenders.

In mid-August, a frustrated Joe Quinn quit as manager. His resignation prompted Von der Ahe to commit another bizarre move. As replacement, Von der Ahe hired saloon keeper and bookie Lou Phelan, a man with absolutely no baseball experience. Phelan's new employment was based solely on nepotism. Chris' lady friend Della Wells, a relative of Phelan, had apparently ordered Von der Ahe to appoint the bartender. Phelan's hiring stunned the local papers. Von der Ahe probably figured Phelan could better keep an eye on his players if he were passing bottles of beer to them from behind a counter. The *Philadelphia Record* wrote of Phelan: "One of his principal qualifications is that he knows less about the National game than Von der Ahe, and that is what Chris wants."

Phelan's contributions to the 1895 season were minimal, at best. Manager Phelan promised to spend his *off-season* learning the fine points of the game! Knowing more about horses than baseball, Phelan presented an incentive salary plan to Von der Ahe for the Browns. The higher the St. Louis team stood in the National League standings at the start of each month, the bigger the bonus. Phelan's idea called for bonuses from first to seventh place. Von der Ahe wasn't exactly warm to the idea, but it didn't matter, because the Browns didn't give the magnate a reason for pennant-race incentives.

With the campaign winding down, Tom Brown, Denny Lyons, and Harry Staley were released. All were ecstatic to escape Herr Von der Ahe's clutches. Then, Von der Ahe went on a September spree. He fined pitcher Kissinger $25 for looking "frightened." He reduced the salary of infielder Ike Samuels. When a crippled Heinie Peitz was told to get in a game and he refused, Von der Ahe and his best catcher exchanged words. Then, Von der Ahe bounced a roustabout, who worked only for beer and a place to sleep under the stands at the park. Before Von der Ahe was finished, he ditched Phelan after six weeks. As replacement, Von der Ahe hired the very best man for the job of managing the St. Louis Browns: a rumpled, meddling, 44-year-old saloon owner named Chris Von der Ahe.

As field boss, Chris Von der Ahe was a disaster. He blew whistles and fixed his gaze on his players with binoculars. Most of his "decisions" were met with no small form of protest. Von der Ahe didn't understand pitching or fielding very well. His entire expertise concerned hitting. While his players batted, Chris yelled out, "Gif it a bost. Gif it a hard bost." Von der Ahe was convinced that scorching grounders were the way to base hits. Having no use for players who hit fly balls, Von der Ahe chided, "Shtop hitting them high fliers. Keep them on the floor! Don't you know them fielders can gatch dose high vuns?" Von der Ahe had a strange ritual. When his players hit the ball in the air, he would gasp and grab his binoculars. Then he'd focus on the opposition fielder and mimic his movements by grabbing his arms and legs. His body would twist like a pretzel while he prayed for a fielder's muff. As the ball settled into the fielder's glove, Von der Ahe often got so excited that he'd topple off the bench. His players had a difficult time containing their laughs.

With Chris "managing" from the bench, the Browns miraculously won the season finale. Overall, though, the 1895 Browns weren't just bad, they were embarrassing. Von der Ahe could take full measure of blame. Perhaps

Chris recalled an old German phrase: "Guilt is a private game, embarrassment requires whole teams." It seemed painfully apparent that Von der Ahe and his Browns were distracted by the imminent opening of the racetrack.

Finally, race day dawned. The ballpark-racetrack configuration was filled with festive flags. Sportsman's contained a flower garden and beer pavilion with red chairs and tables on the right-field side of the park. On the left-field side were bleachers with the horse betting ring in front. Freshly painted white fences lined the outfield. Just a few feet behind the catcher and umpire rested the soft dirt of the race course. The grandstands, painted salmon-pink, were lined with geranium beds. Nearby were water fountains and, to add to the carnival-like atmosphere, a group of stuffed bears! To help pay for the expense, Von der Ahe hired a host of scorecard-peddling boys, soft-drink concessionaires, and beer waiters. On September 30, the Sportsman's Park racetrack opened. The debut was less than auspicious. A young jockey was reportedly killed riding a pony named Little Chris. Newspaper criticism grew louder, again calling for the League to shut down the plan. President Young, however, wavered to inaction, since the races had occurred *after* the scheduled St. Louis home games. League officials claimed they had no jurisdiction over parks in the off-season. The *St. Louis Post-Dispatch* blew the bugle loudest. In a December article entitled "Prostitution of a Ball Park," they wrote

> *Chris Von der Ahe has permitted his base ball park to be turned into the vilest gambling den in the West. Sportsman's Park is now a daily resort of all the rogues of various kinds that the St. Louis police allow to roam at large as long as they "behave themselves." This is a police term which means that the liberty given these gentry is liable to be cut short at any time, if the guardians of the law do not get from their probationists information leading to the capture of the men who do the big criminal jobs.*

Commenting further on the crowds, the *Post-Dispatch* wrote:

> *Von der Ahe's patrons during the base ball season are drawn for the most part from the ranks of the most respectable elements in the city. But if he does not stop this prostitution of his park for the purposes of the thieves and "sure-thing" gamblers, who now have possession of it, the base ball boss can not hope to longer have the patronage of ladies and gentlemen when the base ball season again opens. Respectable people will not go to a resort that several months in the year is given over to the scurvy scum and the flotsam and jetsam of society any more than they will be seen in a place which is part of the year is run as a disreputable house and another part of the year as a cafe.*

Within a week, the racing business changed Chris. He started learning the sights and sounds and used track analogies like "100-to-1 shot" in his speech. Advisors, especially the shrewd Fred Foster, were teaching him about horses and when to listen to tipsters. Von der Ahe quickly bragged he had won $2,000 in one afternoon. The big purse was followed by Von der Ahe's bravado statement that he would buy the Fairgrounds. With both partners flexing their egos, Foster came into Chris' private office one day with an offer. Foster couldn't quite believe Von der Ahe's furious reaction to his proposal to buy one-half interest in the Browns. Von der Ahe's pride and joy were not for sale! He threatened to "trow der race horse gang out of my park."

Von der Ahe wasn't alone in playing the ponies. Early aficionados included Ted Breitenstein and Conrad "Con" Lucid. The latter purchased a broken-down racehorse to go with his broken-down pitching record. Con conned no one with his mound work or his horse sense. St. Louis natives Jack Crooks and Scrappy Bill Joyce also liked to gamble at the track. Both Crooks and Joyce were known for their batting eyes, patiently drawing scores of bases on balls. Would they be able to spot winning horses as well? Crooks, a friend of Foster, cashed eleven of twelve bets on a hot streak. When Crooks tried to tip fellow ballplayers, however, no one took his advice. Perhaps the players believed Crooks had been set up by Foster to bring more business to the track. Ballplayers suffered no moral misgivings about betting on horses. Neither did their boss. Players frequently bet on prize fights, and they could bet on horses. Von der Ahe and partner Fred Foster didn't care who was plunking down money and screaming at the top of their lungs. Business was business. In mid-October, after only weeks of operation, the Von der Ahe-Foster track closed for the season.

Unwilling to learn a lesson on the unpredictability of animals, Von der Ahe sent his Wild West show south for the winter. The resultant incident taxed Von der Ahe's wallet for several hundred unforseen dollars. This time, however, Indians weren't the problem.

In Little Rock, Arkansas, Von der Ahe's showmen unloaded their wagons of people, animals, and gear and then proceeded through town to the grounds. While conferring with local officials, Von der Ahe was informed by a sheriff of a strict town ordinance concerning parades. Getting the show to the grounds would constitute a parade and cost Von der Ahe $300.

Trying to avoid the fee, Von der Ahe said, "Sheriff, how am I to get to the grounds and hotel without being seen? Do you think I'm going to tunnel myself to those places?"

The officials remained adamant about the law, but Von der Ahe quickly hit upon a plan. He ordered his cowboys, scouts, and Indians to unload and then walk to the tent one by one. Two thousand feet would separate each walker, thus avoiding the appearance of a parade. The plan seemed to be working until a few small boys tagged along behind two cowboys escorting a slightly rambunctious steer. The steer, in the rear of the procession, was tamed by the ropes of the cowboys. As a sizable crowd gathered behind the procession, one of the boys became mischievous. To liven up the day, the boy pricked the hind quarters of the steer with a pointed stick. All hell then broke loose.

The steer quickly broke away from the ropes and ran pell-mell down the street. The frightful stampede was on. In the blink of an eye, the crowd scattered like bees. Horses and wagons were thrown by the horns of the steer. Women grabbed children and men grabbed their wives while rushing for the nearest doorways. Vegetable wagons were overturned, with produce littering the street. A milk wagon upset, giving two ladies an unwelcome bath. One lady in a red dress had her clothes stripped off by the steer's horns. She plopped down unceremoniously into the dust, bruised, embarrassed, and in her underwear. Von der Ahe watched the entire spectacle in horror from his hotel window.

"I want three hundred dollars for the parade you made, Mr. Von der Ahe," said the sheriff.

At first the St. Louis owner tried to disagree.

"Makes no difference. The people saw them, and we call that a parade in Arkansas."

Von der Ahe reluctantly paid the parade fee, slapping his money into the hands of the sheriff. Dozens of claimants then converged upon Von der Ahe's hotel room with their stories of woe. The lady who was dressed in red wanted five dollars for her clothes and thirty dollars for her bruises. One townswoman related that the angry steer had stomped on her brood of chickens when it ran into the country. Others claimed numerous damages to their products and bodies.

The Boss President eventually settled the matter with his cowboys and Indians, giving them tickets for their train rides back home. Flabbergasted by the mounting claimants' bills, Von der Ahe asked the sheriff if the steer had finally been captured. When the sheriff replied that the wild animal was under control, Von der Ahe sighed. Chris washed his hands of Wild West shows.

"Thanks be to God. If he had kept running I'd have damages from here to St. Louis."

At the National League winter meeting, the main order of business was to be a discussion of Von der Ahe's Sportsman's Park racetrack. However, the magnates chose to do nothing, claiming that the baseball season had ended when the track opened. Instead, Browns' shortstop Bones Ely spoke at the gathering, causing Von der Ahe as much embarrassment as the runaway steer. Ely presented directors with evidence of Von der Ahe's ridiculous fines. Ely spoke for himself and his teammates Heinie Peitz, Denny Lyons, Red Ehret, and Duff Cooley. He outlined horror stories of players being ordered to play ball when they were crippled or sick. Ely also spoke of Von der Ahe withholding their pay. The shortstop's remarks included sworn affidavits from the players. Catcher Heinie Peitz could not deal with Von der Ahe's gutteral voice, and he was still due two weeks pay and $200 balance when the owner promised him the captaincy of the club. Despite Ely's pleading, the League remained noncommittal to the Browns' grievances. They could have voted to release the players at Von der Ahe's expense.

Within two weeks, Von der Ahe traded malcontent pitcher Ehret and catcher Peitz to Cincinnati. In return, Chris picked up four men: catchers Morgan Murphy and Ed McFarland, outfielder-pitcher Tom Parrott, old-time joker Arlie Latham, and an undisclosed amount of cash. *The Sporting News* couldn't resist the crack that Parrott, a clarinetist, would take up a bugle and announce the running of the horses. In January 1896, Ely rejoined Buckenberger in Pittsburgh when he was traded for shortstop Monte Cross, pitcher Hart, and $750 in cash.

24

Baldwin and Pendleton

Two legal cases greatly impacted Von der Ahe and his 1890s St. Louis Browns: the Mark Baldwin affair and the Pendleton Lease. Both helped destroy Chris' professional relationship with baseball. The Baldwin difficulty, begun by Von der Ahe, dragged on for over seven years in the courts. The Pendleton Lease case kept the participants and their lawyers busy for five years.

Von der Ahe's most serious player challenge came from a wild, right-handed workhorse pitcher named Marcus Elmore Baldwin. The trouble began in the fall of 1890, during the time of the National League and American Association wars. Both sides were stealing players and claiming leftovers from the short-lived Player's League. In stepped Mark Baldwin, recently signed by Pittsburgh of the National League. Baldwin traveled to St. Louis in hopes of persuading two Association players to join him in jumping to the Pittsburgh club. One was St. Louis ace pitcher Silver King; the other was Columbus catcher Jack O'Connor. Baldwin certainly had ample opportunity to talk to the men, especially King, who played with Baldwin on a fall barnstorming tour. When Chris Von der Ahe discovered that Baldwin had been trying to lure away King, possibly at the bidding of the National League, he acted swiftly. On the advice of his attorneys, Von der Ahe had Baldwin arrested in a St. Louis poolroom. Von der Ahe accused the pitcher of conspiracy to break up the Browns. Mark Baldwin spent his next twenty-four hours in jail, but the case was immediately thrown out. As Baldwin stepped out of the courtroom, Von der Ahe had him rearrested on new charges. The cockroaches and bedbugs in the St. Louis jailhouse didn't exactly endear Von der Ahe to Baldwin. In retaliation, the pitcher filed a $20,000 lawsuit in Pittsburgh against Von der Ahe for false arrest and malicious prosecution.

Naturally, the affair received extraordinary attention in St. Louis. *The Sporting News* reported the events in a seriocomic way. In April 1891, the weekly speculated on the supposed charges of Baldwin's bill to the Pittsburgh club about O'Connor. Included in this tongue-in-cheek bill are at least three separate round-trip rail fares from Pittsburgh to St. Louis. According to the charges, Baldwin first had to locate O'Connor, a notorious St. Louis lush, and then pay for his "entertainment," "sundries," and "wine." In another story, the weekly spoofed the entire case, rebuffing Baldwin's charging Von der Ahe for defamation of character. *The Sporting News* transcribed an imaginary courtroom meeting between Chris' attorneys and Mark Baldwin, using the words "highway robbery" and "bribery" to assail Baldwin's less-than-pristine reputation. In the mock trial, the jury deliberated only thirty seconds before rendering a verdict on the *plaintiff: guilty of manslaughter—punishable by death!*

The real case assumed ludicrous elements and was, no less silly than the parodies. Silver King, who had played for the Chicago Player's League Club in 1890, was now involved in a $3,200 contract dispute with the Browns. Not interested in re-signing his onetime ace, Von der Ahe bade good riddance to King, telling reporters that King could easily be replaced, because he could not bat or field. King denied ever being approached by Baldwin. That summer, Von der Ahe hired detective James Randall, who reported Baldwin's enticement of Browns' players Denny Lyons and Jack Boyle with liquor. Randall claimed that Lyons and Boyle were offered $350 down and $750 each when they got to Pittsburgh. Both men would be salaried at $3,500 for the season. In addition, Randall claimed that a telegram had passed from Pittsburgh owner J. Palmer O'Neill to Mark Baldwin.

Mark Baldwin versus Chris Von der Ahe dragged on and on, mostly due to Von der Ahe's lawyers petitioning for numerous delays and Von der Ahe's perpetual absence from the Pittsburgh-based hearings. By Christmas 1892, Baldwin said that one of Chris' attorneys had agreed to end the suit for $1,200. Baldwin later refuted the deal, however, wanting at least $3,500. *The Sporting News,* growing tired of the muddled affair, wrote that the League should take steps to end Baldwin's suit or ban Baldwin from professional baseball. Siding with its hometown owner, the paper wrote, "The crime of bribery is as much an offense as that of larceny or any of the other petty crimes of the universe." The weekly quoted Von der Ahe. "I have never offered Baldwin a single cent to compromise the case. He made a written offer to Nick Young to compromise the suit for $1,000 and I even refused to treat him at that figure. . . . I shall not pay him a cent until I am compelled to."

Baldwin had a chance for on-field revenge during a Fourth of July series in 1893. Pitching for the New York Giants against the Browns in St. Louis, Baldwin lost both his games, 4–3 and 2–1. In the latter affair, Baldwin took a 1–0 lead against Ted Breitenstein into the ninth inning, only to be defeated by three straight hits. The losses greatly upset Baldwin. Reportedly, Baldwin would gladly have given one month's salary to defeat the Browns.

One year later, as Von der Ahe soaked up spring sun in Pittsburgh, he was approached in his private box by Baldwin and a deputy sheriff. Baldwin looked his enemy right in the eye to inform him that he would not be seeing the ball game. The deputy sheriff grabbed the startled Chris and announced he was under arrest for ordering the false imprisonment of Baldwin in St. Louis. Turnabout was fair play. As Von der Ahe was being whisked away, the game went on. Chris didn't languish in the local jail for long. He secured bail when sympathetic Pittsburgh Club President Nimick posted Von der Ahe's bond.

In May 1895, as interest waned in the case, the dispute was supposedly decided in a Pittsburgh courtroom. Von der Ahe's strange behavior probably influenced the jury decision. Extremely anxious on the witness stand, Von der Ahe acted the fool during cross-examination by Baldwin's attorney. "I never pay a man that works for me," gurgled Von der Ahe. The courtroom broke into nervous laughter, including Judge Porter, who composed himself long enough to say:

> *Was the prosecution of Baldwin malicious? If the prosecution was insisted upon under such circumstances and of such character as to be necessarily injurious to the party, then in connection with all other evidence in the case it is to be considered whether it was with a malicious intention. A lack of probable cause does not always carry with it malice. If a man goes to an attorney and lays before him plainly a full statement of the facts in a case and is advised to make information and in good faith upon that advice he does so, it refutes the charge of malice and protects the defendants.*

However, the jury ruled otherwise and decided in favor of Baldwin for $2,500 damages for false imprisonment. Von der Ahe was not in court for the verdict, preferring to take a train back home to St. Louis. Chris instructed his attorneys to telegram him enroute in case of a favorable verdict. There was no such telegram.

Following Von der Ahe's Pittsburgh debacle, the Browns' owner decided to avoid the Steel City altogether. Von der Ahe believed that since a sheriff had said he could not be found in the county, he'd be home free.

The Sporting News called Chris "Von der Ugh! Ugh!" in print and wrote that he made a "holy show of himself" at the trial. "No one is better fitted to wear an apron and pass beer over a counter."

While Von der Ahe's attorneys petitioned for a new trial, Baldwin declared that he would not pitch in the summer of 1895. In fact, Baldwin hadn't pitched in the League in two years. Though victorious, Baldwin seemed unsure of collecting. "I will attach the St. Louis end of the gate receipts every time St. Louis plays a game in the state of Pennsylvania. I will have 12 chances, six in Pittsburgh and six in Philadelphia, and if I don't collect my $2,500 it will be a very queer thing."

A year and a half later, in January 1897, Baldwin had not received his payment from Von der Ahe. Baldwin sued again, and received judgment for $10,000 in damages. As before, Von der Ahe refused to pay. The case eventually went to the Pennsylvania Supreme Court. The high court upheld Baldwin; still, Von der Ahe continued his refusal. Unfortunately, the Baldwin case severely hampered Von der Ahe's contract negotiations with his players. He became very distrustful of ball tossers. Within a year's time, Baldwin would gain sweet revenge on his nemesis; a revenge that would result in Von der Ahe's utter humiliation.

The Pendleton Park Dispute also damaged Von der Ahe's crumbling credibility.

In 1891, war raged between the National League and the American Association. The Association concocted a plan to damage the profits of John Brush's empire in Cincinnati by placing a team at the East End Grounds, or Pendleton Park. Von der Ahe and fellow Association magnates agreed that a new Cincinnati team was vital as a competitive wedge against the National League. To force the issue, Von der Ahe and others financed the Cincinnati operation by signing a five-year lease for the park at $1,200 per annum. Included in the agreement was an indemnity bond signed by Von der Ahe and other Association clubs that insured Chris against loss in the event of the dissolution of the Cincinnati team. The previous lessees, the Cincinnati Gymnasium, were only too happy to transfer the lease.

With the disintegration of the Association and its subsequent absorption into the National League, the Pendleton Lease question was thrown into a tizzy. Just exactly who would pay for an empty ballpark? In June 1892, Mr. E. H. Pendleton, the owner of the grounds, began the first of a series of legal maneuvers to recoup his losses. He named Chris Von der Ahe as directly responsible for back rent. Pendleton refused to recognize the American Association because it had ceased to exist after the 1891 season. He also operated under the assumption that it would be easier to sue one man than several. Von der Ahe was proving an easy mark in court. Word eventually reached other associates—including the Wagners of Washington and Harry Von der Horst of Baltimore—about Pendleton's refusal to recognize the Association. These magnates probably figured they were in the clear. Pendleton won his judgment for the June 1892 suit for $1421.20. By December 1893, Von der Ahe hired an attorney to sue Von der Horst and the Wagners for their share of the judgment. Two years passed, but still Pendleton was without payment. In September 1894, the persistent Pendleton sued Chris again, winning legal judgment. This time the decision meant $1,800. At this stage, the case had the makings of a legal nightmare.

Pendleton demanded his money. Von der Ahe, with his own debts piling up, refused Pendleton until the other magnates paid their share. The brouhaha of Pendleton versus Von der Ahe versus the Wagners and Von der Horst continued for three more years. While Pendleton waited, Von der Ahe went to court in January 1894 to ask for a receiver for the Cincinnati club and an accounting of the management of the Pendleton property. After Von der Ahe's legal posturing failed, he began to attach a portion of the St. Louis gate receipts that belonged to the Wagners for the 1895 season. The case had progressed from a rental dispute to Von der Ahe's refusal to pay gate money. The Brothers Wagner retaliated by withholding St. Louis club receipts when the

Browns played in Washington. Harry Von der Horst, treasurer of the Baltimores, was also a target of Chris' legal attacks. In February 1895, Von der Ahe sued Baltimore for back payment of the Pendleton lease.

The Wagners launched a clever plan. By the summer of 1895, the respective managers of the Browns and Senators joined in the fray. A $2,000 countersuit was brought by the Wagners against Von der Ahe for refusing to share gate receipts. In court, Gus Schmelz represented the Senators; Al Buckenberger spoke for the Browns. Buckenberger stood up for his boss by commenting that St. Louis would refuse to play games with Washington. Schmelz pointed out that section 47 of the League Constitution called for a $1,000 fine for teams that refused to play a scheduled game. Buckenberger responded by quoting section 48: "At the conclusion of each championship game, the home club shall pay to the visiting club fifty per centum of said receipts." The courts had little choice but to declare that each team had a right to their receipts. The standoff, probably calculated by the Wagners and Schmelz, favored everyone but Chris Von der Ahe, who was still in hock to Pendleton.

In March 1896, the five-year Pendleton Park lease expired. Instead of the combatants breathing sighs of relief, however, the controversy continued on. The National League, fearing bad publicity, called an arbitration meeting. The committee met at the 1896 winter League meeting, headed by Messrs. Frank Robison of Cleveland and Arthur Soden of Boston. Von der Ahe was already a pariah in National League circles for his racetrack-ballpark, his willy-nilly selling of players, and his moral character. Naive Chris expected the panel to rule in his favor and pay off the balance of the Pendleton bill. Once again, Von der Ahe was wrong. The League panel concluded that the old Association clubs were indebted to Von der Ahe. Not surprisingly, the Washington, Baltimore, and Louisville clubs balked at the amount. One month after the League ruling, Chris sued Ned Hanlon and the Baltimore club in separate litigation for $800 each. Both lawsuits concerned a bill of exchange signed by Hanlon on July 26, 1896. The wily Hanlon had duped Chris into "borrowing" $800 as a personal loan. In effect, Von der Ahe had secured Baltimore's receipts to pay back Pendleton and then loaned the money right back to Hanlon. The Louisville club argued that the debts were incurred by the old Association Eclipse club and not by the Louisville Colonels. Therefore, Louisville claimed, the debt was null and void. When Von der Ahe met an attorney representing the Wagners, the two could not agree on a settlement amount. In a final act of irony, Von der Ahe discussed the case with John T. Brush, the National League magnate whom the American Association had tried to crush.

The Pendleton mess was finally settled in 1897 by the legal system and the National League arbitration panel. The settlement included a payment from an unnamed source. On January 4, 1897, League magnates ruled that the Baltimore, Louisville, Philadelphia, and Washington clubs each owed a total of $2,087. Later, a court ruled that the Wagner share was higher for their part in the gate receipt controversy.

25

Coney Island of the West

The St. Louis stage comedy continued in the 1896 season. As always, the play starred Chris Von der Ahe, his "Prowns," ball cranks of the city, and local newspapers. This year, the actors used the Von der Ahe-Foster ball yard racetrack and a new attraction as stage props.

As in 1895, the 1896 campaign played itself out in a sea of difficulties. Among the main themes were rumors of sales of the Browns', club infighting and a managerial merry-go-round, Ted Breitenstein's season of tribulation, unpaid ballplayers, and negative news reportage. Like the sword of Damocles, an outstanding bank note for $44,000 in ballpark loans was due to be paid by Von der Ahe.

With baseball and horse racing financial failures, Von der Ahe announced in January 1896 that a new amusement would be added to Sportsman's Park. Reaching back into his German youth for yet another money scheme, Chris boldly proclaimed the construction of a shoot-the-chutes behind the right field fence. Newsmen were stumped. What on earth was shoot-the-chutes? Chris explained the contrivance as a boat, a water slide, and an artificial lake. Passengers would be loaded into a rowboat and taken by elevator to the top of the ride. Von der Ahe picks up the description: "Den de poat shoots down de hill into de lake. But, i'd don't sink. Id yust schoots ofer de vater, und dot's vy dey gall it schootin de schoots." The summertime attraction would be a titillating sensation for couples or kids of all ages. Shoot-the-Chutes cost a quarter. Ladies with a chaperon could ride for free. In the winter, the 750-by-200-foot lake would be used for ice skating.

An architect named Weiss traveled to Philadelphia with Von der Ahe to examine a shoot-the-chutes. The water slide cost Von der Ahe $25,000 to build. Chris was convinced this was a money-making proposition. He expected a $50,000 a year profit for the venture; a whole lot of quarters. As soon as construction began, a fellow in Philadelphia wired Chris claiming patent restrictions and a $10,000 fee to use the idea. Chris balked and told reporters that he would get his own patent.

The water slide quickly became a metaphor for the sinking fortunes of Von der Ahe. Shoot-the-Chutes might as well have been shoot yourself in the foot. In the ride's first three days, St. Louis citizens lined up in droves to try the new thrill. The ecstatic Von der Ahe enjoyed taking the plunge himself. The ride was popular enough to outdraw baseball and racing. Those disenchanted by the Browns could try the shoot-the-chutes. After a while, though, the quarters stopped coming in. By July, the Hebert Street Shoot-the-Chutes Company holding the Boynton patent was applying for an injunction to stop the ride. Hebert Street also sued Von der Ahe for damages. Later, the Koken Iron Works sued Chris for failing to pay for construction. Shoot-the-Chutes sank in less than two seasons.

On a biting cold St. Louis winter evening in 1896, Von der Ahe advertised the grand opening of the skating season. Sportsman's Park was aglow with electric light and boisterous, flush-cheeked skating hopefuls. The romantic German in Von der Ahe recalled the musical vision of the Blue Danube Waltz. The capitalist American in Von der Ahe looked at the tiny skaters as dollar signs. Just before opening the gates, Von der Ahe asked a Negro in his employ to test the ice. Following orders, the man slid across the ice, seemingly with no difficulty, but as Von der Ahe looked on at the edge of the rink, a loud cry arose as the man dipped below the ice. A policeman standing nearby rushed to the scene. With effort, the man was pulled from the chilly waters. "Vell, vat dit you do dat for?" said the angry magnate. "Yah, you rundt ofer it! Dat vas all right. But I nefer toldt you to chump t'roo it, dit I?" The policeman had to prevent Chris from attacking the man. Embarrassed over the unforseen event, Von der Ahe stood outside in the chill, explaining to the skaters that the opening was postponed.

Local and national media continued to lambaste Von der Ahe. Reportage continually called for his ouster from baseball. Von der Ahe was running an amusement park, but the Browns' incessant losing wasn't funny in the least. To add to the festivities, an all-girl band called the Silver Cornets played popular tunes day and night. Numbering two dozen, the Silver Cornets were dressed in long striped skirts with wide sailor hats and leg-of-mutton sleeves. When the Browns were out of town, Sportsman's Park could be rented out for picnics.

One event that was hardly a picnic occurred when the park was rented out for a political speech. The speaker, William Jennings Bryan, was the Democratic candidate for President of the United States. Bryan figured on a large, enthusiastic crowd, intent on listening to one of his "silver standard" oratories. Unfortunately, Mr. Bryan did not figure on Von der Ahe charging admission for the affair. The snafu enraged Bryan, who eventually lost the election to William McKinley.

In time, Von der Ahe was hyping Sportsman's Park as "der Koney

Island des Westens," or the Coney Island of the West. Coney Island boasted Steeplechase Park, the Canals of Venice, Scenic Railway, and a Giant See-Saw, along with bathing houses, dance halls, shooting galleries, freak shows, and eating houses. Von der Ahe's park seemingly featured all of those. Von der Ahe offered railways to get people to the ball yard. His freak show was the Browns.

Still desperate for dollars, partners Von der Ahe and Foster devised an 1896 plan for nightly horse racing. Iron poles 15-feet equidistant around the track were installed with dim electric lights. However, the horses may have well have been racing in the dark. Though admission was free after 8:00 P.M., only the hardiest aficionados showed up. Examples of unrealized profits included a gentlemen whose horses ran first, second, and second in three races. When the man went to collect, the payoff was only $3.00. Von der Ahe soon fell behind in paying his track employees. Dan Donnelly, a Philadelphia bookie operating the track with Foster, quit the business in disgust of Von der Ahe's heavy-handed methods.

Perhaps the only positive story concerning the installation of lights at Sportsman's Park occurred during the playing of an afternoon ball game. On an overcast day, St. Louis crazies were busy guzzling beer and yelling at Umpire Emslie that it was growing rather dark. The umpire paid no heed to the faithful, despite the fact that they tried to set fire to newspapers to get Emslie's attention. Suddenly, Von der Ahe turned on a switch and a bank of electric lights lit up the ball yard. The game continued. This was possibly the first night game in the daytime in major-league history.

It wasn't beneath Von der Ahe to show up at the track as a barker. Taking bets on ball games or racehorses, Chris worked the crowds to much amusement. In time, Chris' "friends" took advantage of the German's ignorance of the horse racing business. Within a few short weeks, Von der Ahe couldn't pick a winning mount to save his life. Horse gamblers could simply write a ticket on the winning horses *after* the race had been decided. Von der Ahe, not realizing the difference, cashed in the ticket.

The new Sportsman's Park now barely resembled a baseball field. The turf was cut to pieces, the grounds were reseeded, and a new diamond had to be laid out thirty feet further from the grandstand. The distance alienated baseball fans. Thanks to Chris Von der Ahe, the sanctity of baseball was disappearing. The sport, with its smell of fresh-roasted peanuts, mugs of beer, the crack of bat meeting ball, and the roar of multitudes, had sunk to a new low.

Forty-two-year-old Harry Diddlebock was pegged to manage the Browns for 1896. Harry was neither a player nor a manager. He was a sports editor. For Von der Ahe, that was enough qualification. For eleven years, Diddlebock served as the head sportswriter at the *Philadelphia Times*. For six years he'd been in charge of the *Philadelphia Inquirer*. Diddlebock also possessed some executive baseball experience, having served in the Eastern and Pennsylvania Leagues as secretary. At first, the local papers in St. Louis were kind to Harry. Without interference, he'd manage the Browns to the first division within a year. With Chris' propensity for signing German players, Von der Ahe and Diddlebock conjured visions of a German empire in St. Louis, wrote the *Cleveland World*. Diddlebock's first job would be to undo Herr Von der Ahe's damage.

Shortly after his December 1895 hiring, Diddlebock was involved in two controversies. Both came before he arrived in St. Louis, trained his men, or managed a game. The biggest involved an impossible $30,000 deal for five of Philadelphia's star players. No money was available in the St. Louis treasury for such a transaction. Diddlebock was Von der Ahe's fall guy in the gossipy mess. The *Philadelphia Press* followed up the bluff with a story of a $110,000 deal by Von der Ahe for nearly all of the Philadelphia team!

Diddlebock was reportedly paid a considerable sum to manage the Browns. Another report concerned Diddlebock's old employer offering Harry $100 a week for his old job back. Most likely, it was a contract ploy by Harry to secure more money from the Browns. The highest paid sporting editor in Philadelphia made only $50 a week.

By mid-February, Harry was off and running as the Browns new manager. He mailed contracts to players and took a skeleton team to Texas to train. Because the Browns demanded better treatment from club management, many remained unsigned. During a spring training trip to Dallas, the ballplayers were presented with small cards. Distributed by Von der Ahe, the cards contained edifying messages. The players must have looked upon the communication as nothing less than ridiculous. Reactions varied. Some may have wadded up the cards and tossed them away. Others may have picked their teeth with them. Perhaps several of the more adventurous players read the words aloud to each other. In so doing, they could mimic the thick German accent of Chris Von der Ahe. Belly laughs followed. These short, terse messages contained rules of conduct for Browns' players to abide by during the upcoming season. The messages were something out of Emily Post. Two rules stood out. Rule 3 stated, "Players must act in a gentlemanly manner and be careful not to socialize with undesirable characters." Rule 5 said, "Drunkenness and gambling will not be tolerated."

In the 1880s and 1890s, ballplayers were anything but gentlemen. They spent sweaty, endless summers traveling about on trains for long distances. Their playing ball times were all too brief. Afterwards, it was quite customary for them to stay together for a few rounds in the poolrooms and bars. Gambling, beer hoisting, and wenching served as popular amusements. Exactly who were the undesirable characters among this crowd? The hypocritical Von der Ahe was running a bar, a ball team, a racetrack, and conducting his personal affairs with hardly the mannerisms of a refined gentleman.

St. Louis' newspapers launched daily assaults on Von der Ahe and his Browns. Von der Ahe promised to hold reporters "pussonally responsible" for attacks on his character. The Boss President threatened to fight his enemies man to man. The local papers were expert at *Schadenfreude*, a German term for deriving enjoyment from the misfortunes of others. Even Von der Ahe's long-time friend Al Spink admitted in print that he now despised the Browns' owner.

Unfortunately, no one gave the Browns a chance. The team had few decent ballplayers. Arlie Latham had been signed for comic relief. With a lame arm, Latham's fielding skills had eroded so badly in Cincinnati that he often just waved his glove at sharply hit grounders.

Spring training typified the lack of seriousness in the players, especially Tom Parrott. An outfielder-pitcher, a joking "Tacky Tom" reported to camp with a matted, full beard. Parrott's growth was said to be five inches in length. The beard looked great on a circus impresario, but not so good on a ballplayer. In an exhibition against Belleview, the score was tied at eight in the ninth inning. Parrott was pitching. The first batter hit a high bounder that caught Tom in his chin. Making a stop with his beard, Parrot stuck his fingers into the tangle to retrieve the ball and throw out the runner. Unfortunately, the ball would not cooperate, so Parrott raced the runner to first base. The runner was safe—by a hair, or several hairs! Taking advantage, the runner kept going while the hapless Parrott chased him around the bases. When Von der Ahe heard of the grooming and fielding indiscretion, he fined his man $25 and made him shave. Many stories exist of men losing balls in the sun, in the lights, or in the web of gloves. Few matched Tom Parrott's experience, which may have added new meaning to the term "hidden ball trick."

The *New York Recorder* gave Baltimore 3–1 odds of capturing the National League pennant. Cleveland was 7–3. Washington was 100–1. St. Louis, wrote the paper, was listed as "write your own tickets." For unexplained reasons, Diddlebock was in absentia for his first St. Louis press gathering at the park. The Browns opened with Ted Breitenstein beating Cy Young and Cleveland, 5–2. That would be the season's highlight. A power struggle quickly developed among Diddlebock, Arlie Latham, and secretary Muckenfuss. With the exception of Latham and outfielder Tom Niland, the players supported Diddlebock. Latham was unpopular with his fellow ballplayers, accusing Diddlebock of drinking to excess. During a Latham-Diddlebock meeting, Arlie told his manager, "From now on we'll divide this work. You do the managing and I'll do the drinking." To complicate matters, the relatives of Von der Ahe's girlfriend Della made their displeasure known against Diddlebock. All reported to boss Von der Ahe with their complaints. Chris wasn't too wild about Harry.

Within a short time, Diddlebock lost all control. In a game against the New York Giants, Ted Breitenstein walked six batters in the first two innings. The Browns' hurler then told Diddlebock to get someone else ready to pitch. In the third, Breitenstein walked two more men and then walked off the field. Diddlebock, angry at being dictated to, chastised Breitenstein, who said; "That's all right, you so-and-so. I'll try these fellows again tomorrow and show you." The Giants were blanked on three hits the next day, thanks to Breitenstein's pitching.

Gambling at the horse track proved too enticing for Diddlebock. In addition to managing, Diddlebock was checking Von der Ahe's racing sheets. Von der Ahe also employed two of Harry's sons for odd jobs around Sportsman's. One night, Diddlebock secured quite a sum in backing a winner. He went out afterward, intending to celebrate in grand style. However, when a policeman discovered Diddlebock on the street at 3:00 A.M., Von der Ahe suspended him. The policeman reported that Harry had bumps on his noggin but was not intoxicated. Immediately, Von der Ahe had a private detective investigate. The detective found that Diddlebock was injured in a fall from a streetcar. The fall resulted from the manager being drunk. With the Browns hopelessly demoralized, losing eleven of twelve games, Von der Ahe fired Diddlebock. Harry managed the Browns for three weeks.

To replace Diddlebock, Von der Ahe temporarily assigned Arlie Latham to the post. Arlie lasted three games, all losses. During one game Latham disagreed with umpire Tim Hurst. In protest, an indignant Arlie slammed his glove to the ground and then kicked it. Hurst then booted Latham's leather. Latham followed suit, and the two took turns kicking the glove all the way to the outfield fence.

Though Latham's days with the club were numbered, he still had one last stunt for Von der Ahe. He described the high-jinks himself in the *New York World* in 1896:

> *We were playing in St. Louis one Fourth of July morning, and it occurred to me that I'd have a little fun with the club owner. During our batting period I got a dynamite bomb from a man in the grand stand, and then, when our side was out, I walked out to third and put it under the base where Chris couldn't see it. I also had got a piece of punk, and, as though tying my shoelace, I lit the fuse of the bomb. Then I pulled down my cap, put my hands on my knees and while shouting "Come on! Get in the game!" I watched it.*
>
> *All of a sudden—boom!*
>
> *I jumped three feet in the air and landed on my back, kicking and writhing. Then I rolled on my side and kept one eye cocked on Von der Ahe. He always carried a bugle with him with which he summoned the special policemen when he needed them. When he saw me fall he put the bugle to his lips and tooted away for dear life. The specials came running from all parts of the stand and surrounded their employer. When he felt he was safe and that no one could shoot him without first killing a guard he got up and yelled:*
>
> *"Who in blazes shoot Laydem?" Then he came down on the field surrounded by his guard and looked at me.*
>
> *Presently I jump up, shook myself and looked old Chris in the eye.*
>
> *"It's all right, Chris," I said; "it didn't go in; it just stunned me."*
>
> *Just then a player with a pail of ice water came running up and threw it*

> *over me. At that the spectators and the players began to roar, and I could see the light of understanding coming into Chris' eyes.*
>
> *"You chackass," he yelled at last, "I fine you $50!"*
>
> *Which he never got.*

Chris reappointed himself field general for two contests. Von der Ahe's managerial stint lasted long enough for the team to endure another tirade about drunken behavior and fines. J. B. Sheridan, a sporting writer with the *St. Louis Post-Dispatch,* noticed the absurdity of the situation. After writing more negative stories about Von der Ahe and his sinking club, Sheridan saw his press pass at the park revoked. The Browns' owner threatened to fine any player who spoke to reporters. Sheridan wasn't finished. The *Post-Dispatch* stories went on unabated. To defeat his ban, Sheridan simply walked up to the ticket booth and purchased a ticket. The move cost the *Post-Dispatch* one quarter.

He didn't deserve the punishment, but first baseman Roger Connor assumed the position as Von der Ahe's manager. After two weeks, Connor's record was so poor that Larry O'Dea was rumored as his successor. O'Dea's full-time job was head barkeep at Von der Ahe's saloon. Connor somehow survived, at least long enough to note that the only good thing about playing ball in St. Louis was that the bleachers and grandstand were quite far removed from the players. Due to ballpark improvements, players couldn't always hear sarcastic remarks from fans. Connor managed for forty-five games, thirty-seven of them losses. By early July, Von der Ahe's Browns were failing, as was the ballpark-racetrack and the Shoot-the-Chutes. Second baseman Quinn and catcher McFarland nursed wounds in a local hospital. Von der Ahe's players were forced to play without pay for six weeks. Chris then fined four men. Outfielder Duff Cooley, out with malaria, was docked pay. Pitcher Bill Kissinger and infielders Monte Cross and Bert Myers were assessed $25 each. Von der Ahe explained they were punished "just to show dem who's dair boss, ain'd I. You bet your life I know my business." That same week, Von der Ahe shipped his best hitter Cooley, to Philadelphia for outfielders Joe Sullivan and Tuck Turner. Eventually, the Browns were paid their salaries, thanks to a reported $5,000 advance from Cincinnati's John Brush.

The Browns also endured interference from Von der Ahe's love interest, Della Wells. While Chris employed Della's kin at the park, Von der Ahe's secretary Stuart Muckenfuss insisted that his boss dump Della, Lou Phelan, Harry Oliver, and the rest of the freeloaders. Von der Ahe did so, but only after a creditor explained that reforming his lifestyle would make it easier to get an extension on his $44,000 loan. The full figure was due in August. Muckenfuss' $100 a month job was said to be in jeopardy after Von der Ahe forbade him from playing the racehorses at the classier Fairgrounds track. In September 1896, Von der Ahe snuck off to Erie, Pennsylvania, and married Della Wells.

While Rome burned, Von der Ahe thought nothing of entertaining his political buddies at Sportsman's Park. One afternoon Von der Ahe insisted that politician Ed Butler sit with him on the hometeam bench. Siding up to manager Roger Connor, Von der Ahe noticed the crowd had spied Butler hobnobbing with the players. Feeling secure with his guest, Von der Ahe turned his attentions to the ball game. Red Donahue was pitching for St. Louis against the Orioles. Unfortunately, there would be no showing off the team. Baltimore batters pasted Donahue's slants all over Sportsman's. Hughie Jennings knocked out a four-baser in the fifth inning. Muttering to Butler, Von der Ahe said, "Vut's der madder mid dot clup, anyhow?" The politician had no response. Then, acting managerial, Von der Ahe grabbed his binoculars and surveyed the diamond. Raising his voice higher, Von der Ahe spoke to Roger Connor. "Vut t'ell is der madder? Your outfield is blaying about three blocks too deep and so is your infield. It's no vunter dey are hitting Donahue. Pull in der whole field!" Noting Von der Ahe's less-than-scientific spyglass methods, Connor rolled his eyes and shot a glance to Butler. The big first baseman said, "Just switch and try the other end and see how they look, Chris." Von der Ahe rearranged the ocular so that his men didn't resemble ants. "Say old boy, der drinks are on me! I vill buy after tis game, even if ve lose."

Into this mess came Tommy Dowd. Acting as player-captain and manager, Dowd tried to make the best of the situation. Because of Von der Ahe's financial condition, the Browns simply couldn't afford to sign any top-notch players. Despite his pessimism, Dowd's charges managed to play .400 ball the rest of the way.

Late in the season, a group of ten hoodlums boarded the Browns' train between Cincinnati and Louisville, looking for trouble. None of them possessed tickets; they swiped passes from the hatbands of the passengers. Second baseman Tommy Dowd was unaware of the pilfering and was reading with his feet propped up on a seat. One of the men approached Dowd for his ticket, but Tommy wasn't in the mood for games. The man left the car and returned with a half dozen of his mates. It wasn't long before a full-scale fight was on. Dowd popped one of the hoods in the nose. Backwards went the man, tumbling his buddies in domino fashion. Tuck Turner, Red Donahue, Monte Cross, and Roger Connor all joined the fray. The sheepish hoods beat a retreat to the toilet room. There was no more trouble, and all the stolen tickets were returned. When the train stopped at Louisville, the hoodlums debarked. Monte Cross punctuated the end of the fight by backing up one of the men against a train car. It was doubtful these hoods ever fought a trainload of ballplayers again. "Buttermilk Tommy" signed on to manage the team again in 1897.

Veteran left-hander Ted Breitenstein's campaign typified the turmoil. In January, St. Louis' best pitcher spurned an offer to toss balls for Chester of the Southern Illinois League. One month later, Ted was in a Baltimore theater, acting as starter in Al Spink's turf drama, *The Derby Winner*. Owner Chris Von der Ahe didn't take kindly to Breitenstein's stage career. Von der Ahe believed that Breit should have been spending time getting in shape for the upcoming season. Perhaps Von der Ahe was jealous of the adulation his pitcher was receiving from members of the National League Champion Baltimore Orioles, who had attended the performance. The Von der Ahe-Breitenstein dispute blew up into a full-blown contract squabble by March. Breitenstein argued his case before the National Board of Arbitration, claiming St. Louis had not reserved him by the March 1 deadline. Incoming manager Harry Diddlebock disagreed and said that talking to Breitenstein constituted an agreement on the "spirit of the law." While Breit held out, Von der Ahe ordered his ace lefty to report to the club by the first of April "in proper condition to play ball." Von der Ahe further stipulated that he, and not Breitenstein, would "be the sole judge" of the pitcher's condition. Chris realized that Breitenstein's southpaw heroics were one of the few drawing cards on the club.

Reluctantly, Breit pitched the whole campaign, leading the team in games, innings, victories, and earned run average. In October, Von der Ahe sold Breit to John Brush's Cincinnati Reds for a reported ten grand. The amount earned Breitenstein an instant nickname: "The $10,000 Beauty." For Breitenstein, the sale meant a reunion of the famous Pretzel Battery with old chum Heinie Peitz. However magnanimous it seemed, Brush's gesture may have been part of a premeditated plan to help Von der Ahe pay off his players' salaries. Von der Ahe had been funneling St. Louis players to the Reds for years. In addition to Breitenstein, pitchers Frank Dwyer and Red Ehret, catcher Heinie Peitz, and outfielder Dummy Hoy were all peddled to Cincinnati.

St. Louis played poorly in every department. They sported a trio of 20-game losing pitchers (Breitenstein, Hart, and Donahue), a weak catcher platoon, a thoroughly jumbled outfield mix, and an infield with only two decent players: Dowd and Roger Connor. St. Louis couldn't beat anybody away from home and finished the season with only forty victories, almost half by Ted Breitenstein.

26

"Let Chris Play Left!"

It didn't seem possible that St. Louis fortunes, or lack thereof, could get much worse in 1897. However, that is precisely what happened. This time, the turmoil included four more managers who ran the club for various intervals. The players survived long stretches without pay and threatened mutiny. Questions arose about exactly who was in charge of the St. Louis club. At a time when the club desperately needed stability, Chris Von der Ahe and secretary Benjamin Muckenfuss did their best to create controversies.

The preseason foreshadowed many of the campaign's problems. During the spring meeting of the National League, many owners expected Von der Ahe's exit from the game. Others expected to supplement the pathetic Browns' roster by giving St. Louis their excess players. The *Washington Post* fired off an editorial that Von der Ahe's Browns were undeserving. The article correctly pointed out that Von der Ahe had released, sold, or exchanged many good men since his arrival in the National League. Secretary Muckenfuss then put his foot in his mouth by exclaiming that Von der Ahe would have nothing to do with signing players. Muckenfuss' statement gave rise to speculation that Edward Becker was running the Browns. When questioned further, Muckenfuss offered a sheepish retort. "The old man will still be boss." Because of a lack of funds, the Tommy Dowd led Browns trained at Sportsman's Park against teams from the Western League. Dowd had resigned himself to the fact that St. Louis was destined for last place in the National League. So did all the sportswriters. On Dowd's training methods, *The Sporting News* quipped,"He will divide them into two teams, and see if they can beat each other."

All of Chris' managers entered hopeless, uncontrollable situations. Tommy Dowd led off the campaign. Poor Tommy had to deal with second baseman Lou Bierbauer, who began the season recovering from a spiked leg. When Bierbauer returned, he saw action in only a dozen games before jumping the team and returning home to Pennsylvania. Von der Ahe then suspended Bierbauer and fined him $250. Pitcher Duke Esper went home to care for his sick child. When Esper rejoined the team, he pitched like *he* was sick. Tom Parrott was sold to St. Paul for a pittance. *The Sporting News* reported that disgusted fans patronized the amateur and semipro clubs in town. The other St. Louis dailies kept up the negative reportage and refused to advertise Browns' games until Von der Ahe settled his accounts with the papers. When Von der Ahe told the news mavens to be damned, reporters vowed not to print any positive stories about the club.

After one scribe asked naive Chris about the uniformity in scorekeeping, Von der Ahe replied, "Now vot do reporters want with uniforms on? Are they stuck on the dames and do they want to show off? Let the players wear the uniforms, but not the reporters."

A flood of nicknames surfaced, including the Done Browns. Von der Ahe himself was pilloried with these unflattering handles: Von der Grab, Von der Ugh Ugh, Tricky Teuton, Jonah, Von der Ha! Ha!, "maggot" instead of magnate, and the Sick Man of Baseball. To pour salt in Chris' wounds, a bill was introduced in the City House of Delegates to license all ballparks in St. Louis for an annual fee of $3,000. After the bill was read to the delegates, they responded with silence and then snickers. Clubs had to pay before the games were held. Noncompliance would result in fines not less than $100 or more than $500. Each day would be a separate offense.

A May game with Louisville illustrates the St. Louis fans' displeasure with Von der Ahe. On a Sunday afternoon, St. Louis catcher Ed McFarland took a turn in left field. In the first inning, McFarland dropped a fly ball, prompting a wise crack from the crowd: "Let Chris play left." The joker's remarks prompted laughter, as the buzz spread through the audience. Then one fan pointed out that Herr Von der Ahe was enjoying the spectacle from his front-row box. With the boss were three lady guests, only one of whom was his wife. This observation prompted a host of catcalls, hissing, and insults about the Browns' amorous owner. "Wher'd you find these misfits?" and "Go hide yourself" were among the milder comments. Chris pretended not to notice the ruckus. Instead, he fixed his gaze straight ahead to watch his club surrender eleven runs in the first two innings. The crowd began to cheer against the locals. After a few minutes of razzing, secretary Muckenfuss came down to the front-row box to whisper something into his boss' ear. Von der Ahe rose and exited the premises. Louisville won the game 14–6. McFarland, hitting well over .300, was traded to Philadelphia a week later. After an 11–4 loss to Boston at Sportsman's Park, the *Globe-Democrat* wrote: "Everybody went away in a bad humor, and some of the oldest and steadiest of the fans resolved never to go to the game again. They will all be there today just the same."

Shortly after these games, Dowd was fired.

Von der Ahe then hired ex-Browns' outfielder and local favorite Hugh Nicol. Tommy Dowd was ticketed for Philadelphia but refused to leave until Von der Ahe had settled all financial affairs with him. During his tenure, Nicol had to endure the trade of Ed McFarland to Philadelphia for pitcher Kid

Carsey and catcher-infielder Mike Grady. Originally, Carsey refused to report to the Browns, prompting Von der Ahe to say, "If he didn't want to work for St. Louis, why did he sign a contract? He'll repent . . . Oh, well, pitchers are queer fellows."

Nicol's first road trip ended with fifteen losses in seventeen games, including a 25–5 mud bath in Boston. Due to injuries and sickness, Nicol was forced to play men out of position. Luckily, few showed to witness the spectacle. During the losing steak, Nicol asked Chris for $10 to purchase some new bats. Chris responded, "Mein Gott, vat do dey vant mit bats? Hay! Dey can't der balloon hit, und vy don'd dey go to der plate un shust stand there mit no bats und haf der umpire yell 'ball,' 'strike,' 'out!' Bats, hey? Ten dollars for bats! Nonsense, poy! Dey don'd need 'em. Guess again!"

Von der Ahe was right. The Browns hardly needed bats. They were dead last in the league in hitting. St. Louis needed bed slats. The Browns proved this by losing to their old workhorse battery of Ted Breitenstein and Heinie Peitz. Breit pitched a 3–0 three-hitter and smacked a triple against his old mates.

Nicol's fate was sealed after a mid-July weekend at Sportsman's Park. During a Saturday game with Brooklyn, rotten St. Louis fans tossed two eggs at umpire Sheridan. The fans were rather displeased with Sheridan's officiating. The umpire demanded police protection. Once a lawman was secured, Von der Ahe rose from his seat to ensure the umpire made it to the dressing room without bodily harm. That evening, manager Nicol complained that Sheridan had cost the Browns the game. St. Louis newspapers played up the incident, helping to generate 6,000 for the Sunday game. This time, however, no umpire could be blamed. The Browns lost 21–4 to Baltimore before howling and disgusted home fans. Von der Ahe had another scapegoat for his team's poor play. Hugh Nicol was deposed after seven weeks.

By mid-season Von der Ahe complained that the entire National League was against him. At dispute was Chris' claim that the League deliberately scheduled fewer Sunday games in St. Louis and Louisville. As a result, the St. Louis organization lost critical revenues. Only five Sunday affairs were scheduled for the two clubs.

Bill Hallman, a scratchy-voiced, off-season vaudevillian was next to manage St. Louis. He tried, but the task proved impossible. The Browns spent time traveling around America playing baseball for free. Since early July, their paydays had been few and far between. The club was drinking and in near mutiny. The losses piled up; eighteen in a row under Hallman's tutelage. In September, Von der Ahe applied to the League for a loan to pay his players. The League promised restitution in full, but *The Sporting News* pointed out that failure to pay salaries constituted franchise forfeiture under the League Constitution. After some time, Edward Becker was believed to have fronted money for the Browns.

Von der Ahe's club even managed to lose games *after* they were won. No umpires showed for the August 1 game at Sportsman's. As was the custom, each team provided a man. For St. Louis, pitcher Red Donahue went behind the plate to call the balls and strikes. Louisville catcher Charlie Dexter worked the field. After repeatedly calling for umpire Donahue to provide new baseballs, Colonels' pitcher Bert Cunningham persisted in rubbing the balls with dirt and "soiling" them. The dirt balls angered the crowd, and Donahue forfeited the game to his own team. Three weeks later, the National League Board reversed Donahue, depriving the Browns of a victory.

Frustrated over losing, Browns' players resorted to pulling pranks on their owner. During one close contest, Von der Ahe observed matters from the bench with his trusty field glasses. Sitting next to Von der Ahe was pitcher Con Lucid. With two on and two out, the batter lifted a fly ball to St. Louis left fielder Dan Lally. As the ball sailed skyward, Von der Ahe grabbed his big eyes and asked Lucid, "I hope Lally gets dot ball. Say, Con, vill he get it?" Thinking fast, Lucid poked the magnate in the ribs and exclaimed, "Get out of the way, Chris. You're in Lally's way!" Startled, Von der Ahe jumped from the bench. Lally let the ball plunk him on the arm. Two runs scored. As soon as Von der Ahe discovered Con's game, he chuckled. "Dot's very goot uf you, Con. You got me twisted, you did. I tot I vos in der vay uf Lally. I guess I'm getting to be a ball crank myself."

Late in this sorry season, infielder Monte Cross' actions spoke for many members of the Browns. So tired was Monte of playing for this ragtag collection that in one game he fell to his knees and prayed forgiveness from the umpire. The puzzled arbiter, not used to such Catholic displays, fined Cross $20. Von der Ahe was tempted to fine Cross more money. After a reporter asked about his shortstop, Von der Ahe said, "Vot you tink of dot Monte Cross making two errors today? His named ought to be schanged to Double Cross."

If Monte Cross was Double Cross, Von der Ahe was Triple Cross. Chris appointed himself manager for the season's remaining fourteen games. It was the third time that Chris had hired himself. St. Louis won just twice with their owner at the helm. So pitiable were these Browns. During one team lecture, Von der Ahe told his men that they should never give away club secrets. "It's a silent head dot keeps your mouth shut," said the German, matter-of-factly. Von der Ahe also advised them to look after each other, especially when fellow ball tossers were down on their luck. Most likely, Von der Ahe wanted to avoid listening to his player's sob stories. "A frient in need iss a frient ven you're broke," he liked to say. At one such fatherly gathering, Tommy Dowd stuffed a handkerchief in his mouth to keep himself from doubling over. Von der Ahe found the hanky none too amusing and fined Dowd $10. When the embarrassment became too much, Muckenfuss was forced to take dictation as Von der Ahe spoke at meetings with the Browns' brain trust. The next day, a somber Muckenfuss relayed owner Von der Ahe's observations to the men. The first order of business for the Browns' secretary would be to try to get the players not to laugh.

The 1897 Browns were such a joke that one of their men is forever linked to a play that probably never happened. According to an inventive sportswriter, ex-Browns' third baseman Mike Grady was patrolling third base one day for the New York Giants. The batter scorched a grounder to Mike that he couldn't handle. Error number one. Grady then threw the ball over the first baseman's head in an effort to get the out. Error number two. As the ball caromed off the grandstand, the base runner slid into third. The relay throw to Grady was perfect. Unfortunately, Grady wasn't. He dropped the ball for error number three. The runner, probably fighting off laughter, scrambled up and headed for home. By this time, Grady and the rest of the Giants composed themselves just long enough to get the base runner in a rundown. However, when the runner dived back into third, Grady again fumbled the ball. Error number four. As the sphere was squirting away, the runner got up quickly and flashed for home. Poor Mike Grady then managed to toss the ball over the head of his catcher. The run scored and Grady was tagged with his fifth error on the play. Later, Grady would claim that the fifth miscue was the result of his chucking the ball over the grandstand in disgust. The story was never verified by the National League, the New York Giants, or *The Sporting News*. Of course, it is only possible to commit one error for every base advanced. However, Grady's play was perpetuated in *Ripley's Believe It or Not!*

With the campaign mercifully about to end, Von der Ahe slapped second baseman Hallman ($200), infielder Mike Grady ($100), and outfielder Dan Lally ($100) with enormous fines for drinking. Von der Ahe suspended Hallman for the final three games. Shortstop Monte Cross was named captain. Then Von der Ahe's groundskeeper, Herman Fenske, convinced the Boss President that in order to trim expenses, the Browns could play without a manager. Von der Ahe agreed and called it "reorganizing."

In the off-season, St. Louis completed a blockbuster trade. The Browns unloaded shortstop Monte Cross, catcher Klondike Douglas, and pitcher Red Donahue to Philadelphia for catcher Jack Clements, pitcher Jack Taylor, and outfielder Tommy Dowd. Cross, Douglas, and Donahue seemed happy to leave the clutches of Von der Ahe. Donahue wasted away in St. Louis, losing fifty-eight games in three years. For Tommy Dowd, the transaction meant an unwelcome reunion with Von der Ahe. Soon afterward, St. Louis spitballer Bill Hart was sold to Pittsburgh for $1,800. The Pirates gave pitcher Jim Hughey in return. For Hart, the trade must have seemed a godsend. Desperate to leave St. Louis from the moment he arrived, Hart lost fifty-six games in two seasons. One could describe unsuccessful curveballers as having pitches that didn't curve. For the unfortunate Hart, his spitballs didn't spit. Von der Ahe had made every player on the St. Louis team expendable for sale or trade. It was hardly a method to create camaraderie. St. Louis ball cranks barely batted an eyelash.

27

Anna Kaiser Versus Della Wells

Von der Ahe's amorous troubles escalated following his divorce from Emma. When the former Mrs. Von der Ahe moved out, Chris' housemaid Anna Kaiser decided that it would be improper to remain as the only woman in the house. Von der Ahe insisted that she stay, conditional to her cleaning the house by day and returning to her parents at night. It didn't quite work out that way. In March 1895, as Anna would later claim, Von der Ahe proposed marriage to her. Von der Ahe was twice Anna's age, and she was younger than his son. The lovesick Anna accepted, although no specific date was set for the wedding. Von der Ahe even promised Anna a trip back to their native Germany. However, Chris was always too busy fixing up the ballpark and the wedding was forever delayed. A marriage so soon after Chris' divorce from Emma would probably cause too much gossip. Anna remained patient with Chris—too patient. On one occasion Von der Ahe's Saint Bernard dog attacked her and bit her in the throat and face. Anna was advised to sue Chris for damages, but she decided that a lawsuit was futile, considering that she was to marry the man. Anna remained convinced of Chris' sincerity. Von der Ahe often wrote tender love letters to Anna in German and would often call her "mein kleines entschen" or "little ducky darling."

Unlike his other escapades, Von der Ahe did not publicize his engagement to Anna Kaiser, keeping the affair a secret. The charade lasted well over a year. Unfortunately for the naive Anna, Von der Ahe was also involved with a lady closer to his own age, Della Wells, a flirtatious and headstrong woman. Della's attraction to Von der Ahe seemed based on his financial standing. The gregarious German always acted like a millionaire with his saloon, grocery, and baseball team. Von der Ahe wore fancy clothes, and his name was frequently mentioned in the papers. Unfortunately, by the middle of the 1890s, creditors constantly hounded Von der Ahe for money. Lawsuits for nonpayment piled up. In July 1896, the relationship blew up when Della found out about a $44,000 credit note being due in August. Smooth-talking Von der Ahe quickly won back Della's favor. Despite the publicity that surrounded Von der Ahe, Anna Kaiser remained unaware of Della Wells. Miss Wells, meanwhile, could not have guessed that her lover was making promises to Anna Kaiser. Von der Ahe always skirted the telltale questions. The story started to unravel one day when Anna and Chris were in Von der Ahe's home. Chris was lying down relaxing, and Anna was reading. As a startled Della Wells entered the room, she asked Anna what she was doing. Anna responded that it was none of Miss Wells' business. Della promptly picked up a chair and bashed her rival. A frightened Anna immediately left the house, followed by a screaming Della and an embarrassed Chris. Anna and Chris climbed into a carriage outside. Della Wells raged at Von der Ahe to come to her, but Chris was going trotting. He would tell Anna on that excursion that he didn't care a hoot for Della Wells. On another occasion, Della visited Chris in his private ballpark box. Anna, following behind, attempted to enter the box of her lover. Anna was rebuffed by Della, the older woman locking the younger woman into the box. After these events, the forceful Della acted quickly. She threatened Chris with a pistol and told him of his imminent demise if he didn't marry her. Della reasoned that a man of Chris Von der Ahe's social standing could not marry a servant girl.

On a September weekend in 1896, Von der Ahe boarded a train and departed St. Louis for environs east. To the gossipy local papers, the reason for the trip was unknown. As was her custom, housekeeper Anna Kaiser left Chris' residence on Friday, to return to her parents. It was to be Miss Kaiser's last day of employment for the Browns' president. The next time Chris stepped off the platform at St. Louis' Union Station, he was a married man. As Von der Ahe announced his betrothal to reporters, they noted the absence of the new bride. Von der Ahe stated that she was Della Wells, who was staying behind in Erie, Pennsylvania. Della was being protected. The new Mrs. Von der Ahe would no longer check into hotel registers as Chris' "niece." Once again, the mercurial Von der Ahe had confounded everyone. The marriage was unknown to Miss Kaiser when she reported for work the next Monday. Browns' secretary Muckenfuss, who had warned Chris that Della was a gold digger, waited for Anna with the news, saddled with the unenviable task of telling the young girl of Chris' marriage to Della. Naturally, Anna was crushed.

Within days, Anna told her story to the *St. Louis Post-Dispatch*. Details had been written in German, in the young girl's diary. Anna was convinced that Chris would marry her. Della Wells threatened Chris into matrimony at gunpoint, but Anna Kaiser had some ammunition of her own. The September 19, 1896, issue of *The Sporting News* headlined,

He Jilted Her
Chris to Be Sued for Breach of Promise
Anna Kaiser, His Former Housekeeper,
will pull Her Little Diary on Him.

Ordinary St. Louis citizens, ignoring the baseball team, now had reason to reach for the sports pages. Von der Ahe's bedroom escapades were the city's hottest gossip. The press quickly pointed out that making love to two different women at the same time and then marrying one of them was not exactly conducive to domestic tranquility.

Anna Kaiser versus Chris Von der Ahe concerned the anguish of a woman scorned. On the advice of her attorney, Kaiser sought $10,000, then $20,000, then $25,000 damages for Von der Ahe's breach of promise. With her fury over Von der Ahe's pretrial tricks, Kaiser's damages kept increasing. In pretrial motions, Von der Ahe requested a change of venue due to scandalous publicity. The request was granted, and the suit moved to St. Charles, Missouri. In March 1897, Von der Ahe submitted a $120 receipt to the court. The receipt, signed by Chris on September 2, 1896, stated: "In payment of every kind and nature of claim to date." However, the judge saw through the ruse when Anna's attorney claimed the receipt was merely for six months' back wages. Von der Ahe's breach of promise did not occur until a week later.[1] Before the matter could be decided, the combatants settled out of court in September 1897. Kaiser reportedly received $3,000 plus court costs from Von der Ahe. In the *same week* of the Kaiser-Von der Ahe settlement, Chris was sued by his attorneys Broadhead and Hezel for unpaid services and by Koken Iron Works for Shoot-the-Chutes materials unpaid. Puzzled creditors found the $3,000 figure highly sensationalized, considering Von der Ahe's financial difficulties. Speculation abounded that the settlement was closer to $250.

The new Von der Ahes moved into Chris' apartment over the saloon at Sportsman's Park. The unusual living arrangement, with the daily sights and smells of baseball, was a novelty for the couple. However, the apartment was hardly a field of dreams. Barely one year after marrying the Browns' President, Della herself was feeling the pressure.

Von der Ahe's slipshod methods of securing money were most suspect. He often slept in his Sportsman's Park apartment. When the bar establishment closed up at night, Von der Ahe would place the money in a box and take it to bed with him. The bartender would arrive in the morning. Upon a prearranged signal, the bartender would whistle to wake his boss. Then Chris would lower the money on a cord through a hole in the ceiling. The idea worked well until some clever crooks learned the secret. Forcing their way into the bar one morning, the robbers simply whistled their way to a profit of a few hundred dollars. By the time the bartender arrived, the crooks were long gone. When the morning man whistled also, Von der Ahe became a bit disoriented by two morning toots. He dropped a shoe through the hole at the startled bartender. Upon waking, Von der Ahe discovered the robbery. Chris called the cops, blamed his bartender, and threatened him with arrest. When the police arrived, Von der Ahe turned soft. Chris reasoned, "Oh, vot der h— I guess it vos vun of mein wives' relatifs. Let der bartender go."

Embarrassing revelations of the Kaiser lawsuit and her husband's debts and legal tribulations made marriage hell for the former Della Wells. By

November 1897, two events occurred that pushed Della over the edge. Mrs. Mary Wells, Della's mother, had been renting property Von der Ahe owned on North Grand Avenue. After nonpayment, Von der Ahe sued Mrs. Wells for $60 back rent; then booted his mother-in-law into the street. Confirming Muckenfuss' observations that the Wells family were sponges, Chris related, "It's all right when you give them all jobs or support them, but when a fellow tries to get rid of them they say you're no good. Yes, I've had too much mother-in-law . . . I had the boys working around here, but I fired them . . . I am not keeping a hotel for the free lodging of my wife's relatives."

During the summer of 1897, Mrs. Wells claimed that she had observed her son-in-law buying a basket downtown and placing a handwritten German note inside. Unaware of his mother-in-law's presence, Von der Ahe hired a messenger to deliver the gift to Anna Kaiser. The basket never arrived at its destination. Along the way, Mrs. Wells intercepted the messenger and the basket. Chris later exclaimed that when he arrived home that night there was a "hell of a dime mit de oldt woman." Despite Anna Kaiser's legal action, Chris was still communicating with his former housekeeper. *The Sporting News* questioned Von der Ahe's fidelity to Della. "If he gets rid of his present wife, Chris will, they say, elope to Germany with Miss Kaiser amid the castles which he has built on the Rhine or in the air."

As the new year began, many people in St. Louis celebrated with songs of Auld Lang Syne. Chris and Della weren't exactly reveling in party spirit. Instead, Von der Ahe decided that constant bickering with his wife forced his hand. He filed for divorce in January of 1898, after less than fifteen months of marriage. There were no children. The bitter divorce action had gossips saying that both parties had used private detectives to obtain evidence on each other. A petition to the court released by Von der Ahe stated that Chris "always treated the defendant with kindness and affection while discharging all obligations of the marriage." In addition, the petition stated,

> *The marriage was unfortunate . . . it was an act of generosity on his part . . . The defendant has habitually absented herself from the home and neglected her duties there, and has been in the habit of meeting persons unknown to the plaintiff . . . She runs up large bills with tradesmen for articles which she does not need . . . She has recently said that she wished the plaintiff was dead so she could have a good time with his money, that she married him for his money, and that she is in the habit of calling him vile names and striking him whenever she feels inclined.*

Mrs. Della Von der Ahe could hardly have been surprised. She bitterly contested her husband by retaining ex-Governor Charles Johnson and filing a countersuit. Della denied the charges and promised juicy tidbits that would make Chris squirm. Doubtless this would be the story of Von der Ahe's love basket to his former housekeeper.

Von der Ahe's method of communicating his disfavor with Della was similar to his lockout of Anna Kaiser. After returning home from shopping one day, Mrs. Von der Ahe discovered entirely new doors and locks on the apartment at the park. Going downstairs, she ran into a housemaid who snootily commented about the impending divorce. Frantic for her husband, Della noticed huge chains around the ball yard. When Della stormed to the saloon, six park employees surrounded her. One man gave her a note written by her husband. The note informed her of her "release," worded in the precise manner of a ballplayer's firing. For a time, Della went without her elaborate boudoir articles. Soon, a trunk of wrinkled clothing was delivered to Mrs. Della Wells Von der Ahe, who was forced to move in with her mother.

When the combatants met in court, Della brought out all the sordid details of her marriage. The Browns' President was often under the effect of intoxicating drink, calling Della vile names and accusing her of frequenting places of ill repute. Von der Ahe punched his wife and threatened to throw her out the window or down the stairs. Whatever the truth of Von der Ahe's estranged relationships, the Browns' magnate would soon suffer a few sleepless nights of his own. The St. Louis courts granted the Von der Ahes a divorce in January 1898.

28

The Browns for Sale

As the Browns stumbled and bumbled on the field in the 1890s and Von der Ahe's personal life dissolved into a morass of troubles, there were reports and rumors of deals to buy the St. Louis baseball club. Most included elaborate plans to reinvolve the baseball citizenry of St. Louis. Von der Ahe was defaulting on his loans to pay off the new ballpark. This permanent loss of revenue would not be in the best interests of the National League. Because of the embarrassment of being forced to sell his team, Von der Ahe desperately tried to suppress the stories. Though many of the meetings were secret, *The Sporting News* continued to report the details. Most likely the paper had an inside source, perhaps a club director, supplying information and speculation on deals. *The Sporting News* wrote numerous Von der Ahe baseball obituaries. The weekly wanted Chris gone and pride restored to the city.

By the early 1890s, the local papers were reporting the sad news of Von der Ahe's finances. Since his baseball beginnings, Chris had done business with the Northwestern Savings Bank, freely taking out loans for his projects without security. However, due to Von der Ahe's investments in the failed American Association and losses from the Player's League, he owed the bank $44,000, of which $29,000 covered losses. Von der Ahe mortgaged his Grand Avenue properties for $15,000 more. The Northwestern Savings Bank had acquired part of Von der Ahe's Sportsman's Park Club and Association stock as extra security. Final payment on the $44,000 note was due in August 1896. Von der Ahe's creditors continued to line up. He was in arrears on the Mark Baldwin and the Pendleton cases. Chris also owed $1,200 in ballpark back taxes. *The Sporting News* reported that with personal debt, Von der Ahe was nearly $70,000 in the red.

Von der Ahe's unusual bargaining style and blustery statements greatly contributed to the dragged-out dealings. In June 1897, Chris boasted that his baseball holdings (for sale) exceeded $250,000. He would not sell unless he could dispose of the ballpark as well. The comments only further exposed

Von der Ahe's idiocy. The Browns certainly weren't worth a quarter of a million dollars. Furthermore, Von der Ahe and the Sportsman's Park Club and Association did not own the park; they leased the grounds from the Lindell Estate at $1,500 per year. Von der Ahe's Sportsman's Park Club and Association owned only the St. Louis Browns franchise. *The Sporting News* joked that the only real estate Von der Ahe owned was his burial plot. Chris was desperate to pay off debts, but he was exceedingly reluctant to sell the team. He fought to prevent his wife and an army of creditors from acquiring his beloved Browns. He may have been forced into negotiations by local newspaper pressure. Under intense cigar smoke and alcoholic drink, negotiations continued. One-upmanship and ego bruising were hallmarks of the deals. Money talked. Those not interested in anything other than publicity, walked.

The first sincere offer was made by Cleveland Spiders' owner Frank DeHaas Robison. A first-class industrialist, Robison earned his fortune in the trolley car business. Two months earlier, his rowdy club had captured the 1895 Temple Cup championship from the Baltimore Orioles. Feeling the power as owner of the best team in the game, Robison made a pitch for the Browns in January 1896. *The Sporting News* reported Robison would buy out the St. Louis franchise for $100,000, disband the Browns, and then transfer his Cleveland club to St. Louis. Cleveland would be frozen out of the National League and replaced with Detroit from the Western League. The National League required the consent of all clubs for the deal to finalize. The story seemed concocted and was denied by both parties, but rumors persisted in the press.

Von der Ahe bristled at implications that he wanted to sell the Browns. A. J. Flanner of *The Sporting News* cornered Chris' son Eddie for a story. When the younger Von der Ahe confessed his father was trying to sell the club, Chris Von der Ahe became livid. The Boss President sought out Flanner. According to umpire Tim Hurst, the following exchange took place.

"Flanner, vot you mean by wridin dot der Browns is for sale?" yelled an irate Chris.

"Your son Eddie told me so, Mr. Von der Ahe," said the reporter.

"You villain, you drawt mein poy on to say dot. Dake off your goat. I am going ter ligck you to an inch of your life," said Von der Ahe.

To show he meant business, the Browns' President removed his garment.

"Chris, you are an old man. Take care. I do not want to hurt you," said Flanner calmly.

"Ach himmel! Vot un insuldt. Olt mans. Olt mans me Chris Von der Ahe, der Poss Bresident of der Browns, der Four Dime Vinners? Yes, I neffer vos so goodt in mein life. Come on Flanner, und I show you who vos der olt man."

With Von der Ahe's words, Flanner departed the scene. It is unclear whether the reporter was intimidated or entertained by Von der Ahe's posturing.

Thanks to Cincinnati magnate John Brush, Von der Ahe was loaned thousands of dollars. Edward Becker, a retired grocer, successful soap manufacturer, and Browns director, was also known to advance Chris money.

Known in the press as Chris' "angel," Becker was believed to have secured 25 percent stock interest in the Browns. He habitually traveled with Von der Ahe to protect his interests. Because of these two men, Von der Ahe received an extension on the $44,000 note due the Northwestern Savings Bank. The National League was not as sympathetic, although certain league magnates were also secretly fronting Chris undisclosed sums.

Sale rumors persisted. The principals included Frank DeHaas Robison and brother M. Stanley, Baltimore magnate Harry Von der Horst, John Brush, New York owner Andrew Freedman, Edward Becker, and Browns' secretary Benjamin S. Muckenfuss. One 1896 plan involved a partnership between Von der Horst and Robison to pool the best players from Baltimore and St. Louis and reform a team in St. Louis. Another Von der Horst-Robison idea involved moving the Browns to New York. However, Gotham real estate prices made the deal prohibitive. When Von der Horst asked Robison to contribute Cleveland players, the Baltimore-Cleveland partnership effectively ended.

Record keeping for the St. Louis organization was convoluted, at best. In November 1896, a shareholder of the Sportsman's Park Club and Association named George Olney inquired about the profits of the club. Olney had bought four shares of stock some five years earlier. Since Von der Ahe still claimed profits of between $10,000 and $25,000 each year, Olney was curious about the stockholders' share of financial returns. To assist him in this money trail, Olney hired an attorney. Unfortunately for Olney, the trail grew cold. When Olney visited Sportsman's Park one day, Von der Ahe flew into a rage and dismissed him from the grounds. Olney then attempted to open negotiations by letter, but received no response. Secretary Muckenfuss likely kept the financial affairs of the Sportsman's Park Club and Association hidden from public view. Rather frustrated, Olney threatened a lawsuit based on gross mismanagement. He cited horse racing, Shoot-the-Chutes, and numerous other unprofitable ventures. Olney also claimed, as did Edward Von der Ahe, that the Browns' owner used some of the money for himself without proper accountability. In fact, the Sportsman's Park Club and Association had always been Chris Von der Ahe's private power club. Year after year he was named president because he held most of the shares. When members realized they had no say in club affairs, they either quit or Von der Ahe demanded their resignation.

Mr. Claud Martin was a member of Chris' board of directors. During a meeting, Chris brought to a vote the subject of fining Tommy Dowd. The ballplayer happened to be a friend of Martin. There were four votes upholding Dowd and one, Von der Ahe's, for fining him.

"Der ayes have id," declared the Boss President. "Dowt is fined $250. It is so ortered, Mr. Secretary."

"Hold on, Mr. President," interrupted Martin, "let us see about this. There were four votes 'no' and but one vote 'aye.' I submit that the 'noes' have it and demand a rising vote."

"Ordter, ordter," stammered Chris. "You are oudt of order, Mardin. Der vos four votes 'no' budt who voted dem? You, Mardin, und Gottlieb Greun und Peck (John Peckington) und Chewlius Lehman. You fellers hold vun share each, vich I give you mit a season bass. Now, I own 196 shares. I deglare Dowt fined $250. Any direktor who vished to vote 'no' vill bleas handt in his share of stock und also his season bass. I, Chris Von der Ahe, am runnin' dis glub und don't you forged it, Mardin."

Another speculative deal involved a partnership between Robison and Brush. Discussions revolved around a straight franchise swap of the St. Louis Browns and the Cleveland Spiders. As a business deal, the idea made sense. Cleveland, despite winning on the field, was a poor baseball town. Because of local law, Sunday games were disallowed, and working-class patronage remained sparse. Toward the end of the 1896 campaign, the half-holiday Saturday law was passed. Ball cranks turned up for Saturday Cleveland games in droves. Conversely, the St. Louis team fared poorly on the diamond. Rabid St. Louis ball cranks, shown a glimmer of a winner, would plop down their quarters to eagerly attend the games. St. Louis would thrive with a good club in the city. The Browns could do no worse in Cleveland. Neither Robison's Cleveland team nor Brush's Cincinnatis would be wrecked in the process. The Western League Indianapolis franchise, a minor-league farm for the Reds, could be used to pool players for the deal. To appease haughty Von der Ahe and save Chris from the humiliation of selling out, Robison wanted to retain Chris as figurehead owner. Financially, Von der Ahe would have no interest and no power. Robison denied the transfer plan, but *The Sporting News* claimed correspondence between Robison and Von der Ahe proved otherwise. Von der Ahe's baseball ownership seemed numbered in days. The National League seemed powerless to stop the transfer. The aloof Von der Ahe reveled in keeping the speculative press guessing. Mused Chris in December of 1896, "Something that will surprise you may happen." At the League meeting in February 1897, Von der Ahe petitioned colleagues for money to help his struggling franchise. Chris' money man was secretary Benjamin Muckenfuss, who had tried all winter to secure donations. The petition failed. Instead, Chris resorted to other methods to raise cash. Any and all players were up for sale; sacrificial lambs for Chris to recoup losses. Von der Ahe was said to be willing to offer Robison in, but only as partial owner.

Over Christmas 1897, there were several other offers to buy the Browns. Cap Anson was prepared to invest his money. Telegramming Von der Ahe, Anson asked Chris to furnish a statement of the club's indebtedness and name a price. Anson's effort went no farther, since Von der Ahe would not provide the information.

Two more concurrent offers surfaced to buy the team. John Brush led a group that tried various methods to secure the Browns. Brush's ideas included persuading other League magnates to purchase shares of Browns' stock. This idea was rejected in November because some magnates believed Brush already had optioned stock from Von der Ahe. Brush wanted to be a major Sportsman's Park Club shareholder in another scheme. Chris would be indebted to Brush for the payment of a $20,000 bond issue and Becker's bank note for $12,000. However, this deal soured when Brush insisted on having Reds' business manager Frank Bancroft stationed at Sportsman's Park to look after Brush's interests. Like the earlier Robison offer, the plan called for Von der Ahe as figurehead owner.

Four prominent St. Louis businessmen made a strong effort to buy Von der Ahe's team in December 1897. The group, known as the St. Louis syndicate, was interested in the Sportsman's Park Club and Association, the leasehold on the ballpark, and the players known as the Browns. The syndicate was composed of Samuel Myerson, Gus Frey, Charles Spink, and George Munson. Myerson and Frey were both presidents of local printing companies; Spink remained business manager of Von der Ahe's nemesis, *The Sporting News*. Munson was once the Browns' secretary. The syndicate was likely seen by Von der Ahe as hostile.

The syndicate's purpose was twofold: buy out and reorganize the Sportsman's Park Club and Association and restore the allegiance of the St. Louis citizenry to the Browns. With the syndicate's financial solvency, a deal seemed probable. Syndicate moguls could easily hype the Browns and regain the lost fan base.

On December 11, 1897, negotiations began, with Frey representing the syndicate and Muckenfuss the Browns. Chris Von der Ahe was curiously absent. Right off the bat, the syndicate made an offer that was quickly rejected by secretary Muckenfuss. At Von der Ahe's insistence, Muckenfuss then read a prepared statement by his boss. The asking price for the St. Louis franchise was $85,000. Two thousand shares of capital stock at $25 apiece totaled $50,000, with the rest of the money to be used for player salaries and ballpark leasehold transfer. Day one of the negotiations ended.

Two days later, the parties met again. This time, Muckenfuss informed the syndicate of Von der Ahe's dealings with Brush for a portion of the holdings. Myerson proposed a five-day period to examine the financial books of the Browns. The syndicate gave a $500 deposit for the audit. Muckenfuss agreed, but when the syndicate began its examination, they discovered Browns' finances were in a most haphazard way. The syndicate insisted on auditing for twenty days. Von der Ahe wanted $5,000 worth of good-faith guarantees. The two parties agreed. Attorneys for the two sides were notified to prepare papers for signature and a final meeting to consummate the deal.

The end of Chris Von der Ahe's ownership of the Browns seemed imminent. The December 17 local papers covered the story, but *The Sporting News* scaled back coverage due to Charles Spink's involvement. At the moment of truth, as syndicate members picked up their pens, Von der Ahe called a halt to the proceedings. He insisted that only 1,715 shares of stock be transferred, instead of 2,000. An additional $10,000 would be required for the sale to become finalized. Was this bluff or bluster? The $85,000 agreed-upon price had now ballooned to $95,000. Realizing the absurdity of dealing with Von der Ahe, the syndicate backed away.

Within two weeks, *The Sporting News* reported on a story filed by rival weekly *Sporting Life*, written by a "B. M. Stuart." *The Sporting News* claimed that Stuart was actually a sour-grapes pseudonym for Benjamin S. Muckenfuss. The inflammatory article named names and told of the inside story of how Von der Ahe offered him a $10,000 commission to sell the Browns. When the $10,000 was tacked on to the asking price by Von der Ahe at the last minute, the syndicate canceled the deal. Naturally, Stuart was furious at Von der Ahe and the syndicate, and bereft of the ten grand. *The Sporting News* reported that Frey's influence had secured a job for Muckenfuss with the Browns in 1894. The whole deal may have been fueled by the $10,000 commission. By the end of the month, *Sporting Life* reported Stuart (Muckenfuss) was a stanch friend of Von der Ahe who really ran the finances of the Browns. Stuart modestly claimed that he would have the herculean task of repairing the Browns' finances once Von der Ahe was removed from baseball. Stuart then named himself Von der Ahe's "logical successor." *The Sporting News* trashed Stuart's claims. They also trumpeted that the press would boom the game following Chris' baseball demise.

Another complicated deal involved a Muckenfuss tip to John Brush to save the Browns. Despite some sympathy from fellow magnates, most viewed Von der Ahe's troubles as entirely self-inflicted. Sometime in 1897, a prominent Philadelphian posed as Chris' friend and secretly wrote letters to Muckenfuss to get the best selling price. Unfortunately for the Philadelphia man, Muckenfuss warned John Brush, who called newspapermen to a hotel and exposed the secret letters. As a reward, Von der Ahe named Muckenfuss the new president of the Browns.

Despite *The Sporting News* comments on Von der Ahe's "characteristic duplicity and contemptible vacillations," Chris met with Myerson at the park in early January 1898. Again, Von der Ahe insisted on an asking price of $95,000. Chris quickly capitulated, and the figure was lowered to $85,000. Though Von der Ahe owned 1,761 shares, the stock was in possession of Edward Becker as security for a $12,000 note. To protect purchasers from Von der Ahe's prior debt, Chris was to present an itemized statement to the syndicate. The transfer would take place by January 4, 1898. Meanwhile, Von der Ahe fondly repeated the statement, "I am the St. Louis Club." Chris was keeping his lawyers busy while doing everything to hold on to his team.

As a new January 15, 1898, bank loan deadline loomed, Von der Ahe stunned everyone by becoming the trustee and preferred creditor of his own club for $91,000! The Sportsman's Park and Club Association filed a chattel deed of trust securing liabilities in excess of $108,000. In force was a stipulation that Von der Ahe sell the club within six months and keep the property insured for $30,000. Thirty other creditors owned claims of between $100 and $3,975. The largest sum was due Anheuser-Busch Brewing. Outside indebtedness was $17,000. Mortgage and judgment bonds against Von der Ahe were not affected by the deed. The voluminous document authorized

Von der Ahe to take charge of his assets within six months. The alternative was a public sale of the Browns on the steps of the courthouse.

Immediately, the Sportsman's Park and Club Association met and again elected Chris principal stockholder. Von der Ahe's trustee scheme infuriated Edward Becker, whose stock would be worthless if preferred claims were paid. Von der Ahe then fired Becker, who was still in possession of all of the Browns stock. The stage was set for a court battle between all principals. John Brush found Browns affairs in such disarray that it was impossible to determine clear title to holdings. The creditors argued that Von der Ahe's claims were fictitious. *The Sporting News* headlined "Slick Scheme," and reported that without credit or cash, Von der Ahe's "conspiracy" was sure to fail. A sheriff's auction concerning all rights, titles, and claims to the St. Louis Browns would commence at the courthouse on February 5.

After the trustee story surfaced, Brush's team dropped its bid for the Browns, citing pending suits, judgments, claims, mortgages, and other encumbrances. The Brush bid was halted despite a certified check of $60,000 that was reported to be on its way to St. Louis.

29

Bread and Water Days

The culmination of Von der Ahe's troubles occurred during the calendar years 1898–1899. His staggering professional and private disasters would finally catch up with him. These calamities would severely test the most hardened of men.

In February 1898, Chris Von der Ahe endured the most embarrassing episode of his long career. The event occurred during the time of his divorce suit from Della, the aborted sale of his team, and his horrendous excuse for a baseball club.

Unbeknownst to Von der Ahe, an early February conference took place at the Carnegie Building in Pittsburgh. At the meeting, attorneys Charles O'Brien and Charles Ashley represented Mark Baldwin. Richard Scandrett and Arthur Fording spoke for their client, W. A. Nimick. The result of the meeting was Scandrett's suggestion that Von der Ahe be removed from St. Louis by force.

On Monday, February 7, a group of gentlemen from the Steel City arrived at Union Station in St. Louis to set up shop at a local hotel. The group was headed by former Pittsburgh Base Ball Club President W. A. Nimick. Attorneys Scandrett and Fording were also present, along with a private detective named Nicholas Bendel. A *Pittsburgh Dispatch* reporter recorded the details. After consulting with Mark Baldwin's St. Louis attorneys, the group set the bold plan into action. The idea was to force Chris Von der Ahe to pay legal debts from two judgments rendered in favor of Baldwin. The method was kidnapping.

Unfortunately for Von der Ahe's bondsman Nimick, nonpayment of the judgment would result in substantial financial loss. The court had ruled that Nimick had thirty days to produce Von der Ahe in person to the sheriff of Allegheny County, Pennsylvania. In the meantime, Von der Ahe had ignored all communications concerning the case.

Now, more than seven years after Baldwin's tampering, a scheme to kidnap the German magnate unfolded in St. Louis. To help set the trap, telegrams arrived from New York addressed to Von der Ahe by New York writer Robert Smith. Von der Ahe believed Smith would call on him in St. Louis. Their meeting would concern player deals with Giants owner Andrew Freedman. On hotel stationery, Smith affixed his signature for a proposed rendezvous with Von der Ahe. Chris took the bait. Instead of greeting Smith, a waiting Von der Ahe was hustled into a carriage by Bendel. The private detective informed Chris of important business discussions. After a ride through the city, the carriage headed to East St. Louis. Bendel then informed Chris that their destination was Pittsburgh. As Von der Ahe struggled for freedom and bellowed with rage, he was handcuffed to detective Bendel. Von der Ahe suffered a smashed hat and a torn coat and vest. The carriage sped over a bridge that connected St. Louis to East St. Louis. On the Illinois side of the Mississippi River, a bridge policeman heard Von der Ahe's cries. When questioned by police, Bendel produced a legal writ of arrest for the unpaid Baldwin judgments. Chris' bumpy carriage ride continued. Meeting up with the rest of the conspirators, Bendel and the group placed Von der Ahe on a Baltimore and Ohio train for Pittsburgh. A Pullman car conductor had been tipped to the plan. Once aboard, a miserable Von der Ahe tried to smash windows. He reportedly consumed $36 worth of wine and food in an effort to expose his enemies and get them thrown off the train. Soon, Chris resigned himself to his fate and bawled like a baby. The B & O chugged east to Pittsburgh. To break the monotony of the twenty-two-hour ride, a breakfast occurred in Cincinnati. Von der Ahe was in no mood to break bread with the scoundrels.

Bendel and Von der Ahe exited the locomotive at Glenwood, Pennsylvania. Bendel's instructions were to transport the fallen magnate to Pittsburgh. Meanwhile, the Scandrett and Fording party sped to the Smokey City. Once at their destination, they delivered an impromptu press conference. To a crush of spectators, Scandrett and Fording triumphantly announced the capture of Von der Ahe. Exaggerating wildly, the men reported that portly Von der Ahe had escaped his captors but was retrieved in the woods by Bendel in Wheeling, West Virginia.

On Tuesday morning, Von der Ahe arrived in Pittsburgh and was promptly led to an Allegheny County jail. A series of legal maneuvers followed. The question of habeas corpus, a law that required a prisoner be brought before a court to decide the legality of his detention, was foremost on the minds of the captors and the captive. At the jail, Bendel and the group met a United States Marshal who surrendered Von der Ahe to Judge Marcus Acheson of United States Circuit Court.

In court, Chris was a sight for sore eyes. After his long ordeal, Von der Ahe appeared a pathetic figure with his unwashed face, rumpled clothes, and puzzled expression. Von der Ahe's day of reckoning over the protracted Baldwin affair was at hand. Chris' attorney, J. Scott Ferguson, declared to Judge Buffington that his client's arrest without due process was in violation of the Constitution. The Judge refused the writ until he could confer with Judge Acheson. A few anxious moments passed before Acheson rendered his decision. The Judge ordered Von der Ahe released on $2,500 bail. Ferguson put up the money and invited Chris to his home to stay the night and change his ratty clothes.

The next day, the packed courtroom was filled with attorneys, spectators, and friends and enemies of the German magnate. Von der Ahe smiled at his well-wishers and frowned at the opposition. Judge Buffington would decide the writ of habeas corpus. The gathering resembled a circus. Again, Ferguson pleaded for his client. After all the testimony was heard, Judge Buffington decided to take the case under advisement. Von der Ahe was again released, with the $3,000 bail bonded by Ferguson. With these delays, the Baldwin camp prepared for contingencies. The laws of Pennsylvania provided that when a judgment for torts was unpaid in which there was false imprisonment, the defendant could be placed in jail until the judgment was satisfied. After 60 days, the defendant could be released by taking the insolvent debtor's oath. Baldwin could simply keep arresting Chris Von der Ahe. When Judge Buffington finally decided that the arrest and transportation to Pittsburgh were legal, Van der Ahe took up residence in jail.

For a man who once hosted lavish banquets for his glorious ballplayers, those bread and water days must have been miserable. Von der Ahe received no special treatment, although he did turn over his diamond stud and ring to the warden for security. Meals consisted of bread and coffee, bacon and bread, and potatoes on tin dishes. Von der Ahe had little appetite. Instead, he spent his days furiously wiring secretary Muckenfuss for money. Had Von der Ahe spied the St. Louis papers, it would have depressed him even more. The headlines outlined details of a man duped into being kidnapped. Little sympathy existed for Von der Ahe's plight. *The Sporting News* intoned: "In style of architecture he belongs to the cherubic, modified by the aldermanic and touched up with the ornate coloring which is most in evidence upon the Dutch barns of Eastern Pennsylvania. In language he is a fricassee, in nationality a conundrum, and in general qualities an uncertainty. He could grow rich on an ash pile, but would go broke on a plantation. 'Der bublic be tamned' was original with him, not with Mr. Vanderbilt . . . "

Back in St. Louis, secretary Muckenfuss sent numerous telegrams to his boss, saying that money was forthcoming. Muckenfuss was merely stalling and trying to protect his job. Friends and associates of Von der Ahe refused to help. The Missouri governor, indignant over the manner of Von der Ahe's treatment, declared that Bendel and his associates would go to prison for their misdeed. Most likely, the governor was merely blustering, upset that a Missouri citizen could be so embarrassed by the State of Pennsylvania. Finally, a gift of $2,000 arrived from an unknown sympathizer. Ex-Congressman John Glover traveled to Pittsburgh, armed with the two grand. Glover met with attorney Ferguson to appeal that the case be taken to the Supreme Court. But $2,000 was hardly enough to spring Von der Ahe from jail. The efforts of Chris Von der Ahe's *enemies* were required to finally bail him out of the mess.

MR. NIMICK: Please Do Us the Favor to Take the Rest of Them!

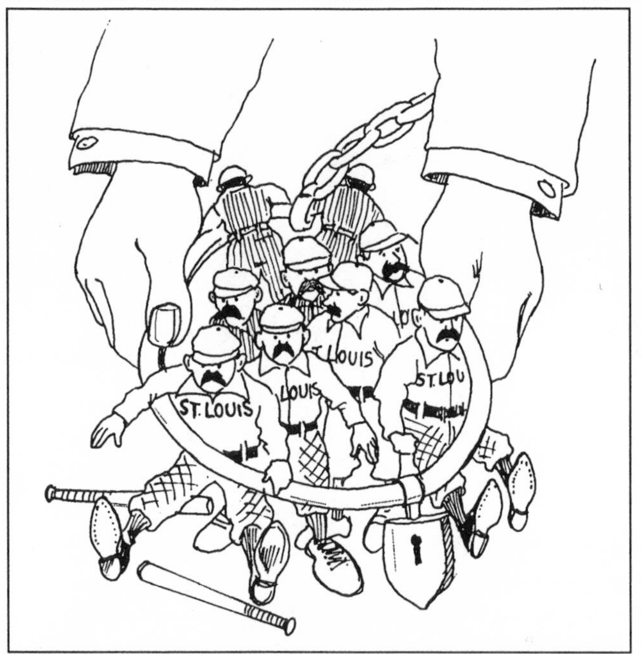

A wave of joy would sweep across a half a dozen towns, should
some good friend of ours kidnap the old St. Louis Browns.
We shouldn't mind the loss at all; we'd gladly part with Chris,
if some Philanthropist would do a favor such as this.

Keep Van Der Ahe and take the browns, and take the shoot-the-chutes
and Sportsman's Park the racing track or anything that suits!
Cart off the whole caboodle, sir, and take it in a hurry!
By doing so'twill save the town an awful lot of worry!

After the Von der Ahe kidnapping episode, the above illustration and poem appeared in the *St. Louis Post-Dispatch.* (*Reprinted with permission of the* St. Louis Post-Dispatch, *copyright 1898.*)

A day at Sportsman's Park. (*Reprinted with permission of the* St. Louis Post-Dispatch, *copyright 1897, and redrawn by Michael D. Arnold.*)

After a lengthy meeting, Cincinnati President John Brush and National League President Nicholas Young determined that the League must take action. The Von der Ahe-Baldwin affair was bad publicity for all concerned. Cautiously, and in secret, the League posted money to free Von der Ahe. In the bargain, Von der Ahe had to agree to get out of baseball, once and for all. To protect its interests, the League determined that a sale of the Browns would not necessarily guarantee membership. The National League would survive without Von der Ahe, but not without the city of St. Louis.

With Browns' misfortunes emanating from Von der Ahe, the League adopted a hands-off policy. John Brush tried to convince League powers to help the Browns, but the League understood that financing St. Louis equated to helping Chris Von der Ahe. Due to financial debt, Von der Ahe no longer controlled the Browns' daily operations. In March 1898, the National League held its annual meeting in St. Louis. Von der Ahe, recently removed from his Pittsburgh debacle, attended the meeting with Benjamin Muckenfuss. Under normal circumstances, the League's spring fete in St. Louis would have served as a triumph for Chris Von der Ahe. Unfortunately, Von der Ahe had long passed from powerful magnate to major-league nonentity. Meeting discussions centered on John Brush's antirowdyism platform. With Brush's help, Von der Ahe was able to secure a $4,000 loan from individual magnates to keep the sinking Browns afloat. The National League exercised its power by installing Muckenfuss as President of the Browns. A notable absentee was Von der Ahe's Brooklyn nemesis Charles Byrne, who had died.

With Von der Ahe sidelined by financial and personal tribulations, Benjamin Muckenfuss assumed full authority of the Browns. Over the winter of 1897–1898, the horse track and Shoot-the-Chutes were removed from Sportsman's Park. With the bleacher improvements, Muckenfuss attempted to restore the park to its original design. Few St. Louis cranks were gullible enough to pay to see broken-down ponies race around a ballfield, nor were they interested in plunging down a water slide. The latter attraction had cost Von der Ahe $30,000. Baseball would be the only game in town. Muckenfuss' first order of business was to hire a manager for the 1898 season.

The choice was Timothy Hurst, an aggressive, redheaded Irishman. A onetime Pennsylvania coal miner, Hurst picked up his toughness from commonplace lunchtime fights on the job. Following his mining days, Hurst pitched some baseball before suffering a sore arm. A physically active man, Hurst competed in boxing and long-distance walking events.

However, it was Hurst's umpiring that earned him his reputation. The veteran Hurst seldom fined players for their on-field tirades. Instead, he simply and subtly insulted them.

Once Hurst scared the daylights out of a transgressing ballplayer. Hurst

> *. . . put his mouth close to the player's ear and said coolly, "Now you're getting a bit chesty, I see you've made a couple of good stops, knocked out a couple of hits and you think you're solid with the crowd. Well, . . . I'll give*

you the key to my room at the hotel, where everything is nice and quiet, and when we get in there alone I'll break that jaw of yours so you can't kick for the rest of the season. I'll see that you go out quietly so you can explain your injury by saying you fell down somewhere."

The player never took the key.

Hurst's methods upset many players and teams, but the National League tolerated his behavior. On August 4, 1897, Hurst's officiating in Cincinnati precipitated a sensational incident that ended his umpiring career. After Hurst made some calls against the home nine, Cincinnati fans grew restless. Not content with hurling epithets at the despised Hurst, one crank tossed a beer stein onto the field. The mug struck Hurst in the back. Recalling that umpire William Quinn had his skull crushed by a beer mug, Hurst picked up the stein and tossed it back into the crowd underhanded, hitting a Cincinnati fireman flush in the face. This action prompted a ballpark riot. Hurst required a police escort to hustle him to safety. For the incident, Hurst was arrested and charged with assault to kill. An official with the Cincinnati club posted a $300 bond, but Hurst skipped town. The fleeing umpire was later plucked out of a crowd at a Pittsburgh-St. Louis game and spent a fitful night on a bed in the jury room. After a $500 bond was paid, Hurst was released. He eventually paid a fine of $100. Hurst would later call the mug tossed at him a premeditated attack. Cincinnati papers branded Hurst a "crook, robber, thief, ex-prize fighter, short-card gambler, drunkard, murderer." The game was Tim Hurst's last as umpire in the League. He was officially released that winter.

Hurst's hiring surprised baseball scribes. Though he promised a decent squad and a hearty training regimen, Hurst's new job wouldn't be easy. With the season less than two months away, no St. Louis players had signed contracts. *The Sporting News* sniped that the task would prove nearly impossible, since the "ruling spirit of the club is jailed at Pittsburgh."

The 1898 Browns started the season red hot. Unfortunately, it wasn't what they had in mind. On Saturday, April 10, Chris Von der Ahe nearly went mad. Barely two months had passed since his Baldwin-induced kidnapping to Pittsburgh. The Browns were entertaining Chicago at Sportsman's Park, and in the bottom of the second inning, a small disturbance broke out in the grandstand. At first, the nearly 4,000 in attendance believed a routine scuffle was taking place. Irritated cries of "Sit down!" and "Put the fighters out!" wafted through the air. Constables would eject the offenders. Soon, however, many spectators started to vacate their seats in a haphazard sort of way. Several minutes passed, and then flames began to lick the seats from below. A fire had broken out in the grandstand.

Ballplayers and umpires, unconcerned at first, now could not help but notice the interruption. Word filtered down to the field, and the game was called. Immediately, the men at play became rescuers, rushing to the stands to warn spectators. Many sat dumbfounded at the curious actions of the excited players. The drama increased with the intensity of the blaze and thick smoke. Despite calm actions by manager Hurst and counterpart Tom Burns of

Chicago, a panic ensued. Amid shouts and screams, heroic players assisted fans to the exits and onto the field in efforts to escape the conflagration. Upended benches were thrown against the grandstand to assist spectators to terra firma. When spectators surged toward the exit between the clubhouse and the saloon, they found the gate closed. The courageous formed a human battering ram to crash through the barrier.

In thirty minutes, the fire reduced the $62,000 park to ashes, burning everything except the right-field bleachers. A day of baseball and sunshine ended in hysteria. No one was killed, but at least 100 people were burned and blistered. Several others suffered leg injuries by jumping from the grandstand. Many were trampled on the narrow, winding stairways. In ruins were the left-field bleachers, the grandstand, the club office building, the saloon and Von der Ahe's apartment above the saloon. The rooftop boxes, used by the directors and reporters, were especially vulnerable during the blaze.

In the aftermath, one man's anguish could scarcely be contained. A frantic Chris Von der Ahe ran around the streets screaming like a madman. He had to be physically restrained by friends. In the fire, Von der Ahe lost all his personal effects, including trophies, correspondence files, and his finery of clothes. Chris' beloved dog Fly had also perished in the blaze. The ticket seller was only able to save about half of the gate receipts. Loss estimates forecast $30,000 to $50,000 in damages. Ballpark insurance covered only $35,000. Von der Ahe estimated losses to his uninsured personal property at $30,000.

The "generally accepted version" was that the fire started when a fan dropped a lighted cigar into a pile of old canvas below the grandstand. It is ironic that a cigar, which Von der Ahe smoked and used as a prop for his successes, would cause such a disaster. Suspicion was easily aroused that the fire was deliberate. Certainly, Chris Von der Ahe had enemies. The National League governing body was hardly his friend. *The Sporting News*, local St. Louis dailies, and newspapers around America were highly critical of his handling of the Browns. Creditors and businessmen alike fought running battles to recover their monies. These enemies had every reason to see Von der Ahe exorcised from baseball, come hell or high water. Ordinary St. Louis citizens, who didn't care a darn about baseball, bad-mouthed the magnate. How difficult would it be to "accidentally" lose a cigar in a pile of brittle, flammable canvas?

As the flames smoldered, St. Louis' de facto President Muckenfuss wired National League President Nick Young to have the home stand transferred to Chicago. Manager Hurst objected to the plan. Desperate for cash and with Von der Ahe's blessing, Hurst organized a gang of construction workers. With many Browns' players, the crew worked through the night. Under electric light, the men removed debris and erected temporary stands for nearly 4,000 people.

Architect Weiss quickly formulated a plan to rebuild Sportsman's Park. The grandstand and clubhouse were priorities. The bar and dressing rooms, previously located under the grandstand, were now redesigned as a new steel structure with orchestra chairs. The three rooftop perches would not be rebuilt. Instead, scribes would have their own boxes near the field. Stairways were designed wider and straighter for future fire safety. A promise was made that a full-house crowd could be emptied in two minutes in case of emergency. New ticket offices would be solid brick. The left-field bleachers would not be restored. A pavilion, covered with wooden benches, would take shape between the stands and the right-field bleachers. The entire job was to be completed in time for the fourth of July. Meanwhile, with the Browns involved in a balancing act with new construction, the team continued its home schedule. As players played and construction workers hammered and hoisted, a new round of lawsuits found their way into Von der Ahe's hands. He was being sued again, this time for personal injuries suffered by spectators at his firetrap. In addition, there were lawsuits concerning building safety violations.

The next day, St. Louis' Renaissance Man awarded himself a new job. He'd been a grocer, bartender, magnate, bandleader, and baseball manager. Suddenly, Von der Ahe assumed foreman duties, supervising a group of carpenters. In the hastily rebuilt ruins, 7,000 gawkers showed up for the Sunday, April 11, affair. Due to the absence of bleachers, ropes were strung along the outfield to contain fans. Both the Colts and Browns agreed beforehand that hits into the crowd counted for three bases. After most of the faithful plopped into their makeshift seats, St. Louis management insisted on 50-cent admission rather than the customary quarter. Late arrivals grumbled over the unannounced price hike.

While some cranks were unhappy, manager Hurst positively fumed. His Browns were humiliated 14–1, making eleven miscues afield and generating only six hits. Said Hurst after the debacle: "We made enough errors to do for a week. Now we'll have winning ball. If not, we'll have other ballplayers." It's likely that the Browns were tired and distracted. Many players, including pitcher "Kid" Carsey, had been awake past midnight helping with the reconstruction. The Colts timed junkballer Carsey's slants to fashion a ten-run fourth inning. Burns' boys knocked six balls beyond the outfield ropes and wowed paying customers with acrobatic, running catches.

Four days after the ballpark fire, the Browns acquired veteran outfielder-first baseman George Decker from Chicago for $1,500. The deal was surprising, considering that Decker was believed to be the first player St. Louis had purchased in four or five years. For most of that time, owner Von der Ahe had been dumping players for cash. The signing of Decker effectively ended the St. Louis career of 24-year-old college lad Mike Mahoney at two games. Mahoney came to the Browns highly recommended by his ex-teammate Dick Harley. A first baseman, Mahoney had been hitless in seven at bats and was considered a poor judge of ground balls. In his two appearances, Mahoney gallantly assisted spectators to safety in the Saturday fire game but made two errors the next day. Of Mahoney and struggling infielder Louis Bierbauer, the

Globe-Democrat wrote, "they have proven themselves fit subjects for utter banishment from league ranks." The Browns followed the newspaper's advice, cutting both within a week. Neither played big-league ball again.

The season continued on a downward spiral. Browns' outfielder Dick Harley was being overworked, according to a local paper. Manager Hurst laughed off the tale and related that no ballplayers are overworked. "When Harley seemed to lack ambition and showed a listlessness in his work, I suggested that he better see the club's physician." said Hurst whose words symbolized the Browns' season. The Browns lacked ambition and were listless in their work. They were also injury-riddled. Harley himself caught a one-hop liner in the face. However, far more damaging elements contributed to another woeful campaign.

As in years past, the St. Louis squad was often forced to play ball games without pay. Because of the depletion of the club payroll, the players toiled without compensation from April 15 to May 19. Only when Tim Hurst chipped in from his own pocket were the men paid. When no payments were forthcoming for the month of July, Hurst had to beg the men to wait a few more days. Naturally, the mood of the club soured early on. Loss piled upon loss. A youngster named Pete Daniels ". . . started in to pitch for the locals [and] fielded his position like an old woman." The Browns were sorely in need of a catcher and an infielder. If truth be known, the team also needed pitchers, first basemen, second basemen, shortstops, and so on.

Attempts to shore up the club failed miserably. In December 1897, Von der Ahe sold pitcher Hart to Pittsburgh for pitcher "Coldwater" Jim Hughey and $1,800 cash. The trade wasn't unusual, but the cash element of the deal was reported with vigor in the St. Louis dailies. Von der Ahe had tried, to keep the $1,800 a secret, especially from creditors. At about the same time, the Browns swapped catchers with Pittsburgh, sending Morgan Murphy away for perennial backup Joe Sugden.

A midsummer trade showcased Hurst's authority and Von der Ahe's diminishing power. Hurst and Muckenfuss attempted to send nonproductive outfielder Ducky Holmes to Baltimore while purchasing outfielder Jake Stenzel and second baseman Joe Quinn for $2,500. The proposed deal infuriated the German because Quinn had made disparaging remarks about his lifestyle and family. Quinn's comments contributed to his 1896 release from the Browns. While Quinn vowed to never play for St. Louis again, Muckenfuss was wiring Chris' displeasure to manager Hurst, telling him to make the deal for just Stenzel. Hurst wouldn't budge saying, "That deal goes or I go." Von der Ahe backed off and Quinn reluctantly became a St. Louis Brown. One month later, the Browns acquired utility man Suter Sullivan for $750 from Wilkes-Barre and first baseman Tommy Tucker from Brooklyn.

The Sporting News didn't help matters. The weekly continued attacking Von der Ahe, writing that St. Louis must "rid itself of the thing that smells to heaven in the nostrils of every honest lover of the game." Those lovers were few and far between in St. Louis.

In early June, the Browns endured a bizarre train trek from St. Louis to Washington, D.C. Their manager didn't quite make the trip. Tim Hurst led his charges into St. Louis' Union Station. When the train stopped for ten minutes in East St. Louis, Hurst debarked with his trusty satchel. The Browns' manager calmly ate a frankfurter, then watched in horror as the train puffed off without him. Hurst had since retired from long-distance walking. To speed to his destination, Hurst boarded a special locomotive to Washington. By odd coincidence, the Browns' train was delayed in a rail wreck. Both parties somehow arrived at the Capital to practice. Hurst's rendezvous with his Browns wasn't exactly triumphant. *The Sporting News* repeated an oft-quoted phrase about St. Louis: "They hurried to the grounds and lost the game."

On the same eastcoast road trip, the Browns' tour of Philadelphia contained a modicum of good cheer. Ball cranks in the City of Brotherly Love showered several Browns with a pregame floral tribute. Honored were Tommy Dowd, Tuck Turner, Dick Harley, Jack Clements, Jack Taylor, and Lave Cross. All of these men had previously spent time wearing Philadelphia uniforms. The players seemed lost behind the multitude of flowers piled up in front of their bench. Third baseman Lave Cross, a fancier of homing pigeons, was startled when he opened his box bouquet and out flew seven birds. The play of the Browns would not be as rosy. St. Louis won only once on the entire trip.

Perhaps outfielder Tommy Dowd let the Philadelphia tribute go to his head. Shortly afterward, manager Hurst fined Dowd and pitcher Pete Daniels $50 for excessive imbibing of alcohol. Unable to learn his lesson, Dowd was slapped with another fine by Hurst for a spree following a trip to the St. Louis Derby horse race. Dowd successfully wagered on a horse named Pink Coat. The horse's name quickly became Dowd's nickname. Hurst admitted that an intoxication clause in the players' contracts had been relatively successful.

30

Sold at Auction

It's unlikely that Von der Ahe found anything amusing in 1898. He frequently threatened to fire Tim Hurst, but the game St. Louis manager stayed on, calling his imminent dismissal so much news talk. Perhaps Von der Ahe's feeble efforts to dispatch Hurst were his final chance at exercising authority.

The courts certainly thought so. In late June 1898, St. Louis management's inability to control the club led the St. Louis Circuit Court to step into the mess. The court took over club expenses for salaries, maintenance, and the purchasing of players. Financial damages and lawsuits incurred after the Sportsman's Park fire effectively ended Von der Ahe's career in the game. But Edward Becker wasn't quitting. In late July, he attempted to purchase the club for $60,000, provided they were debt free. Becker's proviso proved impossible to satisfy. Two weeks later, on August 10, 1898, the Browns were forced by the courts into the hands of a receiver. Benjamin Muckenfuss assumed the unenviable position as treasurer and property administrator of the Browns.

Finally relinquishing his position as magnate, Von der Ahe escaped the pressures of St. Louis to marry his former housekeeper, Anna Kaiser, in Illinois. He was forty-seven years old and attempting his third marriage; she was but twenty-four and marrying for the first time. Von der Ahe listed merchant as his occupation on the marriage license.

The constant ownership turmoil affected the Browns' play, and they finally ended their season by what could charitably be described as going through the motions. Pitcher "Brewery Jack" Taylor exemplified St. Louis' misfortunes. Possessor of a behavioral rather than an occupational nickname, Taylor led the National League in games, games started, complete games, and innings pitched. That was the good news. The sacrificial lamb hurler also paced the circuit in hits allowed, losses, and pitching frustration.

Without good baseball talent evaluators such as Charlie Comiskey and Ted Sullivan, the 1890s' Browns signed a host of supposedly washed-up major leaguers that went on to far better careers after departing. St. Louis also used a veritable pantheon of greenhorn youngsters. After spending years in the game, Von der Ahe reasoned that he could recognize skilled ball tossers. Nothing was further from the truth. In fact, the St. Louis Browns fielded entire squads of fill-in baseball forgettables. The Browns' pathetic won-lost records were the sorry result. Von der Ahe even signed three men who played against the Browns in the World Series of the 1880s.

Outfielder George Gore, who won a batting title in his second year in the big leagues, was a top base stealer and run producer. He appeared opposite St. Louis in the uniforms of the Chicago White Stockings and New York Giants in the 1885, 1886, and 1888 championships. Maybe Von der Ahe figured that Gore's association with seven pennant-winning aggregations in the 1880s would bring the Browns good luck.

Pitcher Pretzels Getzein was about finished by the time St. Louis acquired him in 1892. Getzein had befuddled the Browns in the 1887 Series with Detroit with his drop fastball and his curves. With the Browns, Getzein fooled few batters. Veteran slugger Roger Connor, elected to the Baseball Hall of Fame, probably deserved a better fate than to toil with and manage the Browns. Connor played against St. Louis in the 1888 World Series as a member of the New York Giants.

The Browns employed several major leaguers whose best years were far behind them. Pitcher Pud Galvin was closing out a remarkable Hall of Fame career. Galvin hurled in a handful of games on the 1892 Browns. Pete "The Gladiator" Browning was one of the American Association's best hitters with the early Louisville clubs. Browning admitted he'd made a mistake in signing with St. Louis. Pete played all of two contests with the 1894 Browns. Browning's outfield teammate was Chicken Wolf. He lasted three games with Von der Ahe. Hick Carpenter manned third base for the Cincinnati Association team for eight years before spending his last game with 1892 St. Louis. Jack Glasscock, a talented shortstop, didn't appreciate his tenure with Von der Ahe's 1892–1893 Browns one iota and he didn't hesitate to say so. Germany Smith, another shortstop, played on back-to-back pennant winners with the 1889 Brooklyn Association club and the 1890 Brooklyn National Leaguers. With the 1898 Browns, Smith had trouble hitting his weight. Duke Esper came to St. Louis after having enjoyed pitching on three successive Baltimore Orioles pennant winners. First baseman Tommy Tucker and third baseman Lave Cross, both with the 1898 Browns, spent banner years with their former employers. Finally, outfielder "Handsome Tom" Brown played for the 1895 squad and batted poorly. Brown had been a stalwart in Boston, but his glory days were only memories.

Oddly, Willie Kuehne, a backup infielder with the 1892 Browns, was the inventor of an early pitching machine. The device operated with an adjustable spring attached to a piece of timber. Kuehne's machine reportedly delivered faster-than-human pitches. The 1890s' St. Louis Browns could have used Kuehne's invention—during games! Catcher Heinie Peitz harbored few good feelings for Von der Ahe; he couldn't leave St. Louis fast enough. Outfielders

Duff Cooley and Steve Brodie both gained pennant fame after their departure from St. Louis. Brodie was a member of the Baltimore Orioles, while Cooley starred for the Boston Beaneaters and Philadelphia Athletics.

Young ballplayers, especially garden variety sandlotters, didn't stand a chance with Von der Ahe's Browns, or anyone else. No less than seventeen hopefuls appeared in their only major-league game for the 1890s' Browns. Two unfortunate pitchers, John Wood and John Grimes, pitched three games for the Browns between them. Grimes lost both of his games; Wood never retired a batter. A total of thirty-six men that were signed by Von der Ahe played in less than three ball games in the National League. Quite simply, teams other than St. Louis easily recognized that many of Von der Ahe's signees were hardly major-league material.

Though Von der Ahe's troubles seemed insurmountable, they only mirrored the financial difficulties of the National League. Beginning with the formation of the rival Player's League and the absorption of four American Association clubs, the twelve-team League had become an unmanageable mess. Unlike the late 1880s when baseball boomed, 1890s' attendance at ballparks fell off markedly, due to several factors, most notably too many teams in the circuit, a bottom-heavy league imbalance, and a lack of pennant races. Poor summer weather and the Spanish-American War kept potential sporting interests elsewhere. Another major factor was the syndicate monopoly problem.

Due to legal entanglements, the magnates seemed powerless to solve their own difficulties. A ten-year "consolidation agreement" stipulated that no franchise changes be made during the period. This forced the league into a holding pattern. All the magnates recognized the problem: their enterprises were losing money. However, they could not agree on a plausible solution. Most owners favored an eight-team league, but none were willing to disintegrate their own businesses. Other magnates favored adding four clubs and reorganizing into two leagues. One owner proposed the league dividing into two six-club circuits, the Eastern and Western.

In December 1898, Von der Ahe faced yet another red-letter day. The Mississippi Valley Trust Company filed a foreclosure suit against the Sportsman's Park Club, et al., for failure to pay off bonds in the reconstruction of the ballpark. The Mississippi Valley Trust Company asked to foreclose on all baseball property and the right to sell the Browns' franchise. In effect, Von der Ahe was fighting for his baseball life. Like so many of his recent ventures, Von der Ahe's court appearance ended in his abject disgrace. A judge ruled that Von der Ahe was incompetent and a detriment to the game.

It had not been a good year for Chris Von der Ahe. In January, Von der Ahe's legal manuverings made him trustee of his own club. This effort to stave off the sale of the Browns was successful. Potential club buyers opted out, dismayed by the convoluted record keeping of the Browns. In February, Von der Ahe was spirited away to Pittsburgh as a result of the Baldwin affair. Two months later, Sportsman's Park nearly burned to the ground. Now, in December, Von der Ahe was in the throes of financial flameout. His wealth, once estimated as high as $1 million, had vanished. Von der Ahe's "lavish spending and profligate living" led to his downfall. In later years, Chris Von der Ahe had raked in countless thousands in criticism, but not one penny that would pay off his creditors. Ironically, Von der Ahe's trial defense sealed his doom. Chris stammered and stuttered and argued that he owned the Browns through the St. Louis Baseball Association. When the legal questions pointed toward the Sportsman's Park Club and Association, Von der Ahe denied that this organization owned the St. Louis Browns. Another man's testimony greatly affected the verdict. That man was Alfred Spink.

Over the years, Von der Ahe and Spink had been through thick and thin. Their friendship began in the late 1870s when Spink and Ned Cuthbert convinced the virtually unknown saloon owner to finance a baseball team. Talkative Al tirelessly promoted the semipro Browns and was there for the formation of the American Association. About seven years later, in Spink's own *Sporting News,* the champion Browns were regaled at every opportunity as not only a great baseball team, but a source of local pride. With the steadfast efforts of Charles Comiskey, Von der Ahe's Browns succeeded in the 1880s. In the 1890s, both *The Sporting News* and Von der Ahe were on the slide. Both institutions suffered financially with the formation of the Player's League. As the Browns' winning ways waned, Al Spink believed Von der Ahe had let the city down. He attacked Von der Ahe in print, admitting he despised his old friend. Al Spink eventually left the paper that he founded to embark upon a series of financial flops of his own. Spink's *The Derby Winner* never quite caught the imagination of the theater-going public. After the fiasco, Al tried his hand at homesteading in South Dakota with Ernest Lanigan. Neither man made money. Later in the decade, Spink's efforts at night horse racing were forestalled by a devastating tornado that damaged his South Side track.

At Von der Ahe's trial, Spink regrettably rebuked Chris' testimony. Al correctly told the court that the St. Louis Baseball Association had ceased business operations in 1881. In that year, Von der Ahe had purchased nearly all of the stock. The proceedings ended with the court decision that Von der Ahe's team would be sold at auction on the steps of the St. Louis courthouse.

On March 14, 1899, Von der Ahe lost control of his beloved St. Louis Browns.

The sale of the Browns was not without controversy. Just before the gavel announced the sale to Cleveland magnate Frank DeHaas Robison, the National League held its annual meeting in New York. It was quite a party. The ensuing discussion prompted by the Browns' sale nearly caused two magnates to come to blows. Other owners quelled the fight by holding back the combatants. Frank DeHaas Robison announced that he wanted to sell off his Cleveland franchise to Detroit interests. However, the League nixed Robison's Detroit plan due to the smallish nature of the Detroit population. Robison, having received no better offers for his Cleveland plant, retained his interest.

Finally, the magnates tabled a proposal to expel the St. Louis Browns from the National League. The resolution failed by a 7–4 margin.

The courthouse auction of the Browns mimicked the entanglement that defined Von der Ahe's business and personal finances. The affair was well attended, though Christian Frederick Wilhelm Von der Ahe could not be spotted in the gathering. Numbered among the crowd were Charles Comiskey and Tom Loftus. Neither man bid, so as to not further embarrass Von der Ahe. Benjamin Muckenfuss was finished as Browns' president and court-appointed receiver. When it was over, Edward Becker, the de facto owner of the club, relinquished control of the Browns to a St. Louis attorney named G. A. Gruner for $33,000. The fee included the franchise and lease rights to Sportsman's Park. Becker had almost $20,000 in unsettled claims from Von der Ahe's corporation. The *Post-Dispatch* commented that the club was worth nearly $100,000. Three days later, Gruner, representing Von der Ahe's creditors, sold the Sportsman's Park Club and Association to Frank DeHaas Robison for nearly $40,000.

Frank DeHaas Robison then initiated one of the strangest moves in baseball history. Owning both the Cleveland and St. Louis baseball teams, he transferred the competitive Cleveland Spiders southwest to St. Louis, where he believed they would be a better gate attraction. At the same time, Robison deposited the club that Von der Ahe built in Cleveland. The late spring transfer, threatened for years, effectively wiped out the exhibition season for both clubs. Neither squad fielded a team until late March, due to the turmoil. Robison's franchise swap temporarily solved the problem of bad baseball in St. Louis. Thanks to the inattention paid by Robison, the 1899 Cleveland Spiders played to the worst record in the history of major-league baseball.

31

Back to the Bars

Von der Ahe's exile from baseball could not have been more painful. The cold, calculating anti-Von der Ahe conspiracy involved the National League, the new St. Louis ownership, and virtually every club. Benjamin Muckenfuss and Von der Ahe formally protested to the League. While Muckenfuss zipped off telegrams to President Nicholas Young, Von der Ahe filed a $50,000 damage suit against the National League. When the Pirates arrived in St. Louis for an early season 1899 game, Von der Ahe tried to sue the Pittsburgh club secretary and intended to do the same to the other ten clubs. Before consummation of the Browns' sale, Edward Becker and Von der Ahe took their feud into black and white newsprint. When Becker stated he didn't want Chris "hanging around the park," Von der Ahe returned fire. The National League then stepped in and expelled the old St. Louis club. The American Baseball and Exhibition Company was formed as a corporation to handle baseball affairs in the city. The new St. Louis owner, Frank DeHaas Robison, further humiliated Von der Ahe by changing the team nickname to "Perfectos" and the brown stocking colors to cardinal red. Both moves were designed to erase all vestiges of losing baseball in St. Louis. Robison then issued the final blow: "No beer waiters, peanut vendors or score card boys will annoy patrons during games."

Barely six months after his ignominious departure, Von der Ahe became involved in yet another baseball venture. On September 17–18, 1899, a group of powerful men met in Chicago. Their idea was the proposed formation of the eight-team American Association of Baseball Clubs. Some lampooned it as the Rainbow League. This new stab was directed right at the heart of the National League. The new Association's platform promised honest competition, respect for all contracts, and popular prices. Syndicate baseball and the reserve rule would be banned. Among the leading names involved was St. Louis alderman George Schaefer, who unsuccessfully bid to purchase the Browns in 1898. For three summer months, Schaefer spent countless hours trying to convince would-be promoters to commit to the new organization. Schaefer announced that Adolphus Busch was prepared to invest significant amounts of his beer profits to the St. Louis entry. City native Billy Joyce would manage the club. Old cronies Al Spink and Ted Sullivan backed the league, along with Von der Ahe, Cap Anson, and Francis Richter. Star players John McGraw, Napoleon Lajoie, and Ed Delahanty would go to bat for the Association, as would two ex-Browns, Lave Cross and Dick Harley. Al Spink claimed credit for the idea as editor of the *Post-Dispatch*. Ban Johnson, Charlie Comiskey, and Thomas Loftus showed, but attended the meetings noncommitted. Despite Von der Ahe's presence for the talks, he preferred to remain nearly anonymous. Von der Ahe did donate his Wiman Trophy to be given to the champions of the league.

The proposed sites of the new Association were New York, St. Louis, Milwaukee, Detroit, Chicago, Baltimore, Philadelphia, and Washington. To combat the scheme, the National League formed its own American Association (known as American Association II) and challenged the use of the name. The National League's version would operate as a minor league and charge a quarter for admission. American Association II teams would play their ball games in the home parks of the League while senior circuit clubs were on the road. The National League disputed the new league's name by pointing out that they were formally known as The National League and American Association of Base Ball Clubs. By now the League was quite experienced with baseball competitors. In response, the neophytes changed their name to the New American Association and elected Cap Anson president. Within months, though, the Rainbows disintegrated over rivalries, personality conflicts, and an inability to secure playing fields. In a power struggle, John McGraw feuded with Francis Richter, and the grandiose idea was stillborn. On February 16, 1900, Anson announced that the league had collapsed. Not one pitch was thrown in the league's five months of operation. Chris Von der Ahe's Wiman Trophy was returned to him. Two years later, another attempt at a new American Association failed as well.

With a thriving St. Louis population of nearly 600,000 inhabitants, a better financed American League expanded into St. Louis in 1901. Many of the Rainbow organizers played signifant roles in the new league. As perhaps a backhanded tribute to Von der Ahe, the new American League team called themselves the Browns. Nearly thirty baseball scribes were required to support rabid St. Louis ball fans, again blessed with two major-league clubs.

In the years following the failure of the Rainbows, Chris Von der Ahe was driven into seclusion. In the spring of 1902, his wife Anna filed for divorce. The matter was never carried to conclusion. No longer was he "toast of the town" or "boast of the town." Von der Ahe wasn't even the "roast of the town." Chris Von der Ahe simply lived his days as a St. Louis nonentity, a passé bartender in a city full of suds. An illustration of his lowly stature occurred when Chicago National League manager Tom Loftus visited Sportsman's Park about 1901. Von der Ahe sat in the stands attending the game, but soon grew restless and ambled over to the visiting players' bench to talk over old times with Loftus. Few noticed at all.

After a while, Von der Ahe was back in a new saloon on Grand and St. Louis Avenues. Although Von der Ahe showed little interest in current baseball affairs, he loved to reminisce about the glory days of his old St. Louis Browns! Anyone fortunate (or cursed) enough to meet Chris at a watering hole would be subjected to an earful of tales about his "poys." Chris would talk for hours about his favorite subject. Perhaps Von der Ahe enjoyed singing the German-American song of loss; "Ach du lieber, Augustin," about a man who's robbed of his money, his girl, and his self-respect. Or perhaps he remembered the German-American phrase, "Jung dumb alt schmart" ("too late smart"). When patrons tired of these lamentations, Von der Ahe's business folded. The man who had built a baseball fortune was reduced to handouts from longtime friends Al Spink and Chicago White Sox owner Charlie Comiskey. Ted Sullivan also helped Von der Ahe by giving *The Sporting News* an undisclosed amount of cash to pass to Chris. Like Edward Becker, Sullivan believed Von der Ahe should serve as an object lesson for other magnates.

Nearly a decade after Von der Ahe's removal from baseball, the city of St. Louis experienced a revival for "Der Poss Bresident." Most probably this was due to both the Browns and Cardinals being perennial losers. Chris Von der Ahe had brought the city its only baseball glory.

On May 1, 1907, a baseball banquet took place at the Southern Hotel to commemorate the anniversary of a special St. Louis event. Thirty years earlier, a 0–0 15-inning tie occurred between the National League St. Louis Browns and the Syracuse Stars. The contest was notable due to its length, pitching, and remarkable bare-handed fielding. The dinner was an informal affair, attended by old-timers involved with St. Louis baseball. Among the many invited were A. J. Flanner, Bill Gleason, Henry V. Lucas, George Munson, Charles Spink, and Chris Von der Ahe. Al Spink was absent due to illness. Meeting attendees ordered their sustenance from a brown-colored menu. To honor the ancient Browns, the motto for the evening's festivities became "Let's do things up brown." Thunderous applause followed a nostalgic speech given by Chris Von der Ahe. A *St. Louis Times* reporter would regret that the speech was not transcribed. Everyone seemed impressed, especially since the speaker was nearly destitute. Von der Ahe's days of bartending at various establishments in the city had long passed.

In January 1908, St. Louis papers reported that Von der Ahe was critically ill with pneumonia. He was no longer employed at his old corner saloon-grocery at Grand and St. Louis Avenues. Indeed, Chris was not known to have any business interests in the city. His once extensive real estate holdings had since passed into other hands. Gone were all his saloons, his stonefront residences, and the leasehold flats.

With failing health and failed finances, Von der Ahe filed a petition for bankruptcy in 1908, listing his total assets at $200. That summer, Charles

Spink, the publisher of *The Sporting News*, which helped drive Von der Ahe out of baseball, organized a benefit. The Cardinals played the Browns in a ball game that raised nearly $5,000 for Von der Ahe. To drum up support, the *St. Louis Globe-Democrat* trumpeted Chris as "the man who did much to make baseball the national game." William Medart, a St. Louis sportsman and industrialist, was treasurer for the affair. Donations came from friends and fellow magnates, including Charles Comiskey. When creditors tried to intercept Von der Ahe's money, Charles Spink stepped forward to forestall their efforts.

Monies from the benefit game weren't nearly enough for Von der Ahe. Almost five years later, Von der Ahe was sued by the St. Louis Brewing Association for $850 for debts related to beer purchases. The firm's name was ironic, considering that all three words stood for three of Chris' lifetime passions. "St. Louis" was the city where Von der Ahe lived and flourished. "Brewing" and selling beer helped bring fans in droves to his park. Finally, "Association" was a reminder of his days in the American Association. Sadly, the lawsuit underscored Von der Ahe's propensity to drown his sorrows.

By January 1913, years of drinking were catching up with Chris Von der Ahe. He spent his days bedridden at his home on St. Louis Avenue. His personal physician commented that Von der Ahe's life was tenuous, at best. Charles Comiskey called on his old friend in February. After a few pleasantries, Comiskey asked Von der Ahe how he was doing. "I've got a lot and a nice monument already built for me in Bellefontaine cemetery." The sadness of the two men was palpable. Both cried. The visit ended when the doctor informed Comiskey it was time to leave. Less than four months later, Chris Von der Ahe was dead. Shortly after 3:00 P.M. on June 5, 1913, Chris passed away at his home. The cause of death was dropsy and cirrhosis of the liver. The onetime Browns' owner and baseball impresario was survived by his wife Anna (Kaiser) Von der Ahe.

The sporting world mourned his loss.

Sporting Life headlined: "The Passing of a Base Ball Man Once a Power in Base Ball Famous for Phenomenal Luck, Quaint Sayings and Queer Doings." The weekly also called him the "most written and talked about man in the United States." Charles Comiskey said that Von der Ahe was "the grandest figure baseball has ever known." In their obituaries, newspapers couldn't resist dusting off several of the best anecdotes about Chris Von der Ahe. The *Post-Dispatch* wrote that Von der Ahe was "never lacking for flatterers and hangers-on who would slap him on the back and tell him what a wonderful magnate he was—and drink the wine and smoke the cigars for which he paid." Another Von der Ahe story dealt with a new technology, the telephone. Chris seemed to have a problem understanding the newfangled communication device. Said Von der Ahe's calling friend, "I left an umbrella at your park today. Have you seen it?" Chris placed the phone down for a minute and took a few steps across the room. Holding the umbrella up to the telephone, Von der Ahe said, "Vos dis idt?"

Truth be known, Von der Ahe was a combination of Shakespeare's Sir

John Falstaff and characters from Horatio Alger. (Coincidentally, Falstaff was the name of a local St. Louis beer whose motto was "Eat, drink, and be merry.") Author Alger stressed that through hard work, honesty, and thrift, great financial rewards would follow. Von der Ahe most certainly was a rags-to-riches story. However, only in his pre-baseball days could he be considered thrifty. Big money and Von der Ahe's bigger ego destroyed his Browns.

Local ball fans, friends, and contemporaries squeezed into Von der Ahe's smallish residence for the funeral. Elaborate floral offerings filled the living room. The sermon was delivered by the Reverend Frederick Craft, who eulogized Von der Ahe in a customary baseball motif. Rev. Craft proclaimed that "First base is enlightenment, second base is repentance, third base, faith, and the home plate the heavenly goal! Don't fail to touch second base, for it leads you onward to third. All of us finally reach the home plate, though some may be called out when they slide home." The burial was dignified and ceremonial, indicative of Chris' lofty days in the American Association. *The Sporting News* also commented that "hundreds of old-time ballplayers" attended; they "crowded the streets for blocks and stood with bowed heads." Serving as pallbearers were American League President Ban Johnson, Al Spink, and former Browns Charlie Comiskey, Ted Sullivan, brothers William and Jack Gleason, and George McGinnis. Although Von der Ahe's widow Anna attended, conspicuously absent were Von der Ahe's first wife Emma, son Eddie, and Della Wells Von der Ahe. Chris Von der Ahe was laid to rest under his grandiose monument at Bellefontaine Cemetery.

EPILOGUE

Very little remains of the St. Louis haunts of Chris Von der Ahe. Gone are his Grand and St. Louis Avenue saloon, his houses at Sportsman's Park and on St. Louis Avenue, and the two ballparks where the Browns played.

The saloon was razed in August 1933, shortly after Prohibition ended. The property was then transferred to a dairyman who built a "modern block of stores and offices" on the site. In 1958, the same block contained an insurance company, a finance company, a tailor shop, a barbershop, a haberdashery, a sandwich shop, and, of course, a bar. Von der Ahe could have used a good finance company.

Chevrolet placed an automobile storage lot on Von der Ahe's former residential property at 3617 St. Louis Avenue. Chris Von der Ahe lived in this house from 1884–1896. The old stone property was destroyed in August 1951.

The Herbert Hoover Boy's Club, an educational and recreational institution, rests on the site of the original Sportsman's Park. Baseball is still being played here, though not quite in the fashion it was from the 1870s through 1890s. In 1991, the Bob Broeg Chapter of the Society for American Baseball Research dedicated the site with a plaque. The citation signifies the 125th anniversary from the time Gus Solari laid out the grounds in 1866. The Sportsman's Park built in 1893 is now the location of Beaumont High School. A famous graduate of Beaumont is Earl Weaver, a pepperpot manager who fought just as hard for his team as Charlie Comiskey.

In the famous Sportsman's Park Fire of 1898, Chris Von der Ahe lost his ballpark residence and nearly all his personal effects. What tales these correspondence files could tell! Most likely they contained notes to creditors, wives, girlfriends, league moguls, and players.

The site of Von der Ahe's grave might cause some unsuspecting visitors pause. Adorning Von der Ahe's remains is the bold larger-than-life-sized statue, dressed in his trademark frockcoat. So majestic is this monument that a sarcastic Denver writer captioned it as "Von der Ahe Discovers Illinois." An old legend claims that Von der Ahe foretold the year of his death by having that year chiseled on the monument while he was still alive, but there is no evidence to support the story. Von der Ahe's third wife, Anna Kaiser Behnen, followed him in death in October 1919 and is buried at the Von der Ahe plot. Von der Ahe's first wife Emma and only son Eddie are buried together in a nearby lot at Bellefontaine.

Von der Ahe's Browns spent many an hour embarking and debarking at both Union Stations, the original and its huge replacement built in 1894. The newer building, famous for a 65-foot ceiling and "Grand Hall," still stands, and today it is a magnificent shopping center in downtown St. Louis. The legend of midwest railroad stops being named after Browns' players persisted for years. However, eminent baseball historian Lee Allen debunked this as myth. Allen insisted that although there is a Comiskey and Bushong in Kansas, there were never any such stations named after St. Louis players.

Eddie Von der Ahe died of tuberculosis in 1926 after a long illness. His will, revised just three days before his death, provided a trust fund for the Shriner's Hospital for Crippled Children and the Bethesda Home. After her celebrated divorce from Chris, Emma Von der Ahe lived in St. Louis with relatives and later with her son. She spent the last six years of her life with a friend in Troy, Missouri. Emma passed away in 1938. She was eighty-eight.

All too often, baseball history has judged Chris Von der Ahe as a buffoon. However, he was at least indirectly responsible for many innovations that are commonplace today. His most lasting contribution was his belief that baseball is a sport for the masses. Unlike their stodgy National League rivals, who viewed the game as entertainment for the upper crust, the founders of the American Association envisioned crowds comprised of the common man. Von der Ahe's ballpark beer concessions were a large part of the equation. Beer sales and their inherent profit potential eventually forced the National League to concede to beer at the park and Sunday baseball. Though heavily criticized, Von der Ahe's "Coney Island of the West" ball park foreshadowed today's electronic scoreboards and whiz-bang displays. Von der Ahe was an early innovator in promoting his team through sales of illustrations, china, towels, and cigars. Who else would dare name apartments after his players? Von der Ahe believed strongly, especially in his halcyon days, that words of the Browns' glories should be spread throughout the land. He accomplished this by sending advance men David Reed and George Munson to cities before the Browns arrived. Finally, Von der Ahe offered numerous ballpark promotions, from scorecards to Wild West shows to oompah bands.

It's fascinating to speculate how the Von der Ahe-Comiskey relationship affected the latter's ownership of the Chicago White Sox. As Von der Ahe's baseball empire went down in flames, Comiskey's star rose as he saved his money and planned for the future. Often portrayed as the cheapskate villain of the 1919 World Series scandal, Comiskey likely learned from the tragic lesson of his old boss, Chris Von der Ahe.

Longtime Von der Ahe rival Albert Spalding penned *America's National Game* in 1911. In his book, Spalding offers a "plea for the magnates." This essay attempts to bridge the gap between baseball executives and fans by explaining the difficulties faced by owners.

Spalding tries to dispel the public perception that magnates are "men without a care in the world, except to expend upon their persons and their pleasure the alleged countless coins that flow in an unending stream through the turnstiles of their clubs." The job "wreaks havoc to the health and happiness of the man who understands it, and that the long list of physical and mental wrecks strewn along the shores of Base Ball history tells a story of sacrifice to our national game that is not generally appreciated or known."

These words ring true in the case of Von der Ahe.

Spalding also detailed that criticism from writers, reporters, other magnates, and fans is a constant companion. Magnates are expected to rise above petty annoyances and, above all, support their team. Occasionally, magnates have to stand between the umpire and the mob. At night, magnates are fortunate for a restful sleep. However, interruptions are common by the "ever-ready instrument of torture, the telephone." Unhappy ball cranks often approached the owner at the park to ask the score sardonically.

A delicate psychological balance should exist on the ball club. Managers are required to treat their players fairly. All teams are prone to jealousies and internal squabbles. A failure of good spirit is the failing of a magnate.

Concerning ballparks, Spalding wrote that owners "must provide grounds easily accessible, and fit them up with elaborate grandstand, bleachers, club house and toilets, that shall meet all the requirements of comfort, cleanliness and convenience." The grounds should be located next to trolley or rapid transit lines.

Chris Von der Ahe may have understood the trappings of success and the pressures of failure better than anyone else. Like his perilous sea voyage to America, Von der Ahe survived arguably the most intense criticism ever heaped on a baseball team owner. Much of the criticism was deserved. Perhaps, though, Christian Frederick Wilhelm Von der Ahe was simply a man caught up in the struggles and chaos of nineteenth-century baseball.

Appendices

Appendix A

The Browns under Von der Ahe

YEAR	RECORD	POS	PCT.	MANAGER(S)	W-L RECORD
AMERICAN ASSOCIATION					
1882	37–43	5	.463	Cuthbert	37–43
1883	65–33	2	.663	Sullivan	53–26
				Comiskey	12–7
1884	67–40	4	.626	Williams	51–33
				Comiskey	16–7
1885	79–33	1	.705	Comiskey	79–33
1886	93–46	1	.669	Comiskey	93–46
1887	95–40	1	.704	Comiskey	95–40
1888	92–43	1	.682	Comiskey	92–43
1889	90–45	2	.667	Comiskey	90–45
1890	78–58	3	.573	McCarthy	15–12
				Roseman	7–8
				Kerins	9–8
				Gerhardt	20–16
				Campau	27–14
1891	85–51	2	.625	Comiskey	85–51
NATIONAL LEAGUE					
1892	56–94	11	.373	Glasscock	1–3
				Stricker	6–17
				Crooks	27–33
				Gore	6–9
				Caruthers	16–32
1893	57–75	10	.432	Watkins	57–75
1894	56–76	9	.424	Miller	56–76
1895	39–92	11	.298	Buckenberger	16–34
				Quinn	11–28
				Phelan	11–30
				Von der Ahe	1–0
1896	40–90	11	.308	Diddlebock	7–10
				Latham	0–3
				Von der Ahe	0–2
				Connor	8–37
				Dowd	25–38
1897	29–102	12	.221	Dowd	6–22
				Nicol	8–32
				Hallman	13–36
				Von der Ahe	2–12
1898	39–111	12	.260	Hurst	39–111

Appendix B

Team Statistics 1885–1888

1885 St. Louis Browns
W-79 L-33
Charlie Comiskey
Home: 44–11
Road: 35–22

PITCHERS	G	IP	H	BB	SO	W	L	ERA	SHO
Bob Caruthers	53	482	430	57	190	40	13	2.07	6
Dave Foutz	47	407	351	92	147	33	14	2.63	2
Jumbo McGinnis	13	112	98	19	41	6	6	3.38	3

CATCHERS	G	AB	H	2B	3B	HR	R	RBI	BB	AVG	SA
Doc Bushong	85	300	80	13	5	0	42	21	11	.267	.343
Dan Sullivan	17	60	7	2	0	0	4	3	6	.117	.150
also with Lou-AA	13	44	8	1	0	0	3	4	2	.182	.205
Mike Drissel	6	20	1	0	0	0	0	0	0	.050	.050
Cal Broughton	4	17	1	0	0	0	1	1	0	.059	.059
also with NY-AA	11	41	6	1	0	0	1	1	1	.146	.171
INFIELDERS											
1b-Charlie Comiskey	83	340	87	15	7	2	68	44	14	.256	.359
2b-Sam Barkley	106	418	112	18	10	3	67	53	25	.268	.380
ss-Bill Gleason	112	472	119	9	5	3	79	53	29	.252	.311
3b-Arlie Latham	110	485	100	15	3	1	84	34	18	.206	.256
OUTFIELDERS/PITCHERS											
rf-Hugh Nicol	112	425	88	11	1	0	59	45	34	.207	.238
cf-Curt Welch	112	432	117	18	8	3	84	69	23	.271	.370
lf-Tip O'Neill	52	206	72	7	4	3	44	38	13	.350	.466
ut-Yank Robinson	78	287	75	8	8	0	63	35	29	.261	.345
p 1b-Dave Foutz	65	238	59	6	4	0	42	34	11	.248	.307
p of-Bob Caruthers	60	222	50	10	2	1	37	12	20	.225	.302
p-Jumbo McGinnis	13	50	11	0	0	1	3	7	1	.220	.280

NOTE: Strikeout and stolen base figures not available for batters.

All team stats compiled from *The Great Encyclopedia of 19th Century Major League Baseball*, by David Nemec, and *Total Baseball*, CD-Rom.

1886 St. Louis Browns
W-93 L-46
Charlie Comiskey
Home: 52–18
Road: 41–28

PITCHERS	G	IP	H	BB	SO	W	L	ERA	SHO
Dave Foutz	59	504	418	144	283	41	16	2.11	11
Bob Caruthers	44	387	323	86	166	30	14	2.32	2
Nat Hudson	29	234	224	62	100	16	10	3.03	0
Jumbo McGinnis	10	87	107	27	30	5	5	3.80	1
also with Bal-AA	26	209	235	48	70	11	13	3.48	0
Joe Murphy	1	7	5	3	3	1	0	3.86	0
also with Cin-AA	5	46	50	21	11	2	3	4.89	0
also with St.L-N	4	33	45	16	11	0	4	8.18	0
Yank Robinson	1	9	10	7	1	0	1	3.00	0

CATCHERS	G	AB	H	2B	3B	HR	R	RBI	BB	AVG	SA	SB
Doc Bushong	107	386	86	8	0	1	56	31	31	.223	.251	12
Rudy Kemmler	35	123	17	2	0	0	13	6	8	.138	.154	0
Lou Harding	1	3	1	1	0	0	0	1	0	.333	.667	0
INFIELDERS												
1b-Charlie Comiskey	131	578	147	15	9	3	95	76	10	.254	.327	41
2b-Yank Robinson	133	481	132	26	9	3	89	71	64	.274	.385	51
ss-Bill Gleason	125	524	141	18	5	0	97	61	43	.269	.323	19
3b-Arlie Latham	134	578	174	23	8	1	152	47	55	.301	.374	60
ss-Trick McSorley	5	20	3	3	0	0	1	0	0	.150	.300	0
OUTFIELDERS												
rf-Hugh Nicol	67	253	52	6	3	0	44	19	26	.206	.253	38
cf-Curt Welch	138	563	158	31	13	2	114	95	29	.281	.393	59
lf-Tip O'Neill	138	579	190	28	15	3	106	107	47	.328	.444	9
p of 1b-Dave Foutz	102	414	116	18	9	3	66	59	9	.280	.389	17
p of-Bob Caruthers	87	317	106	21	14	4	91	61	64	.334	.527	26
p of-Nat Hudson	43	150	35	4	1	0	16	17	11	.233	.273	2
p-Joe Murphy	1	3	0	0	0	0	0	0	0	.000	.000	1

NOTE: Strikeout figures not available for batters.

1887 St. Louis Browns
W-95 L-40
Charlie Comiskey
Home: 58–15
Road: 37–25

PITCHERS	G	IP	H	BB	SO	W	L	ERA	SHO
Silver King	46	390	401	109	128	32	12	3.78	2
Bob Caruthers	39	341	337	61	74	29	9	3.30	2
Dave Foutz	40	339	369	90	94	25	12	3.87	1
Nat Hudson	9	67	91	20	15	4	4	4.97	0
Ed Knouff	6	50	40	18	36	4	2	4.50	1
also with Bal-AA	9	63	79	41	27	2	6	7.57	0
Joe Murphy	1	9	13	4	5	1	0	5.00	0
Yank Robinson	1	3	3	3	0	0	0	3.00	0

CATCHERS	G	AB	H	2B	3B	HR	R	RBI	BB	AVG	SA	SB
Jack Boyle	88	350	66	3	1	2	48	41	20	.189	.220	7
Doc Bushong	53	201	51	4	0	0	35	26	11	.254	.274	14
Mike Goodfellow	1	4	0	0	0	0	0	0	0	.000	.000	0
INFIELDERS												
1b-Charlie Comiskey	125	538	180	22	5	4	139	103	27	.335	.416	117
2b-Yank Robinson	125	430	131	32	4	1	102	74	92	.305	.405	75
ss-Bill Gleason	135	598	172	19	1	0	135	76	41	.288	.323	23
3b-Arlie Latham	136	627	198	35	10	2	163	86	45	.316	.413	129
OUTFIELDERS/PITCHERS												
rf-Bob Caruthers	98	364	130	23	11	8	102	73	66	.357	.547	49
cf-Curt Welch	131	544	151	32	7	3	98	108	25	.278	.379	89
lf-Tip O'Neill	124	517	225	52	19	14	167	123	50	.435	.691	30
ut-Dave Foutz	102	423	151	26	13	4	79	108	23	.357	.508	22
p of-Silver King	62	222	46	6	1	0	28	19	24	.207	.243	10
of-Lou Sylvester	29	112	25	4	3	1	20	18	13	.223	.339	13
p-Ed Knouff	15	56	10	4	1	2	4	6	1	.179	.268	1
p-Nat Hudson	13	48	12	2	1	0	7	3	4	.250	.333	0
of-Harry Lyons	2	8	1	0	0	0	2	1	0	.125	.125	2
also with Phil-N	1	4	0	0	0	0	0	0	1	.000	.000	0
p-Joe Murphy	1	6	1	0	0	0	0	0	0	.167	.167	0

NOTE: Strikeout figures not available for batters.

1888 St. Louis Browns
W-92 L-43
Charlie Comiskey
Home: 60-21
Road: 32-22

PITCHERS	G	IP	H	BB	SO	W	L	ERA	SHO
Silver King	66	585	437	76	258	45	21	1.64	6
Nat Hudson	39	333	283	59	130	25	10	2.54	5
Icebox Chamberlain	14	112	61	27	57	11	2	1.61	1
also with Lou-AA	24	196	177	59	119	14	9	2.53	1
Jim Devlin	11	90	82	20	45	6	5	3.19	0
Ed Knouff	9	81	66	37	25	5	4	2.67	0
also with Clev-AA	2	9	8	3	2	0	1	1.00	0
Tommy McCarthy	2	4	3	2	1	0	0	4.15	0
Julie Freeman	1	6	7	4	1	0	1	4.26	0

CATCHERS	G	AB	H	2B	3B	HR	R	RBI	BB	AVG	SA	SB
Jack Boyle	71	257	62	8	1	1	33	23	13	.241	.292	11
Jocko Milligan	63	219	55	6	2	5	19	37	17	.251	.365	3
Tom Dolan	11	36	7	1	0	0	1	1	1	.194	.222	1
INFIELDERS												
1b-Charlie Comiskey	137	576	157	22	5	6	102	83	12	.273	.359	72
2b-Yank Robinson	134	455	105	17	6	3	111	53	116	.231	.314	56
ss-Bill White	76	275	48	2	3	2	31	30	21	.175	.225	6
also with Lou-AA	49	198	55	6	5	1	35	30	7	.278	.374	15
3b-Arlie Latham	133	570	151	19	5	2	119	31	43	.265	.326	109
ss-Ed Herr	43	172	46	7	1	3	21	43	11	.267	.372	9
2b-Chippy McGarr	34	132	31	1	0	0	17	13	6	.235	.242	25
OUTFIELDERS/PITCHERS												
rf-Tommy McCarthy	131	511	140	20	3	1	107	68	38	.274	.331	93
cf-Harry Lyons	123	499	97	10	5	4	66	63	20	.194	259	36
lf-Tip O'Neill	130	529	177	24	10	5	96	98	44	.335	.446	26
p-Silver King	66	207	43	4	6	1	25	14	40	.208	.300	6
p of-Nat Hudson	56	196	50	7	0	2	27	28	18	.255	.321	9
p-Icebox Chamberlain	14	50	5	0	0	1	6	2	3	.100	.180	3
p-Jim Devlin	11	37	11	1	0	0	7	3	4	.297	.324	2
p-Ed Knouff	9	31	3	0	0	0	1	1	3	.097	.097	1
p-Julie Freeman	1	3	1	0	0	0	0	0	0	.333	.333	0

NOTE: Strikeout figures not available for batters.

Appendix C

Lawsuit Abstract

Chris Von der Ahe's preponderance of legal trouble points to his haphazard financial affairs and his combative personality. As his professional career wore on, Von der Ahe was discovered to be an easy target. More than fifty lawsuits are listed here, including over thirty during a five-year period beginning in 1893. Five lawsuits deal with people closest to him: his wife Emma and son Eddie, wife Della Wells, and housemaid/wife Anna Kaiser. At least eight concern disputes with players over non-payment, unfair treatment, tampering, and the "slavery" issue. Von der Ahe also suffered numerous major run-ins with other players such as Charlie Comiskey, Yank Robinson, Arlie Latham, Tommy McCarthy, Silver King, Ted Breitenstein, and Billy Earle. About twenty legal actions are related to non-payment for materials used or services rendered. Tellingly, two of these items were cigars and beer. For reasons unknown, many of the court records today are incomplete, especially the Emma divorce and Von der Ahe's "baseball trial" in 1898. Unless otherwise noted, this material is derived from *The Sporting News* of November 13, 1897, which carried a detailed list of Von der Ahe's legal squabbles. Lawsuit dates are sometimes approximate.

March 1884. Henry Oberbeck, an outfielder, played in four games for the Browns at the end of 1883. Oberbeck sued Von der Ahe $400 for being released unfairly. The case challenged the nature of baseball contracts. Although Oberbeck won the suit, the owners managed to retain their power over ballplayers.

March 19, 1885. Dave Rowe, a 29-year-old outfielder, sued Von der Ahe for $25,000 for being blacklisted and expelled from the American Association. Rowe had not played a solitary game for the Browns. He claimed that he was "good for" ten more years on the diamond at $2,500 per year. Tried in St. Louis, this case captured a lot of attention. Settled out of court.

May 1885. Von der Ahe lost $650 in this suit to the Toledo Association ball club. The case involved Von der Ahe's tampering with Tony Mullane (*Sporting Life*, June 17, 1885)

February 26, 1886. William Green, a taxi operator, transported players to Sportsman's Park in an omnibus. After non-payment by Von der Ahe for services rendered, Green sued for $325. Case settled out of court.

May 16, 1887. A stockholder in the Sportsman's Park Club and Association named William Spinney filed a mandamus suit to compel Von der Ahe to open the books and cash accounts. Spinney received a writ and examined the books.

May 28, 1887. William Green sued Von der Ahe again, this time for $250 for nonpayment. Green testified that he had transported visiting clubs from Union Station to the park for a fee of $5.00. After Green secured judgment, Von der Ahe appealed, and the case was settled. (St. Louis Court Records, case 07381).

July 15, 1887. *The State of Missouri Vs. Chris Von der Ahe* challenged the issue of Sunday baseball. The arguments concerned whether baseball was "labor" or "recreation." Von der Ahe's drinking buddy, ex-Congressman John J. O'Neill, eulogized baseball, and the judge ruled in favor of the Browns' owner. This result was vital to the finances of the Browns, the American Association and, in time, all of professional baseball.

1888. The St. Louis Quarry Company sued Von der Ahe for unpaid bills amounting to $1,493.55. The company had delivered stone to Von der Ahe's property on Grand and St. Louis Avenues. Judgment secured for $1,556.

August 12, 1888. Ball crank John Alyea sought $5,000 damages from Von der Ahe following his alleged injury suffered at Sportsman's Park. He claimed he was hurt due to a falling grandstand. Case was nonsuited.

June 1889. Charles Brandt secured a judgment for $15.75 from Von der Ahe for brick, sand and other material unpaid.

July 1889. Harry Lyons, the Browns' regular center fielder in 1888, tried to recover his share of the pennant money. The amount was $71.40. Von der Ahe testified in court that Lyons didn't earn his share. Lyons batted .194 for the campaign. Judgment secured and Von der Ahe appealed.

May 6, 1890. The Missouri Cigar and Tobacco company sued and secured $25 from Von der Ahe for an unpaid balance on cigars.

1890–1898. Pitcher Mark Baldwin sued Von der Ahe for false arrest after Chris accused Baldwin of conspiracy to bribe Silver King and Jack O'Connor to break their 1891 American Association contracts. Although Baldwin sued for $10,000 and then $20,000, he was eventually awarded $2,500 after two trials (*See* chapters 24 and 29).

November 14, 1890. This suit involved a baseball trade gone sour. William Gray, the Detroit manager, sued Von der Ahe to recover $1,666.67 for the agreed-upon price to release players Bill Higgins, Jake Virtue, and Bobby Wheelock, who had been sold to Von der Ahe in December 1889. One of the men refused Von der Ahe's payment, for which Von der Ahe was given the verdict. Results of the other cases unknown. The case focused much attention on the issue of selling ballplayers, called "slavery" by critics (*See* chapter 17).

1891. With help of his father, a boy named Isaac Laskey sued Von der Ahe for $200 after being run over by Von der Ahe's carriage. The judge awarded $20. The Laskeys appealed and the case was settled out of court. (Case 82937, St. Louis Circuit Court Records.)

June 1892. E. H. Pendleton secured a judgment for $1,421.20 for overdue rent of the Cincinnati ballpark. A host of other lawsuits arose from this particular case (*See* chapter 24).

August 1893. William Pinkston was Von der Ahe's partner for unsuccessful "military and pyrotechnic" exhibitions conducted at the new Sportsman's Park. The failed venture caused numerous lawsuits against both men. To protect himself, it was alleged that Von der Ahe had his employee Ed Goodfellow attach Pinkston's outfit of tents, etc. amounting to $4,396.68. Though Von der Ahe and John Peckington signed security for Goodfellow, this was not sustained in court. Pinkston then sued the bondsman for $8,615 (St. Louis Circuit Court Records, case 94391).

August 1893. Professor Michael Mooney, a manager of the Men's Business Gymnasium, and Al Newton gave boxing and club-swinging exhibitions August 14–22 at Sportsman's Park. Though refused their wages by Von der Ahe, each man secured $61.25 in back pay.

October 24, 1893. Erich Wellman sued Von der Ahe $1,222 for nonpayment of rented costumes. Wellman secured judgment in the case.

1893. Nonpayment for supplies compelled the George A. Rubelman Hardware Co. to sue Von der Ahe. Judgment secured for $53.33.

1893. Samuel C. Davis & Company sued and secured $19.99 from Von der Ahe for nonpayment of unspecified hardware supplies.

1893. The Platt & Thornburg Paint and Glass Co. secured $91.55 for unspecified hardware supplies.

1893. Von der Ahe did not pay for lithographs from Compton & Son Printing Co. The company secured $149.

1893. Dr. Norman B. Carson sued Von der Ahe for $70 for professional services rendered. Case settled out of court.

August 13, 1894. Chris Von der Ahe sued his son for possession of his own Grand Avenue property. After borrowing $11,000 from Eddie, Von der Ahe handed over his deeds as security. Case helped lead to Von der Ahe's divorce from Emma and breakup of the family (*See* chapter 22).

September 14, 1894. E. H. Pendleton sued for the rental of the Cincinnati ballpark for $1,800. Von der Ahe had agreed to pay $1,200 per year rent to fight the National League. However, when the League absorbed the American Association, Von der Ahe and allies tried to avoid payment. Pendleton secured a judgment for $1,800. Von der Ahe then sued his ex-colleagues for their share in the Pendleton debacle (*See* chapter 24).

1894. Clemens Whirlwind, representing an American Indian contingent, sued Von der Ahe for nonpayment after appearing in Buck Taylor's Wild West Show at Sportsman's Park. Probably unsuited (*See* chapter 21).

1895. Emma Von der Ahe filed and was granted a divorce from her husband, Chris, with a $3,150 judgment. Case led to total estrangement from ex-wife and son Eddie (*Emma Von der Ahe vs. Chris Von der Ahe*, Case 099067, St. Louis Court Records, *see* chapter 22).

1895. *The Washington Post* printed a scathing attack on Von der Ahe's personal and business lifestyle. Incensed by the article, Von der Ahe began a $50,000 damage suit against the newspaper. The suit was dropped when the newspaper agreed to make a public retraction.

March 12, 1895. George W. Stevenson, a black man, was standing outside Sportsman's Park when he was shot and then beaten by Von der Ahe. One bullet hit Stevenson's heel. Stevenson had Von der Ahe arrested for felonious assault and filed a $5,000 damage suit. However, the plaintiff had no security for the costs, and the case was dismissed (*See* chapter 23).

1895. Out of action with a knee injury, third baseman Denny Lyons sued Von der Ahe for refusal to pay $360 of salary. Lyons threatened to attach St. Louis club receipts. Result unknown.

November 1895. Eddie Von der Ahe sued the Citizen's Railway Company $20,000 for running him over in 1893. Result unknown.

1896. Mark Baldwin finally received another verdict for $2,500. W. A. Nimick of Pittsburgh was surety for Von der Ahe. However, with Von der Ahe buried in debt and lawsuits, Nimick was unsure he could recover his money. Nimick then filed an affidavit to recover money from the bondsman. Final result led to Von der Ahe's kidnapping in 1898 and eventual ouster from baseball (*See* chapters 24 and 29).

1896. Ed Hanlon's champion Orioles team played a weekday series in St. Louis before small crowds. Baltimore did not clear expenses. Hanlon believed that Von der Ahe would attach receipts to make the Orioles pay for their share of the Pendleton debt. A gullible Von der Ahe then loaned the amount of the receipts to Hanlon. Unaware of this startling transaction, Von der Ahe then files two $800 lawsuits against Hanlon. Results unknown.

1896. Hoyt and Bright sued Von der Ahe for unpaid bills for turnstiles and cancelling machines. When the bill became due, the company began attachment proceedings in Cleveland for $385. Result unknown.

1896. The Mississippi Valley Trust Company sued the Sportsman's Park Club and Association et al. for the failure to pay off bonds. The company told the court that a receiver should be appointed and Von der Ahe removed as president of the Browns.

1896. Bandmaster Weil sued Von der Ahe $250 for failure to pay for music provided at park. The case was heard in St. Charles, Mo. Result unknown.

1896. The Boynton company sued Von der Ahe for patent infringement on Shoot-the-Chutes water slide. Result unknown.

December 1896. In a similar suit, the Aetna Iron Works company sued Von der Ahe for patent violations on the water slide. Amount is $1,372.20. Result unknown (*The Sporting News*, December 19, 1896).

1896. Von der Ahe's former housekeeper, Anna Kaiser, filed a breach of promise for marriage lawsuit for $10,000. When Von der Ahe petitioned that he couldn't get a fair trial in St. Louis due to his besmirched reputation, the case was transferred to St. Charles, Missouri. Case settled out of court in September 1897 for a reported $3,000 and court costs. However, skeptics discount the amount and reported that the figure was closer to $250. The $3,000 settlement amount had Von der Ahe's creditors salivating.

1897. Browns' third base hopeful John Newell broke his arm during the 1893 exhibition season. He sued Von der Ahe for $274.12 in back pay. The court battle took place in Philadelphia. Von der Ahe claimed that Newell was suspended for his inability to run bases or throw a ball. Von der Ahe did not give proper notification of Newell's status during the injuries, which resulted in the Newell judgment.

January 1897. The Pulitzer Publishing company took Von der Ahe to court for advertising baseball games for the Browns. Von der Ahe claimed that his advertising agent was not authorized to contract for the ads. After the judge sustained Von der Ahe, Pulitzer appealed. The St. Louis papers simply refused to run any more ads for upcoming Browns' games until all bills were paid.

August 1897. John Brush, who had been propping up the St. Louis franchise, agreed with Von der Ahe to transfer games to Cincinnati. Consent of other magnates was obtained, but not without considerable trouble. Von der Ahe then tried to annul the agreement. After a Sunday game in St. Louis drew only 5,000 customers, Brush threatened a $1,000 fine. Von der

Ahe backed down, and the second game of the series was played in Cincinnati.

September 1897. In yet another Shoot-the-Chutes lawsuit, the Koken Iron Works sued Von der Ahe for material used to build the contraption.

September 1897. Von der Ahe's own attorneys, Charles Broadhead and Walter Hezel, sued their client and won $876.50 in unpaid lawyer fees. The venue being St. Charles, Von der Ahe refused to appear and lost by default. This Catch-22 illustrates the quandary Von der Ahe had with his lawyers. Von der Ahe's legal eagles lost every case and then sued him for nonpayment.

November 1897. For nonpayment of rent on his property, Von der Ahe evicted and then sued his mother-in-law, Mrs. Mary Wells. Chris claimed $60 for his troubles (*The Sporting News,* November 6, 1897).

January 1898. Chris Von der Ahe filed for and was granted a divorce from Della Wells Von der Ahe.

1898- . A barrage of lawsuits occurred due to the calamitous ballpark fire in April.

December 1898. The foreclosure suit from the Mississippi Valley Trust Company versus the Sportsman's Park Club came to trial. The trust company claimed failure to pay off bonds in reconstruction of the park. This action ended Von der Ahe's baseball enterprise once and for all (Case 11324, St. Louis Circuit Court).

February 1899. After being run out of baseball, Von der Ahe filed a $50,000 lawsuit against the National League. He then threatened all the other clubs with separate suits. These cases never went to trial.

1899. Von der Ahe's estranged son sued his father concerning the 1894 Grand Avenue property dispute. Result unknown.

May 1902. Von der Ahe's third wife, Anna, filed for divorce. However, the couple remained married, since the procedure was never followed through (*St. Louis Post-Dispatch,* May 25, 1902).

1908. Destitute and in ill health, Von der Ahe filed for bankruptcy. On the petition, he listed his total assets at only $200. Charles Spink of *The Sporting News* then organized a special benefit ball game between the local American League Browns and the National League Cardinals. The affair raised an estimated $5,000, not nearly enough to satisfy Von der Ahe's medical bills, creditors, and expenses.

1913. The St. Louis Brewing Association sued Von der Ahe for $850 in the last year of his life. The debts are related to Von der Ahe's failure to pay for beer purchases.

Appendix D

"Chris Sat on the Bench"

Chris Von der Ahe sat on the bench,
    His eyes glued on the game,
And ever and anon poor Chris
    Would give a groan of shame.
Said he: "I had von ball glub vonce—
    A glub both strong and frisky;
Dey von der bennat umsteen times
    Mit Captain Charles Comiskey!
Und now I haf a gang of bums
    Who tink dis all a frolic,
Und blay, id seems to me, like men
    Who haf a visky colic!
I'll fir all blayers of my glub,
    No madder vat deir station,
Who come of dot mean Irish blood
    Und nod from German nation!
I'll keep Ehret, und Herr Breitenstein
    Und Miller, Peitz, und Otten,
Und Kissinger—de rest, I dinks,
    Vos mosd distinkly rotten!
Dot grosser Cooley in left;
    Dot Ely vot blays short,
Dey dings I vos a monkey und
    A vigdim for deir sport!
Dot Sheehan, too, vot stants on firsd,
    He vos an Irish loafer;
He gomes to me from Liddle Rock,
    Und now he lives in clofer!

Dot Quinn, der segond baseman, he
Is somedings of a batter—
Vot of id? He's an Irisher,
Und dot vos vat's der madder!
I haf hired a liddle poy for third;
His name was Valter Kinlock—
I hopes he is a Prussian of
Der Kaiser Wilhelm stock!
Vot's dot? Dot Sheehan muffed a ball?
I'll fine him yust a dwendy!
Vot? Ely fans der vind dwo dimes?
Oh, I haf droubles blendy!
Look at dot Lange! He hits der ball
Und makes dwo long dwo-baggers—
I dell you dot dese German love
To gif poor Chris der staggers!
I'll haf dings all my way negst year,
Und haf a team of vinners—
Nod an Irisher in all der growd,
But good old German sinners!
I'll keep my German pitchers und
Hire Stein und Rhines direkly—
Peitz, Miller, Otten, dey gan gatch;
For firsd I'll get Chake Beckley!
Louis Bierbauer for segond base,
Und Cross for third-a daisy—
Dahlen for shord- now dere's a team
Vill drive der Irish grazy!
Der outfield? Selbach, Stenzel, Shoch!
My team, vos den gombleted—
I'll vin six bennants efery year
Und nefer de defeated!"

Originally appearing in the *Chicago Mail,* this poem was reprinted in *The Sporting News,* Aug. 10, 1895. It serves as wondrous parody of the 1895 St. Louis Browns.

Source Notes

Main Sources

Axelson, Gustav, *"Commy": The Life Story of Charles Comiskey,* 1919.

Egenreither, Richard, "Chris Von der Ahe: Baseball's Pioneering Huckster," *Baseball Research Journal*, 1989.

Lansche, Jerry, *Glory Fades Away*, 1991.

Pearson, Daniel, *Baseball in 1889: Players vs. Owners,* 1993.

Phillips, John, *Uncle Nick's Birthday Party,* 1991.

Pietrusza, David, *Major Leagues,* 1991.

Rygelski, Jim, "Baseball's 'Boss President': Chris von der Ahe and the Nineteenth-Century St. Louis Browns," *Gateway Heritage* 13, 1992.

Seymour, Harold, *Baseball: The Early Years,* 1960.

Spink, Al, *The National Game,* 1910.

Sullivan, Ted, *Humorous Stories of the Ball Field,* 1903.

Tiemann, Robert, *Cardinal Classics*, 1982.

Tiemann, Robert, et al., *Nineteenth Century Stars*, 1989.

Sporting Life.

St. Louis Globe-Democrat.

St. Louis Post-Dispatch.

The Sporting News.

Chapter 1

William Filby and Iva A. Glazer, eds., *Germans to America: Lists of Passengers Arriving at U. S. Ports,* vol. XII., 1990. Sixteen-year old Chris Von der Ahe made the journey from Germany aboard a ship reeking with sickness, food spoilage, and death. If he could survive this odyssey, he could survive anything else.

Olsen, Audrey, *St. Louis Germans, 1850–1920: The Nature of an Immigrant Community and Its Relation to the Assimilation Process*, 1980.

Carter, Gregg Lee, "Baseball in St. Louis, 1867–1875: An Historical Case Study in Civic Pride," *Missouri Historical Society Bulletin*, 1975.

Lampe, Anthony B., "The Background of Professional Baseball in St. Louis," *The Missouri Historical Society Bulletin* VII, 1950.

"The St. Louis Red Stockings: More Than A Footnote," *St. Louis' Favorite Sports, SABR* 22, 1992.

Holt, Brian, "Chris Von der Ahe: Primary sources of 'der Boss President.'" Thesis. St. Louis University, 1994.

St. Louis City Recorder of Deeds, Deed Books #452, p. 228; #61, p. 514; #1375, p. 313. Information provided by Brian Holt.

Personal Interview with Curator of Bellefontaine Cemetery Michael Tiemann, June 25, 1992; Bellefontaine Cemetery records, St. Louis, Missouri. A second child, John F. Von der Ahe, was born in January 1873. However, the infant died six months later. Originally buried in Bethania (Bethlehem) Cemetery, the body was reinterred in Bellefontaine in 1886.

Files of Russell L. Von der Ahe.

Chapter 2

Allen, Lee, *100 Years of Baseball*, 1950.

Axelson, Gustav, *"Commy": The Life Story of Charles Comiskey*, 1919. Although Comiskey later perpetuated that he was the first man to play off the bag, all players did after the 1883 rule when catching one foul bounce was no longer an out.

O'Conner, Richard, *The German-Americans: An Informal History*, 1968.

Seymour, Harold, *Baseball: The Early Years,* 1960.

Spink, Al, *The National Game*, 1910. Sportsman's Park was so named by William Spink.

Gietschier, Steve, "Before 'The Bible of Baseball,'" *St. Louis' Favorite Sport, SABR* 22, 1992.

Missouri Republican.

Rygelski, Jim, "Baseball's 'Boss President': Chris von der Ahe and the Nineteenth-Century St. Louis Browns," *Gateway Heritage* 13, 1992.

St. Louis Republican. Von der Ahe bought 180 shares at $10 a piece.

St. Louis Star and Times.

The Sporting News.

Chapter 3

Lowry, Phillip, *Green Cathedrals* (1992). The Japanese fireworks cannon was at Sportsman's during the 1882 season.

Pearson, Daniel, *Baseball in 1889: Players vs. Owners* (1993).

Pietrusza, David, *Major Leagues* (1991). American Association magnates probably realized that their patrons could spend their extra quarters on beer. The National League had committed a financial blunder by getting rid of Louisville, St. Louis, New York, and Philadelphia. In their place were smaller population cities; Syracuse and Troy in New York, and Worcester and Providence in New England.

Rozensweig, Roy, *Eight Hours for What We Will: Workers and Leisure in an Industrial City, 1870–1920*, 1983.

S.C. Thompson and Hy Turkin, *The Baseball Encyclopedia,* 1951.
Vincent, Ted, *Mudville's Revenge: The Rise and Fall of American Sport,* 1981.

Chapter 4

Axelson, Gustav, *"Commy": The Life Story of Charles Comiskey,* 1919.
Broeg, Bob, *Redbirds: A Century of Cardinals Baseball,* 1987.
Nineteenth Century Stars, 1989.
Pietrusza, David, *Major Leagues*, 1991. The American Association lost all 21 exhibitions against National Leaguers in the spring of 1882. Although the Association didn't fare well on the scoreboard, they won points for their attire. In the early months of that first season, many teams had not yet acquired uniforms. The Association players wore colorful, nonmatching garb. Sandlotters across America soon imitated the Association's style.
Smith, Robert, *Baseball in the Afternoon*, 1993.
__________, *Hits, Runs, and Errors*, 1949.
Tiemann, Robert, *Cardinal Classics, 1982.*
Egenreither, Richard, "Chris Von der Ahe: Baseball's Pioneering Huckster," *Baseball Research Journal*, 1989. "Welt" is German for "world."
New York Clipper.
Orenstein, Joshua, "The Union Association of 1884: A Glorious Failure," *Baseball Research Journal* 19, 1990.
St. Louis Globe-Democrat.
St. Louis Star and Times.
Dellinger, Harold, "Rival Leagues," *Total Baseball CD-Rom, 1992.*

Chapter 5

Nemec, David, *The Beer and Whisky League*, 1994.
Nineteenth Century Stars, 1989.
Orem, Preston, *Baseball from the Newspaper Accounts 1882–1891*, 1966. Umpiring in the 1880s was a tenuous business. Although the Association paid umpires a salary "plus all traveling expenses and hotel bills, not to exceed $3 a day," the Association rarely backed arbiters in disputes. Umpires worked alone; having to run down the foul line on drives to right field. Baserunners took advantage of umpire's limited vision, by cutting from first to third and from second to home plate. Third basemen often grabbed the belts of runners to prevent them from scoring. All this action produced frightful rows from the players and incited cranks in the stands. Umpires could fully expect being cursed at, mobbed, shoved, kicked, and spat upon. Ballpark patrons often became involved with the umpires in delivering expert testimony on the affairs in the field as if they were impartial observers. The Association eventually curtailed this practice and also devised a rule that umpires were subject to fines for entering a saloon or poolroom in uniform. Umpires often traveled and ate meals together on the trains with the players, building friends and enemies over cards games and beer. Because owners didn't particularly care for doubleheaders, umpires were reluctant to call games on account of darkness.

Phillips, John *Uncle Nick's Birthday Party*, 1991.
Seymour, Harold, *Baseball: The Early Years*, 1960.
Sullivan, Ted, *Humorous Stories of the Ball Field*, 1903. Von der Ahe's umpire interference led to the 1884 Association's rules revision on arbiters. The Association President would assign umpires by telegraph, whose identities would not be known until they appeared on the grounds and presented credentials. Umpires could also work no more than four consecutive games in one city.
Voigt, David, *American Baseball*, 1980. Von der Ahe claimed $70,000 in profits for 1883.
Cincinnati Inquirer.
Missouri Republican.
New York Journal.
Rygelski, Jim, "George Washington Bradley," *St. Louis' Favorite Sport SABR 22*, 1992.
Sporting Life.
The Sporting News.

Chapter 6

Allen, Lee, *100 Years of Baseball, 1950.*
Benson, Michael, *Ballparks of North America*, 1989.
Lowry, Phillip, *Green Cathedrals*, 1992. After the 1888 World Series, balls deposited fair into the right field seats were home runs.
Nemec, David, *The Beer and Whisky League*, 1994.
Nineteenth Century Stars, 1989.
Palmer, Harry, *Stories of the Base Ball Field* (1890.
Pietrusza, David, *Major Leagues*, 1991.
Seymour, Harold, *Baseball: The Early Years*, 1960.
Smith, Robert, *Baseball in the Afternoon*, 1993.
Sullivan, Ted, *Humorous Stories of the Ball Field*, 1903.
Voigt, David, *American Baseball*, 1980.
St. Louis Republic.
Sporting Life.
The Sporting News.
Dellinger, Harold, "Rival Leagues," *Total Baseball CD-Rom,* 1992.

Chapter 7

Axelson, Gustav, *""Commy": The Life Story of Charles Comiskey*, 1919. "Kicking" referred to a particularly argumentative tactic that involved kicking up dirt and grass at the umpire or opposition player.
Benson, Michael, *Ballparks of North America*, 1989.
Blount, Roy, ed., *The Fireside Book of Baseball* 4th ed., 1987.
Dickson, Paul *The Dickson Baseball Dictionary*, 1989.
Lansche, Jerry, *Glory Fades Away*, 1991.
Nemec, David, *The Beer and Whisky League*, 1994. The Association improved

enough to win 15 of 27 exhibitions against National Leaguers in the spring of 1885.
Nineteenth Century Stars, 1989.
Pearson, Daniel, *Baseball in 1889: Players vs. Owners*, 1993.
Seymour, Harold, *Baseball: The Early Years*, 1960.
H. Allen Smith and Iva Smith, *Low and Inside*, 1949.
Sullivan, Ted, *Humorous Stories of the Ball Field*, 1903.
Tiemann, Robert, *Cardinal Classics*, 1982.
Vincent, Ted, *Mudville's Revenge: The Rise and Fall of American Sport*, 1981.
Voigt, Davd, *American Baseball*, 1980.
Chicago Tribune. Von der Ahe referred to exhibitions in which players were promised gate receipts.
Missouri Republican.
New York Clipper.
St. Louis Globe-Democrat.
Sporting Life.
The Sporting News.
Baseball Hall of Fame files.

Chapter 8

Cohen, Richard, et al., *The Scrapbook History of Baseball*, 1975.
Kargau, E.D., *Mercantile, Industrial and Professional St. Louis* (1899.
Lansche, Jerry, *Glory Fades Away*, 1991.
Levine, Peter, *A. G. Spalding and the Rise of Baseball*, 1985.
Nemec, David, *The Beer and Whisky League*, 1994.
Reichler, Joseph, ed., *The Baseball Encyclopedia*, 1976.
Tiemann, Robert, *Cardinal Classics*, 1982.
S.C. Thompson and Hy Turkin, *The Baseball Encyclopedia*, 1951.
Lansche, Jerry, "The St. Louis City Series," *St. Louis' Favorite Sport SABR* 22, 1992.
Missouri Republican.

Chapter 9

Alexander, Charles, *Our Game: An American Baseball History*, 1991.
Axelson, Gustav, *"Commy": The Life Story of Charles Comiskey*, 1919.
Lansche, Jerry, *Glory Fades Away*, 1991.
O'Conner, Richard, *The German-Americans: An Informal History*, 1968.
Pearson, Daniel, *Baseball in 1889: Players vs. Owners*, 1993.
Reidenbaugh, Lowell, *The Sporting News First Hundred Years*, 1985.
Seymour, Harold, *Baseball: The Early Years*, 1960.
Tiemann, Robert, *Cardinal Classics*, 1982.
Vincent, Ted, *Mudville's Revenge: The Rise and Fall of American Sport*, 1981.
Wallop, Douglas, *Baseball: An Informal History*, 1969.
Humber, William, "Where Do They All Come From?" *The National Pastime* 12, 1992.

New York World.

Porter, David, "Untold Saga of Europe's Big Leaguers," *The National Pastime* 12, 1992.

Rygelski, Jim, "Baseball's 'Boss President': Chris von der Ahe and the Nineteenth-Century St. Louis Browns," *Gateway Heritage* 13, 1992.

St. Louis Post-Dispatch.

St. Louis Star and Times.

Sporting Life.

The Sporting News.

Chapter 10

Astor, Gerald, *Baseball Hall of Fame 50th Anniversary Book*, 1988.

Axelson, Gustav, *"Commy": The Life Story of Charles Comiskey*, 1919.

Hynd, Noel, *The Giants of the Polo Grounds*, 1988.

Lansche, Jerry, *Glory Fades Away*, 1991.

Lieb, Fred, *The St. Louis Cardinals*, 1944.

Nemec, Davd,*The Beer and Whisky League*, 1994.

Pietrusza, David,*Major Leagues*, 1991.

Reiss, Steven, "A Historical Anthology of Sport in America," in *The Baseball Magnates and Urban Politics in the Progressive Era: 1895–1920,* ed. Reiss, 1984. Gambling remained pervasive in a sport highly conducive to wagering on runs, hits, wins, losses, etc. Although police were assigned to deter gambling and ticket scalping at ball parks, professional bettors enjoyed the protection of local politicians practicing graft.

Seymour, Harold, *Baseball: The Early Years*, 1960.

Smith, Robert, *Hits, Runs, and Errors*, 1949.

Chicago News.

Lansche, Jerry, "The St. Louis City Series," *St. Louis' Favorite Sport SABR* 22, 1992.

St. Louis Post-Dispatch.

The Sporting News. The St. Louis Exchange was willing to wager $10,000 while the Chicago Board of Trade offered one million dollars. Both institutions were bluffing; an example of *The Sporting News* hyping the series.

Chapter 11

Nemec, David, *The Beer and Whisky League*, 1994.

Nineteenth Century Stars, 1989.

Phillips, John, *Uncle Nick's Birthday Party*, 1991.

Seymour, Harold, *Baseball: The Early Years*, 1960. In November 1886, the League and Association voted on critical rules changes for 1887; bases on balls were lowered to five balls, strikes from four to three. In addition, bases on balls counted as hits for the season. The new rules led to astronomical batting averages and robust earned run averages. The rule was repealed for 1888. Tip O'Neill's average of .492 reflects his percentage with base on balls. Adjusted, O'Neill hit .435, still the 2nd highest seasonal batting average ever compiled.

The other high totals reflect the adjustments. Pitchers also had to contend with new pitching slabs, now placed six feet apart. The slabs allowed pitchers to place one foot on the hindmost slab and take a hop, skip, and jump towards home plate.

Tiemann, Robert, *Cardinal Classics*, 1982.

Malloy, Jerry, "The Cuban's Last Stand" *The National Pastime* 11, 1992. Two years earlier, two colored ball teams squared off at Sportsman's Park. For a quarter, fans could watch the undefeated Hoosier Black Socks of Indianapolis play St. Louis' own West Ends.

St. Louis Globe-Democrat. In 1886, the Browns defeated the Cuban Giants 9–3, stopping their reported thirty-five game winning streak. So strong were the "Cubans" that New York's version of the Giants tried to purchase their best player, pitcher George Washington Stovey. When Chicago manager Cap Anson learned of the deal, he boycotted Stovey's signing and the upcoming scheduled games between his White Stockings and the New Yorkers. Professional baseball's color line, not to be broken for sixty more years, is believed to have its genesis here.

St. Louis Post-Dispatch.

St. Louis Star and Times. Von der Ahe loved to boast that he used his influence to help get Noonan elected mayor of St. Louis in 1889.

Sporting Life.

The Sporting News.

"Merrell's Penetrating Oil," advertisement pamphlet.

Chapter 12

Lansche, Jerry, *Glory Fades Away*, 1991.

Lieb, Fred, *The St. Louis Cardinals*, 1944.

Nemec, David, *The Beer and Whisky League*, 1994.

H. Allen Smith and Iva Smith, *Low and Inside*, 1949.

S.C. Thompson and Hy Turkin, *The Baseball Encyclopedia*, 1951.

St. Louis Globe-Democrat. One baseball scribe of this newspaper was Joe Murphy, who also pitched several games for the Browns in 1886–1887.

St. Louis Post-Dispatch.

The Sporting News.

Chapter 13

Nemec, David, *The Beer and Whisky League*, 1994. The only other club that won four consecutive pennants before the Browns was the 1872–1876 Boston Red Stockings of the National Association.

Phillips, John, *Uncle Nick's Birthday Party*, 1991.

Pietrusza, David, *Major Leagues, 1991*.

Seymour, Harold, *Baseball: The Early Years*, 1960.

Tiemann, Robert, *Cardinal Classics*, 1982.

Voigt, David, *American Baseball*, 1980. The 1887 Decoration Day crowd in St. Louis totaled 25,000 people. Thanks to the guarantee system, Von der Ahe realized a profit of $10,000 for the event.

Lipset, Lew, "The Egyptian and the Greyhounds," *The National Pastime*, 1982.

St. Louis Globe-Democrat.

St. Louis Post-Dispatch.

Sporting Life.

The Sporting News.

Chapter 14

Hynd, Noel, *The Giants of the Polo Grounds*, 1988.

Lansche, Jerry, *Glory Fades Away*, 1991.

Spink, Al, *The National Game*, 1910.

S.C. Thompson and Hy Turkin, *The Baseball Encyclopedia*, 1951.

St. Louis Globe-Democrat.

St. Louis Post-Dispatch.

The Sporting News.

Chapter 15

Benson, Michael, *Ballparks of North America*, 1989.

Orem, Preston, *Baseball from the Newspaper Accounts*, 1966.

Pearson, David, *Baseball in 1889: Players vs. Owners*, 1993. Ballpark losses due to fire were considered acceptable risks in the nineteenth century. Byrne had only $7,000 in insurance to cover his $18,000 debt.

Seymour, Harold, *Baseball: The Early Years*, 1960.

Spink, Al, *The National Game*, 1910.

Sullivan, Ted, *Humorous Stories of the Ball Field*, 1903.

Voigt, David, *American Baseball*, 1980. In 1889, the Brooklyn ballclub was also nicknamed the "Bridegrooms" due to several of their players being engaged. So serious was the pennant race that Brooklyn players were said to suspend their lovemaking for the September stretch run. Pitcher Bob Caruthers refused to see his newborn child.

Brooklyn Eagle.

McCue, Andy, "A History of Dodger Ownership," *The National Pastime* 13, 1993.

New York Clipper.

New York Herald.

New York Times.

St. Louis Globe-Democrat.

St. Louis Post-Dispatch.

Sporting Life.

The Sporting News.

Chapter 16

Astor, Gerald, *Baseball Hall of Fame 50th Anniversary Book*, 1988.

Alexander, Charles, *Our Game: An American Baseball History*, 1991.

James, Bill, *The Baseball Book*, 1986.
Seymour, Harold, *Baseball: The Early Years*, 1960.
The Sporting News.
Dellinger, Harold, "Rival Leagues," *Total Baseball CD-Rom,* 1992.

Chapter 17

Phillips, John, *Uncle Nick's Birthday Party*, 1991.
Reidenbaugh, Lowell, *The Sporting News First Hundred Years*, 1985.
Sullivan, Ted, *Humorous Stories of the Ball Field*, 1903. Von der Ahe's claim that Comiskey had part interest in the team is dubious. Von der Ahe once gave Comiskey one share of stock in the Sportsman's Park Club & Association. Although Von der Ahe claimed "signing" nearly all the Browns, Ted Sullivan constantly scouted for players. Comiskey also suggested numerous players to his boss. Naturally, Von der Ahe signed his men. His name was on their paychecks.
Tiemann, Robert, *Cardinal Classics, 1982.*
Philadelphia Enquirer.
St. Louis Post-Dispatch. Munson's bolt to the Player's League hurt Von der Ahe. J. B. Sheridan was eventually hired to fill the post, after numerous St. Louis newsmen turned down the job. Most likely, they were having too much fun lampooning Von der Ahe.
The Sporting News. While suspended, Latham asked Comiskey for $5.00 to do his laundry.

Chapter 18

Phillips, John, *Uncle Nick's Birthday Party*, 1991.
Voigt, David, *American Baseball*, 1980. Owing to blue laws, liqour sales and Sunday ball were left to the locals. In 1892, St. Louis, Cincinnati, and Louisville played Sunday ball. In time, all the National League clubs would play ball on the Sabbath. Fifty-cent prices prevailed, except in standing room only and bleacher seats.
St. Louis Post-Dispatch. Von der Ahe increasingly interfered in team matters but his priorities weren't so much with the Browns as they were with saving the Association.
The Sporting News.
Tiemann, Robert, "The Forgotten Winning Streak of 1891," *Baseball Research Journal* 18, 1989. The 1891 National League race is shrouded in controversy. The New York Giants and Chicago Colts charged other clubs with hippodroming. The Boston pennant look highly suspicious in light of opposition errors and deliberately not playing their best men. Chicago's Cap Anson played an entire home game dressed in white wig and false beard. The race was more convoluted by the fact that Chicago's Albert Spalding (and others) owned stock in multiple teams as a result of the 1890 Player's League War bailout. The Boston pennant victory may well have been contrived. Any team winning the flag that was comprised of King Kelly's men would further drive a nail into the Association's experiment in Cincinnati.
Voigt, David, "Denny Lyons' 52-Game Hitting Streak," *The National Pastime* 13, 1993. Denny Lyons hit in 52 straight games in 1887.

Chapter 19

Phillips, John,*Uncle Nick's Birthday Party*, 1991.
Seymour, Harold, *Baseball: The Early Years*, 1960.
Tiemann, Robert, *Cardinal Classics*, 1982.
Wallop, Douglas, *Baseball: An Informal History*, 1969.
St. Louis Post-Dispatch.
The Sporting News.

Chapter 20

Nineteenth Century Stars, 1989.
The Sporting News.

Chapter 21

Nineteenth Century Stars, 1989.
Reidenbaugh, Lowell, *The Sporting News First Hundred Years*, 1985.
H. Allen Smith and Iva Smith, *Low and Inside*, 1949.
Egenreither, Richard, "Chris Von der Ahe: Baseball's Pioneering Huckster," *Baseball Research Journal*, 1989.
Gietschier, Steve, "Before 'The Bible of Baseball,'" *St. Louis' Favorite Sport SABR* 22, 1992.
St. Louis Globe-Democrat.
St. Louis Republic.
The Sporting News.
Dellinger, Harold, "Rival Leagues," *Total Baseball CD-Rom,* 1992.

Chapter 22

Seymour, Harold, *Baseball: The Early Years*, 1960.
Rygelski, Jim, "Baseball's 'Boss President': Chris von der Ahe and the Nineteenth-Century St. Louis Browns," *Gateway Heritage* 13, 1992.
St. Louis Globe-Democrat.
St. Louis Republic.
The Sporting News.

Chapter 23

Sullivan, Ted, *Humorous Stories of the Ball Field,* 1903.
Diamond, Etan, "Kerry Patch: Irish Immigrant Life in St. Louis." *Gateway Heritage* 12, 1989.
New York World.
Philadelphia Bulletin.
Sporting Life. Dusty sandlot ball and drinking were popular in St. Louis. A certain variation of baseball rules evolved. Third base became the scene of a keg of beer with a big dipper. The name of this liquid refreshment center was curiously called a "German Disturber." By no coincidence, the Browns had a German Disturber of their own.
The Sporting News. Denny Lyons was also suspended without pay for two weeks

for not moving from Von der Ahe's boarding house. He protested claiming that Von der Ahe was trying to rent the flat to someone else. Lyons was supported by manager Buckenberger and his teammates. He would later sue Von der Ahe for nonpayment while he was injured.

Chapter 24

Seymour, Harold, *Baseball: The Early Years*, 1960.

Sporting Life.

The Sporting News. "Attachment" is a law that can give a prejudgment remedy to an aggrieved party when there is substantial fear of fraud. It is used for sales or transfer of assets, between the filing of a lawsuit and final judgment. The plaintiff files a lawsuit claim of damages. If the court decides for the plaintiff, a "writ of attachment" is personally served by a sheriff to a defendant. No writ can be issued without requirement of bond posted by the plaintiff to cover any damages to the defendant. When the property attached is money or movable property, the sheriff will take the property into his custody until further court order. Defendant can retain posession of property by posting bond as well. The courts are very cautious to issue writs in these cases. "Attaching the receipts" at a ballgame would require an application to the court before the game. A sheriff would have to have a writ in his hands in order to sieze gate receipts. In his lifetime, Chris Von der Ahe became very familiar with the threat of attachment.

Chapter 25

Dickson, Paul *The Dickson Baseball Dictionary*, 1989. The baseball term "Arlie Latham" first came into vogue in 1907. This described an infielder making a passing stab at a ground ball. However, "Arlie Latham" was also used to define a particularly loud player or coach or the act of yelling or carrying on in the coaching box to unnerve the opposition pitcher. An "Arlie Latham hit" was a grounder that eluded infielders. Arlie Latham remains a rare ballplayer whose full name became part of baseball lexicon.

Mead, William, *Even the Browns*, 1978.

Pearson, Daniel, *Baseball in 1889: Players vs. Owners*, 1993. Latham shouldn't have spoken ill of anyone, considering he was also accused of throwing games on Comiskey's 1890 Chicago Player's League squad.

Phillips, John *Uncle Nick's Birthday Party*, 1991.

Pietrusza, David, *Lights On!*, 1997.

Egenreither, Richard, "Chris Von der Ahe: Baseball's Pioneering Huckster," *Baseball Research Journal*, 1989.

Philadelphia Bulletin.

St. Louis Post-Dispatch.

Sporting Life.

The Sporting News.

Hall of Fame player files.

Chapter 26

Lieb, Fred, *The St. Louis Cardinals*, 1944.
Phillips, John, *Uncle Nick's Birthday Party*, 1991.
H. Allen Smith and Iva Smith, *Low and Inside*, 1949..
Chicago News.
Egenreither, Richard, "Chris Von der Ahe: Baseball's Pioneering Huckster," *Baseball Research Journal*, 1989.
St. Louis Post-Dispatch.
The Sporting News.

Chapter 27

Philadelphia Bulletin.
St. Louis Post-Dispatch.
The Sporting News. When speaking about his wife's relatives, he was speaking of Joe Oliver, a brother-in-law of Della Wells, whom Von der Ahe hired for the new grocery. Della's brother was also on the Browns' salary list.

Chapter 28

St. Louis Republic.
The Sporting News. Curiously, Al Spink was in the process of gaining control of Von der Ahe's horse race assets. Al Spink was the turf organizer at the South Side, Madison, and Kinloch race tracks in St. Louis.

Chapter 29

Allen, Lee, *The Hot Stove League*, 1955.
Benson, Michael, *Ballparks of North America*, 1989.
Smith, Robert, *Hits, Runs, and Errors*, 1949.
Sullivan, Ted, *Humorous Stories of the Ball Field*, 1903. Sullivan lamented that Von der Ahe's friends and politicos deserted him in his hour of greatest need. Von der Ahe spent large sums of money to get politians elected.
Tiemann, Robert, *Cardinal Classics, 1982.*
Egenreither, Richard, "Chris Von der Ahe: Baseball's Pioneering Huckster," *Baseball Research Journal*, 1989.
Eldred, Rich, "Umpiring in the 1890's," *The Baseball Research Journal* 18, 1989.
Boston Record.
Lipset, Lew, "The Egyptian and the Greyhounds," *The National Pastime*, 1982.
St. Louis Globe-Democrat.
St. Louis Post-Dispatch.
Sporting Life.
The Sporting News.

Chapter 30

Hetrick, J. Thomas, *MISFITS! The Cleveland Spiders in 1899*, 1991.
Pearson, Daniel, *Baseball in 1889: Players vs. Owners*, 1993.
Seymour, Harold, *Baseball: The Early Years*, 1960.

Spink, Al, *The National Game*, 1910.

St. Louis Globe-Democrat. No one defended Chris Von der Ahe at the trial, not even his son Eddie. The younger Von der Ahe had been in court that same year. A judge ruled the Eddie didn't have to pay margin losses on investments in wheat and railroad securites because they were gambling losses.

St. Louis Post-Dispatch.

St. Louis Star.

The Sporting News.

Hall of Fame player files.

Chapter 31

Borst, Bill, *Baseball Through A Knothole- A St. Louis History, 1980*. Shortly before his death, Chris Von der Ahe willed Charlie Comiskey one of his few remaining possessions; the Wiman Trophy. The solid-silver statue was won by the Browns after their 1886 World Series victory over Chicago. When Comiskey became owner of the Chicago White Sox, he kept the trophy in his private office.

Kelsoe, William, *St. Louis Reference Record, 1927*.

Lieb, Fred, *The St. Louis Cardinals*, 1944.

Okkonen, Mark, *Baseball Memories*, 1992.

Pietrusza, David, *Major Leagues*, 1991.

Seymour, Harold, *Baseball: The Early Years*, 1960.

Smith, Robert, *Hits, Runs, and Errors*, 1949.

St. Louis Globe-Democrat.

St. Louis Post-Dispatch.

St. Louis Republican.

St. Louis Star and Times.

Sports Afield.

Sporting Life.

The Sporting News. Several members of the Four-Time Pennant-Winning Browns preceded Chris Von der Ahe in death. Among them were Jack Boyle, (1913), Doc Bushong, (1908), Bob Caruthers, (1911), Dave Foutz, (1897), Harry Lyons, (1912), Chippy McGarr, (1904), Yank Robinson, (1894), and Curt Welch, (1896).

Wagner, Bill, "The League That Never Was," *Baseball Research Journal* 16, 1987.

Dellinger, Harold, "Rival Leagues," *Total Baseball CD-Rom,* 1992.

St. Louis Mercantile Library Association.

Personal Interview with Curator of Bellefontaine Cemetery Michael Tiemann, 25 June 1992. Bellefontaine Cemetery, a large and beautiful rural burial ground in Northwest St. Louis, is the final resting place of many famous Americans. Included in the interments are Senator Thomas Hart Benton (1782–1858), General William Clark (1770–1838) of the Lewis & Clark Expedition, and Captain Isaiah Sellers (1802–1864) who used the pseudonym of "Mark Twain" that was later adopted by Samuel Clemens. The Spink Family Mausoleum contains the remains of Al, Charles, and William.

Bibliography

BOOKS

Alexander, Charles. *Our Game: An American Baseball History.* New York: Henry Holt, 1991.

Allen, Lee. *100 Years of Baseball.* New York: Bartholomew House, 1950.

______. *The Hot Stove League.* New York: A. S. Barnes, 1955.

Astor, Gerald. *The Baseball Hall of Fame 50th Anniversary Book.* New York: Prentice Hall, 1988.

Axelson, G. W. *"Commy" The Life Story of Charles A. Comiskey.* Chicago: Reilly & Lee, 1919.

Benson, Michael. *Ballparks of North America: A Comprehensive Historical Reference to Baseball Grounds, Yards, and Stadiums, 1845 to Present.* Jefferson, NC: McFarland, 1989.

Blount, Roy, ed. *The Fireside Book of Baseball 4th ed.* New York: Simon and Schuster, 1987.

Borst, Bill. *Baseball Through a Knothole—A St. Louis History.* St. Louis: Krank Press, 1980.

Broeg, Bob. *Redbirds: A Century of Cardinals Baseball.* St. Louis: Rivercity Publishers, 1987.

Cohen, Richard M., et al. *The Scrapbook History of Baseball.* Indianapolis, IN: Bobbs-Merrill, 1975.

Dickson, Paul. *The Dickson Baseball Dictionary.* New York: Facts on File, 1989.

Filby, P. William, and Iva A. Glazer, ed. *Germans to America Lists of Passengers Arriving at U. S. Ports.* Wilmington, DE : Scholarly Resources, 1986.

Hetrick, J. Thomas. *MISFITS! The Cleveland Spiders in 1899.* Jefferson, NC: McFarland, 1991.

Hynd, Noel. *The Giants of the Polo Grounds.* Garden City, NY: Doubleday, 1988.

James, Bill. *The Baseball Book.* New York: Villard Books, 1990.

Kargau, E.D. *Mercantile, Industrial and Professional St. Louis.* St. Louis: Nixon-Jones Printing Company, 1899.

Kelsoe, William A. *St. Louis Reference Record.* St. Louis: Von Hoffman Press, 1927.

Lansche, Jerry. *Glory Fades Away: The Nineteenth-Century World Series Rediscovered.* Dallas: Taylor Publishing, 1991.

Levine, Peter. *A.G. Spalding and the Rise of Baseball.* New York: Oxford UP, 1985.

Lieb, Fred. *The St. Louis Cardinals.* St. Louis: Putnam Van Rees Press, 1944.

Lowry, Philip J. *Green Cathedrals.* Cooperstown, NY: Society for American Baseball Research, 1986.

Mead, William B. *Even The Browns.* Chicago: Contemporary Books, 1978.

Nemec, David. *The Beer & Whisky League.* New York: Lyons & Burford, 1994.

O'Conner, Richard. *The German-Americans An Informal History.* Boston: Little, Brown, 1968.

Okkonen, Marc. *Baseball Memories.* New York: Sterling Publishing, 1992.

Olsen, Audrey. *St. Louis Germans, 1850–1920 The Nature of an Immigrant Community and Its Relation to the Assimilation Process.* New York: Arno Press, 1980.

Orem, Preston *Baseball From the Newspaper Accounts, 1882–1891.* Altadena, CA: Private Issue, 1966.

Palmer, Harry. *Stories of the Base Ball Field.* Chicago : Rand McNally, 1890.

Palmer, P., and Thorn, J. (Eds.). (1992). *Total Baseball CD-Rom.* Portland, OR: Creative Media Corporation.

______. (Eds.). (1991). *Total Baseball Second Edition.* New York: Warner Books.

______. (Eds.). (1989). *Total Baseball* New York: Warner Books.

Pearson, Daniel M. *Baseball in 1889: Players vs. Owners.* Bowling Green, OH: Bowling Green University Popular Press, 1993.

Phillips, John. *Uncle Nick's Birthday Party.* (orig. *Fannin' Baseball*) Cabin John, MD: Capital Publishing, 1991.

Pietrusza, David. *Lights On!.* Lanham, MD: Scarecrow Press, 1997.

______. *Major Leagues.* Jefferson, NC: McFarland, 1991.

Reichler, Joseph L., ed. *The Baseball Encyclopedia.* New York: Macmillan, 1976.

Reidenbaugh, Lowell. *The Sporting News First Hundred Years.* St. Louis: Sporting News Publishing, 1985.

Riess, Steven. "A History Anthology of Sport in America." Baseball Magnates and Urban Politics in the Progressive Era: 1895–1920. ed. Riess. Westport, CT: Leisure Press, 1984.

Rozensweig, Roy. *Eight Hours for What We Will: Workers and Leisure in an Industrial City, 1870–1920.* New York: Cambridge UP, 1983.

Seymour, Harold. *Baseball The Early Years.* New York: Oxford UP, 1960.

Smith, H. Allen, and Iva Smith. *Low and Inside.* Garden City, NY: Doubleday, 1949.

Smith, Robert. *Hits, Runs & Errors*. New York: Simon and Schuster, 1949.

______. *Baseball in the Afternoon*. New York: Simon and Schuster, 1993.

Spalding, Albert G. *America's National Game*. Lincoln: University of Nebraska Press, 1992.

Spalding's Official Baseball Guide, New York: A. G. Spalding & Bros., 1892.

Spink, Alfred H. *The National Game*. St. Louis: The National Game Publishing Co., 1910.

Sullivan, Ted. *Humorous Stories of the Ball Field*. Chicago: M. Donahue, 1903.

Thompson, S.C. and Hy Turkin. *The Official Encyclopedia of Baseball*. Cranbury, NJ: A. S. Barnes, 1951.

Tiemann, Bob. *Cardinal Classics*. St. Louis: Baseball Histories, 1982.

Tiemann, Robert L., and Mark Rucker, eds. *Nineteenth Century Stars*. Cleveland: The Society for American Baseball Research, 1989.

Vincent, Ted. *Mudville's Revenge: The Rise and Fall of American Sport*. New York: Seaview Books, 1981.

Voigt, David Q. *American Baseball*. University Park: Pennsylvania State University, 1980.

Wallop, Douglass. *Baseball: An Informal History*. New York: W. W. Norton, 1969.

NEWSPAPERS

Anzeiger des Westens 1886
Boston Record 1897
Brooklyn Eagle 1889
Chicago Inter-Ocean 1886
Chicago Mail 1895
Chicago News 1886, 1897
Chicago Tribune 1885, 1886
Cincinnati Gazette 1885
Cincinnati Inquirer 1916
Cleveland Herald 1884
Cleveland World 1896
Kansas City Times 1889
Louisville Courier-Journal 1892
Missouri Republican 1880, 1883, 1885, 1907
New York Clipper 1882, 1885, 1886, 1889
New York Journal 1912
New York Recorder 1896
New York Sun 1889
New York Times 1870s, 1888, 1889
New York World 1895
Philadelphia Bulletin 1934
Philadelphia Enquirer 1896, 1946

Philadelphia Press 1889, 1896
Philadelphia Record 1895
Pittsburg Dispatch 1898
Sporting Life 1883, 1884, 1885, 1887, 1889, 1896, 1897, 1913, 1916
Sporting Times 1889
St. Louis Chronicle 1894
St. Louis Critic 1886
St. Louis Globe-Democrat 1880, 1882, 1884, 1885, 1886, 1887, 1888, 1890, 1895, 1896, 1897, 1898, 1905, 1908, 1958
St. Louis Post-Dispatch 1886, 1887, 1888, 1889, 1890, 1891, 1893, 1894, 1895, 1896, 1897, 1898, 1899, 1902, 1913, 1951, 1992
St. Louis Republican 1886, 1887, 1895, 1913
St. Louis Star and Times 1907, 1933, 1938
St. Louis Star 1898
St. Louis Star-Sayings 1895
The Sporting News 1886, 1887, 1888, 1889, 1890, 1891, 1892, 1893, 1894, 1895, 1896, 1897, 1898, 1899, 1908, 1913, 1926, 1929, 1941, 1966, 1982
Washington Post 1895, 1897, 1991

PERIODICAL AND OTHER SOURCES

Allen, Lee. "Legends." *Cooperstown Corner,* (1980): 106–108.

Carter, Gregg Lee. "Baseball in St. Louis, 1867–1875: An Historical Case Study in Civic Pride." *Missouri Historical Society Bulletin,* (1975): 253–263.

Diamond, Etan. "Kerry Patch: Irish Immigrant Life in St. Louis." *Gateway Heritage* 2 (1989): 21–30.

Egenriether, Richard. "Chris Von der Ahe: Baseball's Pioneering Huckster." *Baseball Research Journal* (1989):27–31.

Eldred, Rich. "Umpiring in the 1890's." *Baseball Research Journal* 18 (1989): 75.

Gietschier, Steve. "Before the Bible of Baseball: The First Quarter Century of The Sporting News." *St. Louis's Favorite Sport SABR 22* (1992): 31–34.

Hohlt, Brian. "Chris Von der Ahe; Primary sources of 'der Boss President.'" Thesis. St. Louis University, 1994.

Humber, William. "Where Do They All Come From?" *The interNational Pastime* (1992): 26–29.

Lampe, Anthony B. "The Background of Professional Baseball in St. Louis. *The Missouri Historical Society Bulletin,* (1950): 6–34.

Lipset, Lew. "The Egyptian and the Greyhounds." *The National Pastime* (1982): 48.

McCue, Andy. "A History of Dodger Ownership." *The National Pastime* (1993): 34–42.

Malloy, Jerry. "The Cubans' Last Stand." *The National Pastime* (1992): 11–12.

Merrell's Penetrating Oil pamphlet, 1887.

National Baseball Hall of Fame, Cooperstown, New York. Player Files.

Orenstein, Joshua. "The Union Association: A Glorius Failure." *Baseball Research Journal* 19 (1990): 3–6.

Porter, David L. "Untold Saga of Europe's Big Leaguers." *The interNational Pastime* (1992): 70–76.

Recorder of Deeds. St. Louis, Mo.: #452, p. 228; #61, p. 514; #1375, p. 313.

Riley, Matthew J. "Chris Von der Ahe and the St. Louis Baseball Club in the American Association 1882–1891." Thesis. United States Sports Academy 1990.

Rygelski, Jim. "Baseball's 'Boss President': Chris Von der Ahe and the Nineteenth-Century St. Louis Browns." *Gateway Heritage* (1992): 42–53.

Rygelski, Jim. "George Washington Bradley." *St. Louis's Favorite Sport SABR* 22 (1992)

St. Louis Circuit Court Records. "Emma Von der Ahe vs. Chris Von der Ahe." Case 099067. 1895.

St. Louis Circuit Court Records. "Isaac Laskey vs. Chris Von der Ahe." Case 82937. 1891.

St. Louis Circuit Court Records. "Mississippi Valley Trust Co. vs. Sportsman's Park Club and Association." Case 11324. 1898.

St. Louis Circuit Court Records. "St. Louis Brewing Association vs. Chris Von der Ahe." Case 82864. 1913.

St. Louis Circuit Court Records. "William Pinkston vs. Chris Von der Ahe." Case 94391. 1893.

St. Louis Court Records. "William Green vs. Chris Von der Ahe." Case 07381. 1887.

"St. Louis Red Stockings: More Than a Footnote." St. Louis Favorite Sports SABR 22 (1992): 11.

"The St. Louis Merchants' Exchange Collection." *Missouri Historical Society Bulletin* 1 (1949): 53.

Tiemann, Michael. Curator, Bellefntaine Cemetery, St. Louis. Personal Interview. 25 June 1992.

Tiemann, Robert. "The Forgotten Winning Streak of 1891." *Baseball Research Journal* 18 (1989): 2–5.

Voigt, David. "Denny Lyons' 52-Game Hitting Streak." *The National Pastime* 13 (1993): 45.

Von der Ahe, Russell L. Personal Files.

Wagner, Bill. "The League That Never Was." *Baseball Research Journal* 16 (1987): 18–21.

Index

Abbreviations:

AA	American Association
AL	American League
BBC	Base Ball Club
CL	California League
EL	Eastern League
IA	International Association
IL	Interstate League
NA	National Association
NL	National League
NW	Northwestern League
PL	Pennsylvania League
SI	Southern Illinois League
SL	Southern League
TL	Tri-State League
UA	Union Association
WA	Western Association
WL	Western League

About the Author

J. Thomas Hetrick is a baseball writer fascinated by profoundly thorough research and totally lost causes. Following the publication of his critically acclaimed book, *MISFITS! The Cleveland Spiders in 1899*, an in-depth study of major league baseball's worst-ever team, Tom turned his attention to documenting the tragicomic rise and fall of the owner of the St. Louis Browns, Christian Frederick Wilheim Von der Ahe.

Born an "army brat" (Fort Belvoir, Arlington, VA), Hetrick currently resides with his family in Clifton, VA and is employed by MITRE Corporation. He is an active member of SABR (the Society of American Baseball Research) and has presented numerous research papers at regional and national meetings.